RACIAL INEQUALITY IN NEW YORK CITY SINCE 1965

RACIAL INEQUALITY IN NEW YORK CITY SINCE 1965

EDITED BY

BENJAMIN P. BOWSER AND CHELLI DEVADUTT

SUNY PRESS

Cover designed by Matt Schoen.

Published by State University of New York Press, Albany

For information, contact State University of New York Press, Albany, NY
www.sunypress.edu

Library of Congress Cataloging-in-Publication Data

Names: Bowser, Benjamin P., editor. | Devadutt, Chelli, 1944– editor.
Title: Racial inequality in New York City since 1965 / edited by Benjamin P. Bowser and Chelli Devadutt.
Description: Albany : State University of New York Press, [2019] | Includes bibliographical references and index.
Identifiers: LCCN 2018046842 | ISBN 9781438475998 (hardcover) | ISBN 9781438476018 (ebook) | ISBN 9781438476001 (pbk.) Subjects: LCSH: New York (N.Y.)—Race relations—Political aspects. | New York (N.Y.)—Ethnic relations—Political aspects. | Race discrimination—New York (State)—New York. | Minorities—New York (State)—New York—Social conditions. | Minorities—New York (State)—New York—Economic conditions. | New York (N.Y.)—Politics and government.
Classification: LCC F128.9.A1 R33 2019 | DDC 305.8009747/1—dc23
LC record available at https://lccn.loc.gov/2018046842

10 9 8 7 6 5 4 3 2 1

To
Walter W. Stafford

This anthology is inspired by the life and work of Walter Stafford, a man whose spirit and essence permeates this book. Just days before he passed away, still steadfastly committed to his work, he said to his wife, Chelli, "I'm not afraid to die. I want to live, because I love life, and there is so much work to do."

Contents

Illustrations

Maps

Figures

Tables

Foreword

J. Phillip Thompson

Many thanks to Chelli Devadutt and Benjamin Bowser for assembling this needed anthology on racial inequality in New York City. As they note, the city of hope for European immigrants more than a century ago shunned Black immigrants from the Jim Crow Deep South. The city that designed programs and influenced the nation to establish pathways for creating the great White middle-class is today one of America's most racially segregated cities. This is not because New York is one of the most racist cities, far from it; it is because of the operation of the labor market and real estate markets combined with the impact of historical legacies such as inheritance. The challenge of racial inequality goes far beyond city policies. They point to the need to implement federal and state policies that match the power and effect of the federal and state policies that established racial hierarchies in the first place. We are far from that now; the nation has never figured out or had the political will to integrate its schools and neighborhoods racially. Non-whites, Blacks, and Latinos especially, are still concentrated in the worst paying occupations—as they have always been. Wealth disparities between Whites, Blacks, and Latinos are growing, leading to increased residential segregation. This anthology brings together the City's most ardent, authoritative, and intrepid scholars and analysts to probe these issues and more. The result is a thorough overview of the problems confronting New York, and many useful insights on how to make the city better and more democratic.

It is fitting that this volume be dedicated to the memory of Professor Walter Stafford. Walter was a friend, mentor, and inspiration for many students of urban policy and especially young scholars of color, including me. Walter's spirit was infectious; he often laughed when he described his activism in the South during the Civil Rights Movement, while pointing out the intractability of racial segregation in New York City. Two conversations with Walter stick out in my mind. Walter continually emphasized the importance of job training and analysis of labor markets. While activists in the 1980s were focused on housing affordability, Walter made us think about the other side of affordability: what was happening to jobs and incomes in the economy, especially for workers of color. Walter was always on the lookout for new developments and potential paths for economic opportunity.

For example, Walter was one of the early investigators of corporations dealing with inadequacies in public education by developing internal job training programs. He thought that finding new pathways for workforce development ought to be a key topic in addressing inequality—something I continue to believe. Walter read broadly and studied political theory to help conceive new approaches to public policy. He was thrilled with the emergence of critical feminist scholarship in the 1980s. Walter repeatedly stated that feminist thinkers were developing important critiques that paralleled, deepened, and transformed race and class analyses. He was no doubt right about that too. If those of us working on New York policy and politics can come close to Walter's intensity and intellectual curiosity, I think we can change the trajectory of many of the negative trends outlined in this volume.

Can New York City Be a "Fair City" in an Unfair Nation? What Are the Limits?

Chelli Devadutt and Benjamin Bowser pose the question of whether New York City can do for its recent immigrants from Asia, Africa, and Latin America, and for its historic African American and Puerto Rican populations, what it did for European immigrants a century ago. This again raises the question of "city limits." How much can cities do without state and especially national governmental support? What can progressive mayors, like Bill de Blasio in New York, accomplish with a conservative Congress and Donald Trump in the White House? Can New York maintain its public hospitals, refurbish its decaying public housing stock, provide affordable housing to the nearly one million families that need them, make necessary subway upgrades, and make its schools and colleges engines for a 21st century economy without massive federal investment? The short answer is no. New York needs federal support and new directions in federal urban policy. This makes national movement building a priority.

However, there are still many things cities (and states) can do. Cities can digitize the books in libraries and make them available online for everyone with a library card. Cities can foster partnerships between public and private (nonprofit) universities, and teachers' unions, to co-develop massive open online courses (MOOCs) and make them available for students to learn at their own pace. Cities can make the Internet universally accessible and affordable. We can launch practice-based, real-world problem-solving approaches to teaching science, technology, engineering, and math (STEM) or science, technology, reading, engineering, arts and math (STEAM) from preschool to worker retraining programs. Such moves can prepare a skilled workforce for the emerging digital economy. Cities can retrofit buildings (nearly a million in New York City) for energy efficiency, not only to reduce the City's carbon footprint but also to employ a whole generation of green construction workers, maintenance workers, engineers, and designers—all paid for by savings in energy consumption. Cities can propagate different forms of land ownership, such as land trusts, that spread the rewards of rising real estate values from speculators to longtime community residents. Cities can create worker-owned businesses that remove the fear of worker displacement emanating from the spread of technological innovations, and instead, generate greater worker prosperity and perhaps more time for family and learning new skills. Cities can reduce healthcare costs by extensive community engagement in growing and eating healthier food, promoting exercise, addressing mental health issues, reducing social isolation, and increasing community involvement. We are working on these things and lots more. When progressive change reaches the federal government in Washington, D.C., New York City and other progressive cities will have created prototypes for effective national policy change, just as New York City did in inspiring New Deal programs.

Developing the kinds of initiatives described above requires moving beyond stale tropes like "markets can solve every problem" (neo-liberalism), "government can solve every problem" (welfare-statism), or "community participation is the sure cure for inequity" (advocacy planning). There are no roadmaps or magic bullets, particularly as we face an unprecedented pace of technological and climate change. We need to cultivate a spirit of bold innovation and radical open-mindedness across government, the private sector, and civil society if we are to come up with workable solutions to the city's problems. Government also has to defend and enhance its role as the trusted agent of the people. Take energy retrofits in large multi-family buildings, if tenants do not trust their landlords to tell the truth about the dollar savings stemming from energy retrofits, or to share savings fairly with tenants, a trust-worthy government is needed to bridge the divide. The same goes for things as basic as counting who live in New York City. A recent Trump administration decision to put a citizenship question on the United States Census threatens to drive undocumented residents underground, fostering an undercount of residents in cities with large immigrant populations. Such a decision may well hurt New York City politically and financially, but just as important, it undermines trust in government. If the public cannot trust government on issues as basic as counting who resides in the city, it will be that much harder to foster the trust we need to tackle difficult issues in neighborhood policing, fair housing, or racial conflicts.

What Kind of Politics does New York City Need to Create?

There is no racial or ethnic majority in New York City. In this sense, New York is already a prototype for the demographic transition happening nationally. I have observed this learning process underway in New York. White residents, like every other group, are now a minority group. Predominantly White groups had to form coalitions with other race/ethnic groups to be successful on major citywide issues, and they must understand nonwhite perspectives to reach agreements. These are important political skills. While minority status has been the normal experience for nonwhites for generations, it is a radical shift in position for European descendants accustomed to believing that their views of the New York City and nation are "the only views." As Devadutt and Bowser note, for example, the Statue of Liberty symbolized *exclusion* for nonwhite New Yorkers, e.g., particular White historical narratives have been privileged for so long they are considered universal—yet they are not. Another shift brought about by demographic change is that Blacks, Latinos, and Asians have to learn how to value one another as important coalition partners. They can no longer be competitors seeking from powerful White groups more favorable treatment. With greater power, people of color have to learn how to lead Whites, not just their own race/ethnic group. This requires, among other things, dealing with White groups without resentment from the past; it will require listening to and addressing *their* hopes and fears as well. The most important learning I believe is this: no single race/ethnic or issue group can win without the support of other groups. In emerging New York and eventually the nation, Blacks need Whites, Whites need Blacks, and both need Latinos and Asians, and vice-versa. Labor cannot win without environmentalists, and so on. The necessity to work together in solidarity will mean more than racial or ethnic unity. With solidarity, racial justice, gender equality, economic justice, greening the economy, and other goals are fully achievable. Without solidarity, none of these goals is politically feasible. Solidarity cannot be achieved without mutual respect and mutual understanding. It does not come about by ignoring difference but through understanding and engaging difference. In this regard, I want to take a swipe at social scientists, one of my own tribes. We have done such a thorough job of slicing and dicing up "interest groups" that we help confine public dialogue, and shape group identities around narrowly conceived abstractions rather than felt human experiences. We have neglected the shared human qualities of love, forgiveness, nurturing, and other dimensions of the human spirit that are usually the domain of the humanities. For example, we continually confuse the term "desegregation" with "integration." In contrast, Martin L. King, Jr's "beloved community" went well beyond integration. These are communities where residents *intentionally* reach out to different others to get to know and love them.

While the challenges are enormous, I believe that New York City is showing what can happen when young progressive Whites and people of color come together. New York has elected and reelected a genuinely progressive mayor who cares deeply about the issues addressed in this volume. New Yorkers often disagree and debate how to solve problems (this is what is great about democracy), yet there is today more agreement than ever across race/ethnic divides about what the city's problems are—this is in itself a tremendous advance. The young people engaged in studying and debating these issues will soon be leaders of the nation as demographic change makes the nation look a lot like New York, and issues we in New York are struggling with right now will become national issues. We will then have great opportunities to bury racial inequality finally.

Acknowledgments

No one has been better at creating bridges between the day-to-day lives of ordinary New Yorkers, the academy, public policy, and the government than the late Walter Stafford. As a professor at New York University, he moved effortlessly back and forth between the streets, the classroom, and the New York City Council. This book acknowledges his skill, dedication, and role model.

We are grateful for the generous grant facilitated by New York University's vice provost, Ulrich Baer, and his endorsement and support for the Walter Stafford Project on Racial Inequality in NYC. In addition, Ellen Schall, former dean of The Robert F. Wagner School for Public Service, provided invaluable assistance to us. Walter Stafford was on the faculty at the Wagner School for nearly 20 years. It was Dean Schall who introduced us to current Wagner Dean Sherry Glied, who agreed to sponsor and house our project, as well as to provide staff and other resources to ensure our success.

We are grateful to several other New York University faculty and staff supporters. They include: Philip Harper, Iveliza Vazquez, Mike West, LaShawn Jones, Sunil Kunnakkat, Adrienne Prassas, Hannah Alchison, and Victor Rodwin. Robert Hawkins of the McSilver School for Social Work, helped us to obtain a grant from the McSilver Institute on Poverty, Policy, and Research. David Jones, CEO of the New York City Community Services Society, where Walter Stafford was a senior researcher for many years, provided a grant that enabled Jarrett Murphy to research and to write the chapter on New York mayors. This chapter is dedicated to the late Wayne Barrett of the *Village Voice*, who was to be the original author of the chapter. Sadly, Wayne passed away before he could complete it.

We were greatly assisted in our work by a remarkable young intern, Madison Moore, as well as by our graduate assistant, Andrea Gordillo, who is a fantastic researcher, planner, organizer, and communicator. We owe her a great deal for her unflagging commitment to the project. Our thanks to Matt Schoen for conceiving the ingenious book cover.

This was no ordinary writing assignment. By their very nature, anthologies provide broad and comprehensive coverage of topics that no one person has the expertise to cover adequately on their own. To succeed, anthologies must coordinate the work of several specialists. In this process, editors get to know their contributors, and become part of their lives as they write, rewrite and shape their piece of the puzzle. We want to acknowledge every single one of our contributors. They were all expected to make sense of the lives of millions of New Yorkers within the context of their own discipline, and over the extended period of the last half-century. There is nothing in any disciplinary literature that prepares anyone for such a task. We acknowledge that this kind of writing requires imagination, experience, and much reflection and intellectual risk-taking, and we appreciate that this is exactly what we got from our many contributors.

Benjamin Bowser, coeditor

Walter Stafford and I discussed the need for this book in meetings that spanned many decades. We even outlined what such a book would contain. Walter continued to be my eyes and ears on the ground, even after my career took me, a native New Yorker, west to California. Initially, we believed successive generations of scholars would do this work. Yet, 25 years passed, and no one had taken up the baton. We realized it was up to us to follow through. Before we could do that, however, Walter Stafford passed away. Nonetheless, this book has become a reality because of the dedication of the person who was closest to Walter, his wife, Chelli Devadutt. She is an extraordinary networker and planner, and has, in her own right, a broad network of friends and colleagues in the academy, public policy, and in New York community-based organizations. She knew what Walter wanted, and was aware of our historic conversations. It has been an honor to work with her.

Special thanks are due to John Mollenkopf and Mindy Fullilove for the counsel they both provided. I must also acknowledge another New York native son, Arthur Paris. In 1980, Professor Paris and I proposed to do the research behind this project, backed by the Ford Foundation. However, the Foundation decided not to pursue our efforts, and we both had to carry on careers elsewhere. During this time, Nathalia Bowser, my mother, the consummate Harlemite, would stop Walter Stafford on the street, and ask him what he was doing about our research. She would not accept that her son, a social scientist who went off to study communities in other parts of the United States, in Europe, the Caribbean, and Africa, would not study New York, as well. She remained Walter's and my conscience. She also served as a spokesperson for seven decades of voiceless neighbors who came to New

York City and Harlem when it was full of hope, but ended up living in a place that struggled through one of the most challenging periods in the history of Black New York, the years after 1970.

Finally, I want to acknowledge Michael Rinella at SUNY Press. He honored our vision, and was immediately supportive of it, as were a group of anonymous reviewers whose critiques were rigorous, detailed, and helpful. Their suggestions have much improved the final work. We also would like to recognize Terry Oldano, who proofread and edited the book. We are all grateful to her for her thoroughness and skill at making sure that our writing is comprehensible to the broadest range of readers.

Chelli Devadutt, coeditor

I must acknowledge my now-dear friend, Benjamin Bowser. He managed to convince me that I could do something I had never planned to do: co-edit an anthology. This collection of essays on racial inequality in New York City was a vision Ben, and my late husband, Walter Stafford, shared. I was inspired to do this book when I finally understood that it was an opportunity to use the special research approach that Walter had developed toward the end of his life. He wanted to enrich and to expand standard research data, by using the voices and experiences of people on the ground who, on a daily basis, were dealing with the issues this anthology addresses. Ben, gently, but persistently, urged me to do this book. I finally agreed in 2014, six years after Walter passed away. It has been a joy to work with Ben.

Many friends and family have shown a sincere willingness to provide financial, as well as moral, support to our project, and we are most grateful. It is a testimony to their regard for Walter. These individuals include: Florence Amerley Adu, Daisy Maria Auger Dominguez, Larry B. Barrett, Cathy Hawkins, Janet Dewart Bell, Sumati Devadutt, Yrthya Dinzey Flores, Rafe Ellison, Jill Vinjamuri Gettman, Dale Joseph, Bill McAllister, Shabnam Merchant, Daniel Goldstein, Shawn Moore, Stacia Murphy, Mary Nakashian, Ellen Schall, Steven Kelban, Judith Solomon, Gita Stulberg, Ian Schoen, David Schoen, Norma Tan, Deborah Taylor, Kathrin Scheel-Ungerleider, David Vinjamuri, and Michelle Blau Vinjamuri.

I am thankful for the many conversations I had with Bill McAllister, Esmeralda Simmons, Patricia Swann, Mary Nakashian, Alan Taddiken, Kathrin Scheel-Ungerleider, Wayne Winborn, and Sondra Youdelman. They fundamentally shaped my thinking on the Walter Stafford Project.

My daughter, Gita Julianna, has also challenged and inspired my thinking about how important it is to organize to achieve social justice. She is truly her stepfather, Walter's, daughter. My sister, Sumati, is always my pillar of strength whenever I undertake seemingly impossible tasks. Finally, I owe everything to my partner of 23 years, Walter Stafford. He changed the way I see the world, and gave me a life filled with music, art, travel, and laughter.

Introduction

Benjamin P. Bowser and Chelli Devadutt

The Statue of Liberty sits at the foot of New York City's harbor, a quintessential icon for both the city and the nation. The statue is the figure of a welcoming woman, not of a conquering male hero, nor of a benevolent nobleman. Rather than brandishing a sword or a rifle, she holds a torch to light the way for weary refugees. As a gift from France, Lady Liberty underscores a common bond between the United States and France: two nations forged in the revolutionary ideals of freedom and equality. The plaque at the base of the statute reads:

> Give me your tired, your poor, your huddled masses yearning to breathe free, the wretched refuse of your teeming shore. Send these, the homeless, tempest-tossed to me; I lift my lamp beside the golden door! (National Park Service, 2016)

Emma Lazarus, a young woman of Portuguese Sephardic Jewish descent, wrote these words in 1883. In them, she expresses an ideal of equality that makes the U.S. unique among nations. Over time, the pursuit of this ideal has provided New York City with a special character and mission. Early on, New York became the gateway for millions of foreign-born immigrants entering the United States—a place where individuals would become New Yorkers first, and then transform themselves into Americans prepared to disperse throughout the nation.

No one could have anticipated what Emma Lazarus set in motion with the aspirations she expressed in her dedication. However, ambition is one thing, reality is another, and the two are in perpetual conflict. In 1883, such aspirations faced formidable challenges. Women could neither vote, nor own property. The millions of European immigrants sailing into New York harbor were not free to do whatever they wanted. Instead, they entered America as laborers for an emerging manufacturing and industrial economy (Hirschman and Mogford, 2009). They worked twelve-hour shifts, six days a week, often in dangerous and unhealthful conditions. They had no benefits, no vacations, no health insurance, or retirement. Wages started low and were kept that way by employers who replaced one group of ethnic workers with newer arrivals. Each group was willing to work for less than their predecessors. Universal education was still a dream. In effect, Europeans arriving in the United States were a laboring underclass. Their immigrant status was the basis for their social and economic inequality, relative to those born in America, and who came before them (Thernstrom 1994).

Despite the challenge immigrants faced in 1883, things improved over the next century, and many of the aspirations expressed by Emma Lazarus came to pass. By 1960, unions had formed, wages had improved, women had the right to vote and own property, and a five-day workweek and eight-hour workday were law. Health insurance, unemployment benefits, and retirement plans were common worker benefits. Education through the 12th grade was universal. Workers now even had leisure time. After only a few years of work, they could buy a car, move out of worker apartments, and purchase single-family homes in the suburbs.

The ideals embodied in the Statue of Liberty became a reality. The sons, daughters, and grandchildren of immigrants have been assimilated into American society (Alba and Nee, 2003) and became part of the new majority middle class. As their circumstances improved, their identity as immigrants waned. They, their children, and their grandchildren became increasingly indistinguishable from long-term, White native-born Americans.[1] The inequality that had separated these former immigrants from other Americans decreased, as well.

Americans whose parents were immigrants experienced a degree of social mobility they would not have imagined in their native countries. As a result, they developed two strong convictions. First, they believed that anyone, who was disciplined, worked hard and made sacrifices, could advance into the middle class. Second, they concluded that their children would do better than the past generation, and subsequent generations would achieve even more. It was in other countries that family status at birth determined an individual's social mobility. In America, these same people could firmly reject the idea that someone's entire life is prescribed at birth, based solely on social identity, religion, or ethnicity.

However, now, many of the great-great-grandchildren of these immigrants see themselves left behind and facing a cliff of downward mobility ahead. Perhaps, it is time to look more carefully at the existing architecture of social inequality in the nation and New York City. However, the starting point for such an inquiry must be with racial stratification, the foundations on which inequality in the United States started and continues.

Racial Inequality

What about "the tired, the poor and the wretched" who were already here? Emma Lazarus's ideals were not explicit about their status. For many already here, the ideals embodied in the Statue of Liberty, and in Emma Lazarus's words, did not apply. For instance, Native Americans had been eliminated from New York City and State more than a century before her words were inscribed. In 1883, the forced removal of native peoples, from the East coast and then to reservations in the West, was nearly complete, as was the appropriation of their lands.

Before the Civil War, the South had been the most prosperous region of the United States. Slaves did virtually all the manual labor in both agriculture and manufacturing. They were the miners, the steelworkers, and the builders who made it possible for the South to thrive. The 1866 emancipation of slaves freed more than a million workers and artisans who had the craft and language skills to do the industrial work New York and northern states desired. There were no oceans for these workers to cross. Yet these ex-slaves were overlooked in favor of millions of Germans, Irish, Italians, Greeks, Russians, and Eastern Europeans who spoke no English, and were mostly unskilled. Before massive immigration from Europe, Black labor eclipsed European immigrants in both skills and sometimes in numbers in New York City and elsewhere in the nation (Bowser 2007). In New York City, slaves and free Blacks were fourteen percent of the workforce in 1820. They made up one-third of the population and the majority of laborers in Kings County, now Brooklyn, until New York State abolished slavery in 1827 (Rael, 2005).

African Americans living in New York City during European immigration served as an example of how Black labor is overlooked (Sacks, 2005). Blacks faced levels of racial discrimination slaves had experienced in the South. This was despite the fact that African Americans had done these jobs and crafts since the 1600s (Ottley & Weatherby, 1967). It was immigrant workers and their children who got the jobs in all the emerging industries in New York, and other large U.S. cities.

The abolition of slavery was not a ticket into the economy. As Emma Lazarus wrote her poem, the Black Codes, laws that specified what slaves could and could not do, were re-introduced as an elaborate and comprehensive system for guaranteeing White racial supremacy in the South. "Jim Crow" laws would freeze former slaves and poor Whites alike into a form of servitude that would last another century.

As of 1929, and the Great Depression, Blacks from the South and Caribbean were the last hired, rather than the first. They were used only as a reserve labor force. If immigrant workers made wage or benefit demands, employers would threaten to hire Blacks for less, using them as replacement workers during strikes. This century-long history of racial discrimination and subordination in New York City's industrial workforce was in place from 1900 until the eve of World War II (Dodson, Moore, & Yancey, 2000). It was not until the mid-20th century, and the civil rights movement from 1955 through the 1960s, that the goal of racial equality was acknowledged as the same dream stated in Emma Lazarus' words. The 19th-century history of Black exclusion set the stage for racial inequality today.

There is a new challenge, however, in today's brand of racial inequality, and it goes beyond the basic differences between White and Black New Yorkers. Since World War II, Western Europe has become a center of relative affluence, thereby eliminating the historical incentives for massive emigration to the United States. Things have changed in another way since the 1965 Immigrant Act. Immigrants to the United States are primarily from Asia, Latin America, the Caribbean, Africa and Eastern Europe. Except Eastern Europeans, immigrants today are racially distinct from those arriving in the past. The all-important question now is whether these later immigrants will experience the same upward mobility across generations as did the European immigrants who came before them. More specifically, will these people of color from Asia, Africa, and the Caribbean, who cannot pass for White, have the same upward mobility after three generations, as did the earlier waves of Europeans? Based on new changes in the national and New York's regional economy and globalization, partial answers to this question may already be apparent.

Mid-20th Century Assessments

Gunnar Myrdal's *An American Dilemma* (1944) was a landmark assessment, and introduction to racial inequality for the second half of the twentieth century. It was the first comprehensive description of race relations in the United States, summarizing the work of virtually every scholar and researcher who had addressed the issue to date. It documented the systemic subordination of African Americans in all aspects of American life, whether in the South or the North, by describing segregation and discrimination in housing, employment, and education. The book recounted the history, justifications, and costs of caste-like inequality for Blacks and the economic and social costs for

Whites, as well. More importantly, Myrdal's assessment explained how systemic racial inequality runs contrary to American ideals, and, in fact, presented a moral dilemma for Whites, who discriminated against Blacks, willingly or unwillingly. For Myrdal, the most effective way to reduce inequality and to eradicate Blacks' caste-like status in American life was to point out how racism disavows American values and produces an implacable moral problem.

The American dilemma was New York City's dilemma, as well. Until 1964, in broad sections of the city, Blacks could not buy or rent housing, go to school, or gain employment. Well-paying union jobs were closed to them. These inequities provoked Blacks to riot in Harlem in the years 1919, 1935, 1943, and again in 1964 (Grimshaw, 1969). By closing virtually all avenues of social and economic mobility to Blacks, New York City created a situation no different in outcome from what Blacks had experienced in the Jim Crow South.

The effects of racial discrimination were always visible in Harlem, an initially hopeful and vibrant Black community. Many found themselves isolated and hopeless even after fleeing the South (Clarke, 1969; McKay, 1968; Scheiner, 1965). Stores on 125th Street had to be boycotted and picketed in the 1930s before they agreed to employ "Negro" sales clerks. This was thirty years before Martin Luther King Jr.'s marches. Ironically, it was World War II, which brought some relief. Because of the Great Depression and War, European immigrants stopped flowing into the United States just when the war effort required millions of additional workers. Women and Blacks were hired for jobs that previously only White men held. New York City neighborhoods that had been closed to Blacks before the War reluctantly opened to them. Although the race dilemma was still very much alive in New York City after the War, there would be no returning to the more blatant, entrenched pre-war practices of racial discrimination.

After 1960, a new frustration emerged. The changes brought on by the Civil Rights movement had created an occasion for optimism. However, these changes seemed to bypass northern Black communities like New York. Rather than seeing improvements, Black urban communities were in rapid decline, and were characterized increasingly as "ghettos." There was rising unemployment, deteriorating housing, and failing schools (Auletta, 1979; Osofsky, 1963). Amid these frustrations *Youth in the Ghetto* by Kenneth Clark, et al. (1964), was published. It became a blueprint for attacking racial inequality, using education and youth service programs.

The approaches outlined in *Youth in the Ghetto* were piloted in New York City and scaled up for use nationally in President Johnsons' War on Poverty. The conceptual background for *Youth in the Ghetto* was presented in Kenneth Clark's *Dark Ghetto* (1965), which was the New York equivalent of Myrdal's *An American Dilemma*. Clark's *Dark Ghetto* described the racial-caste-like circumstances of Black New Yorkers. However, rather than defining the systemic subordination of Blacks as a moral dilemma between ideals and reality, Clark believed New York's racial quagmire was based on a lack of social power. Blacks did not have the economic or political resources to ameliorate their condition and were dependent upon others who did not have the will or interest to make the necessary changes. That was what made urban racial segregation and poverty unique. In addition, the existence of Black ghettos was as much the result of mental chains on residents' imaginations and aspirations as it was a physical and economic reality.

The Last 50 Years

It is time to reassess what has happened in New York City since the publication of *The Dark Ghetto*. We have to ask ourselves if inequality based on race has decreased, increased or remained the same. We have moved beyond Kenneth Clark's appraisals, as well as Glazer and Moynihan's *Beyond the Melting Pot* (1963). There are other more recent descriptions of race-based social and economic inequality in New York City over the last half century (Bobo, O'Connor, & Tilly, 2001; Curtis & Farnsworth-Jackson, 1977; Federal Reserve Bank of New York, 1999; Mollenkopf & Castells, 1991; Varady, 2005). Collectively, they paint a stark picture. The Kenneth Clark inspired efforts ended years ago. Black and Latino's unemployment have persisted as has the racial, educational achievement gap. Current incarceration rates of Black and Latino young men were unimaginable in the 1960s. Drug abuse and HIV have devastated already troubled communities; most have yet to recover. Current Black family indicators make Moynihan's controversial 1965 assessment seems optimistic. Racial inequality, by any definition, has increased and become more multifaceted, despite the advent and high visibility of a Black middle class.

There is plenty of room for debate on how racial inequality has increased, and why. Since 1965, two generations of scholars and researchers have produced an impressive array of work addressing aspects of race and inequality in New York City. We acknowledge much of this work in subsequent chapters. In fact, over the last half-century, more than 300 books, journal articles, and magazine feature articles have been written on the topics of immigration, race, ethnicity, housing, policing, neighborhoods, schools and the economy in New York City. It does not stop there. For each of these topics, there are additional works on the history, changes, and transformations in the city, thereby doubling the number of publications.

Consequently, there is a virtual mosaic of fragmented knowledge from academic disciplines and sub-disciplines; most are microscopic in view. Those concerned with, and interested in, New York City have worked in disciplinary silos, having few interactions with others outside their specialty. In fact, the literature on New York reflects the physical detachment and dispersion of research and policy institutes, and of university departments throughout the city. What we now know about the city comes in narrow, deep slices. Despite hundreds of studies, we are unable to make a comprehensive statement of how racial inequality has changed in the last 50 years, or of what we can expect in coming decades. There is a pressing need for an overview of race and inequality, one that connects and integrates existing knowledge.

Our goal is not to advocate for a classless society. Perhaps it should be. Instead, what we look toward is much less ambitious. In whatever way social stratification is defined in the United States and New York City, one or the other group should not benefit from it or be disadvantaged by it because of their race or ethnicity. We know enough about ourselves to know that the social constructs of race, ethnicity, and gender have not endowed any group as superior or inferior that then justifies disproportionate power or privilege. The successful integration of millions of European immigrants into American life is the strongest evidence that a level playing field can be produced. This goal is not unreasonable or unachievable.

Symposium and Method

The late Walter Stafford (New York University, Wagner Graduate School of Public Service), Chelli Devadutt, his widow, and Benjamin Bowser originally planned this work as a 25-year retrospective of *The Dark Ghetto*. The timeframe expanded due to teaching, writing, and community service, plus the responsibilities of running agencies and programs. Crises arose, funders were uninterested, and eventually, Walter suffered from poor health. Also, we assumed someone else would do a macro assessment of New York City focusing on racial inequality. Professor Stafford's passing is what finally prompted us to follow through on this project. We believe the best way to accomplish such a large and complex project is to invite experts from a range of fields to contribute to an interdisciplinary anthology. This seems the best way to connect the dots between the many self-contained academic silos to understand a complicated history and contemporary circumstances.

Since 1965, there has been a key shift in the world of research. Academic departments are no longer the primary source for research. Now public policy organizations, city and state government agencies, and social service providers do the bulk of the work on issues related to race and inequality.

As with Clark's *Youth in the Ghetto*, this collection aims to serve as a catalyst for discussion and change moving forward. With this anthology, we hope to assist community agencies, foundations, and city government to find ways to ameliorate racial inequality and make improvements wherever possible.

Our Method

We asked individuals who have written on aspects of race and inequality in New York City to inform us on what research was currently underway, who was doing it, and who among researchers, their students, and colleagues, might be interested in contributing to this anthology. Our advisory board included:

Richard Alba, Graduate Center, CUNY
Elijah Anderson, Yale University
Donald Davis, Columbia University
Nancy Foner, Hunter College
Mindy Fullilove, New School
Philip Harper, New York University
Philip Kasinitz, Graduate Center, CUNY
John Mollenkopf, Grad. Center, CUNY
Arthur Paris, Syracuse University
Emily Rosenbaum, Fordham University
Saskia Sassen, Columbia University

In winter 2015, we set up a website for the project, through the New York University, Wagner Graduate School of Public Service. In January 2016, we emailed a call-for-papers to relevant academic departments, public policy institutes, and organizations whose work focuses on New York City, and asked our advisers to distribute the call-for-papers, as well. We received twelve inquiries, with adviser referrals being our most productive source of names.

We invited inquirers to submit a short abstract of their prospective paper. Next, we listed essential chapters and subsequently matched these chapters with researchers who submitted abstracts, and with the names and specialties of individuals referred to us. We spent winter 2016 discussing our plans with prospective contributors. From these meetings, twenty individuals and teams accepted the challenge of presenting their initial work at a symposium, held at the NYU Wagner School, on October 13 and 14, 2016. Fifteen presentations were made over two days. What distinguished this symposium from others was the decision to have reviewers from three distinct communities participate in each presentation. These reviewers were from public policy organizations, and from community-based and city agencies whose work is research-driven. This particular review process connected academic and public policy specialists, with the end consumers of their research.

One month before the symposium, reviewers received a draft of their assigned symposium paper to read and review. We modeled our approach on the one Walter Stafford used late in his career. He always saw the wisdom of bridging the academic, public policy, and practitioner communities as a way of activating ideas between them. This approach reflects the editors' professional engagements as well in children's services and in public health research.

Each presentation and review session that took place during the October 2016 symposium was videotaped. By December 2016, each presenter was given access to a transcript and video of their session, which made it possible for them to take reviewer comments, concerns, suggestions and needs into consideration when revising their papers. Their final drafts became chapters in this collection during the winter, spring, and summer of 2017. Authors were encouraged to draw upon one another's works when doing their final edits, thereby integrating their knowledge with that from other disciplines. The editors made suggestions to each author, as well.

The chapters in this anthology have been written to be academically sound and thoroughly useful to community and government agencies tasked with addressing race and inequality in New York City. We hope that others will apply the project's methodology to racial inequality in other cities, with the same objectives in mind.

A Chapter Review

Part 1: Structural Underpinnings

This anthology consists of three interrelated sections. The first addresses the structural underpinnings of racial inequality. Inequality is based not on inherent racial differences in mental capacity, nor is it rooted in different biological or physical characteristics. Instead, major economic differences among races, genders, religions are produced by institutional conventions, practices, and government policies in four interrelated sectors: employment (economy), government, education, and housing.

Chapter 1: Economy

The first structural chapter addresses the economy. Employers who discriminate do so through existing hiring, promotion, and termination policies. Consequently, job placement, mobility, and income outcomes are skewed by race. However, racial discrimination is not the only factor that drives racial economic inequality. Wage stratification does so as well. Different classes of workers are compensated with a wide range in salaries. Traditionally, employers justify this kind of job and wage stratification by weighting the importance of a position, the skills it requires, the training needed, the job's difficulty, and the size of the pool of people qualified to do the work. When a type of work is deemed more important, it is understood that more training is required. When fewer people can perform a task, paying a qualified person more is considered appropriate—supply and demand. In this case, the gap between compensation levels by work sectors will increase or decrease. If one class of workers is compensated more, and another is compensated less, overall inequality increases, regardless of race.

When racial participation in the economy varies by sectors, economic inequality increases further. For example, Whites are over represented in sectors such as banking and finance where compensation levels are higher than other sectors. People of color, on the other hand, are over-represented in the food and services sectors, where salary levels are lower. James Parrott addresses these compensation issues in chapter 1, "Inequality in New York City: The Intersection of Race and Class." Wage disparity, where people of color are concentrated in lower-paying sectors, has contributed greatly to the rising racial inequality in New York in the past 50 years.

Chapter 2: Race and Community

The status of neighborhoods and housing are outcomes of changes in the economy. New York City is one of the most diverse cities in the world. Our global economy drives this diversity. The city's streets, buses, subways, and public spaces reflect virtually every social class, race, gender variation, religion, ethnicity, age group, culture, and lifestyle that exists. However, when everyone returns home, New York City is also one of the most racially segregated cities in the nation. Communities and housing show us that we live in a socially stratified economy. Economic inequality drives racial inequality, with different races segregated and insulated from one another. Ingrid Gould Ellen, Jessica Yager, and Maxwell Austensen, from the New York University Furman Center, address this issue in chapter 2, "The Paradox of Inclusion and Segregation in the Nation's Melting Pot."

Chapter 3: Education

Income and racial segregation in housing and communities lead to racial segregation in schools and differential levels of academic achievement by race. In 1965, Kenneth Clark mourned that an entire generation of young people had been lost to substandard education and racial segregation in New York

City schools. In the years between 1940 and 1965, public education failed to provide a level playing field for most Black and Latino children. Norm Fruchter and Christina Mokhtar, of New York University, offer a fifty-year update of educational progress in chapter 3, "New York City School Segregation Then and Now: *Plus Ça Change . . .*"

Despite five city administrations, two generations of teachers, and two sets of major reforms, little has changed about New York City schools. Students from Black and Latino low-income communities are still segregated in poor-performing schools. Racial segregation still results in poverty and reduced academic achievement.

Chapter 3 is followed by an abstract by Adriana Villavicencio, Shifra Goldenberg, and Sarah Klevan, from the NYU Research Alliance for New York City Schools. In this short essay, titled "Understanding and Dismantling Barriers to College and Career Success for Black and Latino Young Men," the authors describe programmatic efforts that could improve academic performance in low-performing schools with low-income students. Implementing these improvements, however, would require two things: bringing the program to scale citywide and generating the political will to implement the steps they outline.

Chapter 4: Government

Besides Federal and State governments, City government has constitutional responsibility for the social wellbeing of its citizens. City governments are responsible for public schools and improving them. Government is the only entity that can influence businesses and employers to act fairly and equitably. In chapter 4, Jarrett Murphy takes a critical look at the five city administrations in place since 1965, and asks the most relevant question, "Do Mayors Matter? Race, Justice and the Men in City Hall, 1965–2017." Murphy describes the mixed results the respective administrations achieved in reducing economic and racial inequality while in office. He underscores the limited power and minimal control city governments have to influence national and regional trends in a local economy. During the New York City fiscal crisis, we saw that state and federal governments are vital for cities to be able to maintain and provide social and human services and to address economic and racial inequalities.

The discussion in part 1 on structural underpinnings set the stage for subsequent chapters. The major forces are summarized that shape the lives of millions of New Yorkers—who makes a living doing what; where people can afford to live; whether their children will do better than their parents, and; the impact a city government can have on people's lives. Part 2 looks at New York City's racial groups that are unequal to Whites and examines two points: the degree of racial inequality each experience and the prospects each faces to reduce these inequities.

Part 2: The Race Mountain

Within only a few generations, European immigrants were able to achieve equity with native White citizens. Now they are indisputably American. Part 2 explores whether the more-recent immigrants from the Caribbean, Latin America, and Asia, as well as African Americans, who were here before 19th-century European immigrants, will be as fortunate.

Chapter 5: African Americans

African Americans have been in New York City for over four hundred years. They have lived through the major social changes of New York as a Dutch and British colony, through U.S. independence. As slaves, laborers, and artisans, Blacks were a major part of New York's mercantile economy, through the rise of industrialism. Throughout the city's history, African Americans have been used as the metric for the base of the race mountain, the bottom of the social hierarchy. They have been the New Yorkers others dare not fall below, as implied in the popularity of the 19th-century minstrel show (Lhamon, 1998). This long history of subordination, of using Blacks as the bottom of New York's social hierarchy, has largely been ignored. This history implies that Blacks have a much more complex and longer route to achieve equity. There is no way African Americans can become racially White as a precondition for parity as in the case of European immigrants. All immigrants who cannot pass for White face this same challenge. Benjamin Bowser of California State University, East Bay, addresses these issues in chapter 5, "African Americans and Racialized Inequality in New York." Gentrification is indicative of only one phase in a complex succession of places Black people have concentrated in New York as a function of their social status.

Chapter 6: Latino Americans

Puerto Ricans and Cubans have been in New York City since the early 1900s, with the largest influx occurring after World War II. Over time, Latino immigrant communities established themselves in Lower Manhattan, East (Spanish) Harlem, and in the South Bronx. No one could have anticipated the number and diversity of Latinos who would immigrate to New York City after 1965. There is a dozen distinct, nation-of-origin Latino communities in New York, arriving from all over the Caribbean, Mexico, and Central and South America.

Latinos also pose a particular challenge when trying to categorize them by race. Some individuals easily pass for White; others have distinct Native American or African ancestry, and others are racially mixed. Some Latinos are upwardly mobile across one or two generations, in the same way, earlier European immigrants were. Others who are of Indian and African ancestry are finding upward mobility more difficult. Hector Cordero-Guzman of City University of New York addresses the Latino situation in chapter 6, "The Evolving Latino Population in New York City."

Chapter 7: West Indian Americans

Caribbean immigrants have come to New York in two waves. The first influx came in the early 1900s, primarily from Jamaica and Barbados. The second wave arrived after the 1965 Immigration and Nationality Act was passed. They come from every island nation in the Caribbean, plus Guyana, speaking English, Spanish or French.

The vast majorities of immigrants from the Caribbean are of African ancestry and are indistinguishable in appearance from African Americans. However, there is an essential question. To what extent have West Indian immigrants reached parity with the White population? If so, it would suggest that their immigrant experience trumps race. Calvin Holder of CUNY Staten Island and Aubrey Bonnett of SUNY Old Westbury address these issues in chapter 7, "Select Socioeconomic Characteristics of West Indian Immigration in New York City."

Chapter 8: Asian Americans

Asians are the fastest-growing group of immigrants in New York City, and are a more complex population to assess. That is because of the large number of countries Asian immigrants come from, each has its own distinct culture. They do not share a common language or history. The majority of these new immigrants are from China, but many come from India, Cambodia, Laos, Pakistan, Korea, the Philippines, Japan, and Vietnam. Their diversity says more about the limited utility of the concept of race than it does about them as immigrants. How can so many different people be thrown into a single fictive classification: Asian American? Anthropologically, the racial categories of White, Black, Native American, and Hispanic are equally fictive and erroneous.

Furthermore, each Asian ethnicity negotiates its own process of becoming American, and each has its own social and economic trajectory. Only time will tell which group will reach social and economic parity with the general population, and when. Howard Shih of the Asian American Federation reviews these complex circumstances in chapter 8, "Asian Americans: Immigration, Diversity, and Disparity."

Chapter 9: Ethnic Conflict

Chapters 5 through 8 focus specifically on the questions of the social and economic disparities African Americans, and Asian, Latino, and Caribbean immigrant New Yorkers have in comparison with White New Yorkers. Chapter 9 addresses a second question. What have been the ethnic conflicts between Black, White, and new immigrants over the last half century? Violence was a major part of interethnic relations in the 19th century. Because of the larger sizes and greater number of ethnic-racial groups today, one could hypothesize that more conflict and violence might have happened in the last half century than in prior periods.

Surprisingly, the authors of the previous chapters, independently, see less violence between groups, rather than more, in the past half-century. There has certainly been conflict and the potential for more remains, but the general lack of riot and open violence has been remarkable. There are intriguing reasons for why this potential for violence has not been actualized.

Part 3: Practice and Policy

Barriers to racial equity have never been removed. As old barriers are challenged and become less effective, new ones replace them. The process of understanding how the new barriers to equity work and then can be challenged starts over again. We have witnessed such a transition in racial oppression in New York since 1970. As racial discrimination in employment and housing were challenged with relative success, criminal justice, drug trafficking, drug addiction and HIV/AIDS, and government divestment became new barriers. At the same time, the barriers to racial equality among Asian, Latino, Caribbean and, African American New Yorkers have never been received passively. People of color have acted invariably to resist them in both organized and unorganized ways. They do not choose to be hapless victims of the discriminatory forces affecting their lives. They act and find ways to improve their plight eventually. In part 3, we examine the new barriers—criminal justice, drug trafficking and abuse, HIV/AIDS, government divestment, and the efforts of those who experience racial barriers to struggle against them.

Chapter 10: Policing—Stop and Frisk

The most recent embodiment of racial discrimination in New York City has been the stop-and-frisk police practice. Officers will stop and frisk young Black and Latino men as a means of discouraging them from carrying weapons and drugs. The stop and frisk policy were conceived to be a preventive measure aimed at reducing violent crimes, drug trafficking, and drug abuse. However, this policy was applied selectively to mostly Black and Latino men. The NYPD made no distinction between the majority of young, law abiding Blacks and Latinos, and the minority of them who break the law.

For law-abiding Blacks and Latinos, stop and frisk has been dangerous, publicly embarrassing, personally humiliating, and an invasion of privacy. The practice has effectively criminalized everyone touched by it, not because these individuals have committed crimes, but because of their race. In this chapter, Natalie Byfield, of St. John's University, assesses the reach of stop and frisk, and the impact of this practice and its replacement.

After Byfield, there is an addendum by Woods and Greenspan entitled, "Race-Based Discrimination in Expert Witness Testimony." They present an unexamined form of racial discrimination that occurs when forensic mental health professionals testify about people of color in criminal and civil cases. Expert witnesses either minimize or ignore person-based qualities, such as brain damage, mental illness, or physical illness. Alternatively, they rely excessively on alleged personal qualities but do not give sufficient attention to the explanatory role of pertinent cultural and environmental factors. Either way, their assessments are wrong. Defendants are either convicted or released based upon faulty testimony.

Chapter 11: Public Health

In the past 50 years, Black and Latino communities in New York have faced two very serious public health crises: the trafficking and use of heroin and crack cocaine, and the HIV/AIDS epidemic. Valuable human, financial and social resources were diverted and exhausted in the struggle against drugs and HIV/AIDS. These resources could have been devoted to civil rights efforts and community advancement. Decades of progress in addressing racial inequality were lost. In that time, drug abuse was erroneously treated as a criminal justice problem, rather than as a public health issue. This only served to heighten the epidemic as the police response became a war on the very communities that were in crisis. The public health response to the rapid spread of HIV/AIDS has been tentative and ineffective as well.

Because of these crises, two generations of young people were lost. Many died from violence, drug overdoses, and disease, or they were sent to jail. A miracle is that hard-hit communities survived; none have recovered from these epidemics and the government "war on drugs." Robert Fullilove of Columbia University, details these crises, what was and was not done about them, and the human cost, in chapter 11, "Public Policy, HIV/AIDS and Destruction of

Community in New York City." Following Fullilove comes an addendum by Gusmano and Rodwin, "Inequalities in Health and Access to Health Services in New York City: Change and Continuity." They bring us up to date on the continuing racial disparity in health care access by race in Manhattan, with implications for the other boroughs. This issue is imminently fixable if given sufficient attention.

Chapter 12: Human Development Index

The title of chapter 12 is "The Five New Yorks: Understanding Inequality by Place and Race in New York City Using the American Human Development Index." Kristen Lewis and Sarah Burd-Sharps of Measures of America, a program of the Social Science Research Council, take a close look at the social and economic variations in communities across the city. They have developed an analytic and descriptive tool to monitor the economic resources and quality of life of communities across time. Having applied their human development index to the issue of racial inequality in New York, they report their results in chapter 12. Their work puts in relief the distinct worlds that New Yorkers live in by race and social class, highlighting the toll that racial barriers have had and the depth of the struggle against them.

Chapter 13: Public Housing

In chapter 13, Victor Bach of The New York Community Services Society writes "Public Housing: New York's Third City." Public housing represents one of the most extensive efforts government has made to address poverty and, indirectly, racial inequality. Subsidized housing was intended to provide decent housing, at rents low-income people could afford. In concept, residents would live in an environment where they could benefit from opportunities for upward mobility. Their children could advance via education. However, this has not happened. Instead, public housing has become a way to warehouse Blacks and Latinos, and the government has lost the will to make public housing work as it was intended originally. The result has been long-term disinvestment.

Chapter 14: Political Participation

African Americans and other people of color can influence government to address racial inequality in two important ways: by exercising their right to vote and by participating directly in government. Before the 1964 Civil Rights Act, Blacks were denied these rights in much of the country. New York City was an exception, however. Any citizen of color could vote. Harlem's Black population not only voted; it eventually got large enough to elect its own representatives. After the 1964 Civil Rights Act and the expansion of the African American and Caribbean populations in New York, the number of Black representatives increased. After 100 years, and the Black Reconstruction in the South (1865–1877), efforts to reduce racial inequality through political participation finally began to pay off. In chapter 14, "Black New Yorkers: 50 Years of Closing the Political Inequality Gap, 1965–2016," John Flateau of CUNY, Medgar Evers College, describes the extent to which Black political representation has been attained in New York City. He describes the struggle it took to achieve this, and the difference it has made in people's lives.

Chapter 15: Social Capital and Inequality

Chapter 15, "Social Capital, Gentrification, and Inequality in New York City," focuses on a question that arises whenever race and inequality are discussed. That is, can Blacks, Latinos, Caribbean and the Asian poor reduce social and economic inequality through their own enterprise and actions? This question and chapter return us full circle to Kenneth Clark's thesis that racial inequality in New York and the nation is an issue of social power and the lack of it. Blacks and other people of color do not have sufficient social and economic capital to end racial discrimination. They are reliant on the resources of others. Authors Rodriguez, Hawkins and Wilkes assess whether leaders of community-based agencies and businesses have sufficient social capital to uplift their communities.

Conclusion and Recommendations

In our conclusion, this book provides plenty of evidence that New York City is very much a dual city. The presumption of Black racial inferiority that is the basis of past racial discrimination and segregation has consigned many African Americans to the lesser of the dual cities. New immigrants, who are now mostly people of color, join them. Indeed, if an underlying global economy drives the dual city divide, then reliance on local government and efforts to influence city government as a way to address inequality are in question. Our history is that local government could compel local businesses to follow laws, and act affirmatively. Government can create good schools and even invest in local labor as part of the common good. However, in globalization, the fortune of any one city or state and local population is incidental to the overall bottom line of multinational corporations. Wherever offices, plants and other facilities are placed is conditional on local governments going along with corporate agendas. If local governments and populations demand too much, a business can always move to less demanding locations.

Businesses in the past century benefitted directly from the labor of millions of workers. Businesses could be held partly accountable for their workers' welfare via regulations and taxation. New York City is potentially such a place. However, today, new business entities employ as few people as possible and can move easily their work to wherever they can pay and be taxed the least. Local governments and workforces cannot apply a great deal of pressure on such entities to collaborate with them to redress the sins of the past. Perhaps, we have just not yet found a way to pressure multinational corporate employers meaningfully. The need to address racial inequality is growing, but our ability to make necessary change appears to be waning. Are we too late? Not hardly.

The good news from chapter 1 is that the inequality of the last half-century has been driven more by federal, state, and municipal public policies than by businesses that are too big to fail. In effect, local government still counts and can be a point of leverage to reduce social class and racial inequality, even if federal and state level governments are in question.

In this conclusion, we review major chapter findings, and summarize authors' recommendations on what can and cannot be done to reduce racial inequality in New York City. Our circumstances limit what one city can do. Perhaps in another 50 years, there will be unforeseen progress toward racial equality, and a new macro-assessment will point us toward improvements and show how they were achieved.

Finally, this single-city, in-depth focus could easily be applied to other cities, as well. We hope that this work will be a catalyst for renewed discussions on ways to lower the height of what we call "the race mountain."

Notes

1. Throughout this book, White and Black are capitalized as nouns and adjectives, designating European American and African American racial-ethnic groups, as is already the case in the common capitalization of Latino, Hispanic, and Asian.

References

Alba, R. & Nee, V. (2003). *Remaking the American mainstream*. Cambridge, MA: Harvard University Press.

Auletta, K. (1979). *The streets were paved with gold*. New York, NY: Vintage Books.

Bobo, L., O'Connor, A., & Tilly, C. (2001). *Urban inequality in the United States: Evidence from four cities*. New York, NY: Russell Sage Foundation.

Bowser, B. (2007). *The Black middle class: Social mobility—and vulnerability*. Boulder, CO: Lynne Rienner Publishers.

Clark, Kenneth B. (1965). *Dark ghetto: Dilemmas of social power*. New York, NY: Harper and Row.

Clarke, John Henrik (Ed.). (1969). *Harlem: A community in transition*. New York, NY: Citadel Press.

Curtis, R., & Farnsworth-Jackson, E. F. (1977). *Inequality in American communities*. New York, NY: Academic Press.

Dodson, H., Moore, C., and, Yancey, R. (2000). *The Black New Yorkers*. New York, NY: John Wiley and Sons.

Federal Reserve Bank of New York. (1999). *Unequal incomes, unequal outcomes?: Economic inequality and measures of well-being: Proceedings of a conference sponsored by the Federal Reserve Bank of New York*. New York, NY: Research and Market Analysis Group of the Federal Reserve Bank of New York.

Glazer, N. & Moynihan, D. P. (1963). *Beyond the melting pot: The Negroes, Puerto Ricans, Jews, Italians, and Irish of New York City*. Cambridge, MA: The MIT Press.

Grimshaw, A. D. 1969. *Racial violence in the United States*. Chicago, IL: Aldine Publishing Company.

Harlem Youth Opportunities Unlimited (HARYOU). (1964). *Youth in the ghetto: A study of the consequences of powerlessness and a blueprint for change*. New York, NY: Century Press.

Hirschman, C. & Mogford, E. (2009). "Immigration and the American industrial revolution from 1880 to 1920." *Social Science Research* 38(4), 897–920.

Lhamon, L. (1998). *Raising Cain: Blackface performance from Jim Crow to Hip Hop*. Cambridge, MA: Harvard University Press.

McKay, Claude. (1968). *Harlem: Negro metropolis*. New York, NY: Harcourt Brace Jovanovich, Inc.

Mollenkopf, John H., and Manuel Castells. (1991). *Dual city: Restructuring New York*. New York, NY: Russell Sage Foundation.

Myrdal, G. (1944). *An American dilemma*. New York, NY: Harper and Row.

National Park Service. (2016). Emma Lazarus. New York, NY: U.S. Department of the Interior.

Osofsky, G. (1963). *Harlem: The making of a ghetto*. New York, NY: Harper Torchbooks.

Ottley, R., & Weatherby, W. (Eds.). (1967). *The Negro in New York: An informal social history 1626–1940*. New York, NY: Praeger Publishers.

Rael, Patrick. (2005). *The long death of slavery*. In I. Berlin and L. Harris (Eds.), *Slavery in New York* (111–46). New York, NY: The New Press.

Sacks, M. (2005). Re-Creating Black New York at century's end. In I. Berlin and L. Harris (Eds.), *Slavery in New York*. New York, NY: The New Press.

Scheiner, S. M. (1965). *Negro mecca: A history of the Negro in New York City: 1865–1920*. New York, NY: New York University Press.

Thernstrom, S. (1994). *Poverty and progress: Social mobility in a 19th century city.* Cambridge, MA: Harvard University Press.
Varady, D. P. (2005). *Desegregating the city: ghettos, enclaves, and inequality.* Albany, NY: State University of New York Press.

PART 1

Structural Underpinnings of Inequality

Chapter 1

Economy

Inequality in New York City

The Intersection of Race and Class

James A. Parrott

Introduction

In a December 2013 speech, President Obama stressed that government programs such as Social Security, the minimum wage, Medicare, and Medicaid, have enabled the United States to build the "largest middle class the world has ever known." Despite this achievement, former President Barack Obama highlighted what he believes is "the defining challenge of our time," namely, income inequality that has been on the rise since the late 1970s. Not everyone has benefited equally from these and other programs. He observed that racial discrimination has "locked millions out of opportunity," and that women "were too often confined to a handful of poorly paid professions." President Obama went on to note that "it was only through painstaking struggle that more women and minorities . . . began to win the right to more fairly and fully participate in the economy" (Obama, 2013).

Ironically, victories in these equality struggles occurred in the late 1970s and early 1980s, just as the political and economic forces fueling polarization were gathering steam. New York City is a case in point. The postwar era of broadly shared prosperity in New York City and elsewhere ended in the 1980s when economic gains began concentrating at the top. Initially, income polarization did not preclude rising real incomes for those in the middle.

However, things changed quickly. The favorable economic picture in 1980s New York soon gave way to corporate downsizing in the 1990s, and a rapid increase in low-wage jobs, beginning in the year 2000. As a result, median family incomes for Blacks, Latinos, and Asians have generally stagnated since 1990. In the 35-year period between 1980 and 2015, real median family incomes for all New Yorkers grew by only 14 percent. The improvement among families of color, however, was much lower than for White families, and much less than the 87 percent growth in real per capita income.[1] Median real earnings for full-time workers rose by only 7 percent. New York City's income growth, concentrated in the hands of the few, meant that living standards for most New Yorkers grew far less than the broader growth in the city's economy would have suggested.

This turnaround in broadly-shared prosperity occurred at the same time the composition of New York's population changed. In 1980, the city's population was comprised of 48 percent persons of color. By 2015, this had risen to 68 percent. The percent of immigrants increased from slightly more than a quarter of the city's workforce in 1980 to 46 percent by 2015. During this period, the share of total income held by the richest one percent more than tripled, from 12 percent to 41 percent. White families remained predominant among the top income quintile, and almost certainly among the top one percent.[2]

This chapter assesses several factors that have contributed to New York City's post–1980 family income and earnings trends based on race and ethnicity. These include: the outmigration of Whites in the 1980s and 1990s; the increased number and share of immigrants; economic transformations affecting the relative growth of specific sectors and occupations; the relative economic position of New York City in that changing landscape, and; the broader national dynamic fueling the continued income polarization since the late 1970s.

The Reversal of Broadly Shared Prosperity in New York City

In the first 35 years following World War II, the United States enjoyed a period of broadly shared prosperity (Facundo, Atkinson, Piketty, & Saez, 2013). For most of this 35-year period, the share of all income flowing to the richest one percent was remarkably constant, at around 10 percent. Living standards rose across the board, the middle class grew, and poverty declined. However, as President Obama noted, Blacks and other people of color, as well as women not part of married couple families, did not share fully in this semblance of shared prosperity (Katznelson, 2005).

Beginning around 1980, income growth started concentrating at the top of the income pyramid. As Atkinson, Stiglitz, Hacker, Pierson, and others have argued, the ensuing income polarization resulted more from policy choices, and the increased political influence of those with greater economic power, than it did from globalization or skills-based technological change (Atkinson, 2015; Hacker & Pierson, 2010; 2012). During this time, labor unions were allowed to weaken, and the purchasing power of minimum wages declined. Industries were being deregulated, notably finance, and the government failed to pass campaign finance laws that would prevent the ever-increasing transformation of economic power into political power. This created, as Kuttner has written, "a self-reinforcing circle of more such policies, and more inequality" (Kuttner, 2016).

As figure 1.1 indicates, throughout the years between 1945 and 1980, the one percent's income share in New York State tracked closely with that of the nation's. In 1946, the one percent's share of all New York income was 16 percent. It fell to an average of 13 percent in the 1960s, and a little above 10 percent in the 1970s. The pre-1980 income tax data needed to estimate New York City's income shares is not available, but conceivably, the top one percent's share in the city generally tracked a little above New York State's.[3]

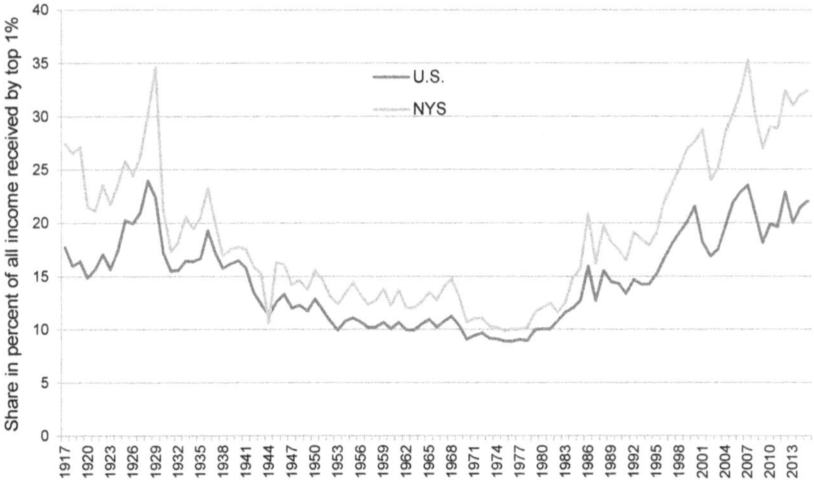

Figure 1.1. 1 percent income share rises sharply after 1970s following three decades of a semblance of "shared prosperity." *Source:* US data, Emmanuel Saez website, table A3, June 2016 update; New York State data, Estelle Sommeiller, Mark Price, and Ellis Wazeter, "Income inequality in the U.S. by state, metropolitan area, and county," Economic Policy Institute, June 16, 2016.

Figure 1.2 shows the one percent income share for New York City, New York State, and the United States since 1980.

It is no surprise that over the past 35 years, the one percent's income share in New York City has risen faster than it has in the nation overall. By 2000, the one percent income share in the city was 35 percent, compared to 22 percent in the United States. By 2015, it had risen to 41 percent, only slightly higher than in 2000 for the entire United States. It should be noted that the share fluctuates in its upward trajectory based on the ups and downs in realized capital gains.

New York City is home to many people working in the highly lucrative finance sector, where compensation has soared commensurate with the growing financialization of the economy. This sector is home to many capital owners who have benefited from the increased capital share of national income. In addition, the city has relatively high concentrations of corporate managers, lawyers and other professionals who have enjoyed large compensation gains.

Gini coefficients, a common statistical measure of income inequality, are based on the Census Bureau's definition of money income. New York City's incomes, based on the Census Ginis, are in fact more unequal than in any of the other 25 largest U.S. cities. However, several cities are not far behind,

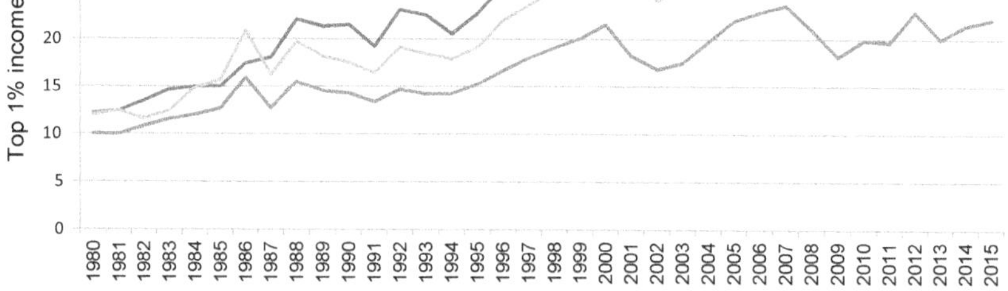

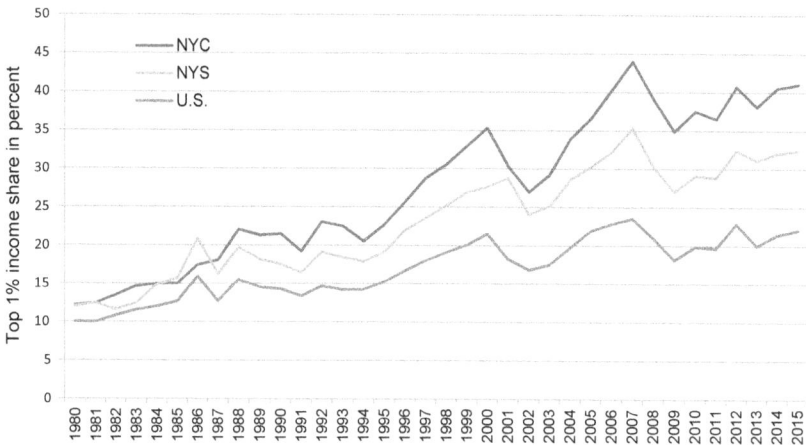

Figure 1.2. The rising share of income going to the top 1 percent since 1980, with the fastest growth in New York City. *Source:* US data, Emmanuel Saez website, table A3, June 2016 update; New York State data, Estelle Sommeiller, Mark Price, and Ellis Wazeter, "Income inequality in the U.S. by state, metropolitan area, and county," Economic Policy Institute, June 16, 2016; New York City data estimates by author based on New York State tax data from the New York City independent budget office.

including Washington, DC, Boston, Dallas, Los Angeles, and Houston (U.S. Bureau of the Census, 2017).

New York City's Changing Population

New York City's population and its composition have changed considerably over the past 35 years. During the 1970s, the city's population declined by over 800,000, sinking to 7.1 million, its lowest level since the 1930s. The out-migration of Whites continued during the 1980s and 1990s, although a steady increase in foreign immigration, buttressed by some domestic in-migration, resulted in net population growth of nearly 21 percent, since 1980. This lifted the city's population to over 8.5 million in 2015. Immigrants accounted for nearly all of the 1.5 million net population increase over this period. The native-born population declined by a little over one percent.

The immigrant portion of New York City's population rose from 24 percent in 1980 to 38 percent in 2015, with the immigrant share of the resident workforce increasing from 27 to 46 percent. Immigrants, who accounted for 88 percent of the nearly 1.3 million total increase in the city's workforce during that period, tend to be concentrated in the working age range. Persons of color comprise 80 percent of the city's immigrant population. So, they represent large shares of the city's non-white, race-ethnicity categories in the resident workforce. Forty-five percent of Black workers are foreign-born, as are 57 percent of Latino workers, and 82 percent of the city's Asian workforce.[4]

Table 1.1 shows that the share of White families in New York City fell sharply between 1980 and 2000, moving even slightly lower by 2015.[5] The

Table 1.1. Distribution of New York City Families by Race/Ethnicity, 1980–2015

	1980	1990	2000	2010	2015
Number, all New York City Families	1,771,000	1,742,000	1,863,000	1,851,000	1,863,000
Shares of all Families	100%	100%	100%	100%	100%
White, Non-Hispanic	54%	44.8%	35.5%	33.1%	32.5%
Black, Non-Hispanic	22.7%	24.8%	24.7%	23.8%	22%
Latino of Any Race	19.7%	23.6%	26.4%	28.4%	28.6%
Asians and All Other Non-Hispanics	3.6%	6.9%	13.4%	14.8%	16.9%

Source: Analysis of 1980–2010 census and 2015 American Community Surveys microdata from IPUMS.

share of Black families rose somewhat between 1990 and 2000, but then returned to the 1980 level in 2015. The share of families who are Latino or Asian grew steadily between 1980 and 2015.

Family Incomes by Race-Ethnicity in Era of Polarization, 1980–2015

The 1980s

In the 1980s, the first decade of pronounced income concentration, median Black and Latino incomes in New York City grew, as did that of Whites. Nevertheless, income gains did accrue disproportionately to those at the high end of the income spectrum. Based on the Census Bureau's Housing and Vacancy Survey, Weitzman noted that the top income decile claimed 42 percent of the total income gains from 1977 to 1986 (Weitzman, 1989). See Figures 1.4 and 1.5 on pages 13 and 14. In fact, during the 1980s, median Black family income grew by one-third, in inflation-adjusted terms, and median Latino family income rose by 27 percent. This was slightly faster than the growth in median White family income (Tobier, 1984).[6]

In the 1980s, the sector including corporate and other production services, expanded (U.S. Bureau of the Census, 1983–2013, 2017). As the economy recovered from the fiscal crisis of the mid-1970s and the loss of 600,000 jobs during that time, well-educated Blacks and Latinos moved into a growing number of new professional and managerial jobs that had opened up.

Black and Latino workers also benefited from the 1980s rebound in city government employment, following the downsizing that had occurred in the immediate wake of the 1975 fiscal crisis. Of the nearly 80,000-strong increase in government jobs in the 1980s, Blacks and Latinos filled well over half of the jobs. The median pay for government jobs in New York City was 25 percent higher than the overall median in 1980, rising to one-third higher in 2015.[7]

The 1990s

In the 1990s, however, the richest one percent again claimed nearly two-thirds of all income growth (figure 1.3), while the inflation-adjusted median incomes of Black, Latino, and Asian families stagnated or declined (table 1.2 on page 10). In part, growth in better-paying jobs was limited by the broader economic transformation in job structure. In the second half of the 1990s, total wage growth was concentrated in high-wage sectors such as finance (Lowenstein, 2016). Native-born Whites were not exempt from the large-scale corporate

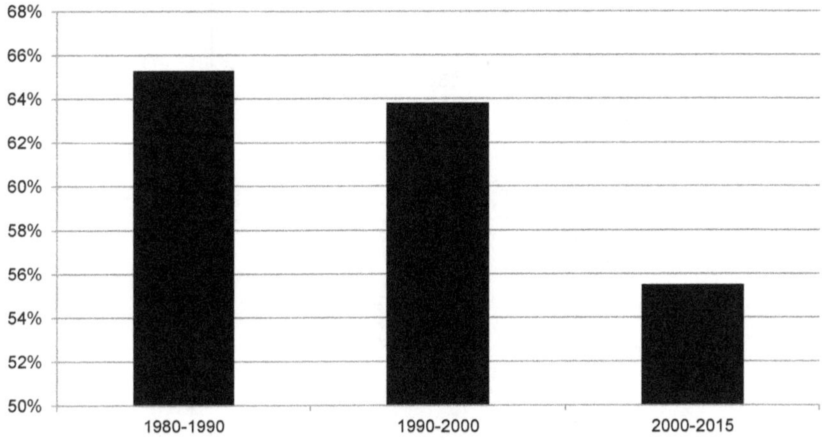

Figure 1.3. Since 1980, 55–65 percent of all income gains have gone to New York City's richest 1 percent. *Source:* Author's estimates based on New York City data in figure 2 and New York State tax data.

downsizing. In the first half of the 1990s, middle-management positions in New York City were reduced dramatically, with over 100,000 administrative support positions disappearing.

The number of native-born Whites holding executive and managerial positions fell by a net of 35,000 in the 1990s, and by over 90,000 in administrative support occupations. The greatest decline was among native-born White women, whose employment numbers fell by more than one-third. In the early 1990s, there was extensive restructuring in the financial sector, resulting in the loss of tens of thousands of middle- and lower-paying jobs. At the same time, top traders and investment bankers were receiving extremely high compensation packages and bonuses. This practice further concentrated income growth at the top levels and encouraged greater risk-taking, speculation, and market and economic instability (Graff, 1995).

During the 1990s, native-born White males lost a net of nearly 50,000 blue-collar jobs, with significant losses in every major occupational grouping. Native-born Black males saw a net loss of nearly 25,000 blue-collar jobs that tended to pay better than low-wage service jobs. Native-born White males lost about 10,000 building service jobs, such as janitors and security guards, and native-born Blacks and Latinos saw a net loss of nearly that number in building services.

Much of the progress Blacks had achieved in the 1980s, securing middle-income government jobs, was undone in the 1990s. In that decade, the

Table 1.2. New York City Median Family Incomes by Race/Ethnicity, 1980–2015

						Change in Median Income				
2015 Dollars	1980	1990	2000	2010	2015	1980–1990	1990–2000	2000–2010	2010–2015	1980–2015
All New York City Families	$55,551	$66,938	$61,616	$59,794	$63,232	20.5%	–8%	–3%	5.7%	13.8%
White, Non-Hispanic	$70,574	$89,309	$89,934	$94,584	$100,151	26.5%	0.7%	5.2%	5.9%	41.9%
Black, Non-Hispanic	$41,916	$56,100	$52,936	$51,097	$56,948	33.8%	–5.6%	–3.5%	11.5%	35.9%
Latino of Any Race	$34,552	$43,988	$44,113	$43,541	$43,006	27.3%	0.3%	–1.3%	–1.2%	24.5%
Asians and All Other Non-Hispanics	$57,184	$65,699	$59,197	$59,794	$60,876	14.9%	–9.9%	1%	1.8%	6.5%

Source: Analysis of 1980–2010 census and 2015 American Community Surveys microdata from IPUMS.

city government reduced employment in social service agencies and the city's public hospital system.[8] Blacks absorbed over 80 percent of the net 50,000-plus decline in government employment in the 1990s.[9]

2000–2015

In the period between 2000 and 2015, median family incomes continued to stagnate for Latinos and Asians, while Blacks saw a moderate increase during that time. The share of all income gains accruing to the richest one percent of the city's workforce moderated, but only slightly. Despite the 2001–2002 and 2008–2009 recessions, New York City saw net resident job growth of 27 percent, adding nearly 900,000 jobs between 2000 and 2014.[10] Growth occurred mainly in three categories: high-wage managerial jobs, which increased 32 percent; middle-wage teaching professions, growing 36 percent, and; low-wage service occupations, including cashiers, household, personal, and food preparation services, and health aides. There was even a net job growth of 70,000 blue-collar jobs, mostly of laborers and drivers. This offset the continued decline among factory occupations like machine operators.

Over this period, the cluster of low-wage service jobs grew by nearly 450,000 jobs or 34 percent. This accounted for half of the city's total job growth. It is worth noting that, for the 1980s and 1990s combined, the low-wage services cluster gained a net of only 16,000 jobs, in part reflecting the loss of over 150,000 administrative support jobs. Still, three low-wage occupational groups grew rapidly from 2000 to 2014, with each adding over 100,000 jobs: health and nursing aides grew by 75 percent; food preparation services increased by 71 percent, and; household and personal services grew by 69 percent. Sales clerks and cashiers added nearly 90,000 jobs, for a 46 percent gain. Building services increased by 67,000 jobs, a growth of 55 percent.

Latinos accounted for a little over half of the net low-wage service job gains that had occurred since the year 2000. Blacks secured about a quarter of the jobs, and Asians obtained a fifth. Whites experienced considerable job growth as well, but they represented only three percent of the low-wage service job growth. Immigrants acquired nearly two-thirds of the low-wage service jobs. Approximately half of the Blacks taking these jobs were foreign-born, while three out of five Latinos and about four out of five Asian workers who moved into these low-wage service jobs were immigrants.

In table 1.3 on page 12, looking back over the period from 2000 to 2010, and then from 2010 to 2014, nearly 60 percent of the total jobs immigrants gained were in low-wage services, and with native-born residents gaining about 40 percent of those jobs. Job growth for Whites was split evenly between high-wage managerial and middle-wage professional jobs. For Blacks, 60

Table 1.3. New York City Job Change by Nativity and Race/Ethnicity, 2000–2010

Job Change, 2000–2010/14		Nativity		Race/Ethnicity			
	Net Job Change	Native-Born	Foreign-Born	Whites	Blacks	Latinos	Asians and Other
Four Occupation Groups	888,727	400,238	488,489	144,859	178,507	383,164	182,197
High-Wage Managerial and Professional	175,660	99,734	75,926	71,345	14,070	32,853	57,393
Middle-Wage Professional	196,601	129,894	66,707	73,874	32,568	50,542	39,618
Middle-Wage Blue Collar	70,315	10,735	59,580	−13,633	23,289	62,689	−2,030
Low-Wage Services	446,151	159,874	286,277	13,273	108,581	237,080	87,217
Shares of Change within Occupation Groups, 2000–2010/14							
Four Occupation Groups	100%	45%	55%	16.3%	20.1%	43.1%	20.5%
High-Wage Managerial and Professional	100%	56.8%	43.2%	40.6%	8%	18.7%	32.7%
Middle-Wage Professional	100%	66.1%	33.9%	37.6%	16.6%	25.7%	20.2%
Middle-Wage Blue Collar	100%	15.3%	84.7%	−19.4%	33.1%	89.2%	−2.9%
Low-Wage Services	100%	35.8%	64.2%	3%	24.3%	53.1%	19.5%
Shares of Change across Occupation Groups, 2000–2010/14							
Four Occupation Groups	100%	100%	100%	100%	100%	100%	100%
High-Wage Managerial and Professional	19.8%	24.9%	15.5%	49.3%	7.9%	8.6%	31.5%
Middle-Wage Professional	22.1%	32.5%	13.7%	51%	18.2%	13.2%	21.7%
Middle-Wage Blue Collar	7.9%	2.7%	12.2%	−9.4%	13%	16.4%	−1.1%
Low-Wage Services	50.2%	39.9%	58.6%	9.2%	60.8%	61.9%	47.9%

Source: Analysis of 2000 census and 2010/2014 American Community Surveys microdata.

percent of the job growth was in low-wage services and only eight percent in high-wage managerial and professional jobs. At nine percent, Latinos had a slightly greater share of job growth in the high-wage managerial positions, and a little over 60 percent in low-wage services. Almost a third of the job growth among Asians was in high-wage managerial positions, and slightly over a fifth was in middle-wage professional jobs.

Local government employment was slightly lower in 2016 than it was in 1990, with human services contracting contributing 84,000 jobs, largely in the nonprofit, and low-paying, social assistance sector. White males hold about five percent of the city's social assistance jobs, while persons of color account for 76 percent of them, and white women hold 19 percent (Parrott, 2017b).

No Convergence of Median Family Incomes by Race

In 1980, the median income of Black families in New York City was only 59 percent that of White families. Median family income for Latinos was 49 percent that of White families. Median Asian family income was 81 percent of Whites, but in 1980, the share of Asian families in New York City was still relatively small: less than four percent. During the 1980s, the faster growth in median Black family income compared to White family income, enabled the black-to-white median ratio to notch up to 63 percent by 1990. As figure 1.4

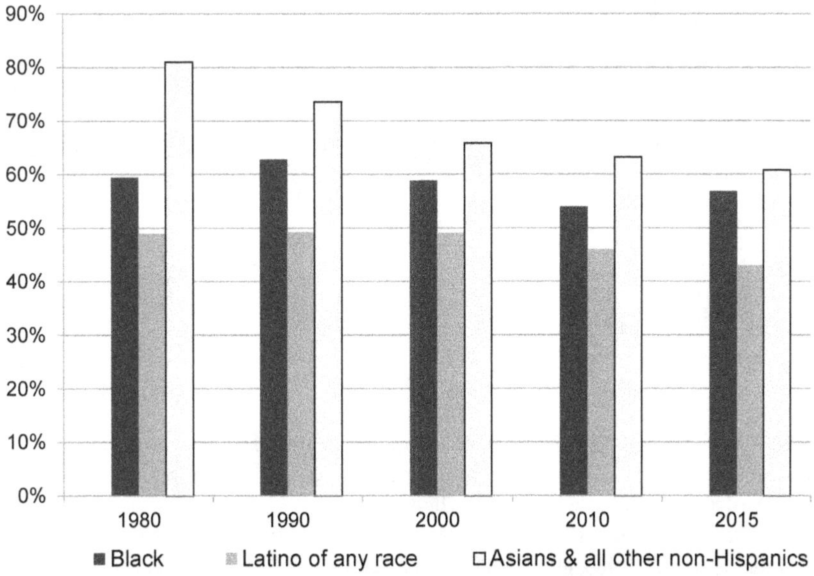

Figure 1.4. New York City median family incomes relative to whites, 1980–2015. *Source:* Analysis of 1980–2010 census and 2015 American Community Surveys microdata from IPUMS.

demonstrates, that was the only time in the four-time intervals between 1980 and 2015 when the ratio of Black, Latino or Asian median family incomes improved in comparison to median White family incomes.

Trends Among Income Ranges by Race-Ethnicity

Another way to examine trends in family income is to divide the income spectrum into three groups, low-, middle-, and high-income, and to categorize income in the constant dollar ranges over time. Using New York City incomes from 2010 as the benchmark, the first four deciles of all family income groups are designated as the low-income group, the next four deciles as the middle-income group, and the top two deciles as the high-income group. Figure 1.5 presents

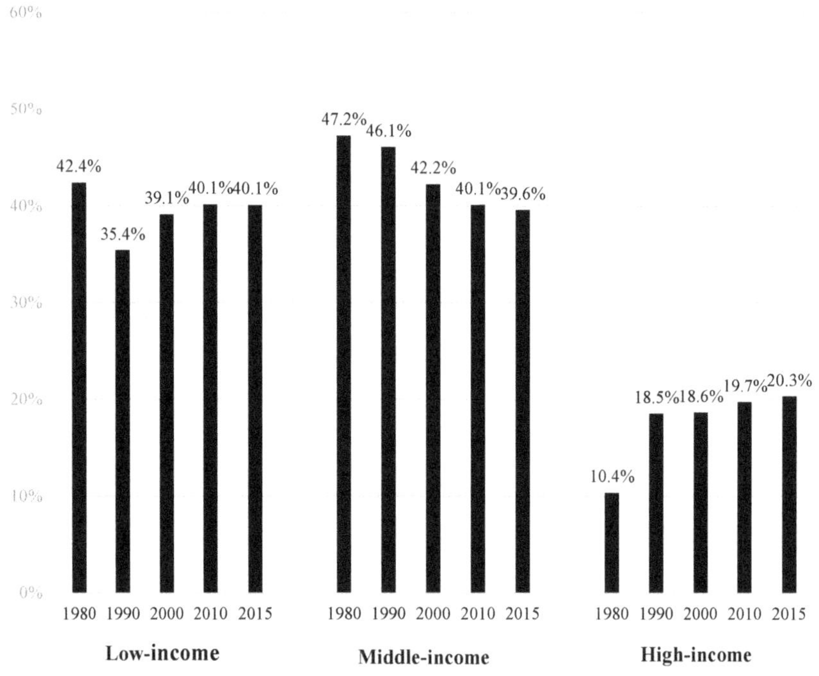

Figure 1.5. Share of all New York City families in low-, middle-, and high-income groups, 1980–2015. Low-income families are those with incomes up to $46,748 (the fortieth percentile in 2010); middle-income families have incomes from above $46,748 up to $130,460 (the eightieth percentile in 2010); high-income families have incomes above $130,460, all in 2015 dollars. *Source:* Analysis of census and American Community Surveys microdata supplied by IPUMS.

the results for all New York City families. Given the strong real median income growth that took place in the 1980s, it is not surprising that this decade saw the largest decline in the share of families in the low-income group and the largest increase in the share of families in the high-income group. In net terms, roughly seven percent of families moved from the low- to the middle-income group, and eight percent of New York City families migrated upward from the mid-income group to the high-income group.

Since 1990, there has been little net income improvement for New York City families. During the 1990s, four percent of families moved downward from the middle- to the low-income group, and in the 2000 to 2010 period, one percent of families moved downward from the middle- to the low-income group. During this same time, one percent of families moved upward from the middle- to the high-income group. From 2010 to 2015 period, a half-percent of families moved up from the middle- to the high-income group.

Consistent with the trends in median family incomes, Whites in 1980 had by far the greatest share of families in the high-income group. In fact, the share of White families in the high-income group more than doubled between 1980 and 2015. Black families experienced substantial income gains in the 1980s, as well, with 13 percent fewer Black families in the low-income group in 1990, than there were in 1980. Black families also increased six percent in the middle-income group and increased by seven percent in the high-income group. The 1990s saw a backslide with approximately three percent of Black families slipping from the middle- to the low-income group. However, there was some improvement in the period between 2010 and 2015, with a slight decline in the share of Black families in the low-income group, as well as increases in the proportion of Black families in the middle- and high-income groups.

Latino and Asian families saw their biggest gains in the 1980s, too, with the number of Latino families in the low-income group holding steady from 1990 on. They also have shown a very gradual shift from the middle- to the high-income group since the 1980s. Asians experienced almost a complete reversal in the 1990s, losing most of what they had gained in the 1980s. Since 2000, the share of Asian families in the low-income group has stabilized, and there has been steady movement from the middle- to the high-income group.

To review, both the low- and middle-income groups comprised 40 percent of the whole, respectively, and the high-income group contained 20 percent. White families tend to have higher incomes, with nearly 40 percent in the middle- and high-income groups, and a little over 20 percent in the low-income group. Asians nearly match the city's overall pattern of income distribution, with 40 percent in low- and middle-income groups, and 20 percent in the high-income group. The share of Blacks in the high-income group is about one-third less than the city distribution overall, and fairly similar shares of Blacks are in the low- and middle-income groups.

Latinos overall have the lowest incomes among the four race-ethnic categories. The share of Latinos in the high-income group is less than half the citywide distribution, and over half of Latinos are in the low-income range. About 40 percent are in the middle-income group. It should be said that, within the top 20 percent of families designated high-income, incomes are highly concentrated at the very top. These families are not only within the top one percent but also within the richest tenth of the top one percent. They are actually among the 370 richest tax filers in the city.[11]

Comparing Trends in Median Earnings by Race-Ethnicity

The growing economic disparity across race-ethnic groups is also apparent in New York City resident worker earnings. Figure 1.6 shows a comparison of the median earnings of White full-time workers compared to those of Blacks, Latinos, and Asians. Relative earnings have declined for these latter three groups, with Latinos experiencing the greatest relative declines. The ratio of Latino median earnings to Whites has fallen from 68 percent in 1980 to 48 percent in 2014. For Blacks, the relative earnings ratio dropped from 78 percent to 62 percent, over the same period. While Asians saw the largest drop in relative median family income, from 80 percent in 1980 to 60 percent in 2014, the overall decline in Asian earnings was six percent, relative to Whites, receding from 70 percent in 1980, to 64 percent in 2014.

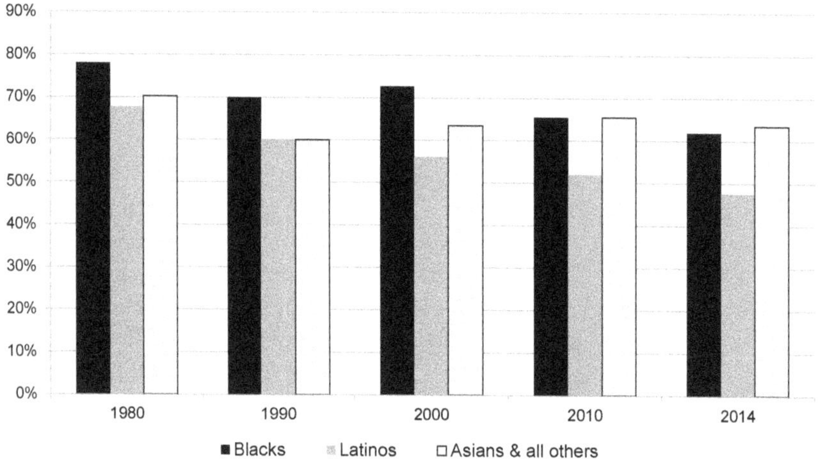

Figure 1.6. New York City earnings relative to whites, 1980–2014. *Source:* Analysis of census and American Community Surveys data provided by IPUMS.

It is worth noting that in the period from 1980 to 2014, the increases in the number of Black, Latino, and Asian resident workers were much greater than the increases in the number of families in each case. According to Census and ACS data on the resident workforce, the number of Black workers rose by 39 percent from 1980 to 2014, with a 129 percent increase in the number of Latino workers, and a 422 percent increase in the number of Asian workers. The number of White workers fell by 11 percent, much smaller than the 36 percent decline in the number of White families. In the absence of a detailed analysis of why these disparities occurred, one could speculate that the differences might be the result of some combination of increased labor force participation, particularly by women, and an increase in the number of non-family households.

Growing Earnings Disparities

There is also evidence of growing earnings disparities between high- and low-wage, full-time workers in New York City, since 1980. According to the data in figure 1.7, the median earnings for all full-time resident workers increased by seven percent from 1980 to 2014. At the same time, lower-wage workers in the first quartile in the earnings distribution, i.e., the 25th percentile experienced a

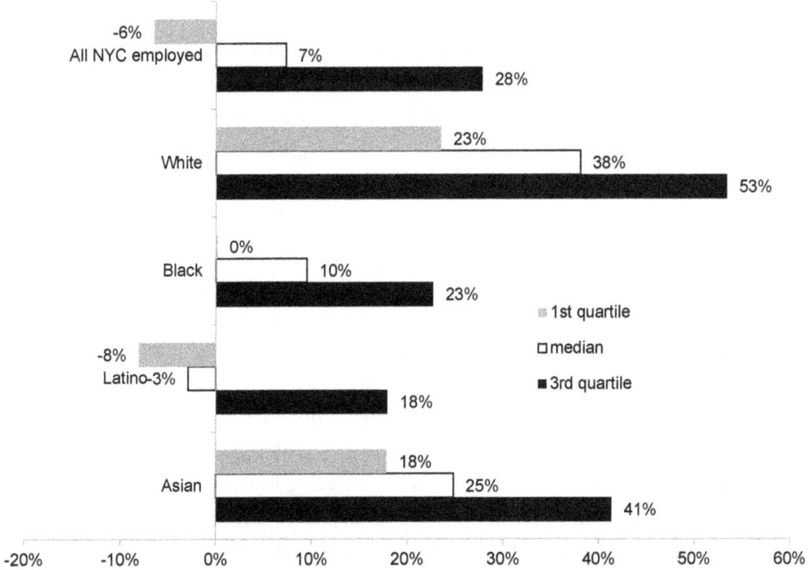

Figure 1.7. New York City resident full-time worker earnings, 1980–2014. Analysis of 1980–2010 *Source:* Census data and 2014 ACS data provided by IPUMS-USA, University of Minnesota. www. ipums.org.

six percent earnings drop. Higher-wage workers in the third quartile, the 75th percentile, saw a 28 percent earnings gain. In 2014, the first quartile earnings level was $23,800, the median $43,500, and the third quartile earnings level was $77,700.

Figure 1.7 indicates a pattern of greater growth as one proceeds up the earnings scale, and this remains consistent for each of the four race-ethnic categories. Whites made greater gains at each wage level than did any of the other three groups. These relatively strong wage gains for Whites, both in the first quartile and at the median, are most likely the result of the loss of lower-paying service jobs during the 1980s and 1990s when Whites were moving out of the city in large numbers. The decline for Latino workers in the first quartile, as well as in median earnings, are probably the result of the influx of recent immigrants, and the substantial growth in low-wage jobs that have occurred since the year 2000. The city's Asian workforce experienced fairly solid growth at all three earnings levels but saw the greatest disparity between the third and first quartile earnings levels. In 2014, third quartile earnings for Asian workers was $72,500, three-and-a-half times the first quartile's $20,700.[12]

The Positive Economic Effects

As of early 2017, New York City has seen eight years of recovery and expansion, and job growth has surpassed that of the nation. The city's economy has experienced broad-based growth in industries such as professional services, technology, and construction. This is the first expansion the city has seen in over fifty years that has not been driven primarily by a booming financial sector. In fact, the securities industry share of total wages in New York City fell from 22 percent in 2000, and 25 percent in 2007, to 19 percent in 2015 (Lowenstein, 2016). For the first time since the 1980s, New York City's growth has raised the wages and incomes of Blacks and Latinos. The city's population continues to grow, and mounting real estate pressures are pushing out some low-income families whose incomes are not keeping pace with rising rents.

The official unemployment rate, 4.6 percent, measured based on a three-month moving average, is at its lowest since late 2006. The only other time it was that low was at the beginning of the modern BLS data series in 1976 (NYS Depart of Labor, 2017). Unemployment rates remain higher for Blacks and Latinos than for Whites, but unemployment rates have been coming down across the board. For the last half of 2016, the employment-to-population ratio for Black males was 58.7 percent: higher than it has been in many years.[13]

From mid-2010 to mid-2016, payroll employment grew by over 15 percent in New York City. Several industries up and down the pay spectrum have achieved significant job gains. One hundred thousand high-wage professional and information sector jobs were added in this period. Industries offering middle-income jobs, including construction, educational services, and health care, have net 140,000 new jobs. Low-wage industries continue to grow rapidly, increasing by nearly one-fourth from 2010 to 2016. These are led by food services and home health care services that together added over 140,000 jobs.[14]

From 2000 to 2013, real median hourly wages for New York City resident workers declined by 1.7 percent. Workers at the top of the wage spectrum were the only ones to see significant wage gains over that period, with wages at the eightieth percentile, rising by 8.7 percent. Sustained, strong job growth and receding unemployment have lifted city workers' fortunes across the board. From 2013 to 2016, the median hourly wage rose by 8.4 percent for all workers. Black and Latino workers have fared better than Whites and Asians during this three-year period. While the median wage for Asian workers declined by 2.5 percent, and the median for Whites increased by 2.4 percent, the median wage for Latino workers jumped by 10.8 percent and for Black workers by 14.5 percent.[15]

Since 2000, there has been a rapid increase in the share of New York City resident workers with four-year college degrees. Migration flows could be a contributing factor in this, with more highly educated in-migrants taking the place of less-educated out-migrants. From 2000 to 2016, there has been a jump from 35 percent to 49 percent of the city workforce holding a four-year college degree or higher. The share of the workforce with a high school diploma or less dropped from 45 percent to 33 percent. The intermediate category, those with some college, saw their share drop from 20 to 18 percent.[16]

The 2015 ACS data for New York City, as well as for the nation overall, showed relatively strong income growth in 2015. The 5.2 percent increase in median U.S. household income is the largest annual gain since Census Bureau record-keeping began in 1967 (Tankersley, 2016). In New York City, median family incomes for Blacks rose more between 2011 and 2015, 8.7 percent, and for Asians, 10.6 percent, than for Whites, which was 7.3 percent. Latino families saw a 6.1 percent income gain (ACS data).

Conclusion

Several data sources have agreed that, since 1980, much of the income growth among New York residents have amassed among the richest one percent of the population. While some families of color have moved into the top one-fifth of New York City earners, and real median family incomes have increased moderately, most of those gains were achieved in the 1980s. Although the current economic expansion has begun to translate into noteworthy income and wage gains for many New Yorkers, as it did in the 1980s, income levels for families of color are not any higher than in 1990. They actually have fallen, relative to White family median incomes.

This analysis has underlined three sets of factors that together shape the intersection of race and class in New York City. First, the demographic changes are resulting from the out-migration of Whites, and the significant in-migration of the foreign-born, most of whom are persons of color. Second, economic transformations in relative industry and occupational growth are stimulating New York City's evolving role in the national and international economy. Third, a widespread national political dynamic is fueling post-1980 income polarization.

These three factors are difficult to disentangle, but the extreme polarization of income growth could be the most profound development to date. The 87 percent growth in per capita income from 1980 to 2015, compared to the 14 percent increase in median family income over the same 35-year period, is an apt illustration.

More than two-thirds of New York City's population are persons of color, many of whom are foreign-born. Forty-two percent of the resident workforce holds either middle- or high-wage professional and managerial occupations. Forty-two percent of families of color have penetrated the top income quintile, and of the 40 percent of people who are in the middle-income quintile, two-thirds are persons of color. However, polarization is still evident in that the living standards of those in the middle significantly lag behind the growth in total income, and the broader productivity gains are driving that income growth. Despite the 87 percent real per capita income growth in New York City since 1980, the poverty rate, as measured by the federal poverty standard, has not dropped since then. Four out of five of those in the 40 percent, low-income family segment, which would be considered poverty or near poverty, are persons of color.

As a hardship measure, the federal poverty standard is notoriously inadequate, particularly in high-cost-of-living areas like New York City. University of Washington researchers estimate that 42 percent of New York City households lack sufficient income to meet minimum basic family needs. Costs include shelter, food, clothing, transportation, childcare, healthcare, and taxes. Looking at individual groups, 61 percent of Latino households, 49 percent of Asian households, and 47 percent of Black households lack sufficient income to cover the costs of living in New York City. On the other hand, only 24 percent of White households are in the same situation (Pearce, Manzer, & Segar, 2014).

Today, local job growth is more concentrated within low-wage industries than it was in the 1980s. Forty percent of job growth since 2010 has occurred in industries with average annual wages under $40,000. Although wages are starting to rise at the bottom of the earnings scale, the career ladder presents fewer opportunities for today's worker to reach the middle class. Due to policy changes in recent decades, and because of insufficient policy responses to the rise of exploitative labor practices, low-wage workers have lost benefits and many employment rights and protections. Noted labor standards expert, David Weil, calls this a "fissure" labor market.

Labor market fissuring encompasses a range of employer practices. These may include increased reliance on temporary workers and contractors, intentionally misclassifying workers as independent contractors, or more nefarious efforts by some employers resulting in systematic wage theft (Bernhardt et al., 2009; Bobo, 2009; Weil, 2014).

We must ask then: "How can the benefits of economic growth be distributed more broadly?" There are clear limits to what local entities can do. Therefore, cities need policy reforms on the national level if they hope to make a perceptible dent in income polarization. The Federal actions instituted under former-President Obama had begun to take effect before he left office. The "2017 Economic Report of the President" indicated that Obama's policies had reduced market-generated inequality more significantly than any policies since the Great Society programs in the mid-1960s. The combined impact of tax policy changes, and the Affordable Care Act's taxing of the rich to pay for expanded health coverage brought about a 20 percent reduction in the ratio of average income of the top one percent related to the bottom 20 percent.[17]

Pathbreaking research by the Harvard-Stanford Equality of Opportunity Project suggests that several local factors can affect intergenerational mobility. For instance, it has long been accepted that having better schools and achieving lower rates of violent crime will affect economic growth. In addition, the progressivity of tax credits, state and local income tax levels, and reduced income and race segregation can all have positive effects (Chetty, Hendren, Kline, & Saez, 2014).

In 2016, New York City began its phase-in of a $15 minimum wage for the state. This change could reduce poverty, and near-poverty, by as much as 750,000 persons, according to research by the City's Center for Economic Opportunity (Mayor's Office of Operations, 2016). New York City's current mayor, Bill de Blasio, has taken steps to raise the wages of thousands of low-wage, nonprofit workers employed under city-funded human services contracts (Parrott, 2017a).

De Blasio has demonstrated, in fact, that large local governments can do many things to bolster the economic futures of low-income communities. In his first year in office, he instituted universal pre-K education, enhancing not only the long-term educational prospects for four-year-olds from low-income families but also saving childcare costs for their parents. In addition, he increased funding for a range of human services, such as homelessness prevention, as well as for programs benefitting immigrants, youth, and seniors. He embarked on an ambitious affordable housing program, made significant investments in public housing, and appointed members to the body that regulates rents for 1.1 million apartments. These appointees have held rent increases to one percent during his first three years in office (Parrott, 2016).

New York City could do even more with a supportive state government, not to mention the right changes in national policies affecting unions, affordable housing, retirement savings, mass transit investments, and forward-looking environmental policies.

Notes

Unless otherwise noted, New York City median family income analysis utilized in this chapter is based on Fiscal Policy Institute analysis of 1980–2010 Census and 2015 American Community Survey microdata provided by IPUMS: IPUMS-USA, University of Minnesota, www.ipums.org (Integrated Public Use Microdata Series).

1. Analysis based on income data expressed in 2015 constant dollars. Growth in real per capita income estimated by the author using New York State income tax data for New York City residents available from either the NYS Department of Taxation and Finance or the New York City Independent Budget Office.

2. See figure 1.2 for the share of total New York City income going to the richest one percent.

3. For decades, the city has accounted for nearly half of total state income.

4. Fiscal Policy Institute analysis of 1980–2000 Census and 2005/07 and 2010/14 American Community Survey microdata from IPUMS.

5. In this analysis, families are categorized by the race/ethnicity of the head of household.

6. In a 1984 report prepared for the Community Service Society, New York University professor Emanuel Tobier presented Census Bureau data showing that there was a 41 percent increase in New York City median family incomes in the 1950s, and a 24 percent real increase in the 1960s. In the 1970s, however, real median family incomes fell by nearly 10 percent. Blacks shared in the 1960s increase, with a real median income gain of 26 percent, and shared in the income deterioration sustained in the 1970s, with a 10 percent decline.

7. Fiscal Policy Institute analysis of 1980–2010 Census and 2014 American Community Survey microdata from IPUMS. Earnings analyzed for resident workers 18 years and older, employed 31 or more hours per week.

8. Walter Stafford pointed this out to the author in the late 1990s.

9. Fiscal Policy Institute analysis of 1980–2010 Census and 2014 American Community Survey microdata from IPUMS.

10. Fiscal Policy Institute analysis of 1980–2000 Census and 2005/07 and 2010/14 American Community Survey microdata from IPUMS. The 2010/14 pooled ACS data will be referred to here as 2014 data.

11. There were 37,273 New York City tax filers in the top one percent in 2014, according to tax data New York City Independent Budget Office, NYC Residents' Income and Tax Liability, Tax Year 2014 http://www.ibo.nyc.ny.us/fiscalhistory.html.

12. Fiscal Policy Institute analysis of 1980–2010 Census and 2014 American Community Survey microdata from IPUMS. Earnings analyzed for resident workers 18 years and older, employed 31 or more hours per week.

13. Fiscal Policy Institute analysis of microdata from the Current Population Survey, July–December 2016.

14. Analysis by the author of New York State Department of Labor Quarterly Census of Employment and Wage data, quarter 2, 2010 and 2016.

15. Fiscal Policy Institute analysis of Current Population Survey microdata.

16. Fiscal Policy Institute analysis of Current Population Survey microdata.

17. *Economic Report of the President, 2017*, Chapter 3, "Progress Reducing Inequality."

References

Atkinson, A. B. (2015). *Inequality: What can be done?* Cambridge, MA: Harvard University Press.

Bernhardt, A., et al. (2009). *Broken laws, unprotected workers: Violations of employment and labor laws in America's cities*. Los Angeles: Center for Urban Economic Development, National Employment Law Project, and UCLA Institute for Research on Labor and Employment.

Bobo, K. (2009). *Wage theft in America: Why millions of working Americans are not getting paid—and what we can do about it*. New York, NY: The New Press.

Chetty, R., Hendren, N., Kline, P., & Saez, E. (2014). Where is the land of opportunity? the geography of intergenerational mobility in the United States. *Quarterly Journal of Economics, 129*(4), 1553–1623.

Facundo, A., Atkinson, A. B., Piketty, T., & Saez, E. (2013). The top 1 percent in international and historical perspective. *Journal of Economic Perspectives, 27*(3), 3–20.

Graff, B. I. (1995). Employment trends in the security brokers and dealers industry. *Monthly Labor Review, 118*(9), 20–29.

Hacker, J. S., & Pierson, P. (2010). *Winner-take-all politics: How Washington made the rich richer—and turned its back on the middle class*. New York, NY: Simon & Schuster.

Katznelson, I. (2005). *When affirmative action was White*. New York, NY: W.W. Norton.

Kuttner, R. (2016). The new inequality debate. *The American Prospect*, Vol. 27, No. 1, Winter.

Lowenstein, R. (2016). *A quarter century of economic change in New York City: A (very) brief history*. Paper presented at the Walter Stafford Symposium, New York University.

Mayor's Office of Operations. (2016). *CEO poverty measure 2005–2014, an annual report*. Retrieved from New York: The Mayor's Office for Economic Opportunity, April 2016. https://www1.nyc.gov/assets/opportunity/pdf/16_poverty_measure_report.pdf.

NYS Depart of Labor. (2017). Seasonally adjusted Labor Force data for New York City through Feb. 2017. Retrieved from https://labor.ny.gov/stats/LSLAUS.shtm.

Obama, B. (2013). *Remarks by the President on Economic Mobility*. Retrieved from Obama White House Archives Washington, DC: https://obamawhitehouse.archives.gov/the-press-office/2013/12/04/remarks-president-economic-mobility

Parrott, J. A. (2016). Going local in the fight against inequality, what progressives can learn from de Blasio's policies in New York City. *The American Prospect*, Vol. 27, No. 4 (Fall), 17–19.

Parrott, J. A. (2017a). *Briefing on Mayor de Blasio's preliminary FY 2018 NYC budget: Budgeting cautiously under a Washington cloud*. Retrieved from New York, N.Y.: Fiscal Policy Institute. http://fiscalpolicy.org/wp-content/uploads/2017/03/Parrott-BudgetBriefingNYC2017-FINAL.pdf.

Parrott, J. A. (2017b). *Undervalued & underpaid: How New York State shortchanges nonprofit human services providers and their workers*. New York, NY: Restore Opportunity Now.

Pearce, D. M., Manzer, L., & Segar, K. (2014). *Overlooked and undercounted: The struggle to make ends meet in New York City*. Retrieved from New York, N.Y.: The United Way of New York City. http://selfsufficiencystandard.org/sites/default/files/selfsuff/docs/NYC2014.pdf.

Stiglitz, J. E. (2012). *The price of inequality: How today's divided society endangers our future*. New York, NY: W. W. Norton & Company.

Tankersley, J. (2016, September 13). U.S. household incomes soared in 2015, recording biggest gain in decades. *The Washington Post*.

Tobier, E. (1984). *The changing face of poverty, trends in New York City's population in poverty: 1960–1990*. New York, N.Y.: Community Service Society of New York.

U.S. Bureau of the Census. (1983–2013). *1980–2010 census microdata*. Retrieved from: www.ipums.org.

U.S. Bureau of the Census. (2017). *2015 American Community survey microdata*.

Weil, D. 2014. *The fissured workplace: Why work became so bad for so many and what can be done to improve it*. Cambridge, MA: Harvard University Press.

Weitzman, P. 1989. *Worlds apart: Housing, race/ethnicity and income in New York City, 1978–1987*. New York, NY: Community Service Society of New York.

Chapter 2

Housing

The Paradox of Inclusion and Segregation in the Nation's Melting Pot

Ingrid Gould Ellen, Jessica Yager, and Maxwell Austensen

New York City is known for its diversity. Throughout its history, the city has welcomed waves of new immigrants. Its residents pride themselves on the diversity of the city's population, neighborhoods, and culture. In 2010, no single racial group constituted more than 33 percent of the city's population, and immigrants comprised 37 percent of the population. Conversely, New York City has consistently been one of the most racially segregated cities in the nation and has become more so over time. Segregation levels have barely changed in New York since 1980, yet Black/White segregation has declined in most other cities around the country.

Segregation such as this has its consequences. Black and Hispanic New Yorkers live in neighborhoods with higher poverty levels, lower-performing schools, and a greater degree of violence than their White and Asian counterparts do. There are some more encouraging trends, as well. Poverty concentration has declined in the city, at the same time it has risen around the country, and by some measures, the lives of racial groups in different neighborhoods have converged.

After providing a brief overview of the existing research on segregation trends and consequences, this chapter will describe how segregation patterns in New York City have changed over time, and what those patterns signify for the neighborhoods that New Yorkers of different races call home. We conclude with a brief discussion of how New York City could respond to help reduce the integration barriers that currently exist.

Background

It has been five decades since the Fair Housing Act was passed. Nevertheless, Whites and members of other racial/ethnic groups continue to live in separate and distinct neighborhoods. Although on average, Black/White segregation has fallen steadily, it has persisted in many cities. Segregation levels among Hispanics and Asians have remained constant since 1980. On the national level, concentrated poverty has been more volatile, rising during the 1980s, dropping in the 1990s, and then rising again in the 2000s.

Recent Trends in Racial Segregation

Since 1980, Black/White segregation has fallen slowly, but consistently, in most metro areas[1] around the country (Farley & Frey, 1994; Logan & Stults, 2011). Still, in 2010, Blacks and Whites rarely shared neighborhoods. At that time, on average, Whites tended to live in neighborhoods with only a small share of minorities, and Blacks lived in neighborhoods with high concentrations of minorities, but few Whites (Logan and Stults, 2011).

Despite the rapid rise of Hispanic and Asian populations in the country, the extent of their segregation from Whites has remained largely unchanged since 1980 (De la Roca, Ellen, & O'Regan, 2014; Rugh & Massey, 2014). However, as their numbers have enlarged, both Asians and Hispanics find themselves living in areas populated more and more by members of their own culture. Hispanics are also faced with increasing isolation rates, so that now they have reached the rate documented for Blacks in 2010 (De la Roca, Ellen, & O'Regan, 2014).

These averages, however, conceal significant variations that exist in racial segregation trends across jurisdictions. Using 1970 to 2010 census data, Rugh and Massey (2014) discovered that broadly integrated metro areas shared several characteristics. These areas had minority populations with relatively high socioeconomic status. In addition, there were low levels of racial prejudice, low immigration rates, and lenient zoning codes. Other research has shown that segregation dropped faster in metro areas with small Black populations (Logan, 2013; Massey & Gross, 1991). Metropolitan areas with a sizeable, poor, Black population showed the highest levels of Black/White segregation in 2010 (measured by dissimilarity index). These included Detroit, Milwaukee, New York, Newark, Chicago, Philadelphia, Miami, Cleveland, St. Louis, and Nassau-Suffolk, New York (Logan and Stults, 2011, 6–7; Rugh & Massey, 2014).

Metropolitan poverty concentration trends fluctuate more across decades. They increased between 1970 and 1990, fell during the 1990s, and rose again during the 2000s. Specifically, the percentage of poor people living in extreme poverty neighborhoods (areas where at least 40 percent of the population is poor) rose almost four percentage points, from 12.7 percent to 16.4 percent, during the 1990s, dropped to 11.4 percent in 2000. It then rose again to 14.1 percent by 2014 (Iceland & Hernandez, 2016). Jargowsky had similar findings (1997, 2013). Both Whites and Blacks were affected by this trend. The number of poor Blacks living in high-poverty neighborhoods decreased from 1980 to the present, while the share of poor Whites living in concentrated poverty increased. Nevertheless, poor Blacks were far more likely to live in high-poverty neighborhoods than were poor Whites (23.1 percent versus 8.2 percent in 2010–14).

The Case of New York City

When researchers looked at segregation shifts in New York City neighborhoods, they noted that, for the most part, Black residents had been excluded from the increasingly integrated tracts (Flores & Lobo, 2013; Rosenbaum & Argeros, 2005). Flores and Lobo (2013) examined forty years of neighborhood transitions in New York City. They observed that, over time, the White-dominant neighborhoods became more integrated and remained stable but did not include Blacks. Flores and Lobo go on to report that neighborhoods occupied by Whites and non-Black minorities comprised 13 percent of the city's neighborhoods overall in 1970, and 27 percent in 2010. Neighborhoods shared by Whites and Blacks comprised 15 percent of all neighborhoods in the city, down from 22 percent in 1970. These locations were judged less stable, and more prone to transition to all-minority. All-minority tracts were deemed least likely to transition to integrated, had the highest poverty rates, and offered the fewest amenities to residents.

Others researchers corroborate this finding. Many have found that in New York City, access to neighborhood amenities is unequal, based on race. Of households with children, Whites live in the most advantageous neighborhoods, native-born Blacks live in the poorest-quality neighborhoods, and foreign-born Black, as well as native and foreign-born Hispanic households, live in neighborhoods ranking somewhere in the middle (Rosenbaum & Friedman, 2001).

Consequences of Segregation

As segregation in the United States persists, there is a growing body of research exploring how living in segregated environments affects residents. Using data from the 1990 Census, Cutler, et al. (1997) found that African Americans living in metro areas with higher levels of segregation had worse outcomes across a variety of measures. These individuals had lower high school graduation rates, lower employment rates, lower earnings, and women had a higher likelihood of becoming a single mother. Researchers controlled for individual characteristics (age, race, ethnicity, and gender), and city characteristics (size, median income, non-White population, region), and the results held firm. The studies showed that segregation led to inferior outcomes, it did not simply correlate with those outcomes. Additional inquiries revealed a range of negative results for Black residents living in highly segregated metropolitan areas (Ananat, 2011; Ellen, 2000).

Research also has shown that Hispanics living in more segregated metropolitan areas tend to reside in neighborhoods with higher poverty rates, lower shares of college-educated residents, lower-performing schools, and higher levels of violence. This is compared to Hispanics living in less segregated areas (De la Roca et al., 2014; Steil, De la Roca, & Ellen, 2015). These disparities appear to make a difference in life opportunities. Twenty- to thirty-year-old, native-born Hispanics, are less likely to graduate from college, have lower employment rates, earn less money, and are more likely to be single mothers (Steil et al., 2015).

When considering economic segregation, some studies have suggested that growing up in high-poverty neighborhoods decreases children's opportunities in life (Sharkey & Faber, 2014). Most recently, researchers Chetty, Hendren, and Katz (2016) have evaluated the effects of the Moving to Opportunity experiment, a program in which the U.S. Department of Housing and Urban Development makes it possible for households living in high-poverty areas to move to lower-poverty areas, by providing them with vouchers. Their study revealed that children under the age of 13 whose households moved to a more prosperous area were more likely: (1) to attend college; (2) to earn more as an adult, and; (3) to live in a lower-poverty neighborhood as an adult. These children also were less likely to be single mothers. It is worth noting, however, that for children who moved when they were 13 or older, the effects were "slightly negative" (Chetty et al., 2016, 858).

How Segregated is New York City?

Trends in Racial Segregation

The dissimilarity index most commonly measures segregation. This index measures how evenly two different groups are distributed across neighborhoods within a metropolitan area. To interpret an index, one can identify the proportion of one group that would need to move to achieve a uniform distribution of different groups across neighborhoods in a city. For instance, table 2.1 shows that levels of segregation between White and non-White residents in New York City have remained largely unchanged since 1980. Like most researchers, we use census tracts as a proxy for neighborhoods. The tracts, drawn by the Census Bureau, house an average of 4,000 people.[2]

Between 1980 and 2010, the average Black/White dissimilarity index in metropolitan areas around the country fell from 73.1 to 59.4. During this same period, racial segregation remained virtually unchanged in New York. In New York City, the Black/White dissimilarity index remained at around 83, between 1980 and 2000, and then fell slightly to 81.6 in 2010. This means that 81.6 percent of White or Black New Yorkers would have to move to a different neighborhood for Blacks and Whites to be distributed equally across neighborhoods. Similarly, Asian segregation remained unchanged between 1980 and 2010, with the Asian/White dissimilarity index staying between 48 and 50. The Hispanic/White dissimilarity index rose slightly between 1980 and 2000, from almost 64 to 67, before dipping to just below 66 in 2010.

Table 2.1. Racial Dissimilarity and Isolation Indices in New York City

	1980	1990	2000	2010
Dissimilarity				
Asian-White	49.7	48.8	49.6	50.7
Black-White	82.5	83.8	83.2	81.6
Hispanic-White	63.8	65.8	66.9	65.8
Isolation				
Asian	16.9	21.8	28.1	33.2
Black	64.4	64.3	62.1	57.7
Hispanic	41.7	45.3	48.1	48.0
White	78.4	73.1	66.3	62.6

Source: Neighborhood Change Database.

During this same period, other large cities in the U.S. saw substantial declines in Black/White segregation. In Los Angeles, for example, the Black/White dissimilarity index fell from 85 to 67; in Chicago, it fell from 91 to 83.[3] Figure 2.1 shows changes in the Black/White dissimilarity index for the ten largest cities in the United States. The figure underscores how little change has occurred in New York, compared to the sizeable declines in all other large cities. By 2010, the city attained the second highest Black/White dissimilarity index among the ten largest cities, up from fourth highest in 1980. It is unclear why Black/White segregation in New York persists to this degree. New York City is less of an outlier concerning change in Hispanic/White segregation, although in 2010, it did have the highest Hispanic/White segregation level among the large cities (see figure 2.2).

Over the last 30 years, there has been little change in the degree to which White New Yorkers have been segregated from New Yorkers of other races. Despite the city's population becoming more diverse, racial groups more commonly live in neighborhoods with others of their same group. Table 2.1, which indicates the isolation index for New York City, shows the proportion

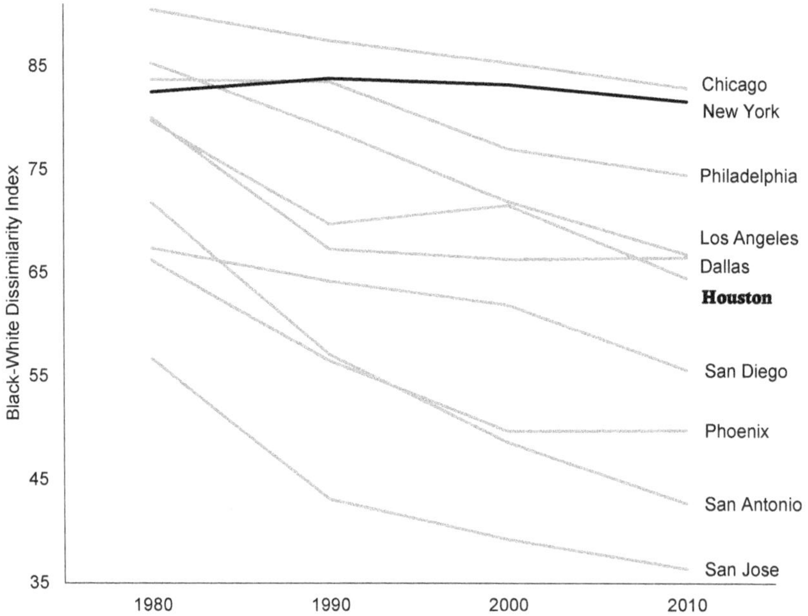

Figure 2.1. Changes in black-white dissimilarity index for the ten largest US cities. *Source:* Neighborhood Change Database.

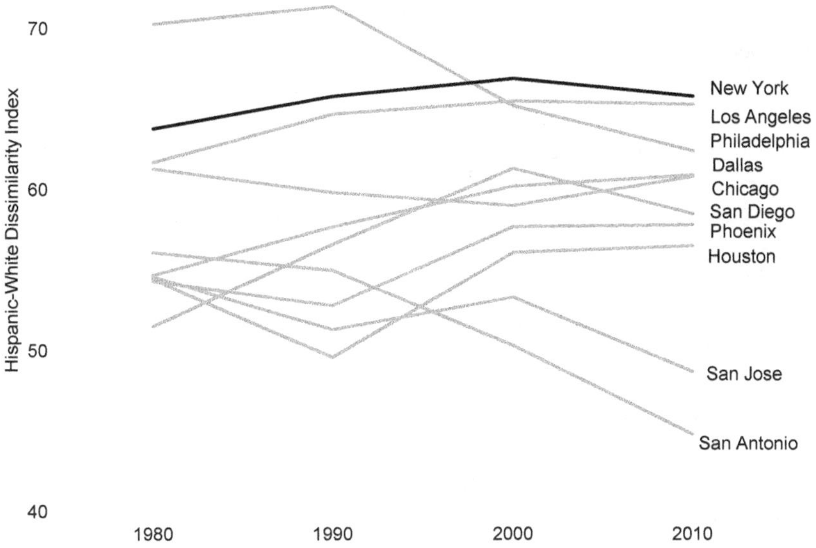

Figure 2.2. Changes in Hispanic-white dissimilarity index for the ten largest US cities. *Source:* Neighborhood Change Database.

of a typical resident's racial group in each neighborhood's population. For example, table 2.1 shows that in 2010, the average Hispanic resident of New York City lived in a census tract that was 48 percent Hispanic. The isolation index naturally grows or shrinks as the population of a given group grows/shrinks in the city, even if their distribution remains constant.

Not surprisingly then, Asian and Hispanic New Yorkers grew more isolated as their numbers increased. Asian New Yorkers experienced the largest increase in population share and the largest increase in isolation between 1980 and 2010. In 1980, the typical Asian resident was living in a neighborhood with 17 percent Asian population. By 2010, that share grew to 33 percent. During this same period, Hispanic New Yorkers experienced a much smaller increase in isolation, as well as an increase in population share. In 1980, the typical Hispanic New Yorker was living in a neighborhood that was 42 percent Hispanic. In both 2000 and 2010, it had grown to 48 percent. It is also of interest that, in 2010, Hispanics accounted for a larger share of the city's population than did Blacks, and Hispanics were only about five percentage points below Whites. The typical Hispanic New Yorker lives in a neighborhood with a much smaller share of neighbors who are co-ethnics than do members of either of the other two groups.

Between 1980 and 2010, the White population share in New York City dropped by 19 percentage points, and the White isolation index fell from 78.4 to 62.6. In 2010, most White New Yorkers continued to live in neighborhoods where the majority of residents were of their same race. In 2010, White New Yorkers lived in neighborhoods that were 63 percent White, even though they comprised only one-third of the city's population.

During the period between 1980 and 2010, the Black isolation index fell from 64.4 to 57.7, despite the fact that the Black population share remained roughly constant. The change occurred because Blacks and other minority groups mixed more as their populations grew. Black New Yorkers in 2010 were more likely to live with Asians, and even more commonly, with Hispanics, than they were in 1980. By contrast, Black New Yorkers were less likely to live with Whites in 2010 than they were in 1980.

In short, changes in the isolation index reveal that New York City residents continue to live in neighborhoods where their own racial and ethnic groups are over-represented. As New York City has become more diverse, White and Black New Yorkers are living in less racially isolated neighborhoods. However, on average, members of both groups continue to live in neighborhoods where a majority of the residents is of the same race.

It is worth noting that, New York City's dissimilarity and isolation indices may overstate the degree of segregation that exists, relative to other cities, because of the city has a higher residential density. The typical census tract in the United States covers about two square miles. In New York, the typical census tract covers less than a tenth of a square mile. As a result, the dissimilarity and isolation indices consider many New Yorkers living in very close proximity to one another, actually to be living in different neighborhoods. The common segregation indices also may understate segregation because they consider every neighborhood isolated. They do not take into account the clustering of census tracts in which one racial or ethnic group predominates. Map 2.1 highlights the neighborhoods in which more than half of the residents identify as belonging to one group, and each other group makes up less than 20 percent of residents. The map clearly shows a very high level of clustering in New York City.

Measures of Integration

Another way to capture changes in residential spatial patterns, by race, is to track the share of a population living in racially integrated neighborhoods. Table 2.2 pinpoints what share of the population of different groups lives in racially integrated tracts. We define these as census tracts in which at least 20

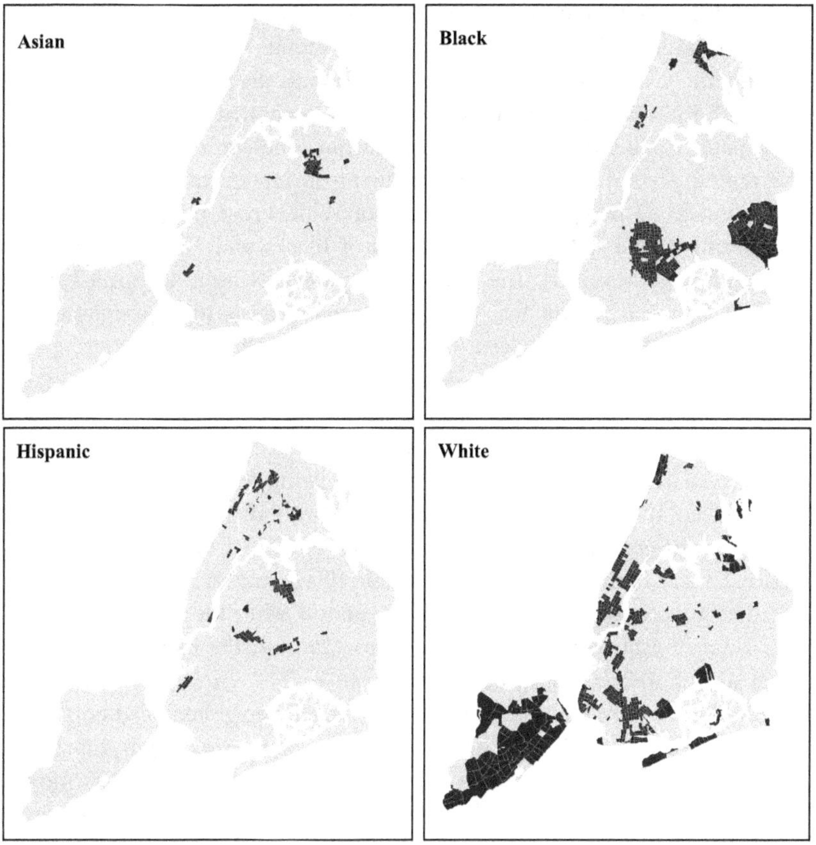

Map 2.1. Predominant racial/ethnic group by census tract in New York City, 2010. *Source:* Neighborhood Change Database.

Table 2.2. Share of Population Living in Integrated Tracts in New York City

	1980	1990	2000	2010
Total Population	22.3%	20.8%	25.6%	26.1%
Asian	38.2%	36.7%	43.1%	41.7%
Black	15.7%	12.1%	10.6%	10.5%
Hispanic	34.2%	25.3%	24.3%	22.1%
White	19.7%	20.9%	32.0%	34.6%

Source: Neighborhood Change Database.

percent of the population is White, and at least 20 percent of the population belongs to at least one other racial or ethnic group.

As the city became more racially and ethnically diverse between 1980 and 2010, the share of New Yorkers living in integrated tracts rose from 22 to 26 percent. This increase, however, did not hold for all groups. In these intervening years, the share of Asians living in integrated tracts rose from 38 percent to 42 percent, and the share of Whites rose from 20 percent to 35 percent. At the same time, the shares of Blacks and Hispanics living in integrated tracts declined. The share of Hispanics living in integrated tracts dropped from 34 percent in 1980, to 22 percent by 2010. Throughout this period, Black New Yorkers were the least likely of all four ethnic groups to live in integrated tracts. Sixteen percent of Blacks lived in integrated tracts in 1980, but only 10.5 percent in 2010. As noted earlier, even though Black New Yorkers were living in more diverse neighborhoods in 2010 than they had been in 1980, they were less likely to be living with Whites.

Indeed, the growth in integrated neighborhoods in the city was driven entirely by the growth in White/Asian and White/mixed-race neighborhoods. Figure 2.3 shows that the number of White/Black and White/Hispanic integrated neighborhoods declined during this period, while the number of White/mixed neighborhoods climbed from 69 to 129, and the number of White/Asian neighborhoods ballooned from seven to 217. In 2010, White/Asian neighborhoods were the largest category of racially integrated neighborhoods.

Virtually all of the neighborhoods that emerged as newly integrated during this time shifted that way because minority group members moved into mostly White tracts, not the reverse. This is consistent with the Flores and Lobo analysis (2013). Despite growing concern about the gentrification

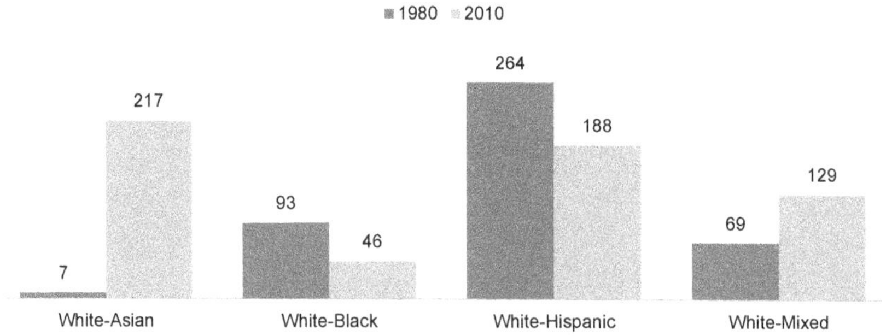

Figure 2.3. Integrated neighborhoods by type in New York City, 1980 and 2010. *Source:* Neighborhood Change Database.

of largely Black neighborhoods, 90 percent of the tracts that became newly integrated during this period had been predominantly White tracts in 1980.

Stability is key when considering integration. Is racial integration merely transitory? Alternatively, to paraphrase Saul Alinsky, is it more accurately the period between the first minority moving in and the last White moving out (Alinsky & Sanders, 1970)? Of the 432 tracts that were integrated racially in 1980, only 118 (27 percent) remained racially integrated in 2010. Eighty percent of those that were no longer racially integrated transitioned to either mixed-minority, majority Hispanic, or majority Black. However, racially integrated neighborhoods do change somewhat slowly and appear to be growing more stable over time. Of the New York City census tracts that were integrated racially in 1980, 60 percent remained racially integrated in 1990. Of the city tracts that were integrated racially in 2000, a full 73 percent remained integrated in 2010.

Does Racial Segregation Produce Separate but Equal Neighborhoods?

Ethnic concentration on its own is not inherently harmful. It becomes detrimental, though, when segregation reduces residential options and leads to inequities in the resources and services available to the groups living in these neighborhoods. Unfortunately, this seems to be the case in New York City. Our analysis below demonstrates that segregation in New York City has resulted in members of some racial groups, in particular, Blacks and Hispanics, living in dramatically different neighborhoods than other New Yorkers. These differences are measured by poverty rate, the share of adults with college degrees, school performance, crime, and access to parks and subways.

Racial Differences in Exposure Rates to Neighborhood Characteristics

Table 2.3 on page 36 presents the average exposure to poverty for different racial groups in 1980 and 2010, or during the five-year span between 2006 and 2010.[4] Specifically, the table shows the average poverty rate, by census neighborhood, that Whites, Blacks, Hispanics, and Asians faced in 1980, as well as during the years 2006 to 2010. The table indicates that large disparities remain in how different racial groups are exposed to poverty. In the years between 2006 and 2010, the typical Hispanic New Yorker lived in a neighborhood with a poverty rate of 25 percent, and the typical Black New Yorker lived in a neighborhood with a poverty rate of 22 percent. By contrast, the typical Asian and White New Yorkers lived in neighborhoods with 16 and 13 percent poverty rates, respectively.

Although these large disparities still exist, they have decreased significantly in the past 30 years. In 1980, the typical White New Yorker lived in a neighborhood with a poverty rate nearly 18 percent lower than the neighborhood a typical Black New Yorker lived in. By 2010, that gap had shrunk to fewer than ten percentage points. The gap shrank because the average Black and Hispanic New Yorkers are now living in neighborhoods with lower poverty than they had in 1980. At that time, they lived in neighborhoods with poverty rates of 30 percent. Also, between 1980 and 2010, White New Yorkers saw a slight increase in exposure to poverty.

One also finds discrepancies across groups when examining their exposure to college-educated adults. In the five-year span between 2006 and 2010, both Black and Hispanic New Yorkers on average lived in neighborhoods in which 22 percent of adults had college degrees. By contrast, Asian and White New Yorkers lived in neighborhoods with average college-educated shares of 34 and 45 percent, respectively.

Despite these wide differences, however, all racial groups have seen substantial gains in the share of college-educated adults in their neighborhoods. Between 1980 and 2010, the typical Black and Hispanic New York neighborhoods, saw the share of college-educated residents rise by 13 percentage points in 1980 and 12 percentage points in 2010. In White and Asian neighborhoods, the gains were even larger: 15 percentage points in 1980 and 24 percentage points in 2010.

Segregation in New York City has also meant that Black and Hispanic children live near lower-performing schools. This is not so for the typical White or Asian child. Table 2.4 illustrates this for the year 2014. In the elementary schools that White and Asian children lived near, over half the children scored at proficient levels on statewide math tests. By contrast, Black

Table 2.3. Typical Neighborhood Poverty Rate and Share of Adults with College Degrees by Race/Ethnicity in New York City, 1980 and 2006–2010

	Poverty Rate		Share of Adults with College Degrees	
	1980	2006–10	1980	2006–10
Asian	16.5%	16.2%	19.2%	33.8%
Black	29.5%	22.4%	8.7%	21.9%
Hispanic	29.9%	25.0%	10.1%	22.2%
White	11.9%	13.2%	20.6%	44.9%

Source: Neighborhood Change Database.

Table 2.4. Typical Neighborhood Conditions by Race/Ethnicity in New York City

	Fourth Grade Students in 2014 Proficient In		Crimes per 1,000 Residents per Year (2010–14)		Residential Units in 2014 Within	
	English Language Arts	Math	Violent	Property	¼ Mile of a Park	½ Mile of a Subway/ Rail Entrance
Asian	41.1%	54.7%	3.6	8.9	65.4%	68.7%
Black	22.0%	26.6%	6.9	8.8	72.1%	62.6%
Hispanic	25.4%	34.0%	5.9	8.2	78.3%	76.1%
White	44.3%	54.2%	2.9	9.7	68.4%	67.2%

Sources: Neighborhood Change Database; New York City Police Department; U.S. Census Bureau; New York City Department of Education; New York City Department of Transportation; New York City Department of City Planning; New York City Department of Parks and Recreation; New York State Office of Parks, Recreation, and Historic Preservation; PLUTO; and New York University's Furman Center.

and Hispanic children lived near schools in which only 27 percent and 34 percent of children scored proficient in math, respectively. To be sure, test scores are not a complete or ideal measure of school quality, but they are used widely by researchers as a rough proxy for school performance.

Different groups also experience very different levels of safety in their neighborhoods. Table 2.4 shows this. Between 2010 and 2014, the typical Black New Yorker lived in a neighborhood with an average of 6.9 violent crimes per 1,000 residents per year, while the typical Hispanic neighborhood averaged 5.9 violent crimes per 1,000 residents. In sharp contrast, during these same years, the average violent crime rates for the typical Asian and White New Yorkers were 3.6 and 2.9 violent crimes per 1,000 residents. That is roughly half the violence faced by their Black and Hispanic counterparts. Interestingly, when it comes to property crime, rates were slightly lower in Black and Hispanic neighborhoods than they were in other New York communities.

Proximity to parks and subways is another neighborhood variable shown in table 2.4. In this case, the disparities among racial groups are smaller. In fact, more of the city's Hispanic residents live close to both parks and subways than any other group.

Trends in Poverty Concentration/Segregation

We have seen that New York City has made less progress than other large cities in reducing racial segregation, or at least segregation between Blacks and Whites. However, it has experienced *larger* reductions in the spatial segregation of the poor. Poor New Yorkers are much less likely to be living in areas of concentrated poverty today than they were in 1980. Figure 2.4 compares the share of the city's poor population that was living in high-poverty tracts and extreme-poverty tracts in 1980 and 2010. The share for both tracts dropped significantly. Forty-two percent of poor New Yorkers were living in high-poverty tracts in 2010, down from 54 percent in 1980, and 20 percent of poor New Yorkers were living in extreme-poverty tracts in 2010, down from 34 percent in 1980.

These changes are the direct result of greatly reduced poverty in high-poverty neighborhoods, and of modest increases in poverty in low-poverty neighborhoods. In other words, people living in poverty are more dispersed throughout the city.

Map 2.2 shows the geography of these changes and highlights the census tracts that saw increases and decreases in poverty rates over this 30-year period. The figure shows that Manhattan and North Brooklyn have seen reductions in poverty, while neighborhoods in Southern Brooklyn, Staten Island, Northern Queens, and the Eastern portions of the Bronx have seen some increases in poverty.

Poor households are still more likely than other households to live in high-poverty neighborhoods where fewer opportunities and resources are

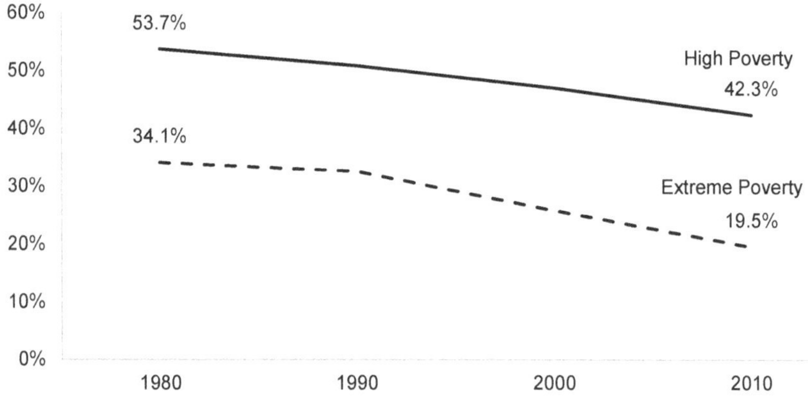

Figure 2.4. Share of population below poverty line living in concentrated poverty in New York City, 1980–2010. *Source:* Neighborhood Change Database.

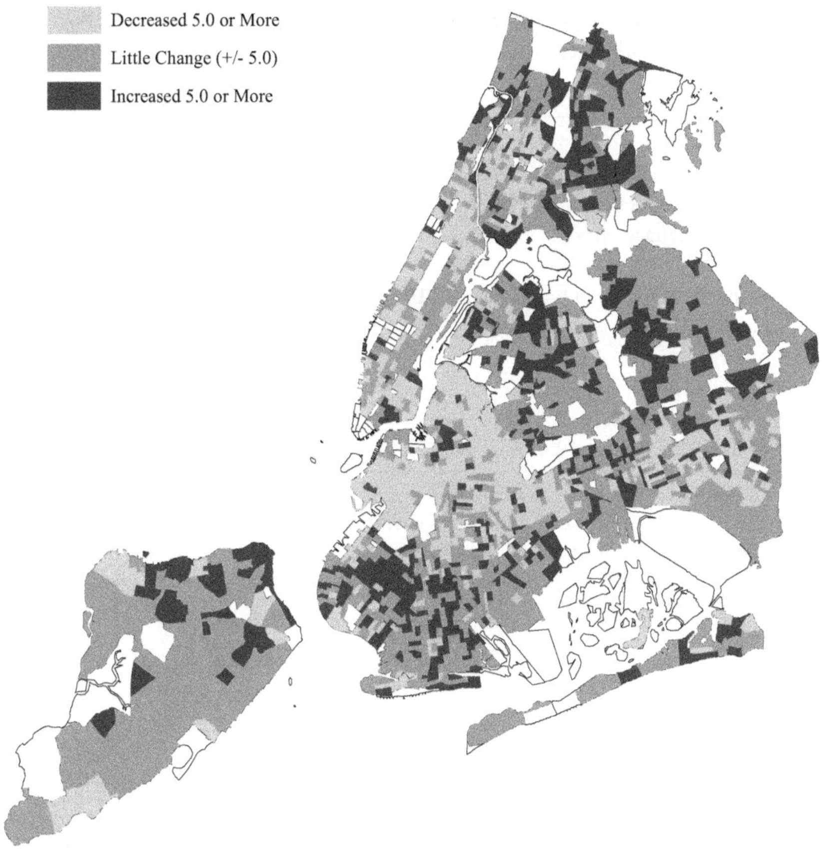

Map 2.2. Percentage point change in poverty rate by census tract, 1980 to 2006–2010. *Source:* Neighborhood Change Database.

available. Table 2.5 on page 40 points out that poor New Yorkers live in neighborhoods with lower-performing schools, fewer college-educated residents, and higher violent crime rates than do their non-poor counterparts. New Yorkers who live below the poverty line do experience some of the same neighborhood advantages that Black and Hispanic New Yorkers do. In particular, they live in areas with lower property crime rates and are more likely to live near parks and subways, as well.

Table 2.5. Typical Neighborhood Characteristics by Individual Poverty Status in New York City

	Below Poverty Line	Above Poverty Line
Poverty Rate (2006–10)	28%	17%
Adults with College Degrees (2006–10)	23%	33%
Fourth Grade Students in 2014 Proficient in		
English Language Arts	26%	35%
Math	34%	44%
Crimes per 1,000 Residents per Year (2010–14)		
Violent	6.1	4.5
Property	8.6	8.9
Residential Units in 2014 within		
Half Mile of a Park	78%	70%
Half Mile of a Subway/Rail Entrance	77%	66%

Sources: Neighborhood Change Database; New York City Police Department; U.S. Census Bureau; New York City Department of Education; New York City Department of Transportation; New York City Department of City Planning; New York City Department of Parks and Recreation; New York State Office of Parks, Recreation, and Historic Preservation; PLUTO; and New York University's Furman Center.

Explaining the Trends

We are left with a question. Why has New York City seen reduced poverty concentration at the same time its Black/White segregation levels remain high? One explanation might be that non-poor households are more open to sharing neighborhoods with the poor as that population becomes more racially diverse. In other words, higher-income "gentrifiers" are more willing to move into high-poverty neighborhoods when those high-poverty neighborhoods are more mixed racially. However, empirical patterns do not support this contention. Poorer Black and poor Hispanics live in lower-poverty neighborhoods today than they did in 1980. Meanwhile, poor Asian and poor White New Yorkers live in slightly higher-poverty neighborhoods than they did in 1980.

Another explanation could be that the poor who are living in high-poverty neighborhoods are more likely to exit poverty today than they were in earlier decades. Without individual-level data, it is difficult, if not impossible, to determine if this is true. Some research suggests that much of the demographic change taking place in the city's changing neighborhoods is due to the shifting composition of in-movers, not the changing circumstances of longer-term residents (NYU Furman Center, 2016).

Table 2.6. Racial/Ethnic Dissimilarity Indices in New York City, 2010

	Total Population	Non-Public Housing Population
Asian-White	50.7	50.9
Black-White	81.6	81.8
Hispanic-White	65.8	65.4

Note: To calculate the non-public housing population we subtract the public housing population in 2014 from 2010 total populations. Sources: Neighborhood Change Database, picture of subsidized households, 2014.

Now, it is not clear why Black/White segregation is falling in most cities, but not in New York. One theory is that New York City's large number of public housing units is responsible for the lack of change in Black/White segregation. The residents of public housing in New York are disproportionately Black and Hispanic. Together, they comprise 91 percent of all public housing residents and are clustered in large developments that often constitute a full census tract. Table 2.6 reveals, however, that the population *not* living in New York City's public housing is just as segregated racially as the full population. The concentration of minority residents in public housing does not seem to explain the city's levels of racial segregation.

It could be that the small size of census tracts in New York explains the high and sustained levels of Black/White segregation in the city. Perhaps in other cities, where census tracts are bigger, it is more common for Blacks and Whites to live in the same census tracts. However, in these census tracts, we live in separate enclaves. Given the small size of tracts in New York, those separate enclaves show up as separate neighborhoods. Finally, the large share of Black New Yorkers who are foreign-born might contribute to higher levels of segregation because they cluster in Black, Hispanic and Asian communities. These issues need to be explored further.

Implications for Public Policy

Our analysis has shown that housing in New York City is far from integrated. Different racial groups remain substantially segregated from each other, and non-White New Yorkers continue to live in areas with lower-performing schools, higher crime, and more poverty. However, there is no doubt progress has been made. The city's housing market has boomed, in part because rapid property appreciation has pushed higher-income households to consider living in previously lower-income areas. The city has more racially integrated neighborhoods than it did in 1980, and New Yorkers of all races are living in neighborhoods with lower crime rates, better-performing schools, and lower rates of poverty than they were in 1980.

Furthermore, similar numbers of people live in poverty in New York City, yet poverty concentration has fallen. Oddly, poverty concentration has been rising in other cities. Still, substantial barriers to housing access continue to exist, and New Yorkers of different races live in very different neighborhoods.

While there is no quick or easy fix, we have a few suggestions for moving forward. First, city officials should make it a priority to reduce disparities in neighborhood opportunities. The city should be working to improve schools, and to reduce violent crime everywhere. In addition, the government needs to scrutinize the decisions it makes about resource allocation and policies, to ensure they ameliorate, rather than reinforce, racial and ethnic disparities in neighborhood conditions. For example, the city has regulations in place that constrain new housing development, such as zoning controls and historic districts. These regulations also discourage developers from creating a more diverse housing stock, by limiting shared and small units. They suppress supply and drive up prices.

Naturally, some of these controls are appropriate. However, city officials should look at whether these regulations are applied equitably across the city. They should consider whether, in some instances, they are causing or exacerbating racial segregation. Officials should review whether the regulations are still appropriate for today's city, with its severe housing needs and technological improvements over the last century. City officials should also be on the lookout for implicit policy implementation bias that affects communities of color, even if those policies achieve larger city goals. The city needs to scrutinize neutral policies to see if they are having a disproportionately negative impact on non-White New Yorkers, and they should explore the role these policies play in reinforcing existing racial disparities in the city.

The city must use its existing tools to create and preserve affordable housing in a diverse set of neighborhoods. The housing market itself is a major impediment to economic mobility in New York City. The city has an extremely low vacancy rate, and rents in many neighborhoods are growing out of reach for most New Yorkers. The city has used zoning policy (its Inclusionary Housing Program), and property tax incentives (the 421a Property Tax Exemption), to encourage people to develop affordable housing opportunities throughout the city. The resources it devotes to direct subsidies dwarf what other cities are spending (Ellen & O'Flaherty, 2013). The city must address substantial challenges before it can implement these measures, given the high cost of land.

As rents increase in the neighborhoods low-income New Yorkers occupy, the city can attempt to preserve the places that are now among the most economically and racially diverse parts of the city. The city should be focusing its resources on protecting the economic and racial diversity of those neighborhoods as they go through their changes. There are several new tools and approaches that the city could experiment with. It could develop housing on sites that were formerly environmentally hazardous, but have now been cleaned up. Alternatively, the city could adopt new forms of shared housing.

City officials must ensure that those New Yorkers who receive rent vouchers should be able to access a wide range of neighborhoods. Currently, voucher holders are highly concentrated in high-poverty neighborhoods, with lower-performing schools (Ellen & Horn, 2011; Horn, et al., 2014). Mayor Bill de Blasio's administration has said that it intends to seek permission from the U.S. Department of Housing and Urban Development (HUD) to use a higher payment standard that would provide voucher holders with access to higher-income neighborhoods (Been & Olatoye, 2016).

The city should put policies in place to help voucher holders move into a broader set of neighborhoods. They could provide counseling and search assistance so households would know about viable neighborhoods. Officials could link voucher holders to units in inclusionary housing, 421a developments in higher-cost parts of the city. They also could develop new strategies for recruiting property owners to accept vouchers.

The city should ensure open access to its own housing programs; remove unnecessary access barriers, such as overreliance on credit score as a tenant selection criterion (City of New York, 2016). Similarly, the city should use caution when monitoring how criminal background information is used in tenant selection for subsidized housing. New York City requires that private owners of subsidized housing conduct a criminal background check for all applicants. The city deems applicants ineligible only if they have been convicted previously of "fraud in connection to any government housing program," or if the applicant "is a criminal fugitive." Making owners responsible gives them leeway to determine how they will use other criminal background information in tenant selection (NYC Department of Housing Preservation and Development, and NYC Housing Development Corporation, 2016, 49). However, owners must disclose to the city any criteria they have used to disqualify tenants. The city should scrutinize this information to ensure that owners are not erecting unnecessary barriers to subsidized housing access, by recent HUD guidance on the use of criminal history in tenant selection.[5]

New York City has antidiscrimination laws on the books that extend beyond the protections provided by the federal Fair Housing Act. The city also has a local Human Rights Commission dedicated to enforcing these laws, and it provides support to legal services offices that litigate discrimination cases.

Historically, the federal government has provided support to these offices. However, in light of the Trump administration's on-the-record skepticism about such fair housing standards, the city must be the one to provide the resources needed to eradicate racial discrimination in its housing market.

New York City has long been an innovator in the realm of affordable housing. Now it must be the leader in defining what fair housing truly means, and how fairness can be achieved in the context of a high-cost, growing city.

Notes

1. Much of the research on segregation trends focuses on metropolitan areas, but large central cities tend to exhibit levels of segregation similar to their metro areas. Our data analysis in this chapter is based on data about New York City, not the entire New York City metro area.

2. We restrict our view to only those tracts with at least 200 people and where less than 30 percent of the population resides in group quarters such as dormitories and correctional facilities. There were 2,078 census tracts in New York City in 2010 that fit these requirements.

3. The share of Black residents fell between 1980 and 2010 in Los Angeles and Chicago, while the share remained stable in New York.

4. It is not possible to get neighborhood-level estimates of poverty or economic conditions in 2010; instead, we use the five-year average from 2006–2010 released by the Census Bureau through the American Community Survey.

5. In 2016, HUD issued detailed guidance on the fair housing implications of the use of criminal history in tenant selection, highlighting when a "facially-neutral" practice might have discriminatory effects by imposing a disparate impact on individuals of a particular race (U.S. Department of Housing and Urban Development 2016, 2). HUD cautioned that "blanket prohibition on any person with any conviction record—no matter *when* the conviction occurred, *what the underlying conduct* entailed, or what the convicted person has *done since*"—are likely not tailored enough to demonstrate the policy is "necessary" to serve the government's interest (U.S. Department of Housing and Urban Development 2016, 6). HUD also suggested that it would investigate claims that criminal history policies have a discriminatory effect based on race where data shows that Hispanic and Black individuals disproportionately fit the criminal history criteria relative to White individuals. HUD also made clear that use of arrest history in tenant selection would very likely violate the Fair Housing Act.

References

Alinsky, S. D., & Sanders, M. K. (1970). *The professional radical: conversations with Saul Alinsky*. New York, NY: Harper & Row.

Ananat, E. (2011). The wrong side of the tracks: The causal effects of racial segregation on urban poverty and inequality. *American Economic Journal: Applied Economics, 3*(2), 34–66.

Been, V., & Olatoye, S. (2016). Comment on proposed rule: Establishing a more effective fair market rent system; using small area fair market rents in housing choice voucher program instead of the current 50th percentile FMRs. Retrieved from https://www.regulations.gov/document?D=HUD-2016-0063-0078.

Chetty, R., Hendren, N., & Katz, L. F. (2016). The effects of exposure to better neighborhoods on children: New evidence from the moving to opportunity experiment. *The American Economic Review, 106*(4), 855–902.

Cutler, D. M., Glaeser, E. L., & Vigdor, J. L. (1997). *The Rise and decline of the American ghetto*. Cambridge, MA: National Bureau of Economic Research.

De la Roca, J., Ellen, I. G., & O'Regan, K. M. (2014). Race and neighborhoods in the 21st century: What does segregation mean today? *Regional Science and Urban Economics, 47*, 138–51.

Ellen, I. G. (2000). *Sharing America's neighborhoods*. Cambridge, MA: Harvard University Press.

Ellen, I. G., & Horn, K. (Eds.). (2011). *Do households with housing assistance have access to high quality public schools? Evidence from New York City*. Washington, DC: Poverty & Race Research Action Council.

Ellen, I., & O'Flaherty, B. (2013). How New York Housing Policies Are Different—and Maybe Why. In A. Beveridge, & D. Halle (Eds.), *New York City-Los Angeles: The Uncertain Future*. Oxford: Oxford University Press, pp. 286–309.

Farley, R., & Frey, W. H. (1994). Changes in the segregation of Whites from Blacks during the 1980s: Small steps toward a more integrated society. *American Sociological Review*, 59(1): 23–45.

Flores, R. J. O., & Lobo, A. P. (2013). The reassertion of a Black/non-Black color line: The Rise in integrated neighborhoods without Blacks in New York City, 1970–2010. *Journal of Urban Affairs, 35*(3), 255–82.

Horn, K. M., Ingrid Gould Ellen, and Amy Ellen Schwartz. (2014). Do housing choice voucher holders live near good schools? *Journal of Housing Economics, 23*(28–40).

Iceland, J., & Hernandez, E. (2016). Understanding trends in concentrated poverty: 1980–2014. *Social Science Research*, 62: 75–79.

Jargowsky, P. A. (1997). *Poverty and place: Ghettos, barrios, and the American city*. New York, NY: Russell Sage Foundation.

Jargowsky, P. A. (2013). *Concentration of poverty in the new millennium: Changes in prevalence, composition, and location in high poverty neighborhoods*. New Brunswick, NJ: The Century Foundation and Rutgers Center for Urban Research and Education.

Logan, J. R. (2013). The persistence of segregation in the 21st century metropolis. *City & Community, 12*(2), 160–68.

Logan, J. R., & Stults, B. (2011). *The Persistence of segregation in the metropolis: New findings from the 2010 census*. Washington, D.C.: Census Brief prepared for Project US2010.

Massey, D. S., & Gross, A. B. (1991). Explaining trends in racial segregation, 1970–1980. *Urban Affairs Review, 27*(1), 13–35.

NYU Furman Center. (2016). *State of New York City's housing and neighborhoods in 2015.* New York, NY: NYU Furman Center.

Rosenbaum, E., & Argeros, G. (2005). Holding the line: Housing turnover and the persistence of racial/ethnic segregation in New York City. *Journal of Urban Affairs, 27*(3), 261–81.

Rosenbaum, E., & Friedman, S. (2001). Differences in the locational attainment of immigrant and native-born households with children in New York City. *Demography, 38*(3), 337–48.

Rugh, J. S., & Massey, D. S. (2014). Segregation in post-civil rights America. *Du Bois Review: Social Science Research on Race, 11*(2), 205–32.

Sharkey, P., & Faber, J. (2014). Where, when, why, and for whom do residential contexts matter? Moving away from the dichotomous understanding of neighborhood effects. *Annual Review of Sociology, 40*, 559–79.

Steil, J., De la Roca, J., & Ellen, I. G. (2015). *Desvinculado y Desigual* Is segregation harmful to Latinos? *The Annals of the American Academy of Political and Social Science, 660* (1), 57–76.

Chapter 3

Education

New York City School Segregation Then and Now

Plus Ça Change

Norm Fruchter and Christina Mokhtar

District Segregation: 1973–74 and 2013–14[1]

In a 2013 study, researchers James Kucsera and Gary Oldfield determined that New York State's schools are the most racially and ethnically segregated in the country and that the New York City (NYC) school system is a major contributor to this hyper-segregation (2014). However, after the election of Mayor Bill de Blasio in 2013, teachers, students, parents, researchers, elected officials and advocacy organizations across New York City intensified their efforts to desegregate and diversify the city's schools (Fessenden, May 11, 2012; James, 2016; Ladner & Torres, December 15, 2017; Veiga, 2017). These efforts were aided by several new developments. For instance, the New York State Education Department (NYSED) awarded grants to two NYC community school districts to foster increased student diversity within their schools. Several small schools of choice developed new admissions policies to maintain their schools' ethnic and racial diversity, and successfully petitioned the city's Department of Education (DOE) to approve those policies.

Potentially Integrable and Hyper-Segregated Districts

In light of these efforts, we decided to examine the levels of segregation, as measured by the percent of Black and Latino students in the city's schools (Harris, 2015). We evaluated information across community school districts, using 2013–14 data from the New York City Department of Education's *Demographic Snapshots* (NYC Department of Education, 2016). Our analysis revealed that fifteen of the 32 community school districts had Black and Latino student populations below the citywide average of 68.5 percent. Conversely, they had White and Asian populations of at least 32 percent. We hypothesized that those fifteen districts had the potential to diversify their student populations if they would employ controlled school choice policies or other programs that combined parent choice and district assignment policies. This depended on their schools' locations, and the availability of within-district public transportation (Alves, November 1, 2016).

Table 3.1 lists the traditionally advantaged and more recently re-gentrified NYC neighborhoods that comprise these fifteen districts. The table arrays the neighborhoods from the lowest to highest percentages of Black and Latino student populations in 2013–14 and specifies their component neighborhoods. The fifteen districts comprised 53.5 percent of the overall citywide student population in 2013–14. We refer to those districts as "potentially integrable" throughout this chapter.[2]

Although we characterize these districts as having the potential to diversify, many of them contain racially/ethnically homogenous enclaves whose schools have historically been very segregated. When a district makes an effort to reduce such segregation, its actions are often met with considerable opposition.

Table 3.1. School Districts with Lowest Percentages of Black and Latino Students by Neighborhood, 2013–2014

District	Black and Latino Students	Neighborhoods
26	29.4	Bayside, Fresh Meadows, Douglaston, Floral Park
20	29.8	Bay Ridge, Bensonhurst, Borough Park, Dycker Heights
25	37.6	Flushing, Whitestone, College Point
31	39.6	Staten Island
21	41	Coney Island, Brighton Beach, Bensonhurst
28	50.6	Forest Hills, Rego Park, Kew Gardens, Jamaica
2	51	Greenwich Village, Tribeca, Soho, Midtown
22	51.4	Ditmas Park, Midwood, Sheeshead Bay
15	56	Park Slope, Carroll Gardens, Sunset Park, Red Hook
1	58.2	Lower East Side
3	60.3	Upper West Side
30	60.8	Astoria, Long Island City, Jackson Heights, Sunnyside
27	63	Far Rockaway, Howard Beach, Woodhaven
24	65.3	Ridgewood, Corona, Elmhurst, Masbeth, Little Village
13	68	Bedford Stuyvesant
Citywide Average	68.5	

Source: New York City Department of Education, demographic snapshots, and annual enrollment snapshots.

Hypersegregated Districts

In 2013–14, student populations in the remaining seventeen community school districts were more than 80 percent Black and Latino. In eleven of those districts, Black and Latino enrollment exceeded 90 percent. These seventeen districts comprised 37.4 percent of the overall citywide student population during these years.[3] Because these districts enroll very small numbers of White and Asian students, it is difficult to increase diversity and reduce the racial isolation in their segregated schools. Only major systemic policy changes involving new district boundaries, or cross-district student assignment, could reduce the deep-seated segregation of the districts. We refer to these districts as hypersegregated throughout this chapter.

Table 3.2 arrays these districts from the highest to lowest percentages of their Black and Latino student enrollments and specifies their corresponding neighborhoods.

Table 3.2. School Districts with Highest Percentages of Black and Latino Students by Neighborhood, 2013–2014

District	Black and Latino Students	Neighborhoods
23	97.1	Ocean Hill, Brownsville
9	97.1	Grand Concourse, Morrisania, Tremont
7	97	South Bronx
16	96.5	Bedford-Stuyvesant
32	96	Bushwick
12	95.5	Crotona Park, West Farms, Belmont
18	95.5	Flatbush, Canarsie
6	94.4	Washington Heights, Inwood, North Harlem
17	93.4	Prospect Heights, East Flatbush, Crown Heights
5	91.7	Central Harlem
19	90.9	East New York
4	88.4	East Harlem
8	88	Hunts Point, Soundview, Throgs Neck
10	85.5	Riverdale, Fordham, Belmont, Kingsbridge
11	83.7	Pelham Parkway, Eastchester, Woodlawn, Coop City
14	83.2	Williamsburg, Greenpoint
29	80.6	Cambria Heights, Laurelton, Rosedale, St. Albans
Citywide Average	68.5	

Source: New York City Department of Education, demographic snapshots, and annual enrollment snapshots, 2014.

Changes in Segregation from 1973–74 to 2013–14

Next, we examined how Black and Latino student segregation has changed in the city's community school districts over the past 40 years. In our analysis, we compared data from two watershed school years. The first was 1973–74, three years after the New York State legislature decentralized the city school system and created the 32 community school districts, and the second was 2013–14, the last operative year of the Bloomberg administration's systemic school reforms.[4]

At the citywide level, in 1973–74, the Black and Latino student population in community school districts was 66.5 percent. That is two percentage points lower than the 68.5 percent system-wide Black and Latino population in 2013–14. The White and Asian citywide percentages were 33.5 percent in 1973–74, and 29.8 percent in 2013–14.[5] This small increase in the Black and Latino student population, and the corresponding, a somewhat larger decrease in the number of White and Asian students during this time, masks significant changes at the community school district level. Table 3.3 details the Black and Latino populations in 1973–74 and 2013–14, in community school districts, both above and below the citywide averages.

As Table 3.3 indicates, in 1973–74, Black and Latino student populations were below the citywide average in fourteen community school districts. In our terms, these districts were potentially integrable. There were fifteen such districts in 2013–14, which is a negligible increase. Conversely, eighteen districts were hypersegregated in 1973–74, while there were 17 such districts in 2013–14. Fourteen of those eighteen hypersegregated districts in 1973–74 (Districts 4, 5, and 6 in Manhattan; Districts 14, 16, 17, 19, 23 and 32 in Brooklyn; Districts 7, 8, 9 and 12 in the Bronx, and; District 29 in Queens) were still hypersegregated in 2013–14. Throughout this 40-year span, hyper-segregation remained in almost all of the markedly segregated community school districts that served the majority of the system's Black and Latino students.

Increased Segregation at the District Level

Although there was negligible change in the system's hyper-segregation from 1973–74 to 2013–14, a considerable change occurred in some districts, as illustrated on the map 3.1. Three districts, two in the Bronx (Districts 10 and 11), and one in Brooklyn (District 18) that were potentially integrable in 1973–74 became hypersegregated by 2013–14, due to substantial increases in their Black and Latino populations (See table 3.4 on page 53). Seven districts, including four in Queens (Districts 24, 25, 27, and 30), two in Brooklyn (Districts 21 and 22), and one in Staten Island (District 31), also saw substan-

Table 3.3. Black/Latino Enrollment by School District, 1973–1974 and 2013–2014[1]

District (1974)	Black and Latino Students (1974)	District (2014)	Black and Latino Students (2014)	District (1974)	Black and Latino Students (1974)	District (2014)	Black and Latino Students (2014)
Below the Citywide Average % of Black and Latino Students:				Above the Citywide Average % of Black and Latino Students:			
City Avg.	66.5	City Avg.	68.5	15	71.7	29	80.6
31	14	26	29.4	29	76.6	14	83.2
25	21.8	20	29.8	8	81.5	11	83.7
22	22.1	25	37.6	6	83.8	10	85.5
26	22.9	31	39.6	3	86	8	88
20	285.9	21	41	1	86.9	4	88.4
21	30.6	28	50.6	32	88.2	19	90.9
24	35.5	2	51	14	89.6	5	91.7
30	41.6	22	51.4	19	90.1	17	93.4
27	42.3	15	56	17	91.4	6	94.4
2	46.7	1	58.2	9	95.9	18	95.5
18	52.7	3	60.3	13	96.7	12	95.5
11	57.1	30	60.8	12	97.5	32	96
10	60.9	27	63	4	98.5	16	96.5
28	61.8	24	65.3	7	98.7	7	97
		13	68	2	98.9	9	97.1
				23	99.2	23	97.1
				16	99.7		

Sources: New York City municipal archives of the school system's Series 1480: Office of Student Information, school profiles, 1973–1974; New York City Department of Education; demographic snapshots; annual enrollment snapshots, 2014.

1. For the archive data (1973–1974): Citywide figures for race/ethnicity are for elementary level students only. District-wide data for race/ethnicity includes all eighth graders, as well as all students in earlier grades, and excludes high schools. For 2013–2014 Department of Education data: Citywide and district figures for race/ethnicity include all students from pre-K–12.

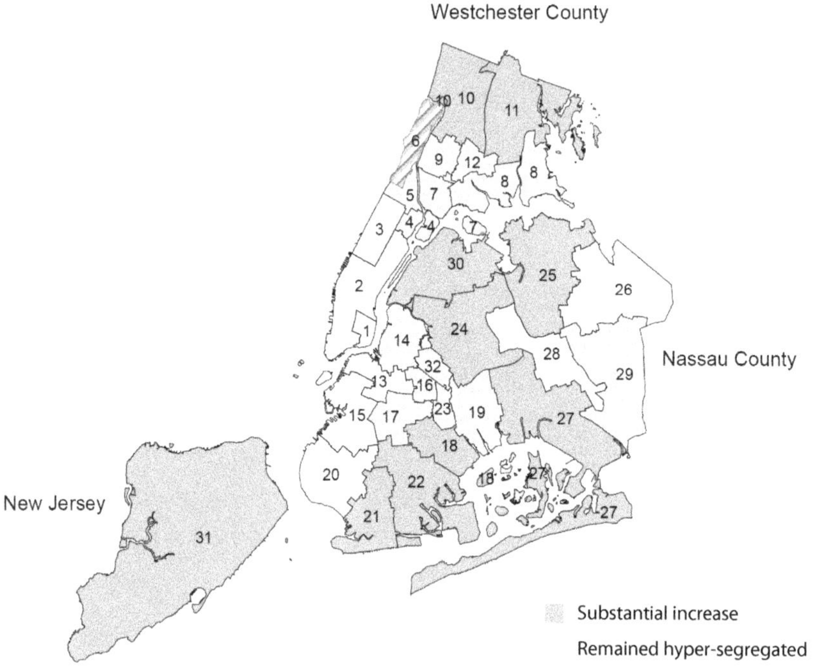

Map 3.1. School districts with substantial increases in black and Latino student populations and school districts that remained hyper-segregated, 1973–1974 to 2013–2014. *Note:* District 6 experienced both a substantial increase and remained hyper-segregated.

tial increases in their Black and Latino populations in the period spanning 1973–74 to 2013–14, but they remained potentially integrable. District 6 was hypersegregated in both 1973–74 and 2013–14 and experienced a significant increase in its Black and Latino populations across the 40-year time span (see table 3.4). The map 3.1 plots these district increases and highlights the districts that were hypersegregated in both 1973–74 and 2013–14, 40 years later.

Most of these districts are in neighborhoods that border or are close to their adjacent suburbs: Westchester to the north of the Bronx; Nassau County to the east of Brooklyn and Queens, and; New Jersey to the west of Staten Island. The substantial increases in the Black and Latino student populations in these districts, from 1973–74 to 2013–14, suggest a great number of people moved from traditional inner-city neighborhoods to the city's peripheral, semi-suburban areas during this time.

Table 3.4. School Districts with Substantial Increases in Black and Latino Student Populations by Borough and Neighborhood, 1973–1974 to 2013–2014[1]

Borough	District	Neighborhood	% Point Increase
Queens	24	Ridgewood, Corona, Elmhurst, Maspeth, Little Village	29.8
	25	Flushing, Whitestone, College Point	15.8
	27	Far Rockaway, Howard Beach, Woodhaven	20.7
	30	Astoria, Long Island City, Jackson Heights, Sunnyside	19.2
Brooklyn	18	Flatbush, Canarsie	42.8
	21	Coney Island, Brighton Beach, Bensonhurst	10.4
	22	Ditmas Park, Midwood, Mill Basin, Sheepshead Bay	29.3
Bronx	10	Fordham, Belmont, Kingsbridge, Riverdale	24.6
	11	Coop City, Eastchester, Woodlawn, City Island	26.6
Manhattan	6	Washington Heights, Inwood, North Harlem	10.6
Staten Island	31	Staten Island	25.6

Sources: New York City municipal archives of the school system's Series 1480: Office of Student Information, school profiles, 1973–1974; New York City Department of Education; demographic snapshots; annual enrollment snapshots, 2014.

1. For the archive data (1973–1974): Citywide figures for race/ethnicity are for elementary level students only. District-wide data for race/ethnicity includes all eighth graders, as well as all students in earlier grades, and excludes high schools. For 2013–2014 Department of Education data: Citywide and district figures for race/ethnicity include all students from pre-K–12.

Decreased Segregation at the District Level

Several community school districts saw sharp reductions in segregation, as indicated in table 3.5 on page 54. During this same 40-year span, four districts, two in Manhattan (Districts 1 and 3) and two in Brooklyn (Districts 13 and 15), shifted from being hypersegregated in 1973–74, to potentially integrable in 2013–14. This was because their Black and Latino populations dropped considerably. District 4 in Manhattan, a hypersegregated district in 1973–74,

Table 3.5. School Districts with Substantial Decreases in Black and Latino Student Populations by Borough and Neighborhood, 1973–1974 to 2013–2014

Borough	District	Neighborhood	% Point Decrease
Manhattan	1	Lower East Side	-28.7
	3	Upper West Side	-25.7
	4	East Harlem	-10.1
Brooklyn	13	Bedford Stuyvesant	-28.7
	15	Park Slope, Carroll Gardens, Sunset Park, Red Hook	-15.7
Queens	28	Forest Hills, Rego Park, Kew Gardens, Jamaica	-11.2

Sources: New York City municipal archives of the school system's Series 1480: Office of Student Information, School Profiles, 1973–1974; New York City Department of Education; demographic snapshots; annual enrollment snapshots, 2014.

1. For the archive data (1973–1974): District-wide data for race/ethnicity includes all eighth graders, as well as all students in earlier grades, and excludes high schools. For 2013–2014 Department of Education data: District figures for race/ethnicity include all students from pre-K–12.

and District 28 in Queens, a potentially integrable district in 1973–74, also experienced sizable decreases in their Black and Latino student populations, but not enough to shift their classifications.

Starting in the 1970s, there was a substantial out-migration of Black and Latino populations in these neighborhoods, with the possible exception of the Queens neighborhoods in District 28. There was a corresponding in-migration of White and Asian populations occurring at the same time.[6]

Because Black and Latino families were moving from traditional inner-city neighborhoods, segregation expanded in many of the community school districts' residential areas that bordered the city's suburbs. On the other hand, White and Asian families moved into traditional inner-city neighborhoods, thereby reducing segregation in the community school districts serving those neighborhoods. Most of the districts that were hypersegregated in 1973–74 remained hypersegregated in 2013–14. Those districts continue to serve the majority of the system's Black and Latino students.

Because race is highly correlated with test scores, not only in New York City but also in urban areas across the country, Black and Latino students in segregated schools and districts tend to perform poorly on standardized tests. Our analysis of the relationship between the racial/ethnic composition of community school districts, and the English Language Arts (ELA) outcomes in 1973–74, yields strong negative Pearson's correlations of $r = -.900$ for Grade 3, $r = -.933$ for Grade 5, and $r = -.920$ for Grade 8 students meeting the ELA standards. For the 2013–14 school year, the corresponding Pearson's correlations were $r = -.867$, $r = -.856$, and $r = -.909$ for the same three grades.

All six correlations were negative, and statistically very significant ($p = < .01$), which means that for both 1973–74 and 2013–14, school districts with the higher proportion of Black and Latino students, saw lower ELA proficiency. Conversely, the less segregated a district, the higher its ELA proficiency. When one asks how much has changed over the past 40 years for NYC's Black and Latino students, the answer is both predictable and grim: not very much.

Correlation is Not Causation

However, correlation is not causation. We know from studies by the city's Independent Budget Office (IBO), that the city's most segregated schools are often poorly resourced and staffed by the newest and least experienced teachers. As a result, these schools encounter very high levels of teacher mobility (Chapman, 2016; Johnson, Subramanian, Wilks, & Domanico, 2013; Roy, 2014). Students in the hypersegregated schools face major gaps in educational opportunities because inequitable resource distribution and disparate staffing policies mean students are denied the instructional support that is critical to their academic success. To make matters worse, hypersegregated schools are often allocated larger percentages of students with challenging instructional needs. Many students require special education services, and are English Language Learners (ELLs). Then, there are so-called "over the counter students" who are not at a school out of choice, but because they missed the choice process deadline (Arvidsson, Fruchter, & Mokhtar, 2013). In addition, the city's hypersegregated districts have the fewest Gifted and Talented (G & T) programs and enroll an extremely low percentage of students into accelerated and intensive learning curricula such as Advanced Placement (AP).

Studies of NYC high school selection shows that segregated middle schools send very few of their students to the city's nine specialized high schools, or to the larger tier of highly selective and high-performing high schools.[7] A study from the New Schools Center for NYC Affairs found that 60 percent of all seventh graders that were admitted to the specialized high schools, came from 45 highly selective middle schools that enrolled extremely low percentages of Black and Latino students (Mader, Cory, & Royo, 2016).

Studies of school discipline policies show that Black and Latino students who attend segregated schools face disproportionate rates of suspensions and expulsions (N.Y. Civil Liberties Union, 2016; U.S. Department of Education, 2016). These indicators of disparate resource provision, inequitable teacher, and student assignment policies, and disproportionate disciplinary outcomes compound the damage that a lack of diversity imposes on hypersegregated schools and classrooms.

Citywide Forces

An underlying economic framework generates and sustains both school segregation and the substandard academic outcomes within hypersegregated schools and districts. When we analyzed the relationship between the racial/ethnic composition of community school districts and the extent of student/family poverty within those districts, we uncovered strong positive Pearson's correlations of r = .943 for 1973–74 and r = .790 for 2013–14. Both year's correlations were positive, and statistically significant (p = <.01). The more segregated a district, that is, the higher the proportion of Black and Latino students, the higher the level of student/family poverty within that district. This finding does not imply causation, however. In our view, the extent of school system hyper-segregation and student/family poverty reflect the fundamental economic, political and social forces reshaping the city, and its school system over the past 40 years.[8]

Three primary developments have reshaped the city's neighborhoods: the globalization of industry, finance, and trade; the technical revolutions in communications, computing, automation and media, and; the resulting concentrations of expanding wealth. Commercial and residential development have transformed the city's traditional financial district and created newly rich Manhattan neighborhoods such as Battery Park City, Tribeca, and Soho. Greenwich Village, the Lower East Side, and much of midtown and the Upper West Side have experienced record booms in housing prices and rental costs. Similar intensive development is reshaping Manhattan's Harlem and East Harlem districts, and transforming Brooklyn neighborhoods such as Park Slope, Carroll Gardens, Windsor Terrace, Gowanus, Williamsburg, and Bedford-Stuyvesant.

Change in district-level student populations is a product of the ongoing citywide transformation. Through the 40-year span of our analysis, these developments have uprooted traditional Black and Latino neighborhoods and pushed many of their inhabitants to the city's peripheries as they search for affordable housing. Similarly, burgeoning increases in family income and wealth have spurred an influx of White and Asian families into traditional Black and Latino neighborhoods. The processes of dislocation and relocation have shifted several community school districts from hypersegregated to potentially integrable while intensifying or sustaining the hyper-segregation of several other districts. Our research suggests that the degree of segregation can be reduced and the extent of school diversity significantly increased in at least a dozen, and perhaps more, of the potentially integrable school districts. Unfortunately, the important gains this reduction could produce for students will not benefit those districts serving the majority of the city's Black and Latino students that are still, after 40 years, hypersegregated.

To reduce segregation significantly, integrated schooling advocates would have to engage the larger economic, political, and social forces that drive the flow of capital, corporate and commercial development, and infrastructure investment within the city. Regrettably, our school system continues to reflect the racial inequities manifest in every other NYC sector.

Systemic Reforms Since 1970

Two major reform efforts dominated the city school system during the past 40 years: decentralization and market-based corrections. Neither reform was designed to increase diversity in schools or to reduce school segregation. The recent policy and advocacy activities are the first since the 1960s. Decentralization and market-based reform were introduced to increase student achievement and, implicitly or explicitly, to reduce the citywide racial achievement gap. This section examines the extent to which these two reform efforts have improved student achievement in the past 40 years, with a particular focus on the system's Black and Latino students in hypersegregated community school districts.

Decentralization: 1970–2002

From the 1950s to the 1970s, African-American children of the great migration from southern states, and Puerto Ricans from the Commonwealth of Puerto Rico transformed the composition of NYC's schools. In 1955, the city's school system was 72 percent White: by 1975, it was almost 70 percent Black, Latino, predominantly Puerto Rican, and Asian (Anker, 1983). This transformation coincided with a landmark change in the public education law. In 1954, the U.S. Supreme Court unanimously ruled, in *Brown v. Board of Education,* that state laws establishing separate public schools for Black and White students, were unconstitutional, and subsequently ordered states to desegregate "with all deliberate speed."

The *Brown* decision escalated demands by Black and Latino constituencies to integrate the city's schools. The decade following *Brown* saw a succession of marches, rallies, protests, even a takeover of the citywide Board of Education, all demanding the integration of the city's schools. Their objective was to improve the schooling conditions and academic outcomes for the system's Black and Latino students. This persistent activism culminated in a one-day school boycott in 1964, in which some 464,000 students, almost 45 percent of the system's students, stayed home to protest the city's failure to integrate its schools (Lewis, 2013).

However, this decade of protest failed to persuade the Board of Education, and the city's political leaders, to move meaningfully towards integration. As a result, the demands of Black and Latino constituencies evolved from integration to community control. Since integration seemed politically unachievable, they argued, local communities of color should have the power to control, determine, and improve their children's schooling. Widespread community agitation, combined with the support of Mayor John Lindsay, and funding from the Ford Foundation, inspired the city to establish three community control demonstration districts. They were governed by locally elected school boards: Ocean Hill/Brownsville in Brooklyn, IS 201 in Harlem, and the Two Bridges neighborhood in Manhattan's Lower East Side.

In its initial year of local governance, 1967–68, the community board of the Ocean Hill/Brownsville district voted to transfer 19 professionals, a mix of teachers, assistant principals, and one principal out of the district, because they were obstructing the new board's policies. The city's teachers union, United Federation of Teachers (UFT), immediately and vocally demanded their reinstatement. During the summer of 1968, the conflict intensified, and in September, the UFT called a citywide strike that closed most of the city's schools for six weeks. Embattled Black and Latino parents and community members kept some schools open by organizing Freedom Schools, and other efforts to educate their students during the strike. They then occupied the schools at night to keep the police from closing them down.

It became a polarizing, citywide struggle. The teachers' union accused community control leaders of anti-Semitism, protests repeatedly developed into fights at several school sites, and the police ringed many schools with police helicopters circling overhead. Once the teachers returned to work, the New York State legislature stepped in to de-escalate the conflict. In April 1969, the legislature passed a bill to decentralize the NYC school system, and new state law was born (Brier, 2014; Isaacs, 2014; Lewis, 2013; Perlstein, 2004).

The decentralization law proved a limited and unsuccessful compromise among community control advocates, the teachers union, and the defenders of the professionally dominated city educational bureaucracy. The new law created 31 community school districts; a 32nd district was added a few years later. Each district was headed by a nine-member, locally elected board, and given the power to appoint a district superintendent as well as the principals of each district's elementary and middle schools. A seven-person board, comprised of two members appointed by the mayor, and five members appointed by the borough presidents, governed the central administration. This board administered the city's high schools, as well as the entire system's fiscal operations, personnel, transportation, special education, curriculum and instruction, professional development, school meals, and contract negotiations with several employee organizations, including the powerful unions for teachers and supervisors.

Dysfunctional Central Board and Local District Corruption

Conventional wisdom says that a combination of a politically toxic central board and corrupt and incompetent local community boards devastated New York City's public education. This may be overstated, but it is not entirely inaccurate. The seven-member, citywide Board of Education displayed a mix of naked ambition, petty rivalries, and constantly shifting political alliances. These not only demeaned the board's legitimacy but also besmirched the reputation of public education throughout the city. The hoped-for board consensus, with its consistent policies and improved educational outcomes for students, were just a fantasy.

Design and Implementation Failures

In our view, decentralization failed precisely because of the central board dysfunction and local district corruption. This was the result of the new law's design and implementation failures. Decentralization, for example, required establishing boundaries for the new community school districts. The law mandated four criteria for creating new districts: a suitable size for efficiency, which the law defined as having at least 20,000 enrolled students; a convenient location for pupil attendance; a "reasonable" number of pupils, and; "heterogeneity," meaning appropriate representation of racial/ethnic and socioeconomic segments of the pupil population. Two of these requirements conflicted. The 20,000-student enrollment mandate meant that most new districts had to include several adjacent neighborhoods. As a result, those who drew the boundaries often yoked together neighborhoods with very different racial/ethnic concentrations. These forced pairings compromised the new law's heterogeneity requirement, and created fierce conflicts between Black, Latino, and White neighborhoods (Demas, 1971; Phenix, 2008).[9]

Several predominantly White neighborhoods, for example, consistently elected disproportionate majorities to their district school boards. They could mobilize the funding, the volunteers, organizational resources, and nonprofit and religious networks needed to mount successful electoral efforts. Several of these under-representative school boards oversaw districts where Whites were predominant, and schools were well-resourced, well-maintained, appropriately staffed, and produced good academic outcomes. However, districts where schools served predominantly Black and Latino students, often lacked critical resources, were poorly maintained and were staffed by a rotating collection of new and often ineffective teachers. Predictably, such neglected schools produced poor academic outcomes. These inequitable conditions led to acrimony among districts, pitted constituencies against each other, and turned many district school board meetings into recurring battlegrounds.

Another design failure of the education law was its unequal division of power between the central administration and the community school districts. In this case, the central administration was given the greater power. For instance, it had a monopoly on all contract negotiations and dealings with the school system's unions. These discouraged and very often limited instructional innovations by individual districts.

In a system of more than one thousand schools and one million students, there were the inevitable nodes of innovative and effective instructional and administrative practices, at school and district levels, and within the community districts. However, the central administration never evaluated, publicized, or attempted to adapt and share the innovations. Instead, the administrators consistently refused to approve, publicize, and adapt successful district practices, or to discuss them during negotiations with the unions. The central administration also routinely ignored the decentralization law's requirement to consult with community school districts in union contract bargaining (McGrail, 1976).

The law was deficient in another way. Elected community school board members were generally limited in their knowledge of education policy or effective schooling practices. They required training, which was called for in the decentralization law. However, the central administration did not provide this training until the advent of the Crew administration, which was very late in the decentralization era. For most of that time, the central administration allowed community board members to struggle through complex political, legal, financial, and educational dilemmas on their own. This arrangement endorsed inexperience and encouraged failure. Because accountability was completely top-down and unidirectional, the community boards could not hold the central administration accountable for the failures, multiple lapses, and obvious inequities it imposed on the community school boards.

In our view, the central administration's worst failure was its refusal to intervene to improve school performance in hypersegregated community school districts that consistently produced dismal student outcomes. From

1970 to 2002, the operative years of decentralization, only two of the eight chancellors who served for more than two years intervened to try to improve disastrous district-level academic outcomes in the hypersegregated districts. Although different central administrations were fully aware of the degree of incompetence, political corruption and inept instructional practices in those districts, only two chancellors mounted efforts to improve the persistent educational failures.

These two exceptions were the Macchiarola (1978–83) and Crew (1995–99) administrations. Frank Macchiarola championed school improvement efforts based on the Effective Schools Research Movement, pioneered by Ronald Edmonds, a Harvard University professor. In Edmonds' research, the schools were effective in providing an education to their Black and Latino students. Therefore, the nation's proven unwillingness to educate effectively all students of color had to be a massive failure of political will.

Under the direction of Edmonds, Macchiarola initiated two pilot programs based on effective schools research. He introduced a systemic effort to end social promotion by denying grade advancement to students who failed to meet new citywide standards ("promotional gates") in Grades 4 and 7. Though the pilot School Improvement Programs showed promising results initially, the program's overly bureaucratic implementation process, and the premature death of Edmonds led to discontinuing the program. The Promotional Policy effort showed similar encouraging results, to begin with, but subsequent research found increasingly limited and diminishing outcomes. The program was quietly phased out (Amin, Chellman, Lockwood, et al., 2004).

The Rudy Crew administration launched several system-wide innovations. Crew adapted English models to develop a comprehensive Early Childhood Literacy Assessment System (ECLAS) that mandated its use throughout the system's beginning grades. Crew's administration implemented a successful experiment in performance-driven budgeting that linked budget allocations to schools' instructional strategies and academic outcomes. Under Crew's leadership, district directors of operations designed Galaxy, a software system that linked central and district fiscal allocations and allowed schools to reconfigure their budgets regularly (Siegel & Fruchter, 2002; Stiefel, Schwartz, Portas, & Kim, 2003).

Finally, Crew removed failing schools from their districts and subsumed them into a Chancellor's district in which district management controlled personnel allocation, teacher time, curriculum and instructional strategies. The Chancellor's District absorbed more than 50 of the school system's most poorly performing schools, most of them within hypersegregated districts, and produced significant improvements in academic performance (Phenix, Siegel, Zaltsman, & Fruchter, 2004).

Unfortunately, the Crew administration's innovations did not survive the escalating citywide disgust with the failures of the central board, the decentralized districts, and ultimately, decentralization itself. Mayor Rudy Giuliani forced Crew out over a dispute about vouchers, and decentralization became history.

System Restructuring through Market Mechanisms: 2002–13

Michael Bloomberg was elected mayor in 2001 and persuaded the New York State legislature to end decentralization in 2002. With his School's Chancellor, Joel Klein, Bloomberg terminated the 32 school districts elected community boards, and fundamentally reshaped the central administration. This system-wide restructuring took different forms as the mayor and the chancellor experimented with "creative confusion" (Haimson, 2010) to disrupt the previous system's governance and instructional infrastructure.

The 32 districts were first grouped into ten overarching regions, each run by a Regional Superintendent, with separate Regional Operations Centers to deal with all non-instructional issues. When this arrangement failed to resolve the numerous problems that transcended this instructional/operational binary, the regional system was scrapped, and a series of instructional networks were established. The system's schools were given the option to join one of these networks, which provided experienced professionals to give both instructional and non-instructional support to all schools.

The Bloomberg reforms had three market principles at their core:

- **Autonomy**—The Bloomberg-Klein administration sought to collapse the distance between system leadership and individual schools by conferring broad freedom of authority and operation on the system's school principals;
- **Accountability**—The Bloomberg-Klein administration sought to condition school-level autonomy on successful academic performance as the determinative measure of educational success, and to root that measure in test score gains;
- **Choice**—The Bloomberg-Klein administration sought to establish choice of school as the core level of parent and student participation, and to increase participants' options by creating hundreds of new schools and closing failing schools.

Autonomy

The Bloomberg-Klein administration defined autonomy as the empowerment of the school system's 1,800 school principals to determine their schools instructional policies and practices, their staffing and budgets. This also included the power to select the instructional networks that, under contract, provided coaching, professional development, resources, and strategic support to help improve school performance and student outcomes.

A 2015 study by the Annenberg Institute for School Reform (AISR) at Brown University examined the effects of these networks on academic outcomes throughout the city system. The study found that school-level student demographics predicted academic performance far more strongly than network membership did. In addition, when key student demographic variables such as poverty, the percentages of students receiving special education services, and the percentage of English Language Learners were held constant at the citywide average, the Bloomberg-Klein instructional networks had very little effect on student academic performance, except possibly for high school graduation rates (Fruchter, Arvidsson, Mokhtar, & Beam, 2015).

During the second year of the Bill de Blasio administration, which succeeded Bloomberg's term, Schools Chancellor Carmen Fariña eliminated the system-wide instructional networks, and increased the administrative powers, staffs, budgets, and oversight of the superintendents of the community school districts.

Accountability

There has been little agreement on the extent to which the Bloomberg administration's market-based reforms improved the city schools. The mayor and his Schools Chancellor cloaked their reforms in a framework of equity, declaring that their efforts to close the racial achievement gap would complete the civil rights revolution in NYC. To systematize accountability, the Bloomberg administration introduced school performance measures that weighted test score outcomes and used solitary standardized proficiency-based tests to assess school effectiveness.

At the same time, they developed metrics to either compare supposedly similar schools to reward or sanction schools that exceeded or fell below expectations. Schools that performed poorly on a regular basis were sanctioned, and eventually phased out, while schools that are more proficient were rewarded with increased levels of autonomy. During the twelve years Mayor Bloomberg held office, his accountability reforms pitted schools against each other, and resulted in fiercely contested closings of more than 150 schools.

During the initial years of the competitive accountability system, test scores did improve. However, in 2009, the state recalibrated its test results, because researchers had found the scores to be inflated. As a result, the city's outcomes fell dramatically. Evidence regarding how much the racial achievement gap dropped is more straightforward. One only has to look at what is called commonly the nation's report card, done by the Trial Urban District Assessment (TUDA), a city-level disaggregation of the National Assessment of Educational Progress (NAEP) to find out. NAEP is designed to inform the nation of broad trends in student performance. Its reputation for high standards, validity, and reliability is well established, because it is based on representative samples of students, and has no individual or school-level performance implications.

In the early 2000s, the NAEP TUDA was disaggregated for the 20 large urban districts it assesses around the country. Since then, NYC students have consistently scored in the middle of the achievement distribution in both Math and Reading. In addition to ranking each participating city's results, NAEP also calibrates their achievement score gaps by race and ethnicity. Fourth and eighth grade Reading and Math are TUDA's testing foci at the elementary and middle grades. TUDA revealed that the very large performance gaps between Black and Latino students, compared to White students, did not significantly diminish on any subject or level. That includes between 2002 and 2015 for Grade 4 Reading; between 2003 and 2015 for Grade 8 Reading, and for Grade 4 and Grade 8 Math (Institute of Education Sciences, 2015a, 2015b).

In 2015, the TUDA Grade 4 Math average score differential was 22 points lower for Black students than it was for White students and 17 points lower for Latino students than for White students. These performance gaps had not changed significantly from those in 2003. Grade 8 Math saw even higher gaps in 2015: Black students scoring 33 points lower than White students, and Latino students scoring 26 points lower than White students. Again, there had been little change from 2003 levels (Institute of Education Sciences, 2015c; 2015d).

In 2015, Black students' average Grade 4 Reading scores were 26 points lower than those of White students and Latino students' scores were 28 points lower than those of White students. These gaps were very similar to those found in 2002. In 2015, Grade 8 Reading, Black students' average scores were 29 points lower than those of White students, and Latino students' reading scores were 22 points lower. Similarly, these gaps had changed little from those in 2003. These TUDA results demonstrate that Mayor Bloomberg's reforms did not affect the persistent racial achievement gap that his administration had pledged it would eliminate.

The Bloomberg era did achieve some improvement in high school graduation rates. Beginning four years after the Bloomberg reform efforts began, from 2007 to 2013, the June four-year graduation rates for Black, Latino, and White students all increased. They went from 47.8 percent to 56.0 percent for Black students, from 43.5 percent to 53.6 percent for Latino students, and from 69.0 percent to 76.4 percent for White students (NYC Department of Education, 2015).

The Bloomberg administration opened more than four hundred high schools and closed more than 150. Opening some comprehensive, small high schools, and closing many others may well have contributed to these increases (Bloom, Thompson, & Unterman, 2010; Bloom & Unterman, 2013; Kemple, 2015). However, the gaps between Blacks and Latinos, and White students in four-year high school graduation rates remained essentially the same in the years from 2007 to 2013. The gap between Black and White students decreased by only 0.8 percentage-points, while the gap between Latino and White students decreased by 2.7 percentage points. Despite these gains in overall graduation rates, the substantial graduation gaps between Black and Latino students, and White students were not closed by very much.

> One of the ultimate goals of high school matriculation is to prepare students for college. The Bloomberg administration's efforts to improve high school preparation were, however, inadequate. An AISR study, *Is Demography Still Destiny?* from 2012, affirmed that, for NYC high school graduates, there was a robust correlation between college readiness and the neighborhood a student lived in.
>
> The Bloomberg administration repeatedly claimed that demography was not destiny, and it insisted that their reforms would break the links between residential neighborhood conditions and schooling outcomes. However, the AISR study found that both the racial composition and the average income of a student's home neighborhood were very strong predictors of how college-ready a student would be when graduating from high school. Moreover, the disparities between neighborhoods were enormous. An overwhelming number of the neighborhoods whose students posted very low college-readiness rates were located in the hypersegregated community school districts. (Fruchter, Hester, Mokhtar, & Shahn, 2012)

Choice

The Bloomberg administration's failure to reduce the racial achievement gap in both graduation outcomes and college readiness rates, lead us to point out the limitations of another key Bloomberg initiative: the effort to expand high school choice. We have noted how the Bloomberg administration planned to increase overall high school effectiveness by creating more than four hundred new high schools and closing over 150 poor performers. This team also recalibrated the universal high school selection process that matched student preferences with an ultimate school assignment. The adapted algorithm was patterned after the one used by prospective interns and medical schools. The new selection method standardized high school choice expanded the percentage of students placed into one of their top three choices and eliminated the margins of manipulation present in the previous system (Abdulkadiroğlu, Pathak, & Roth, 2005).

The AISR college-readiness study showed that, even when a system is more responsive to a student's choice of high school, it does not reduce the racial achievement gap in college readiness, a key measure of high school quality. Choice, by itself, is not the panacea that Chubb and Moe proclaimed in 1990 (Chubb & Moe, 1990). New York City's universal high school selection process assumed the following: 1) all students and family members approach the selection process with equal access to necessary information; 2) all students have equal family and social networks; and 3) all students have the same institutional connections one needs to make an effective choice among more than five hundred school and program options. This self-help approach to high school selection only affirms the fallacy of the neutral starting line, which assumes that hundreds of years of racism, White supremacy, and socioeconomic oppression play no role in limiting student and family capacity to choose (Sattin-Bajaj, 2014).

The Bloomberg high school reforms did accomplish two things: 1) students had more high schools to choose from, and 2) because of the new selection process, the overwhelming majority of middle school students were able to attend one of their top three high school choices. However, as the Annenberg Institute's *Demography/Destiny* study demonstrated, despite access to either of these advances, the racial gap in high school performance did not narrow.

The Annenberg Institute study of the NYC Department of Education's instructional support networks also examined high school segregation in the years 2002 and 2012. The study concluded that, except for a small increase in Asian student segregation, the extent of high school segregation was much the same in both years. The Bloomberg high school reforms did not succeed in reducing the racial gaps in high school achievement or in reducing the hyper-segregation of the school system's Black and Latino students.

Ultimately, the Bloomberg reforms served to bolster existing family advantages and boost the choice system's ability to serve higher-income aspirations. The expanded choice at the high school level underlined the inequalities that separate families and students across the city by race/ethnicity and income. More and better choices alone cannot produce equity. Instead, added choice only reaffirms and rewards privilege, opportunity, and advantage. To be charitable, one could conclude that the Bloomberg administration confused a dream to increase equity for all with the reality of improving opportunities only for some.

Postscript

In this chapter, we have aimed to demonstrate both the continuity and the shifts in New York City's school segregation across the past 40 years. We have offered views on why the major systemic reforms that dominated city schooling during these years, namely governance change and market-based change, failed to reduce segregation and improve the schooling outcomes of the majority of the system's Black and Latino students. We conclude with some thoughts on what might reduce the persistent segregation in New York City's school systems, and what could improve schooling outcomes for all students, particularly for Black and Latino students in hypersegregated schools and districts.

In recent decades, school choice has expanded within the city system. There has been a rapid growth in available charter schools, and students now can list their school preferences. The days of others assigning someone to a school, based on geography, are gone in public schools. Now, there is even a small, but growing, degree of choice at the elementary school level, considerable school choice at the middle school level, and almost universal choice at the high school level. However, none of these choice options promote socioeconomic or racial diversity or equalize opportunity.

Here is one example of how a Mayor and a School's Chancellor could advance significant integration in schools. The Mayor and the Chancellor could issue a comprehensive statement defining the many benefits of integrated schooling. The Chancellor could develop an Equity Audit detailing the extent of school segregation within each community district, and strongly encourage the fifteen districts we define as potentially integrable, to reduce the extent of segregation in their district's elementary and middle schools, and to set a timetable for such district action. The central administration could support this integration mandate by developing a typology of initiatives, such as controlled choice, magnet schools, lottery-driven schools of choice, paired schools, dual-language schools, or other diversity models used by school districts around the country. A new central bureau could provide information, guidance, expertise, and support to districts working to increase integration.

For several decades, the city's high school system has assigned students to schools using an almost universal choice system. Within our hypothetical example, the Mayor and the Chancellor could increase high school integration by requiring all high schools to do the following. They can reserve a certain percentage of their seats for students who receive special education services, ELLs (English Language Learners) and OTC (Over the Counter) students, in proportion to their enrollment in the citywide high school system. These seats could then be filled through a computerized selection process. These mostly low-income students of color together comprise about 40 percent of the citywide high school population. By reserving 40 percent of the seats for these students in each high school, they would immediately expand integration within the city system.

These are two examples of the many possibilities that exist for increasing integration, although they do hint at the immense difficulties such endeavors might encounter. No doubt, there would be an immediate firestorm of opposition. The challenge is to mobilize thoughtfully and strategically the political will needed to withstand the predictable tsunami of opposition.

However, successfully withstanding such opposition and achieving significant levels of integration in the fifteen potentially integrable districts will do little to alter the opportunity gaps within the seventeen hypersegregated school districts. Magnet-school choice programs, or school pairings, focused on the boundary areas between integrable and hypersegregated districts, could draw some students from segregated schools to schools near the borders of integrable districts. Establishing more dual-language schools or redrawing district boundaries might further contribute to desegregation. However, for most of the schools within those hypersegregated districts, the measures chosen by the 1960s-style community control proponents still constitute the major educational option: segregated schools must be improved from within.

This chapter was written during the third year of the Bill de Blasio administration. His campaign mantra, *A Tale of Two Cities*, aptly describes the differences that exist between the potentially integrable districts, and the hypersegregated districts our study discusses. The De Blasio administration's initial system-wide reforms, which include universal full-day, pre-kindergarten classes, and community schools focus on more than one hundred of the system's most poorly performing schools, illustrate the scale and scope of what needs to be done to improve education in the hypersegregated districts. We must do much more if we want to set right the past 50 years of pervasive school segregation and reverse the damaging effects it has had on both the students in the hypersegregated districts, and by extension, on every student in the city's schools.

Notes

1. Because the school system's school year starts in September and ends the following June, the school year actually covers parts of two years, 1973–74 or 2013–14, for example. Our text uses the double year format throughout the chapter.

2. NYC DOE racial/ethnic classifications for the 2013–14 data include: (1) Black, (2) Hispanic, (3) Asian, (4) White, and (5) Other. The authors use the term Latino rather than Hispanic. The classification "Other" refers to students who do not identify themselves as Black, Hispanic, Asian or White (e.g., students of mixed origin, Native American students, etc.). In 2014, "Other" students made up 1.7 percent of all students. Citywide and district figures include all students from PK-12.

3. Note that the 32 Districts across Tables 3.1 and 3.2 do not comprise 100 percent of citywide student populations in 2013–14, because District 75 (special education), District 79 (alternative high schools and programs) and Charter Schools are not included. The complete breakdown follows:

Citywide in 2014: 1,104,479 students.

Table 3.1: School Districts with Lowest Percentages of Black and Latino Students by Neighborhood, 2013–14: 590,592 (53.5 percent)

Table 3.2: School Districts with Highest Percentages of Black and Latino Students by Neighborhood, 2013–14: 413,104 (37.4 percent)

District 75: 23,304 students (2.1 percent)

District 79: 5,574 (0.5 percent)

District 84 (charters): 71,905 (6.5 percent)

4. In 1970, the city school system was decentralized and reorganized into 32 community school districts, each governed by locally elected school boards. Because the start-up years of citywide decentralization required the establishment of new administrative procedures and data collection, we chose the 1973–74 school year as our initial comparison year. We use 2013–14, because it brackets a 40-year timespan and because it was the last operative school year for the Bloomberg-era market-based reforms.

5. In 2013–14, "Other" students made up 1.7 percent of the citywide student population.

6. Note that the changes we identify are changes in community school district student populations, rather than changes in overall populations. There is a predictable lag in school district student population change versus overall population change. The

movement of young couples and young families, for example, often initiates gentrification. The children of those families reach school age and enroll in their new schools some years after their parents/caregivers have settled into their new neighborhoods.

7. The specialized high schools of the NYC school system include:

The Bronx High School of Science

The Brooklyn Latin School

Brooklyn Technical High School

Fiorello H. LaGuardia High School of Music & Art and Performing Arts High School for Mathematics, Science and Engineering at the City College of New York

High School of American Studies at Lehman College

Queens High School for the Sciences at York College

Staten Island Technical High School

Stuyvesant High School

8. Due to data limitations, the 1973–74 data relies on eligibility for free lunch as a proxy for student/family poverty, while the 2013–14 data uses eligibility for free and reduced-price lunch for that year's poverty measure.

9. In Manhattan, for example, District 3's new boundaries joined the White and relatively high-income sections of the Upper West Side with the southern flank of Harlem, whose schools served an almost completely Black, and relatively low-income, student population. The tensions this pairing created continue to this day. A similar combination in District 8 in the Bronx, grouped the low-income Latino neighborhoods of Hunts Point with the largely White working class neighborhoods of Sound View, and the predominantly White neighborhoods of Throgs Neck. In Brooklyn's District 15, the largely White brownstone neighborhoods of Carroll Gardens and Park Slope were linked with the predominantly Black neighborhood of Red Hook, and the predominantly Latino neighborhood of Sunset Park. In District 28 in Queens, the boundary designers combined the predominantly White neighborhoods of Forest Hills, Rego Park and Kew Gardens, with the predominantly Black neighborhoods of South Jamaica and Springfield Gardens.

References

Abdulkadiroğlu, A., Pathak, P. A., & Roth, A. E. (2005). The New York City high school match. *American Economic Review, 95*(2), 364–67.

Alves, M. (November 1, 2016). *Potential strategies for improvement of the New York City high school application process.* Fordham Law School.

Amin, K., Chellman, C., Lockwood, D., et al. (2004). *First, do no harm: A Response to the proposed New York City Third Grade Retention Policy.* New York, NY: Institute for Education & Social Policy, NYU and National Center for Schools and Communities, Fordham University.

Anker, I. (1983). Educational Redlining. In J. P. Vitteritti (Ed.), *Across the river: Politics and education in the city* (p. 6). New York, NY: Holmes & Meier.

Arvidsson, T. S., Fruchter, N., & Mokhtar, C. (2013). *Over the counter, under the radar: Inequitably distributing New York City's late-enrolling high school students.* New York, NY: Annenberg Institute for School Reform at Brown University.

Bloom, H. S., Thompson, S. L., & Unterman, R. (2010). *Transforming the high school experience: How New York City's new small schools are boosting student achievement and graduation rates.* New York, NY: MDRC.

Bloom, H. S., & Unterman, R. (2013). *Sustained progress: New findings about the effectiveness and operation of small public high schools of choice in New York City.* New York, NY: MDRC.

Brier, S. (2014). The ideological and organizational origins of the united federation of teachers' opposition to the community control movement in the New York City Public Schools, 1960–68. *Labour/Le Travail, 73,* 179–93.

Chapman, B. (2016, March 27). City schools shut out minority students from resources. *New York Daily News.* Retrieved from http://www.nydailynews.com/new-york/education/city-schools-shut-minority-students-resources-article-1.2578859.

Chubb, J. E., & Moe, T. M. (1990). *Politics, markets, and America's schools.* Washington, DC: The Brookings Institution.

Demas, B. H. (1971). *The school Lections: A critique of the 1969 New York City School Decentralization Law.* New York, NY: City University of New York, Institute for Community Studies.

Fessenden, F. (May 11, 2012). A portrait of segregation in New York City's schools. *New York Times.* Retrieved from http://www.nytimes.com/interactive/2012/05/11/nyregion/segregation-in-new-york-city-public-schools.html?_r=0.

Fruchter, N., Arvidsson, T. S., Mokhtar, C., & Beam, J. (2015). *Demographics and performance in New York City's School networks: An initial inquiry.* New York, NY: Annenberg Institute for School Reform at Brown University.

Fruchter, N., Hester, M., Mokhtar, C., & Shahn, Z. (2012). *Is demography still destiny? Neighborhood demographics and public high school students' readiness for college in New York City.* New York, NY: Annenberg Institute for School Reform at Brown University.

Haimson, L. (2010). Chapter 1, Children first: A short history. *NYC Schools under Bloomberg/Klein: What parents, teachers and policymakers need to know* (p. 15). New York, NY: Lulu.com.

Harris, E. A. (2015, December 15). School segregation persists in gentrifying neighborhoods, maps suggest. *The New York Times.*

Institute of Education Sciences. (2015a). The nation's report card, 2015 mathematics trial urban district snapshot report, New York City, grade 4, public schools.

Retrieved from https://nces.ed.gov/nationsreportcard/subject/publications/dst2015/pdf/2016049XN4.pdf.

Institute of Education Sciences. (2015b). The nation's report card, 2015 mathematics trial urban district snapshot report, New York City, grade 8, public schools. Retrieved from https://nces.ed.gov/nationsreportcard/subject/publications/dst2015/pdf/2016049XN8.pdf.

Institute of Education Sciences. (2015c). The nation's report card, 2015 reading trial urban district snapshot report, New York City, grade 4, public schools. Retrieved from https://nces.ed.gov/nationsreportcard/subject/publications/dst2015/pdf/2016048XN4.pdf.

Institute of Education Sciences. (2015d). The Nation's Report Card, 2015 Reading Trial Urban District Snapshot Report, New York City, Grade 8, Public Schools. Retrieved from https://nces.ed.gov/nationsreportcard/subject/publications/dst2015/pdf/2016048xn8.pdf.

Isaacs, C. S. (2014). *Inside Ocean Hill–Brownsville: A teacher's education, 1968–69*. Albany, NY: Excelsior Editions.

James, L. (2016). Public advocate for the City of New York Letitia James Calls for Chief Diversity Officer for NYC Public Schools. Retrieved from http://pubadvocate.nyc.gov/news/articles/pa-james-calls-chief-diversity-officer-nyc-public-schools.

Johnson, G., Subramanian, S., Wilks, A., & Domanico, R. (2013). *Availability and distribution of selected program resources in New York City High Schools*. New York, NY: New York City Independent Budget Office.

Kemple, J. J. (2015). *High School closures in New York City: Impacts on students' academic outcomes, attendance, and mobility*. New York, NY: The Research Alliance for New York City Schools, New York University.

Kucsera, J., & Orfield, G. (2014). *New York State's extreme school segregation: Inequality, inaction and a damaged future*. Los Angeles, CA: The Civil Rights Project, UCLA.

Ladner, B., & Torres, R. (Decemer 15, 2017, December 15). What would it take to integrate our schools? *The New York Times*. Retrieved from http://www.nytimes.com/2015/12/15/opinion/what-would-it-take-to-integrate-our-schools.html?_r=0.

Lewis, H. (2013). *New York City Public Schools from Brownsville to Bloomberg*. New York, NY: Teachers College Press.

Mader, N., Cory, B., & Royo, C. (2016). *Diversity in New York's specialized schools: A deeper data dive*. New York, NY: The New School, Center for New York City Affairs.

McGrail, K. R. (1976). New York City School decentralization: The respective powers of the City Board of Education and the Community School Boards. *Fordham Urban Law Journal, 5*(2), 239–78.

N.Y. Civil Liberties Union. (2016). New data show outsized police role and racial disparities in school discipline. Retrieved from http://www.nyclu.org/news/new-data-show-outsized-police-role-and-racial-disparities-school-discipline.

NYC Department of Education. (2015). Graduation results, cohorts of 2001 through 2011 (Classes of 2005 through 2015) graduation outcomes. Retrieved from http://schools.nyc.gov/Accountability/data/GraduationDropoutReports/default.htm.

NYC Department of Education. (2016). Demographic snapshots. Retrieved from http://schools.nyc.gov/Accountability/data/default.htm.

Perlstein, D. H. (2004). *Justice, justice: school politics and the eclipse of liberalism*. New York, NY: Peter Lang Inc.

Phenix, D. (2008). *Data for the people, public education data use in a community base: AERA working paper*. New York, NY: Annenberg Institute for School Reform at Brown University.

Phenix, D., Siegel, D., Zaltsman, A., & Fruchter, N. (2004). *Virtual District, real improvement: a retrospective evaluation of the chancellor's district, 1996–2003*. New York, NY: Institute for Education and Social Policy, New York University.

Roy, J. (2014). *Demographics and work experience: A statistical portrait of New York City's public school teachers*. New York, NY: New York City Independent Budget Office, Schools Brief.

Sattin-Bajaj, C. (2014). *Unaccompanied minors: Immigrant youth, school choice and the pursuit of equity*. Cambridge, MA: Harvard Educational Press.

Siegel, D., & Fruchter, N. (2002). *Final Report: Evaluation of the performance driven budgeting initiative of the New York City Board of Education (1997–2000)*. New York, NY: Institute for Education and Social Policy, New York University.

Stiefel, L., Schwartz, A. E., Portas, C., & Kim, D. Y. (2003). School budgeting and school performance: The impact of New York City's performance driven budgeting initiative. *Journal of Education Finance, 28*, 403–24.

U.S. Department of Education. (2016). *2013–14 Civil rights data collection, a first look: Key data highlights on equity and opportunity gaps in our nation's public schools*. Washington, DC: Office for Civil Rights Retrieved from https://www2.ed.gov/about/offices/list/ocr/docs/2013-14-first-look.pdf.

Veiga, C. (2017). Desegregation as a human right: New York City—Councilman proposes "Office of School Diversity." *Chalkbeat*. Retrieved from http://www.chalkbeat.org/posts/ny/2016/11/29/desegregation-as-a-human-right-new-york-city-councilman-proposes-office-of-school-diversity/.

— EDUCATION ADDENDUM —

Improving School Culture to Reduce Educational Disparities for Black and Latino Young Men

Adriana Villavicencio, Shifra Goldenberg, and Sarah Klevan

Black and Latino young men face educational disparities that begin early in life. These disparities are the result of complicated, intersecting factors they experience, both in and out of school. New York City has developed a new approach designed to address these inequities. By investing in the high school experience, the city hopes to make a difference for a substantial portion of Black and Latino young men.

In 2012, NYC launched its Expanded Success Initiative (ESI), which provided 40 high schools with the financial resources and professional development they needed to create or expand programs to support Black and Latino students. The decision to invest in high schools was motivated partially by student data the city had collected. They found that, even among students who received the highest scores on the state's eighth grade English Language Arts exam, a substantial racial and gender gap had emerged by the time these students completed their high school careers (Villavicencio, Bhattacharya, & Guidry, 2013). Although it was discouraging to learn that high-performing students could fall behind, the data suggested that high schools could make a positive difference by doing more for their male students of color.

After completing a longitudinal study of ESI, in addition to conducting hundreds of interviews with school leaders and teachers, the Research Alliance found that many schools participating in the program had focused their efforts on improving school culture. Their goal was to create a more supportive and welcoming environment for Black and Latino young men. A growing body of research suggests that a positive school culture enhances a student's day-to-day experiences, and plays a role in raising student achievement (Bryk, Sebring, Allensworth, Easton, & Luppescu, 2010; Fergus, Noguera, & Martin,

2014; Kraft, Marinell, & Shen-Wei Yee, 2016; Thapa, Cohen, Guffey, & Higgins-D'Alessandro, 2013). ESI participants concentrated on four specific areas:

- **Developing Culturally Relevant Education (CRE).** After received training in CRE, educators adopted a variety of approaches to make the curriculum and instruction more relevant to students' everyday lives. They fostered an environment that affirms cultural backgrounds and addressed underlying teacher biases toward students.
- **Adopting Restorative Approaches to Discipline.** Rather than relying so heavily on suspension as a form of discipline, educators began to implement new practices, such as peer mediation and conflict resolution training. Their goal was to build positive relationships with students to foster a stronger sense of community at school.
- **Promoting Strong Relationships in Schools.** Educators introduced mentoring and advisory programs that were designed to strengthen relationships between students and staff, as well as between students and their peers. The peer mentorship campaign, in particular, provided struggling students with academic support.
- **Providing Early Support for Postsecondary Goals.** Educators shifted their perspective from preparing for high school graduation to enhancing college readiness. They sought to strengthen each student's belief that they belong in college. They also assisted students in taking the concrete steps involved in preparing for, and applying to, college.

There is a growing recognition that many young men of color feel alienated, rather than embraced, by their schools. There also is substantial evidence that school culture can affect student achievement. The strategies tested in ESI schools are worth examining more closely. ESI educators believe the new approaches they are using have improved their curriculum and instruction, have reduced the use of suspensions, have strengthened relationships in schools, and have encouraged a college-bound identity for Black and Latino males. Additional research might reveal whether school culture interventions encourage additional outcomes, such as graduation achievement and college enrollment, and ultimately, whether the educational disparities facing young men of color can be reduced in New York City.

References

Bryk, A. S., Sebring, P. B., Allensworth, E., Easton, J. Q., & Luppescu, S. (2010). *Organizing schools for improvement: Lessons from Chicago*. Chicago: University of Chicago Press.

Fergus, E., Noguera, P., & Martin, M. (2014). *Schooling for resilience: Improving the life trajectory of Black and Latino Boys*. Cambridge, MA: Harvard Education Press.

Kraft, M. A., Marinell, W. H., & Shen-Wei Yee, D. (2016). School organizational contexts, teacher turnover, and student achievement: Evidence from panel data. *American Educational Research Journal, 53*(5), 1411–49.

Thapa, A., Cohen, J., Guffey, S., & Higgins-D'Alessandro, A. (2013). A review of school climate research. *Review of Educational Research, 83*(3), 357–385.

Villavicencio, A., Bhattacharya, D., & Guidry, B. (2013). Moving the needle: Exploring key levers to boost college readiness among Black and Latino Males in New York City. Retrieved from http://steinhardt.nyu.edu/research_alliance/publications/moving_the_needle.

Chapter 4

Government

Do Mayors Matter?

Race, Justice, and the Men in City Hall, 1965–2017

JARRETT MURPHY[1]

September 16, 1992 was sunny in the city of New York, with highs in the 80s. New Yorkers awoke to the results of the federal primaries that had taken place the day before, to the latest polling in the three-way presidential race, and to news from abroad that the European Monetary System was about to collapse. It had been three years and four days since David N. Dinkins had defeated three-term incumbent Ed Koch in the 1989 primary. Dinkins was en route to becoming the first Black mayor of the nation's greatest city: a milestone in New York City's, and the country's fitful quest for racial equality. This particular Wednesday would attain a different sort of milestone.

The city's largest police union, the Patrolmen's Benevolent Association (PBA), had called for a demonstration that day to protest the mayor's proposal for a civilian-only Civilian Complaint Review Board (CCRB). From its beginning, the CCRB's mission has been to investigate and recommend discipline in those cases of alleged police misconduct that do not rise to the level of criminal charges. These may include complaints of discourtesy or use of excessive force.[2] In 1989, the 12-person board consisted of six civilian members, appointed by the mayor, and six non-uniformed NYPD employees, appointed by the police commissioner. People had expressed concerns that the official police presence on the board undermined its independence. Dinkins then went to the City Council to introduce a bill to relieve the NYPD of their slots on the panel (McKinley Jr., 1992).

Dinkins and others who supported an all-civilian CCRB argued that the existing board have been unable to render credible judgments or to ease concerns in Black and Latino communities about police overreach. A strong case for reform emerged because of the Tompkins Square Park incident in 1988. At that time, a four-hour battle occurred during which dozens of cops went berserk with their nightsticks, pummeling reporters and passersby, spewing racial epithets and profanity, covering their badges to elude complaints. The CCRB managed to make disciplinary recommendations against a mere 17 officers. In the end, only 13 were punished (NYCLU, 1990).

The police union's objection to Dinkins' CCRB proposal was the same as it had been under a different mayor three decades earlier. First, the union believed it was unfair to cops. Second, the proposal would interfere with public safety. In their minds, politically appointed civilians should not have the right to play Monday-morning quarterback on street interactions where officers had to make snap decisions amid uncertainty and potential danger.

The CCRB was not the only gripe the PBA brought to City Hall that day. The union was upset that the Dinkins administration had resisted their push to give officers the option of carrying 9mm pistols, rather than the traditional revolvers. The union argued that this change was necessary to prevent police from being outgunned by drug dealers. They were upset that the mayor had impaneled a commission to investigate police corruption, based on a litany of reports about criminal rings within the NYPD (McKinley, 1992). The PBA was especially angry about the way Dinkins had handled the Kiko Garcia incident that summer. During a reported scuffle, a plainclothes officer had shot and killed a known drug dealer. Amid rising tensions that summer, Dinkins visited the Garcia family to ask for their help in keeping things calm. The mayor said he was trying to prevent a riot. However, officers thought he was coddling a man who had tried to kill a cop (Finder, 1992).

All these complaints found their way to City Hall that day. At an official rally site along the western edge of City Hall Park, some 4,000 PBA members and supporters gathered to hear speeches, and to protest the CCRB proposal, as well as the other allegedly anti-police steps that had been taken by the Dinkins administration. There were 6,000 other police on hand who either skipped or left the official rally. Many of these officers, in an overwhelmingly White male crowd, rushed the City Hall steps, jumping on cars, and yelling, "Take the Hall! Take the Hall!" They appeared oblivious to the 300-strong, on-duty NYPD force, ostensibly present to keep order. When the NYPD's highest-ranking uniformed officer ordered them to back off, they ignored him. Even the pleas from the head of the PBA were ineffective.

Officers blocked traffic on the Brooklyn Bridge and assaulted reporters, leading one lieutenant to order a news photographer off the bridge, because he could not guarantee his safety. A Black council member said some of the off-duty cops called her a "nigger," and a Black TV news camera operator made a similar complaint. Some reporters who covered the event said they did not hear any racial epithets, but the signs some officers carried were obvious in their racial tones (McKinley, 1992). "The mayor," read one, "is on crack." Some posters depicted the mayor as having a large Afro. One infamous placard described the dignified Dinkins as a "washroom attendant" (Purdum, 1992).

In the aftermath, the mayor had harsh words for the unruly demonstrators. However, he reserved his strongest remarks for one of the headline speakers at the official rally on Murray Street. "He's clearly, clearly an opportunist," Dinkins said. "He's seizing upon a fragile circumstance in our city for his own political gain." He was talking about Rudy Giuliani, the Republican whom Dinkins narrowly beat in 1989, and was sure to face again in 1993. At the main demonstration, Giuliani had bellowed through a megaphone, denouncing Dinkins' arguments as "bullshit! bullshit!" and shouting, "The reason the morale of the police department of the City of New York is so low is one reason and one reason alone: David Dinkins!" The cops roared lustily.

Although the two rivals did not come face to face that day, the 1992 police riot reflected the tug of war between multiracial aspiration and the White-ethnic backlash. Such are the fundamental facts of mayoral politics in New York City over the last half-century.

Race has been a defining political factor in New York City since 1626 when a group of White men purchased Manhattan Island from the Lenape Indians. One legend says that Wall Street was given its name because it runs along what was once a fortified border protecting the city from Native American intrusion. A slave revolt in 1712 killed nine Whites and led to a crackdown on the rather-limited rights then enjoyed by New Yorkers in bondage. The worst unrest in U.S. history occurred in New York in 1863, when racial and class grievances became violent in the Draft Riots.

The role of race in the city changed dramatically in 1965. By that year, the Second Great Migration of southern Blacks to northern cities had reached its peak. Congress passed an immigration law that induced Asian, African, and South American immigrants to come to the city, and the face of New York was changed subsequently over the next decades. Nineteen sixty-five was also the year Congress passed the Voting Rights Act, the most significant legislation of the civil rights era,[3] and also approved the most important pieces of President Johnson's Great Society, which briefly and dramatically altered the role government played in mitigating social injustice. Black nationalists, and more radical civil-rights activists gained prominence, alongside establishment Black figures. At the same time, the Vietnam War was escalating dramatically, setting the stage for the domestic political crisis that would split the New Deal coalition of blue-collar Whites from White progressives and Blacks.

Nineteen sixty-five was also when New York voters elected Mayor John Lindsay, a liberal Republican congressional representative. He was the first New York City mayor to grapple with modern racial politics. The six mayors who followed him have wrestled with many of the same issues, though they have employed drastically different approaches.

It is not simple to evaluate how much each of these mayors mattered to the overall state of race equity in the city. We must weigh their intentions versus their results, as well as each mayor's use of nuts-and-bolts policy versus the softer power of symbol and messaging. All this has to be done while noting the limitations and expectations of each era. In this context, we must treat racial justice as something woven into the deeper political health and economic profile of the city, not as an isolated quality, which each mayor shapes.

John Lindsay: Standing for Justice, Triggering a Backlash

John Lindsay, a leader in civil rights, was the first Republican to enter City Hall since Fiorello LaGuardia. He won the mayoralty twice, in 1965 and again four years later. Both times, he won without getting a majority of the votes cast. The intense racial conflict and social upheaval that existed during Lindsay's mayoralty was something that changed the city's politics of race forever. He waged many fights over racial justice and was damaged badly by them. Some battles he chose, others chose him. People have depicted Lindsay's inability to manage these crises as an indictment of his leadership skills, and perhaps a censure of liberalism itself. However, repeatedly, Lindsay appears to have taken the path most consistent with an aggressive pursuit of racial justice. There were many reasons he could not control how others played their part in the drama. Despite this, Lindsay's critics rarely suggested an alternate path he could have taken that would have satisfied the yearning for justice with less disruption or friction.

As a congressional representative from Manhattan's Silk Stocking district, Lindsay had championed civil rights legislation. He entered office promising systemic reform of many aspects of city government, especially those with embedded racial disparities. In his first year in office, Lindsay created an all-civilian police complaint review board. The police union fought back, getting a referendum on the November ballot, and using a campaign based on fear of crime to urge voters to reject Lindsay's board. The campaign was racially tinged. Lindsay was soundly defeated, in a year when there was a broader backlash to the struggle for Black civil rights. The Civilian Complaint Review Board (CCRB) returned to all-police leadership.

When Lindsay ran for mayor, school quality in Black neighborhoods was an issue of increasing concern. Although *Brown vs. Board of Education* had been enacted a decade earlier, there was a growing pessimism that racial integration of schools was politically or pragmatically possible. Many Black parents sensed a lack of dedication or skill among the overwhelmingly White teachers assigned to majority-Black schools. For some parents, the only way to ensure quality was to seize control of the system, to permit communities to run their own schools, to hire teachers and assign principals who were adequately committed to educating local children.

Lindsay and the United Federation of Teachers were open to the principle of greater community power. However, a Ford Foundation-backed experiment in community control in the Ocean Hill-Brownsville district exposed a gap between what more radical elements in the community-control movement wanted, and what Lindsay was able to get the UFT to give. When the Black-run school district fired some White teachers, the union saw a threat to hard-won workplace protections and fought to get them reinstated. The argument soon deteriorated into an ugly confrontation involving threats of violence, anti-Semitic and racist rhetoric, and three separate teachers' strikes. It did lasting damage to relations between Blacks and Jews, long-time allies on the city's left, and exposed Lindsay's inability to mediate passionate desires for social equality with the larger needs of the city.

Lindsay faced another firestorm later in his term when his administration proposed a "scatter-site" public housing development in Forest Hills, Queens (Newfield & Barrett, 1988). Much of the large subsidized housing development was aimed at senior citizens, but a portion was set aside for Blacks, as well. This touched off a local revolt in which opponents conveyed a mix of blatant racism, and of more subtle racism couched in concerns about crime and property values. Politicians, such as Congressman Ed Koch, a once-reliable resident of the far left, sensed changing political winds, so they sided with the local opponents. In the end, a young lawyer named Mario Cuomo brokered a compromise, and a smaller-scale development was built. This incident further damaged Lindsay's already dismal standing among outer-borough Whites, who were already angry over everything from strikes to snowstorms that had occurred during the progressive mayor's term.

Lindsay's social policy was aligned closely with President Johnson's Great Society, including the formation of community groups to dispense social services and to build political power in low-income neighborhoods. A few of those groups wasted money, but others were successful in cultivating a new generation of Black community leadership. Lindsay made aggressive use of federal money to expand social programs, boosting job training and Head Start, and expanding the welfare rolls. Lindsay believed that the demographic changes hitting the city required a more expansive safety net. The increase in lower-income Black and Latino populations was significant at a time when manufacturing employment was decreasing rapidly. Lindsay successfully fought for cities in New York to be treated better in state and federal budgets, rallying his fellow mayors to lobby for more largesse. Despite Lindsay's reputation as a reckless spendthrift, it seems that New York's approach to social spending was not that different from other U.S. cities in that era.

Social spending was how urban America dealt with the cumulative shockwaves of suburbanization, migration, and deindustrialization. Sometimes those forces, and the tensions and frustrations they bred, exploded into violence. Major riots shook Los Angeles (1964), Chicago (1965) and Newark (1966). As a result, in 1967, Lyndon Johnson appointed the National Advisory Commission on Civil Disorders to study the causes of the unrest. The commission was known popularly as the Kerner Commission, named for its chair, Illinois Governor, Otto Kerner. John Lindsay served as it's vice chair. He had an outsized role in shaping the panel's final report, in particular, a boldly worded summary that included lines such as: "What White Americans have never fully understood—but what the Negro can never forget is that White society is implicated deeply in the ghetto. White institutions created it, white institutions maintain it, and white society condones it." Johnson ignored the report. In fact, some of its conclusions may seem simplistic to modern eyes. Nonetheless, it is remarkable that a politician with aspirations for national office (Lindsay was already touted as presidential material, and would run unsuccessfully for the White House in 1972) would steer a presidential commission to implicate so starkly White people in cultivating Black poverty, disempowerment, and rage.

Some critics of the Kerner Commission argue that its report overlooked the real reason for the riots in Los Angeles, Chicago, and Newark. These critics believed the police had held back from crushing the revolt at its earliest and most manageable stage. Lindsay's New York, however, provides the antithesis to this critique. Under the liberal Republican mayor, the NYPD sought a mediated outcome to street confrontations, no longer charging in with helmets on and nightsticks lashing. With this softer approach, the city experienced minimum unrest during the Lindsay years. Lindsay himself has been credited with maintaining some of that peace, because he had the habit of walking through Black neighborhoods, displaying a level of comfort that was unusual for a White man at that time.

On April 4, 1968, Lindsay was at a theater when he received word that Dr. Martin Luther King, Jr. had been assassinated. He rushed first to Gracie

Mansion, and then to Harlem. Despite warnings from his staff, he wandered into a crowd quaking with grief. He made no speech, but instead embraced people one by one, putting his hand on one shoulder to say, "I'm so sorry," then on another to say, "This is terrible." He encountered some hostility but still pressed on. To be sure, there was some unrest in New York that night, but it did not come close to the scale of what occurred in other cities in the U.S., some of which were scarred for decades by the damage that was wrought. That night, as articulated in Pete Hamill's appreciation of Lindsay, "Tanks rolled through American streets. Not in New York."

Other communities were finding their voice in New York, and Lindsay responded to their concerns, as well. At one point, a Puerto Rican activist group called the Young Lords, swept trash into the streets to block traffic, and to draw attention to the abysmal sanitation services in East Harlem. They also occupied a church where a pastor had impeded plans for food distribution, in addition to taking over part of a hospital. Lindsay aides brokered compromises that averted violence and, in most cases, Lindsay responded to legitimate community needs. Critics would accuse Lindsay of incentivizing violent tactics by caving to such illegal protests, but the mayor actually recognized that it was more important to do what was right for people in need than it was to worry about the optics of the moment.

Before Lindsay even occupied City Hall, historian Arthur Mann said that he was "the first New York mayor to really have to care about incorporating the Negro into the American dream." Indeed, Blacks had been only six percent of the city's population in 1940, but by 1968, their presence had increased to 20 percent. While he did not succeed in ending injustice or in equalizing access to opportunity, he did demonstrate that he cared deeply about people of color. He was willing to take profound political, and on his finest evening, personal risks to put the power of city government behind them.

However, his commitment had an ironic consequence that ultimately reshaped New York City politics forever. Historian Vincent Cannato's conclusion was, "The longest lasting consequence of the Lindsay years on the city's political landscape has been the rise of the White ethnic sensibility" (Cannato, 2001, p. 575). Others, who were even more favorably disposed to Lindsay, agreed. "Lindsay was great on race, not so great on class," wrote Jack Newfield, when the former mayor died in late 2000.

A few months before Lindsay squeaked through to win a second term, writer Pete Hamill diagnosed the problem that would bedevil progressive politicians for the next five decades (Hamill, 2010). He said, "The working-class white man sees injustice and politicking everywhere in this town now, with himself in the role of victim. He does not like John Lindsay because he feels Lindsay is only concerned about the needs of Blacks; he sees Lindsay walking the streets of the ghetto or opening a privately-financed housing project in East Harlem or delivering lectures about tolerance and brotherhood, and he wonders what it all means to him."

Abe Beame: A Higher Profile for Blacks in Crisis City

Historians and scholars of municipal government and finance still debate how much responsibility Lindsay bears for the fiscal crisis that consumed the one-term mayoralty of his successor, Abe Beame. The increased borrowing and spending that swelled the city budget began under Lindsay's predecessor, Robert Wagner. During his first term, Lindsay used skillful political maneuvering to secure both new taxes, and federal and state aid that would help balance the city's books more responsibly. However, support from outside the city waned after 1969, and there was pressure to resort to gimmicks. Abe Beame, comptroller during Lindsay's second term, could not avoid blame for the funny bookkeeping.

Backstory aside, the enormity of the fiscal challenge became clear as soon as Beame took office. The crisis cost the city thousands of jobs, as well as many of the services that Lindsay and other expansionist mayors had put in place to address problems with a distinctly racial skew. For example, during Beame's tenure, tuition was re-imposed at City University of New York (CUNY) schools, an educational lifeline to New Yorkers of color.

A dull, yet dutiful, clubhouse politician, Beame brought none of Lindsay's charisma or crusading spirit to City Hall. Perhaps that is the reason little is remembered about Beame's mayoralty, beyond the fiscal crisis. When it comes to matters of race, a Beame observer said that Beame felt torn between two priorities. He wanted to carry out an agenda of racial justice if only to solidify the Democratic Party's standing in emerging communities. At the same time, he needed to satisfy the outer-borough White ethnics who formed his base of power.

Blacks helped make Beame mayor, providing crucial support in the 1973 race against Herman Badillo. In exchange, Beame promised to serve only one term to make way for Percy Sutton, the Manhattan borough president so that Sutton could become the city's first Black mayor in 1977. Beame also vowed to appoint the city's first deputy mayor. The latter promise was one Beame kept, although his first two picks, Harlem lawyer David Dinkins and State Senator Joseph Galiber, were sidelined by minor scandals. Beame settled on Paul Gibson, Jr., an airline executive with past City Hall experience (Martin, 2014). The move was opposed by the *New York Times* editorial page, which hilariously argued, "We have been happy to see the once balanced ticket of Irishman, Italian and Jew vanish in the designation of candidates for New

York City's top elective offices. We hope no counterpart of that unworthy standard will now emerge in filling appointive posts." Beame also appointed the first woman, Lucille Mason Rose, a woman of color, to be deputy mayor when Gibson left in 1977 (Barron, 1987).

By some counts, Beame hired more people of color for top city jobs than Lindsay did. He tried to avoid perpetuating past discriminatory hiring practices after the worst of the fiscal crisis was over, and the laid-off staff was rehired, Beame resisted moves by President Carter to cut welfare programs in ways the mayor thought would hurt low-income people, especially Blacks. He instituted regulations that required firms contracting with the city to commit to broader minority hiring. He fired the Black head of the city hospitals because of budget problems, a move that irked some Black activists, but brought in the civil-rights activist and singer Marion Logan to chair the Human Rights Commission.

After the 1977 blackout, Beame created 2,000 temporary, clean up jobs for "ghetto youth." Concurrently, he faced lawsuits over the conditions in which thousands of the people arrested during the riots, the vast majority of whom were Black or Latino, were held.[4] These riots, plus the Son of Sam killing spree, and the general rise in fear of crime led a desperate Beame to abandon his principled opposition to the death penalty during his 1977 mayoral campaign. He had earlier abandoned his 1973 pledge to make way for Sutton, as well.

It is probably at this stage that Beame realized he would not be able to claim a significant Black or Latino vote in the crowded Democratic primary, which featured both Sutton and Badillo. The Beame era had made Blacks much more pessimistic about the future. A poll in August 1977 indicated that 40 percent of Blacks thought the city would be a significantly worse place in a decade, compared with 39 percent who thought it would be better. In 1973, on the verge of Beame's winning City Hall, only 25 percent of Black New Yorkers were that pessimistic.

On primary day, Beame placed third behind Congressman Ed Koch and Secretary of State Mario Cuomo. Koch had sided with the angry Whites in Forest Hills and had made his support of the death penalty a focus of his 1977 campaign. He won the subsequent runoff against Cuomo, in part because the Black political class supported him. According to Jack Newfield and Wayne Barrett's masterful *City for Sale*, Koch won over the likes of Charles Rangel, Major Owens, and Carl McCall. He promised that "Blacks will have jobs at the highest levels of my administration," vowing to keep Harlem's struggling Sydenham Hospital open, and pledging he would stop using the term "poverty pimps" to describe neighborhood administrators of anti-poverty programs. He broke both vows (Newfield & Barrett, 1988, pp. 136–38).

Ed Koch: Rebuilding, and Tearing Down

By the time he was elected mayor, Ed Koch had spent the better part of a decade resetting his relationship with the movement for racial equity. A veteran of the Freedom Rides, and a reliably pro-civil-rights Congressman in the 1960s, Koch had come out against the scattered-site housing development at Forest Hills. In both 1973 and 1977, he highlighted his support for the death penalty. This was an issue over which the mayor had no power, but it played into fear of crime, especially in the white community. Some biographers have attributed Koch's evolution to his feeling that, by the late 1960s, overt anti-Semitism had become part of mainstream black civil-rights advocacy.[5]

More than one observer has told anecdotes about Koch exhibiting overt racism or at least a distressing comfort with people using racial slurs. Personal feelings aside, Koch's political instincts undoubtedly helped him to sense the ideological shift-taking place in both the city and the country. The Kennedy and Johnson eras were giving way to that of Richard Nixon, and Lindsay's day of bold hopes and soaring rhetoric was fading. Whatever the motivation, Koch was the first, true White-ethnic candidate. He was positioned perfectly to benefit from the lingering White backlash to the civil-rights movement and the Great Society.

In New York City, those two movements had been followed by, and to some degree received the blame for, the city's devastating fiscal crisis. Therefore, Koch was able to oppose civil-rights advocates without being opposed to civil rights. He would embed those views within an agenda of sound management and clean government. His 1977 slogan, "After eight years of charisma and four years of the clubhouse, why not try competence?" reflected this approach. In Koch's framing, he was the grown-up in the room, and his duty was to put people back in their place since their overreaching demands had brought the city to the brink of social and economic crisis. In his 1984 book, *Mayor*, Koch recalled the early days of this approach in a chapter called, "Setting the Tone," where he described, with obvious glee, his first efforts to demonstrate that "my administration was not going to take crap from any group." To wit:

> The second opportunity to make this point clear arose when a group of Blacks who said they were ministers arrived at City Hall. They wanted all the federal city jobs to go to nonwhites. They wanted all the federal money and who-knows-what-else-and-how-much to go only to nonwhites. Their demands were ridiculous . . . So these fifteen 'clergymen' became very demanding and threatening. I said "I am not going to do it. You do whatever you want to do. Goodbye' (Koch, 1984, pp. 70–71).

When the ministers staged a sit-in, Koch ordered them arrested. "The fact is that I was denounced by Shirley Chisholm on the floor of Congress for that action," Koch wrote. "But I happen to think it is to my credit—and people remember it." In his later book, *Citizen Koch*, the mayor wrote, "I have often felt like the one voice of reason in debating the positions of many of our Black leaders—civic, political and religious."

There was a lot more to Koch than bluster and posturing. His policies followed the same theme. He cut services for the poor so he could get the city's budget balanced ahead of schedule. He centralized programs partially to cut out the "poverty pimps." In the process, these cuts ran roughshod over programs that had done a great deal of good. In addition, contrary to his campaign promise, he shuttered Sydenham hospital in 1980, a move he much later admitted was a terrible mistake.

The mayor did appoint Blacks to city jobs at a reasonably high rate (Berg, 2007, p. 130). He claimed that Blacks received a higher share of city jobs under him than they had under his three predecessors combined (Rauch & Koch, 1984, p. 40).[6] Although Koch avoided positioning any appointments as "diversity" picks, when he named Benjamin Ward to be the city's first Black commissioner of police, he told the press: "He's Black. There is no question about that. If that is helpful, isn't that nice?"

Some racial incidents occurred on Koch's watch, and his responses were always unpredictable. In 1983, he appointed a special counsel to investigate the death of graffiti artist, Michael Stewart, who had been held in police custody. He expressed sympathy with subway shooter Bernard Goetz and denounced a grand jury that indicted the cop who shot and killed Eleanor Bumpurs, in 1984. When Michael Griffith was killed in Belt Parkway traffic after being beaten by White kids in Howard Beach, Koch reacted with outrage to what he called a "lynching." In 1989, Yusef Hawkins was shot and killed after an encounter with a White mob in Bensonhurst. Koch condemned this incident, but then criticized Blacks for inflaming tensions by protesting the killing. "The question is: Do you want to be helpful to reduce the tensions or do you want to escalate the tensions?" he asked. "It is just as wrong to march into Bensonhurst as it would be to march into Harlem after that young woman in the jogging case. The Harlem community was not involved in that." One of the more ironic reactions to Koch's comments came from Rudy Giuliani, who accused the mayor of "politicizing this unfortunate incident."

Some of the racial animus that dogged Koch's mayoralty stemmed from his penchant for bypassing established power brokers in the Black community. He circumvented not only rabble-rousers like Sharpton but also avoided longtime leaders such as Carl McCall and Charles Rangel. These men were likely as upset about being sidelined as they were about the substance of the mayor's moves. It is hard to evaluate the wisdom of Koch's approach without speculating on what could have been different if Koch had chosen an alternate path. Would his policies have changed, or just his packaging? Moreover, would different packaging at least have suggested to Black New Yorkers that their mayor was not inherently opposed to them?

We can say with certainty what Koch's circumvention did not do. It did not result in a new generation of Black leaders rising up to challenge the older generation that Koch isolated for 12 years. Neither did it result in an effective anti-Koch coalition. Black leaders who backed Koch in 1977 mounted no concerted challenge to him in 1981, when Koch had both the Republican and Democratic lines for re-election. There was a glimmer of hope in 1985 when a Black/Latino coalition was built around Herman Badillo, but the Black leadership backed Assemblyman Denny Farrell instead, whom Koch destroyed in the primary. This phenomenon of divided minority leadership would recur under mayors Giuliani and Bloomberg, and in a different way, with Mayor Bill de Blasio. This helps to explain the survival of White mayors in an increasingly nonwhite city.

Municipal corruption allegations consumed the latter part of Koch's mayoralty. The scandals, the growing racial tensions, and the length of time he had been mayor set the scene for Koch's humbling defeat in the 1989 Democratic primary. Koch's reputation enjoyed a relatively fast and broad rebound, however, even faster than any of his predecessors, except La Guardia. In part, this was because Koch and his contemporary critics all mellowed a bit with age. However, it also reflected a recognition of Koch's longer-lasting contributions to the city, in particular, his housing plan.

Early in his tenure, Koch focused some attention on the parts of the city most ravaged by the crisis years. These neighborhoods had achieved some national notoriety. They did so through events like President Carter's visit to Charlotte Street in the Bronx. However, his most significant work began much later, when in 1985, he launched the Ten Year Plan, a $5 billion initiative that aimed to build or preserve 250,000 units of affordable housing. The plan was a brilliant solution to a confluence of needs. First, the mayor needed to remove from the city's books tens of thousands of properties that had been seized for tax delinquency. Second, Koch wanted to do something about the lack of affordable housing in New York, as the local economy was recovering and rents rising. Third, there had been a call to revitalize neighborhoods that had been enervated by the crisis years.

The plan was a long-term success, bridging the Dinkins administration, and into the Giuliani years. It helped to bring several parts of New York back from the brink. Most of the areas targeted by the Plan, and most of the tenants who occupied the structures built by it, were Blacks and Latinos.

Koch's vision had enormous benefits for some of the very communities he had alienated through much of his mayoralty. Other Koch policies explicitly aimed to foment gentrification, which has now transformed some of the same neighborhoods his housing plan restored. However, for a generation at least, his Plan made New York City a place where thousands of people of color could gain a decent foothold.

David Dinkins: A Milestone, Undermined

More than once, David Dinkins encountered obstacles that kept him from making Black political history in New York City. His bid to become the city's first Black deputy mayor ended ignominiously in 1974 when it was revealed he had failed to pay some federal taxes. Dinkins always said it had been an oversight, which he corrected immediately. In the circumstances, he accepted an appointment as City Clerk instead, but he soon sought higher elective office.[7] In 1977, when Percy Sutton ran for mayor, Dinkins ran for the office Sutton was vacating, that is, Manhattan borough president, which had been occupied by a Black person since 1954. Naturally, he expected the support of the Harlem political establishment. "What I did not know and did not understand," Dinkins writes in his memoir, "was that Percy and some of his supporters did not want me to run. They felt that two Black men on the ticket would be too much, that some White folks would look at the slate and not want to put political control of the city in so many Black hands." Treated as persona non grata by his lifelong allies, Dinkins lost, and failed again on his second attempt, in 1981. He finally won the office in 1985.

Another Black politician's loss set Dinkins on the path to his greatest triumph. In 1988, Reverend Jesse Jackson ran the most competitive campaign for the presidency ever mounted by a Black candidate. He did not win the nomination or even the New York State primary, but he did win the vote in New York City. That was a remarkable feat, given that Mayor Koch had launched attacks against the candidate who had four years earlier slurred the five boroughs as "Hymietown." It occurred to some of Dinkins' advisers that Jackson had demonstrated that a Black candidate could win a Democratic primary in New York City. Dinkins, reluctant at first, took their advice, and ran. In an upset on primary day, Dinkins defeated Koch by a comfortable margin.

The race had been interjected forcefully into the late stages of the campaign, when Yusef Hawkins, a 16-year-old Black man, was shot and killed in Bensonhurst, Brooklyn. A protest march was met with violence, and Koch blamed the protesters. In the general election campaign against

Rudolph Giuliani, the race was more than a subtext. Giuliani's people raised questions about Dinkins' ties to Sonny Carson, Louis Farrakhan, and Yasser Arafat. Dinkins eked out a narrow victory, one Giuliani's associates contend was stolen via fraud (Strober & Strober, 2007, pp. 85–86).

Dinkins' achievement was historic, but his timing was terrible. He took power as the crack, AIDS, and homelessness crises were peaking, and as the U.S. economy were slipping into recession.[8] This presented him with a budget crisis that restricted his ability to implement social programs he had hoped to launch. It also complicated the changes he did try to make, such as a more welcoming policy at city homeless shelters. The so-called "Dinkins Surge" at shelters, overwhelmed the system, providing support to the skeptics' warnings that people would flock to the shelters if eligibility standards were lowered. Of course, the deepening financial and social shocks hitting the city also might have played a role. Dinkins tightened up shelter-entry rules in response. Despite the challenges, Dinkins did launch supportive housing for homeless people with drug or mental-health issues, shored up the lagging public-health system with community clinics, and launched the city's first program for minority- and women-owned businesses.

He also was the force behind the "Safe Streets, Safe City" program that expanded the police force and largely provided the manpower in later years that Giuliani and Mayor Bloomberg used to bring the city's crime rate down. Crime had been rising for years when Dinkins took office. Although initially, he was skeptical about whether more cops would help (Karmen, 2000, p. 101), he still commissioned a report on NYPD manpower needs during his first year. This came before the *New York Post's* infamous "Dave, Do Something" headline appeared in September 1990. He moved to expand the force. In 1992 and 1993, crime fell in all seven major felony categories, initiating the crime reduction that his successors extended, and received so much credit for.

The mayor's substantive record, not just as a government manager, but also as an arbiter of the city's inevitable social tensions, suffered because of two racially polarizing incidents. In 1990, there was a Korean grocery store boycott, when Black activist Sonny Carson led eight months of protests outside a store where a black customer claimed she had been beaten. There were threats and isolated violent incidents. A court order required the protesters to back off so customers could get to the store, but the city refused to enforce it, trying to mediate instead.

The second incident was the Crown Heights riots of August 1991, in which Blacks, Jews, and police clashed for three days after a Hasidic motorist struck and killed a Black child and, in the subsequent eruption of anger, a mob of Blacks stabbed and killed a Hasidic student. Dinkins was criticized for not ordering a stronger police response on the first day of unrest. Some people alleged that the mayor had consciously decided to let Black youths "vent" their anger. Just before the 1993 election, a report Governor Cuomo had commissioned was published. The *New York Times* described it as "a scathing portrait of ineptitude and miscommunication." The report found that Dinkins had failed to get an accurate picture of the situation on the streets, and as a result, did not issue orders that might have prevented some of the violence.

His critics provided two explanations for Dinkins' performance. The first claimed that the mayor was dangerously tolerant of Black rage. The second held that Dinkins was simply an inept manager. Both fit neatly with stereotypes often held toward Blacks, and therefore, they were precisely the kind of allegation Dinkins, as a racial pioneer, had tried hard to avoid. While he could have done a better job of avoiding the labels in Flatbush and Crown Heights, the misconceptions about crime rates during his mayoralty illustrate that Dinkins faced enormous odds in trying to prove that he was qualified for the job.

The mayor was faced with an even larger quandary. He needed to legitimize the hope that the city's Black communities had invested in him, while also governing as a mayor for all New York's communities. For Dinkins, this was a political and moral imperative. As the 1993 election approached, the *New York Times* published that Dinkins was failing on both fronts. Reporter Jonathan P. Hicks wrote, "Black neighborhood leaders say that an erosion in enthusiasm toward the Mayor is the result of the high expectations that his election produced. Many hoped for a boom in jobs, a refurbishing of the city's tattered infrastructure and the stimulation of economic development in the city's predominantly black neighborhoods" (1993).

Indeed, some people theorized that it was not White voters who voted Dinkins out after one term. Instead, Black voters though they preferred Dinkins to Giuliani, were no longer enthused enough by Dinkins to prompt them to get out and vote. His tactical blunders in Crown Heights and Flatbush hurt his reputation, but in truth, it may have been a strategic decision that cost Dinkins his mayoralty. According to David Jones, Dinkins shot down proposals his campaign advisers made to carry out a strong registration and get-out-the-vote drive in Black neighborhoods. He failed to do this because he was worried people might think he was focused on only one shard in what he called "New York's Gorgeous Mosaic."[9]

Dinkins' 1989 election was a high point for Black political aspirations in the city, but his time in office illustrates the unique challenges facing mayors closely associated with the quest for racial justice. Beset by unexpected events that overwhelmed his sensible policy moves, and unable to master the imagery of command when crisis struck, Dinkins was forced from office, and a new, disastrous era for racial inequality began.

Rudy Giuliani: The Great White Hope

An old friend, and now a congressional representative, Peter King, recollects that, as a young man in the 1960s, Rudolph W. Giuliani was a radical on race, not only supporting the civil-rights movement but also openly and passionately sympathizing with Black nationalists who advocated the use of violence. Some observers have theorized that Giuliani was influenced greatly by the all-White world he grew up in. His close, nearly homogenous, circle of friends and advisers ingrained in him a deep discomfort around people of color, and issues of race. It is certainly conceivable that Giuliani, like many people, was shaped by the whiteness of his formative years, but this does not fully explain the trajectory of his views on race, which seems to have evolved in a retrograde fashion during his adulthood. The most critical juncture in that evolution came in 1989 when Giuliani expected his opponent in the mayoral race would be a conservative White Democrat seeking re-election (Newfield, 2007, p. 62).[10] Instead, he became the last man standing between the city's Black community and the pioneering prize of a Black mayor.

After losing narrowly to David Dinkins in 1989, Giuliani said he resented that he was labeled a racist, merely for advocating for his own candidacy. "A white candidate can't criticize a Black candidate in this city without getting defamed as a racist," he complained at one point (Newfield, 2007, p. 65). The feeling that one's opponents are "playing the race card," that advocates for racial justice are themselves being unfair, is the lifeblood of White ethnic resentment. If Lindsay had inadvertently created that sentiment, Beame had managed it, and Koch had capitalized on it, then Giuliani filled a pump with it, and sprayed it all over the city. Even as the city was blossoming, people of color were being marginalized during Giuliani's incredibly polarizing eight years.

The tone was set during the 1993 campaign. An internal vulnerability study prepared for Giuliani's campaign had concluded the following. "Simply put, Dinkins won't have to work hard at painting Giuliani as a racist," pointing to incidents like the Jackie Mason "schvartze" episode back in 1989. People advised Rudy to turn the racial ammunition he had handed Dinkins, into a liability for him: at every turn, Giuliani should paint Dinkins as the "racial polarizer." Even when pressed to apologize for this role in the 1992 police riot, Giuliani suggested the mayor needed to apologize first for exaggerating the bad behavior at the rally. His only regret about the City Hall rally, he said shortly before the election, was "the fact that false statements have been made about this" (Barrett, 2000, p. 262). The Republican won by 53,000 voters, just a shade more than Dinkins' 47,000-vote margin four years earlier.[11]

Like Koch before him, Giuliani refused to meet with many Black leaders after taking office. That meant more than the Al Sharptons of the world. He snubbed Carl McCall, the state comptroller, as well. LaGuardia biographer, Thomas Kessner, told a *Newsday* columnist that Giuliani seemed to have "a permanent disagreement with a whole part of the city," referring to Blacks. In interviews with Wayne Barrett, two Black political allies, one-time State Senator Ada Smith, and former Brooklyn Republican leader, Arthur Bramwell, devastated Giuliani's approach to race relations. His "relationship with the black community is nonexistent" was Smith's take. "I don't think he has any empathy for Blacks," was Bramwell's opinion (Barrett, 2000, p. 327). The tone was set early in the administration when one of the mayor's top aides, Dennison Young, wrote a memo to another Giuliani aide assuring that "two white guys" have run New York City for as long as anyone could remember. In his first two weeks in office, Giuliani closed the eight liaison offices that had maintained a channel of communication between City Hall and major ethnic groups (Barrett, 2000, p. 292). "Blacks were outsiders by definition," according to Barrett.

This attitude shaped mayoral policy. During his first term, Giuliani sharply reined in welfare and other benefits, imposing punitive sanctions and launching the Work Experience Program, which dispatched thousands of mostly Black or Latino people to pick up garbage in city parks. He sharply cut funding to public hospitals, a lifeline for Black and Brown New York. He adopted a punitive approach to homelessness.

There were fewer Blacks in the city workforce under Giuliani (Barrett, 2000, p. 323), who never expressed any support for the virtue of a diverse government. Journalist Michael Powell found that, by 1996, the city workforce had 4,600 fewer Blacks, and 387 more Whites than when Giuliani took office. This was partly because Giuliani stopped advertising city jobs in Black newspapers (Newfield, 2007, p. 68). During his administration, both the parks and fire departments took actions that became the subject of federal racial discrimination lawsuits. The city eventually settled. Giuliani ended the program Dinkins had launched to encourage minority- and women-led businesses to contract with the city (Barrett, 2000, p. 292). He cut funding to CUNY, a school system that primarily serves students of color. Desperate to impress right-wing Republicans, Giuliani bizarrely asked state legislators to reduce aid to the city, and he resisted efforts to force the state to pay its fair share in support of city schools. He put the city's creation of affordable housing into neutral. The sole counterpoint to Giuliani's cruelty was his opposition to the national Republican crackdown on immigrants.

Of course, Giuliani's mayoralty was defined most clearly by his policing policy. The central theme of Giuliani's candidate biography was law and order, which also anchored his critique of Dinkins's leadership quality. The mayor's reputation for driving down crime in New York City is the lynchpin of his legacy. It is a policy victory for which he shares credit with Dinkins; his first NYPD commissioner, Bill Bratton; the visionary police strategist, Jack Maple; the 1990s economic boom; the nationwide drop in urban crime, and; the courage of community groups who chased drug dealers from their corners.

His policing policy provides the most powerful, if not the only, rationale for arguing that the Giuliani years were anything short of policy and political disaster for Black New York. In his view, reduced crime levels saved the lives of thousands of Blacks who might have been murder victims if old trends had prevailed. Less crime protected the health and livelihoods of others who would otherwise have been victims of nonfatal violence. It made the lives of thousands of Blacks better, because they might otherwise have been arrested and imprisoned for those crimes, and it improved Black neighborhoods. When asked by the *Washington Post* what he had done for Blacks, Giuliani's response was very blunt: "They are alive, how about we start with that?" was his reply.

That is an interesting argument. However, it assumes that the unavoidable price for all these benefits was the heavy-handed policing the NYPD inaugurated under the prosecutor-mayor. Blacks paid an outsized toll for the steep fall in crime. Arrests, which disproportionately affect Blacks and Latinos, soared 17 percent under Giuliani. This increase was driven by a nearly 50 percent leap in misdemeanor busts for low-level, "quality of life" crimes such as public urination or turnstile jumping. Complaints to the Civilian Complaint Review Board jumped, though Giuliani cut its funding. The use of the stop-and-frisk tactic expanded, with communities of color targeted to the degree that crime rates could not explain (New York Attorney General, 2013). In addition, there was a series of high-profile incidents in which innocent Blacks and Latinos were injured severely or killed by the police. Giuliani gravely harmed race relations in New York because of the way he handled those incidents.

In late 1994, Officer Frank Livoti used a banned chokehold on a Bronx man named Anthony Baez, who died a short time later. Giuliani, who typically registered opinions on all manner of events in his city, was silent about the killing. All the same, his handpicked chief of uniformed cops praised Livoti's career, which, in fact, had been checkered by past complaints of brutality. Abner Louima was beaten and sodomized in a precinct bathroom in the middle of the 1997 mayoral campaign. Giuliani quickly condemned the attack, and appointed a panel, including outspoken NYPD critics, to recommend reforms. This helped quell the crisis. Nonetheless, after the election, and with a smirk, Giuliani ignored the panel's recommendations.

No incident better reflected the pitfalls of Giuliani's approach to crime fighting than the 1999 shooting death of Amadou Diallo, in the Bronx. The episode involved the Street Crimes Unit (SCU), a plainclothes outfit developed by NYPD Commissioner Howard Safir that cultivated a warrior ethos with its slogan, "We Own the Night." Local precincts provided minimal oversight to the SCU, which was often staffed by officers with relatively little experience or training. An SCU team approached Diallo, an unarmed vendor returning to his home, looking for a rape suspect whom he did not resemble. Calling to him from the street, they asked him to turn around. He reached for his wallet, probably because that is what he had been asked to do by cops before. The four cops fired 41 bullets at him, striking him 19 times. When more cops arrived at the scene, they turned his apartment inside out looking for something nefarious to pin on the man their colleagues had just gunned down. They found nothing. The shooting touched off huge protests, but Giuliani dismissed the complaints. He labeled the event a tragedy, avoiding even the use of the word "mistake." He mocked the protests, even as more and more of the city's political leadership submitted to civil disobedience arrest. He sided with a judge's outrageous decision to move the trial of the cops who killed Diallo from the Bronx to Albany and cheered the verdict when the officers were acquitted.

Then there was Patrick Dorismond, a security guard who bristled at an undercover cop asking him for drugs. He was shot after scuffling with the detective.[12] This occurred in the year 2000, in the midst of Giuliani's campaign for the U.S. Senate. Faced with a case in which a hardworking man had been killed after refusing to commit a crime, Giuliani launched a vicious attack on the dead man's character. He released Dorismond's sealed juvenile record. He unearthed a series of arrests that had never led to convictions. He said Dorismond "was no altar boy," when, in fact, he had been an altar boy. He had even attended the same Catholic high-school Giuliani had attended (Strober & Strober, 2007, p. 324).

In the Dorismond episode, Giuliani displayed such unrestrained cruelty that it seemed as if the mayor were decompensating. This impression was deepened only in the weeks that followed as Giuliani flaunted his extramarital affair, told his wife through the media that he was seeking a divorce, announced a diagnosis of prostate cancer, and withdrew from the Senate race. His approval rating sank as low as 37 percent. By the following fall, his popularity had recovered. However, Giuliani's national viability, so long an object of local media fascination, seemed gone. The mayor's stoicism and eloquence on September 11, 2001, changed that. Even Black New Yorkers, according to the Quinnipiac Poll, approved of the mayor's performance in the weeks after the terrorist attack.

Nevertheless, even in the afterglow of his finest hour, there was a distinct racial dimension to New Yorkers' views of Rudy Giuliani. When the mayor launched a gambit to rescind term limits, and either serve a slightly longer second term or be allowed to run for a third term, a poll indicated 67 percent of Whites approved of the mayor staying on, and 53 percent of Latinos did, as well. However, 74 percent of Blacks told pollsters they wanted Giuliani to leave office, as planned, on the last day. They had seen quite enough.

Giuliani's 1993 campaign slogan had been, "One City, One Standard," suggesting that the tough-love candidate merely wanted a level playing field. What could be fairer than that? The tagline implied that other candidates, namely David Dinkins, instead promoted a double standard. It was a brilliant way to tap into White resentment of programs and policies that were meant to address systemic racism. It played into the notion that White progressives were driven by guilt to accept anti-social behavior by people of color: the squeegee men, aggressive panhandlers, illegal street vendors, graffiti artists and drug dealers of New York City's urban nightmare.

Giuliani's eight years in office proved the shallowness of that critique and the hollowness of that effort. In no way were Blacks offered a place in his "one city." By adverse example, the era confirmed how important a mayor could be to achieving racial justice in New York.

Michael Bloomberg:
The Un-Ethnic White

It is acknowledged widely that Michael Bloomberg's wealth insulated him from the pressures and temptations of catering to the city's donor class. His wealth had another effect, too. Bloomberg did not have to depend on the same White-ethnic coalition as Koch and Giuliani had to wield power. While Bloomberg enjoyed a great deal of support from those segments of the city, his financial power meant he would not have to pander to the power brokers in those communities. His philanthropic activities secured him goodwill across many sectors of New York. His media connections won him favorable treatment, especially by the city's editorial boards. In addition, his campaign war chest dissuaded candidates in the White-ethnic world from challenging him. The most promising White-ethnic politician of Bloomberg's era, Anthony Weiner, opted not to challenge the mayor in 2009, when the incumbent was most vulnerable, presumably because of the mayor's checkbook.

Bloomberg also understood that he won the 2001 election primarily because of a rift within the Democratic coalition. Democrats Fernando Ferrer and Mark Green waged a brief, but nasty, campaign to win a runoff election for their party's mayoral nomination. Green's allies were accused of playing to White fears about Ferrer's association with Al Sharpton. Green won the runoff and enjoyed a huge lead over Bloomberg, but in the last weeks of October, recriminations from the runoff campaign mounted. Bloomberg soon took the lead among Latinos, and Green saw weakened support from Blacks. Bloomberg ended up winning by about 35,000 votes.

That rift, and the memories of Giuliani's racial hostility encouraged Bloomberg to form alliances across both party and race lines, and he skillfully capitalized on the opportunity. On either election night or election eve, Bloomberg called Sharpton, and said, "Hello, this is Michael Bloomberg. I want you to know it will be different with me as mayor. We will not agree on everything, but you will have access to City Hall." Sharpton, speaking to Bloomberg biographer, Joyce Purnick, recalled Sharpton saying, "I was stunned. It was clearly a reversal in how City Hall was going to deal with us" (Purnick, 2009, p. 119). Within two months of his taking office, Bloomberg met with all the city's Black and Latino leaders (Newfield, 2007, p. 87). The day after the election, he huddled with Ferrer, and with union chief, Dennis Rivera, two leaders of the city's Latino community. Then he invited Sharpton to a dinner where they were photographed together. "The handshake that implied political and maybe even financial support neutralized Sharpton and turned him into a sometime-ally," Purnick observed. Bloomberg told her: "Rudy had the same albatross around his neck for years with Sharpton, and if he'd done that once it would have gone away. The fact of the matter is when you have a racial problem, Sharpton's on your side quieting things down" (Purnick, 2009, p. 134).

Bloomberg did his bit to achieve racial "quiet," too. When cops raided the wrong apartment in Harlem one day in 2003, their concussion grenade terrified 57-year-old Alberta Spruill, and she died hours later. Giuliani would have instinctively leaped to the police officers' defense, or at the very least insisted that he was withholding judgment until all facts were in. Instead, Bloomberg's police commissioner, Ray Kelly, immediately apologized, reassigned the lieutenant who had overseen the operation and ordered an examination of the use of such grenades. At the woman's funeral a week later, the mayor said, "At least in this case, existing practices failed . . . As mayor, I failed to protect someone." The mayor used a similar approach in other instances during his first term, leading his 2005 opponent, Ferrer, to give him credit: "Mike Bloomberg did not go down the path of exacerbating racial tensions in this city. And as a New Yorker, Mike, I thank you for that."

The billionaire mayor continued using the same approach in his second term. In November 2006, the unarmed, 23-year-old Sean Bell was killed in a hail of 50 police bullets outside a strip club in Queens. Bloomberg's initial response was cautious. Later in the day, he said in a statement, "We know that the NYPD officers on the scene had reason to believe that an altercation involving a firearm was about to happen and were trying to stop it." However, a day later, flanked by Black leaders at a press conference, Bloomberg called the shooting "unacceptable" and "inexplicable," and said, "It sounds to me like excessive force was used." Once again, he calmed the waters.[13]

Bloomberg also attempted to connect with Latino voters by speaking Spanish from the mayoral podium. It was an acknowledgment of the community's importance that seemed at once earnest, and politically perceptive, even if it was linguistically poor.

While Bloomberg avoided racial-polarization in high-profile incidents, day-to-day law enforcement under his administration began to show distinct racial disparities. Arrests for low-level marijuana possession, overwhelmingly involving young men of color, were spiking. The use of the "stop, question and frisk" policy, which dated back to the Giuliani days, was increasing dramatically. Incidents rose from 97,000 in 2002, to 300,000 in 2004, to 500,000 in 2006, and to nearly 700,000 in 2011. Blacks and Latinos made up the vast majority of stops, which rarely led to an arrest, a summons, or the recovery of a weapon. The numerical rise could partially be the result of better record keeping. It cannot be ignored, however, that during the Bloomberg era the NYPD became much more aggressive about stopping young men of color on a thin pretext. This intrusive policy stoked fury in some communities. By the time a federal judge ruled that the NYPD's use of stop-and-frisk was unconstitutional, Bloomberg and Kelly had already begun to rein it in. From 2011 to 2013, Bloomberg's last year in office, the number of reported encounters fell about 72 percent.

Bloomberg's record on schools is similarly complex. The mayor invested huge political capital in attempting to improve a system primarily used by students of color. He should get credit for that. He won mayoral control in 2002, reorganized the entire system three times, increased the use of standardized tests, ended social promotion, closed big high schools and opened small ones, and boosted charter schools: an education option that enjoys more support among Blacks than among Whites. He sought to improve the high-school graduation rate. While huge racial gaps remained at the end of Bloomberg's term, Blacks and Hispanics did make massive gains, posting a graduation rate in 2012 of 59.8 and 57.5 percent, respectively, compared to 40.1 percent and 37.4 percent, respectively, in 2005.[14]

Sometimes, the mayor seemed more interested in good numbers than in truly better outcomes. In 2011, a change in state tests led to a huge drop in city scores. Clearly, massive numbers of students needed remedial help. At that point, Bloomberg's chancellor, Joel Klein, cut a backroom deal with state officials to escape any mandated extra instruction. School discipline during the Bloomberg years displayed distinct racial skews, and the mayor's charter school co-locations and school closures rankled thousands of parents, including many parents of color.

A dozen years in office gave Bloomberg ample time to impact race-sensitive policies, across the board. He oversaw a massive campaign of surveillance and infiltration of the city's Muslim community, but also defended critical principles of tolerance when he stood up for the "Ground Zero" mosque. He launched the Young Men's Initiative, which still exists today. It was created as an interdisciplinary effort to break through the education, career, health, family and justice-system obstacles young men of color face in New York City. He boosted efforts to give minority contractors a bigger piece of the city's procurement pie but resisted calls to reform FDNY's blatantly racialized recruiting approach. His efforts to improve public health, through the smoking ban and restrictions on trans fats, likely had a disproportionate benefit for the Black and Latino communities, which tend to suffer the adverse effects of those health threats more acutely.[15]

Politically, Bloomberg benefited, as had Koch, from the split between Latinos and Blacks, with the Black political elite keeping Ferrer at arms-length in 2005, and Latino leadership showing little enthusiasm for Bill Thompson in 2009.[16]

Stop-and-frisk was a dark stain on Bloomberg's time as mayor, even more striking because of how Bloomberg generally tried to avoid stoking racial tensions from the mayoral podium. The wrongheaded policy likely survived as long as it did thanks to a combination of Bloombergian traits. He delegated a tremendous amount of authority to commissioners, especially NYPD boss Kelly. In addition, his social circle insulated him from the people who could have alerted him to how much of a legal and political problem stop-and-frisk was creating.

Bloomberg's greatest impact on race equity in the city, however, may have been physical. The mayor's support for real estate development transformed much of New York City. Black and brown neighborhoods saw some of the most dramatic changes, made in direct response to policy moves. While gentrification has been a reality in New York since the 1970s, Bloomberg enthusiastically presided over a wave of development that uprooted low-income people, many of them black and Latino. It has yet to stop.

Bill de Blasio and the Vanishing City

Bill de Blasio, like Lindsay before him, entered office at a time of emboldened demands for racial justice. The 2012 Florida killing of unarmed teenager, Trayvon Martin, turned up the heat on a simmering national debate over race and privilege, a debate that seemed to begin almost as soon as Barack Obama assumed the presidency. When the wanna-be security guard who slew Martin, was acquitted of murder in 2013, the Black Lives Matter movement was born.

By this time, there was a debate going on in New York City over the racial impact of stop-and-frisk policies. There was also a growing alarm over the effect of development and gentrification on communities of color in the city. Bill de Blasio's rise amid these currents was no coincidence: on the contrary, he rose because of them. De Blasio's platform emphasized two priorities: rolling back stop-and-frisk, and ending the "tale of two cities." Being the husband of a Black woman and the father of two biracial children, gave him a personal stake in those issues. The most successful television commercial of the campaign, hands down, was a simple spot in which de Blasio's large Afro-wearing teenage son, Dante, spoke into the camera about his father's plans, especially those regarding stop-and-frisk.

For most of the 2013 campaign, de Blasio ran far back in the pack, well behind City Council Speaker Christine Quinn, former City Comptroller William Thompson, and former Congressman Anthony Weiner. De Blasio, then the city's public advocate, vied with Comptroller John Liu for fourth place in most surveys. The ground shifted dramatically late in the race. Weiner faced a new sex scandal, a devastating campaign finance board ruling neutralized Liu, and de Blasio TV ads began hitting the airwaves just as people were starting to pay close attention. By primary day, de Blasio's only serious rival was Thompson, who had come close to being the city's second Black mayor just four years earlier. Riding a plurality of Black support, de Blasio won the primary outright. In last-minute polls for the general election in November, de Blasio got 85 to 90 percent support among Blacks and Latinos. On Election Day, he beat Republican, Joe Lhota, with 73 percent of the vote.

De Blasio's inauguration on January 1, 2014, revolved around two themes. First, there was a denunciation of injustice, with singer and activist Harry Belafonte decrying the city's role in creating the prison-industrial complex. Second, a minister's benediction referred to New York as a plantation. The *New York Times* editorial board denounced the rhetoric as "graceless and smug." The new mayor did not distance himself from it.

De Blasio moved quickly to reverse Bloomberg policies. He moved to settle lawsuits over trespassing arrests, stop-and-frisk, and FDNY hiring. He named an inspector general to the NYPD. He appointed several Blacks to high-level positions in his administration, such as corporation counsel, general counsel, homeless services commissioner, the parks commissioner, head of the Economic Development Corporation, and the New York City Housing Authority chair. Though some Latino activists criticized City Hall for failing to include as many Latinos in the administration as hoped, de Blasio did name Latinas to a deputy mayorship, the head of child welfare, and the chancellorship of the school system. He signed off on creating a municipal ID card that was especially valuable to undocumented immigrants, benefiting many New Yorkers, including thousands of Black and Latino immigrants.

Unfortunately, outside events soon strained de Blasio's ability to reconcile the expectation for progress generated by his campaign, with the limits of his power or political vision.[17] In July of 2014, Eric Garner, a Black civilian, died on a Staten Island street, after being violently restrained by a White NYPD officer. Onlookers filmed the incident. Police-reform advocates shifted their focus from stop-and-frisk to denouncing the low-level enforcement known as broken windows. Cops approached Garner because they suspected him of selling unpackaged and untaxed cigarettes, exactly the kind of crime that epitomized broken windows. A month later, a black teenager, Michael Brown, died at the hands of a White cop in Ferguson, Missouri. Even though the NYPD had nothing to do with that death, the protests over that killing increased local pressure for police reform. Meanwhile, the *New York Times* and the U.S. Attorney's Office delivered devastating reports on how detainees and inmates, overwhelmingly Black and Latino, were being treated at city jails on Rikers Island. The Justice Department filed suit later in the year because they were unsatisfied with the city's response to the report.

De Blasio moved ahead with reforms, announcing in November of 2014 that the city would stop arresting people found with small amounts of marijuana. When a grand jury in Missouri declined to indict the officer who shot Brown, the national outcry for more significant reforms grew louder. December 2014 saw the gravest crisis of de Blasio's first term. Early in the month, a local grand jury declined to indict the cop whose chokehold killed Eric Garner. As protests erupted, de Blasio spoke at Staten Island:

> [First Lady] Chirlane [McRae] and I have had to talk to Dante for years, about the dangers he may face. A good young man, a law-abiding young man, who would never think to do anything wrong, and yet, because of a history that still hangs over us, the dangers he may face—we've had to literally train him, as families have all over this city for decades, in how to take special care in any encounter he has with the police officers who are there to protect him. . . . There are so many families in this city who feel that each and every night—is my child safe? And not just from some of the painful realities—crime and violence in some of our neighborhoods—but are they safe from the very people they want to have faith in as their protectors? (Office of the Mayor, 2014)

Police unions and their supporters pounced, accusing the mayor of "throwing them under a bus." Three weeks later, on the Saturday before Christmas, a man named Ismaaiyl Brinsley shot his ex-girlfriend in the stomach in Baltimore, and posted on Instagram the message, "I'm Putting Wings on Pigs Today." He drove up to New York, where he found officers Wenjian Liu and Rafael Ramos sitting in an NYPD cruiser. He murdered them, ran a few blocks, and killed himself. Outside the hospital where the officers were transported, the head of the patrolmen's union said, "There is blood on many hands tonight—those that incited violence on the streets under the guise of protest that tried to tear down what New York police officers did every day. That blood on the hands starts on the steps of City Hall, in the office of the mayor." He did not once mention the person who had actually killed the cops. Inside Woodhull Medical Center, as de Blasio walked the hallway toward a press conference, officers who were there, turned their backs on him. The same thing occurred at the funerals for the two officers. Early the following year, cops engaged in a work slowdown, sharply cutting the number of arrests.[18] It looked as if de Blasio had come close to suffering a mutiny by the nation's largest law enforcement force.

De Blasio faced unique obstacles when attempting to introduce aggressive criminal justice reform. Crime is the most loaded political issue in the city. The surest way to catch New Yorkers' attention is to warn, "We are heading back to the bad old days." De Blasio came to office burdened by the expectation that he was an incompetent manager who would quickly lose control of law and order. It was clear that the tabloid press would pounce on any signal that crime was increasing. The tabloids spent much of the first three years of de Blasio's mayoralty sounding the alarm on crime sprees that never really materialized. They did not need a real crisis to blame de Blasio for creating one.

From the outset, the mayor knew he was going to have to tread very carefully in that minefield. This partially explains why he brought in Commissioner William Bratton. His commitment to broken windows continued, as well. In doing so, he shielded himself from charges that he had a soft touch or a loose hand on crime. Bratton's importance increased after the Liu and Ramos killings. He convinced police to end their on-the-job protests. In the months that followed, de Blasio took a different trajectory on criminal justice reform. He emphasized a crackdown on gun crimes, including the launch of a special courtroom aimed at getting more convictions. After another cop killing, he called for restrictions on bail. For months, he resisted calls to close Rikers Island. He relented on the eve of a clarion call for closure by a blue-ribbon commission. After Bratton's departure in the summer of 2016, de Blasio did emphasize his Neighborhood Policing Initiative, which stressed community relations over arrests, but he refused to back away from broken windows.

As he approached the 2017 election, it appeared that de Blasio had accomplished a difficult feat. He had succeeded in disappointing Blacks and other progressive advocates who had hoped for more profound criminal justice reform, and he had angered the police and their allies for embracing reform too aggressively. In some ways, de Blasio's dilemma mirrored the one that had faced Lindsay. In trying to satisfy everyone with his promise for a better world, he ended up satisfying no one at all.

A Changing Landscape for Racial Justice

De Blasio, however, faced a very different city than John Lindsay did, and was met with a deeper racial challenge than other mayors. His 2013 campaign succeeded not simply by personalizing the mayor's concerns about stop-and-frisk, but also by tapping into the fear that New York was becoming unaffordable to a large swathe of the current population. De Blasio's "tale of two cities" theme was not primarily a story of Black and White, but of the very wealthy versus everyone else.

New York City has always been a relatively expensive place to live, and its neighborhoods have long been shaped and reshaped by ethnic succession. Nevertheless, there have been stunning demographic changes in the last 15 years, all driven by living expenses. Neighborhoods once populated exclusively by low-income Blacks and Latinos, have now been transformed by an influx of wealthier Whites, along with upscale development and boutique retail establishments (NYU Furman Center, 2016). Although some low-income residents have welcomed these changes, people are witnessing the evolution with increasing alarm. Some of the worry is cultural. There is a fear that places essential to Black and Latino community life are being sterilized of Black and Latino identities. In fact, the deepest fears are of a more practical nature. With 60,000 people already occupying homeless shelters, it is clear that the local real estate market is pricing people out of their own abodes (NYC Dept. Homeless Services, 2017).

This state of affairs is not an accident, and it is not purely the product of outside forces. It is true that, throughout the country and around the world, new urbanism is driving people of means back into the cities. The yawning income inequality gives elites the ability to reshape the economic order of neighborhoods, and in truth, whole cities. For New York City, policy choices of past mayors helped to create the dynamic that de Blasio now faces.

Some of the contributing policies were well-intentioned, like Koch's housing plan, which stabilized some of the very neighborhoods that are now at the epicenter of gentrification. Others were indirect, like the steps that led to a decrease in crime. The result was that many of the neighborhoods became more attractive for development. Many policies had a clear and deliberate impact. Mayor Bloomberg's unrestrained support for development, from the Brooklyn waterfront to Harlem, had a profound effect on city neighborhoods. Bloomberg rezoned 40 percent of New York City (Bagli, 2013), and his re-zonings reinforced stark disparities. White, middle-class Staten Island was largely downzoned, preventing multiunit buildings. Black Harlem was up-zoned to permit more dense development, thus incentivizing luxury building.

De Blasio promised to address this situation by constructing and preserving 200,000 units of affordable housing (Housing and Economic Development, 2014). His bid to rezone 12 to 15 city neighborhoods to permit denser construction is at the heart of his housing plan (Office of the Mayor, 2015). Through a new policy mechanism known as mandatory inclusionary housing (NYC Dept. of Planning, 2016), some of that new construction is to be set aside for low- and moderate-income residents. By increasing the supply of market-rate and "affordable" housing, de Blasio's team argues they can reduce the pressure on these New Yorkers.

Critics have their doubts and wonder whether the new construction will displace more low-income people than the affordable housing will serve. Little is known about how re-zonings increase the risk of displacement. What is known, however, is that the preponderance of people living in the neighborhoods de Blasio has selected for development are Black and Latino. The fact that the groups who most ardently supported de Blasio, and his pledge to end the tale of two cities, are now in the crosshairs of his controversial development plan, is a dangerous irony for the mayor (Savitch-Lew, 2017).

The racial reality of gentrification and displacement in New York implicates an aspect of mayoral power that is not examined often. John Lindsay's walking the streets of Harlem on the night of MLK's death had symbolic power, just as Rudy Giuliani's slur of Patrick Dorismond had heft. Programs and policies, from schools to policing, obviously affect the degree to which New York City provides justice. The underlying character of the city, the composite of who is able to live there, is just as important. The mayor shapes that, not exclusively, but significantly.

In the next 50 years, when the record of the next several mayors is examined, it is likely that the policy battle over policing that has dominated racial politics since John Lindsay will be of secondary interest. People will be more interested in whether each mayor did everything they could to keep New York City racially and economically diverse in light of the homogenizing power of capital.

What Difference, a Mayor?

The question of whether mayors have "mattered" in New York City's quest for racial equity is different from the question of whether that quest has made sufficient progress over the last five decades. The latter question is one of net gain. The former is about the ebbs and flows of progress under seven very different leaders. One looks at the longitude and latitude at the end of the journey. The other examines the radar track of the entire, very bumpy flight.

The history is clear. Mayors do matter, very much, to the city's ability to deliver some measure of racial equity. They matter in different ways: as policymakers, as moral leaders, as shapers of the city at large. They are not the only thing that matters because they operate in a political and economic context where other leaders and outside events help to form the landscape. Their intentions matter, but the purity of their hopes does not always translate into real change. Their impact is often unclear, until years after they have left office.

There is, without a doubt, an impact. There may or may not be a Republican's or Democrat's way to take out the garbage, but there certainly is no way to run a colossus like New York and not affect how different communities fare against, and with, one another.

Notes

1. This chapter is dedicated to my late mentor, hero and friend Wayne Barrett, who dedicated his life to pursuing truth and justice for all New Yorkers, and who was uniquely aware of the role race played in that story.

2. Through its many forms over the past 70 years, the CCRB has never had the power to actually *impose* discipline. That remains the purview of the NYPD commissioner. Some commissioners have exhibited a pronounced tendency to dial down the punishments recommended by the board, or in some cases, order no disciplinary action at all.

3. While threats to Black voting rights are stereotyped as a Southern custom, two of New York's five boroughs ended up on the list of U.S. counties that had histories of racial barriers to voting. As a result, all changes to voting practices required pre-approval by the Justice Department, under Part 5 of the Voting Rights Act.

4. The racialized reaction to the riots was rather overt. *Newsweek* devoted extensive coverage to the unrest, including a headline that quoted a cop on the scene: "They're coming across Bushwick Avenue like Buffalos."

5. Koch told *New Yorker* reporter Ken Auletta, "I find the Black community very anti-Semitic."

6. Koch claimed in his book, *Mayor*, that he had appointed Blacks to 27 percent of the 135 top positions controlled by the mayor, compared with 5 percent by Mayor Wagner, 10 percent by Lindsay and 12 percent by Beame.

7. Dinkins was already an elected official, of sorts, in that he had served since 1969 as a Democratic district leader.

8. The 1990–91 recession formally began in July 1990, seven months into Dinkins' term. Officially, it only lasted until the following March, but it was followed by a "jobless" recovery.

9. Interview with David Jones, June 5, 2017.

10. According to Jack Newfield, in 1989, Giuliani predicted he would get 50 percent of the Black vote when he faced Koch.

11. Dinkins was also undermined by Gov. Mario Cuomo's decision to support a Staten Island secession referendum—sure to energize conservative voters—to coincide with the mayoral vote.

12. The police operation that led to Dorismond's death was called Operation Condor. It apparently did not trouble NYPD brass to share that title with the 1970s campaign of torture and extrajudicial killing in Latin America.

13. Bloomberg also led a police force that was increasingly diverse.

14. From 2005 to 2012, the graduation rate for Asian students rose from 66.3 percent to 82.1 percent, and for white students from 64.0 percent to 78.1 percent.

15. In a low moment for both organizations, the NAACP and Hispanic Federation opposed Bloomberg's ban on massive sodas, more concerned about the proposed ban's impact on mom-and-pop stores than the toll diabetes takes in communities of color.

16. Interview with John Mollenkopf, May 26, 2017.

17. That was actually his 2013 campaign slogan: Progress.

18. The move backfired, slightly, because crime fell in spite of the reduced police activity.

References

Bagli, C. V. (2013, December 15). Going out with building boom, mayor pushes billions in projects. *The New York Times*.

Barrett, W. (2000). *Rudy!: An investigative biography of Rudolph Giuliani*. New York, NY: Basic Books.

Barron, J. (1987). Lucille Mason Rose, first woman named as a deputy mayor. Retrieved from http://www.nytimes.com/1987/08/18/obituaries/lucille-mason-rose-first-woman-named-as-a-deputy-mayor.html.

Berg, B. (2007). *New York City politics: Governing gotham*. New Brunswick, N.J.: Rutgers University Press.

Cannato, V. J. (2001). *The ungovernable city: John Lindsay and his struggle to save New York*. New York, NY: Basic Books.

Finder, A. (1992, September 11). In Washington Heights, Dinkins defends actions after shooting. *The New York Times*.

Hamill, P. (2010). Revolt of the white lower middle class. In S. Roberts (Ed.), *America's mayor: John Lindsay and the reinvention of New York*. New York, NY: Columbia University Press.

Hicks, J. (1993, October 4). Disappointed black voters could damage Dinkins's bid. *The New York Times*.

Housing and Economic Development. (2014). Housing New York, NY: a five-borough ten year plan. Retrieved from http://www1.nyc.gov/assets/housing/downloads/pdf/housing_plan.pdf.

Karmen, A. (2000). *New York murder mystery: The true story behind the crime crash of the 1990s*. New York, NY: New York University Press.

Martin, D. (2014). Paul Gibson Jr., New York City's first black deputy mayor, is dead at 86. Retrieved from https://www.nytimes.com/2014/07/17/nyregion/paul-gibson-jr-new-york-citys-first-black-deputy-mayor-is-dead-at-86.html?_r=0.

McKinley Jr., J. C. (1992, September 17). Officers rally and Dinkins is their target. *The New York Times*.

McKinley Jr., J. C. (1992, September 16). Police panel: Shadow of 60's hangs over council. *The New York Times*.

New York Attorney General. (2013). Report: Stop and frisk. Retrieved from https://ag.ny.gov/sites/default/files/pdfs/bureaus/civil_rights/stp_frsk.pdf.

Newfield, J. (2007). *The full Rudy: The man, the myth, the mania*. New York, NY: Nation Books.

Newfield, J., & Barrett, W. (1988). *City for sale: Ed Koch and the betrayal of New York*. New York, NY: Harper and Row.

NYC Dept. Homeless Services. (2017). Daily report. Retrieved from https://www1.nyc.gov/assets/dhs/downloads/pdf/dailyreport.pdf.

NYC Dept. of Planning. (2016). Encouraging housing production, affordability and quality. Retrieved from http://www1.nyc.gov/site/planning/plans/mih/mandatory-inclusionary-housing.page.

NYCLU. (1990). Police abuse: The need for civilian investigation and oversight. Retrieved from https://www.nyclu.org/sites/default/files/publications/Police%20Abuse%20The%20Need%20for%20Civilian%20Investigation%20and%20Oversight.pdf.

NYU Furman Center. (2016). Report analyzes New York City's gentrifying neighborhoods and finds dramatic demographic shifts. Retrieved from http://furmancenter.org/thestoop/entry/new-report-analyzes-new-york-citys-gentrifying-neighborhoods-and-finds-dram.

Office of the Mayor. (2014). Mayor de Blasio holds media availability at Mt. Sinai United Christian Church on Staten Island. Retrieved from http://www1.nyc.gov/office-of-the-mayor/news/542-14/transcript-mayor-de-blasio-holds-media-availability-mt-sinai-united-christian-church-staten.

Office of the Mayor. (2015). State of the city: Mayor de Blasio puts affordable housing at center of 2015 agenda to fight inequality. Retrieved from http://www1.nyc.gov/office-of-the-mayor/news/088-15/state-the-city-mayor-de-blasio-puts-affordable-housing-center-2015-agenda-fight#/0.

Purdum, T. S. (1992, September 19). Slurs from police are not new to Dinkins. *The New York Times*.

Purnick, J. (2009). Mike Bloomberg: Monday, power, politics. New York, NY: Public affairs.

Rauch, W., & Koch, E. (1984). *Mayor*. New York, NY: Simon and Schuster.

Savitch-Lew, A. (2017, January 10). Will rezoning cause or resist displacement? Data paints an incomplete picture. City Limits (citylimits.org).

Strober, D. H., & Strober, G. S. (2007). *Giuliani, flawed or flawless (the oral biography).* New York, NY: John Wiley & Sons.

PART 2

The Race Mountains

Introduction to Part 2

Hector R. Cordero-Guzmán

While New York City has always been described as an immigrant city, at a macro-economic level, New York City is also a "Global City" (Abu-Lughod, 1999; Sassen, 1991). The globalization of markets, capital, labor, production and consumption now shape the economy of New York City and its social structure. Market expansion and integration, and the development of global production chains have connected local and global firms and economies. They have generated both positive and negative impacts on local economies and people. Advances in technology, telecommunications and transportation have facilitated spatial adjustments and connected firms, but also they have connected communities and people in more flexible and effective ways. As firms globalize and translocate, workforces have done the same. We see increased flexibility of work and the proliferation of subcontracting arrangements.

The Global city also brings with it increasing dimensions of polarization that are better captured in the image of New York City as a "Dual City" (Mollenkopf & Castells, 1991; Smith & Michael, 2012). The dual city makes the connection between the evolving structure of the economy and demographic change in local labor markets, industries, and firms. In turn, changes in these entities affect social class and the racial division of labor. The main argument is that there is a core population with articulated economic interests followed by subordinate immigrant and ethnic minority groups competing for work.

The growth of temporary workers, labor brokers, and a range of other labor market intermediaries continually connects workers and employers. In which case, the labor force must be flexible. This flexibility has costs to workers. There is declining unionization, declining bargaining power and a declining ability of workers to protect themselves from abuse. There is a decline in their ability to collectively bargain for better working conditions, wages, benefits and other forms of compensation.

In a globalized economy, there are multiple back and forth exchanges between immigrants and the many global sending communities. Local and transnational ties to communities in their home country sustain migrations that are more recent. At the same time, new migrants navigate through racialized politics, assimilation, labor markets, and the social structures of receiving areas like New York City. While growing international migration, corporate globalization, and social globalization can bring communities together, they do not protect them from marginalization and exploitation. Native minority populations are turned into labor reserves as new groups are absorbed into the labor market. New groups also face continuous racialization as they seek to integrate themselves into New York City's social fabric.

The outcome of all these changes is continuity in succession and competition by racial\ethnic\national origin based succession and competition (Waldinger, 1996). There is also continuing tensions and pressures between assimilation and acculturation (Torres, 1995). This helps us understand the positioning of different groups in the evolving "social and racial pecking order." As Mollenkopf and Castells argue: "Blacks were able to expand their access to jobs in government, social services, and a few corporate services, expanding their middle class. In particular, public service provided a path for upward mobility in income and occupation. In contrast, Latinos are concentrated in sectors like durable manufacturing that have declined rapidly in recent decades" (Mollenkopf & Castells, 1991, p. 15). As new groups enter the city, they provide labor, goods and capital. They repopulate communities in decline and they help to "push-up" those that came before them. However, in a racially stratified city, new immigrants of color enter New York City and interact with existing marginalized "native minority" populations. As newcomers, they may pursue education and economic opportunities, but, at the same time, they are racialized and treated as "second class citizens."

Part 2 looks in detail at how African American, Latino, Caribbean immigrants and native-born Asians have emerged from the older economies to the global and dual city. It also describes the extent that racial inequality continued as an outcome of the forces described in part 1 and above.

References

Abu-Lughod, J. L. (1999). *New York, Chicago, and Los Angeles: America's global cities.* Minneapolis, MN: University of Minnesota Press.

Mollenkopf, J. H., & Castells, M. (Eds.). (1991). *Dual city: Restructuring New York.* New York, NY: Russel Sage Foundation.

Sassen, S. (1991). *The global city: New York, London, Tokyo*. Princeton, NJ: Princeton University Press.

Smith, P. M., & Michael, M. (2012). *Remaking urban citizenship: Organizations, institutions and the right to the city*. New Brunswick, NJ: Transaction Publishers.

Torres, A. (1995). *Between the melting pot and the mosaic: African Americans and Puerto Ricans in the New York political economy*. Philadelphia, PA: Temple University Press.

Waldinger, R. (1996). *Still the promised city? African-Americans and new immigrants in postindustrial New York*. Cambridge, MA: Harvard University Press.

Chapter 5

African Americans

African Americans and Racialized Inequality in New York City

Benjamin P. Bowser

The racialization of social stratification and the subsequent social and economic inequalities in our society can be traced directly back to slavery in the Western Hemisphere. When analyzing the contemporary social status and economic participation of slave descendants in Brazil, Mexico, Cuba, Venezuela, and the United States, it is virtually impossible to speak of race without acknowledging inequality or to discuss social class without recognizing the reality of race (Adalberto Aguirre & Baker, 2008). The Western historical record consistently finds people of visible African ancestry at the bottom of the social hierarchy. This legacy of slavery is very much the case in the United States today (Lovejoy & Bowser, 2013).

This chapter reviews how social and economic inequality in New York City is a continuing outcome of the city's history of slavery. This chapter focuses on indicators that signal whether racial inequality is increasing or decreasing; where and when racially distinct communities locate, form, and disperse. The goal of this analysis is to put racial inequality, and gentrification, which is a primary outcome, into an actionable social context. Census population statistics will provide the necessary background to see who lived when, where and for how long. The chapter is divided into three parts. First, it provides a basic historical review of racialization. Second, it offers a foundational perspective from the past century. Third, this chapter suggests several public policy implications based on this study's research findings.

Harlems before Harlem

Wall Street is the administrative heart of the nation's largest banks and investment firms. So it is all the more ironic that an African burial site stands at the foot of Wall Street. The site takes us back to 1626, when Dutch settlers arrived on Manhattan Island, closely followed by the import of the first African slaves (Berlin & Harris, 2005, p. 22). The Dutch first brought slaves from Curacao and Barbados, to address acute labor shortages. At that time, the North American brand of slavery was still evolving, so the earliest slaves were treated very much like Dutch laborers. As property of the Dutch West India Company, slaves served as municipal workers whose first task was to build and maintain farms, wharves, mills, roads, and the Wall Street fortifications. They cleared land north of the walls and then worked that land as farm laborers. They also worked as household servants, doing the cooking, cleaning, serving, and emptying of chamber pots. These early slaves lived in their masters' basements, attics, and in "Negro kitchens" behind the homes (Berlin & Harris, 2005, p. 75). In these formative years, "Negroes and Indians were brought, sold and hired from the auction block," on Wall Street, along with White indentured servants (Ottley & Weatherby, 1967, p. 19).

In 1644, 11 Blacks and their wives were freed because of "long and faithful services" (Ottley & Weatherby, 1967, p. 4). They were given land and were expected to make annual payments consisting of 22.5 bushels of corn, wheat, beans, plus one fat pig. The land they received consisted of 130 acres in a tangled swamp known as Greenwich Village, near what is currently Washington Square. This first freed Black community was located strategically between the Dutch settlement to the south and Indian raiders to the north. Because the community was so isolated, it became the earliest refuge for freed Blacks in New Amsterdam. It remained a Black enclave for almost two centuries, as the city grew around it, and extended north (Ottley & Weatherby, 1967).

By 1664, at the beginning of British rule over New York, there were several Black settlements on Manhattan Island, south of what is now 14th Street. The burial ground was part of a settlement near Broadway and Duane Streets, northwest of Wall Street. Approximately 15,000 freed and enslaved Africans were buried in this cemetery during the years 1690 to 1794 (Berlin & Harris, 2005). The community predated the burial grounds by many years and remained in this location for well over one hundred years. In addition to the site in Greenwich Village, there was a Black settlement on Catherine Street, just north of what is now the entrance to the Brooklyn Bridge (Ottley & Weatherby, 1967, p. 75).

The Catherine Street settlement was initially just a swamp as well. Although there is no record of when the community was first settled, it became infamous by 1800. In its market, slaves from as far away as New Jersey and Long Island competed with local slaves. They danced on six-foot-wide boards to the beat of other Black men "patting juba": foot stamping and beating their hands against their legs (White, 2005, p. 167). Catherine Street attracted White men looking for a good time because it was known for its dance cellars, gambling, salons, and prostitution.

By 1800, the blocks west of Catherine Street became the infamous Five Points District, filled with over-crowded wooden tenements. After 1825, freed Blacks built a fourth community called Seneca Village, located between 85th and 88th Streets, on 7th Avenue. This was an area in what is now Central Park, southwest of the reservoir. Within fifteen years, homes, barns, farms, schools, and churches had been built (Quigley, 2005, p. 268).

By 1911, Mary White Ovington identified five Black residential areas before Harlem: Greenwich Village, the Upper East Side, and three areas of the West Side (1971). The first were the slums around 34th Street, west of 8th Avenue (McKay, 1968). The second was San Juan Hill in the blocks between 53rd and 65th Streets, the area near what is now Lincoln Center (Ottley & Weatherby, 1967, p. 145). Near Broadway, south of 116th Street was the third enclave. Another area on the East Side, Blacks lived off 3rd Avenue, just south of 100th Street.

There were additional Black communities formed in the outer boroughs. Before the Civil War, well-off, freed Blacks fled Manhattan to Weeksville, in Brooklyn, which eventually became Bedford Stuyvesant. Individuals wanted to get away from Manhattan's congestion, as well as from the contempt and resentment shown them by Irish and German immigrants (Johnson, 1968, p. 59). During the 1863 Draft Riots, Blacks were hunted down in lower Manhattan and lynched on sight. In addition, there was Sandy Ground, in the Rossville area of southwest Staten Island. Freed Blacks purchased land there the year after slavery was outlawed (1827) in New York State. Sandy Ground became a major stop on the Underground Railroad. It may be the oldest continuously settled free-Black community in the U.S. Descendants of the original settlers still live there. Undoubtedly, there were other Black settlements in the five boroughs of New York that are unknown to us.

What Happened to These Harlems?

All of the Black communities that existed on Manhattan Island before Harlem's formation disappeared, along with their memories. These had not been temporary renter communities. Blacks held title to the properties around Washington Square, in Seneca Village, Weeksville, and Sandy Ground. Other than Seneca Village and Wall Street, all the districts had been in existence for at least one hundred years. A law that was passed can explain their demise, in part.

After the 1714 Insurrection, when a group of slaves attempted to kill their masters and burn their properties, the British passed a law. It stated that "No Negro, Indian or Mulatto made free hereafter was to enjoy, hold, or possess houses, land, tenements, or hereditaments within this colony" (Ottley & Weatherby, 1967, p. 24). This law was in place for one hundred years, well into the 1800s.

The dissolution of Seneca Village is of particular interest. In 1855, Mayor Fernando Wood, who had deep ties to the South, took over the village by eminent domain, to start Central Park (Quigley, 2005). It required two years of effort, plus force on his part, to remove Seneca Village's residents. However, there was a more fundamental and abiding reason for the demise of these communities. Their residents were considered racially inferior to others: a status inherited from slavery. Therefore, where Blacks lived was of little consequence.

Racial attitudes in nineteenth-century New York were determined largely by the South and slavery. New York City became the banking center for the South (Quigley, 2005, p. 266), and New York banks invested in the expansion of southern cotton production and loaned money to planters to enlarge their plantations, and to buy slaves. The banks facilitated the shipping of southern cotton through the port of New York, to England. Concurrently, New York's freed Black communities were a source of anti-slave abolitionist agitation. Freed Blacks lived close to downtown and were an offense to the city's many wealthy southern visitors.

While Blacks, slave and free, had been New York's primary source of labor and artisans for two centuries, employers grew increasingly reluctant to hire them for the new manufacturing jobs. At some point, businesses decided not to employ Blacks at all in newly emerging industries (Richardson 2001). The city's manufacturers replaced both slave and bonded servants, after abolishing both, with hundreds of thousands of German and Irish immigrants. They too quickly learned the rules of American racism and perceived Blacks as direct competitors for their jobs.

It is important to note that African slaves were the most volatile labor force in this nation's colonial history (Foner & Lewis, 1989). If European immigration had not occurred, Blacks would have dominated the nation's industrial labor force. After 1865, Blacks would have been in strategic positions in the emerging manufacturing and industrial economy, which was central to the future of New York City (Bowser, 2007). Also, if there had been no alternate workforce, Blacks would have continued to fill the hundreds of service, crafts, and artisanal jobs they had held in previous centuries.

There was another reason Black labor was unwelcome. Former slaves had struggled for their freedom and fought in the Civil War. They could not be exploited easily or expected to be a docile labor force. Therefore, a substitute labor force was sought (Richardson, 2001). Moreover, immigrants' inevitable demands for higher wages could be tempered by the threat that Blacks would replace them. As a result, Blacks found themselves consigned to the bottom of the social and economic hierarchy, with immigrants only one-step above them. Consequently, the racial caste hierarchy, originating in the South, became intrinsic to class stratification in New York City, as well.

Furthermore, immigrant violence against Blacks was relentless. It was not safe to be Black in downtown Manhattan. By the 1860 census, only 85 of 10,000–plus Blacks in New York owned real estate, and there were almost no Black artisans left working on Manhattan Island (Bernstein, 2005, p. 299). There was a constant fear of anti-Black rioting wherever Blacks lived in lower Manhattan. In 1904, the African American realtor, Philip A. Payton, Jr., began leasing Harlem-based apartments to Blacks, which motivated many to move there. At the same time, Blacks living on the West Side, near 34th Street, were displaced by construction of the first Pennsylvania train station.

The Harlems before Harlem tells us a great deal about the evolution of racial inequality in New York. Black and immigrant communities provide perfect case studies on how race and social hierarchy intersected to stratify the city along racial lines. This history suggests several propositions:

> **Proposition One:** Black communities were formed on the immediate outskirts of settled areas that had little or no land value: in tangled swamps (Greenwich Village, Catherine Street, and Sandy Ground), in uncleared land (Wall Street and Seneca Village), and in overbuilt housing (Harlem and Weeksville).

> **Proposition Two:** Each community was founded by freed Blacks, who were granted land or who purchased it. Citywide racial discrimination in housing meant a perpetual housing shortage for Blacks. Black pioneers who moved into new communities were succeeded by the less well off. Over-crowding became inevitable. In addition, immigrants lived close by and competed for the same housing.

> **Proposition Three:** A citywide system of social status evolved. The lower the perceived status of a resident, the less control they had over their own residential living space. Black residential land use was the least respected, followed closely by immigrant residential land use. On the other hand, the higher-status New Yorkers, namely, native Whites, could enjoy minimal disruption of their land use and could sustain residential longevity. Higher-status groups could eclipse the land use of lower-status groups, for whatever purpose.
>
> **Proposition Four:** Eventually, the city grew beyond each Black enclave. Land values increased and became attractive to private development (Greenwich Village). Black domains were repurposed for business (Wall Street), and for public infrastructure projects such as Penn Station (West Side), the Brooklyn Bridge (Catherine Street) and Highway 13 (Sandy Ground), the Cross-Bronx Expressway (South Bronx), and Lincoln Center. Gentrification, or repurposed land use, was the final phase of removing lower-status residents.

Do these nineteenth-century propositions apply equally to the twentieth century? By looking at four generations across the city's development, we take a long view that is critical to understanding what is happening in the twenty-first century, as well.

~

In 1910, there was sufficient development in the city, and progress in the census, to begin tracking the city's modern composition. Manhattan, below 59th Street, was already intensely developed for business, commerce, shipping, and manufacturing. As one traveled up the island, working-class tenements gave way to apartment buildings, which in turn became increasingly rural open space above 110th Street. Figure 5.1 shows the 1910 census population distribution of native and foreign-born White and Black residents by Manhattan Assembly Districts. It should be noted as well that these three groups of New Yorkers were economically stratified; Native Whites were at the top followed by foreign-born Whites with Blacks at the bottom of the income and jobs hierarchy. Assembly Districts run from the historic southern tip of Manhattan, northward to the then-rural, undeveloped top of the island beginning around 146th Street.

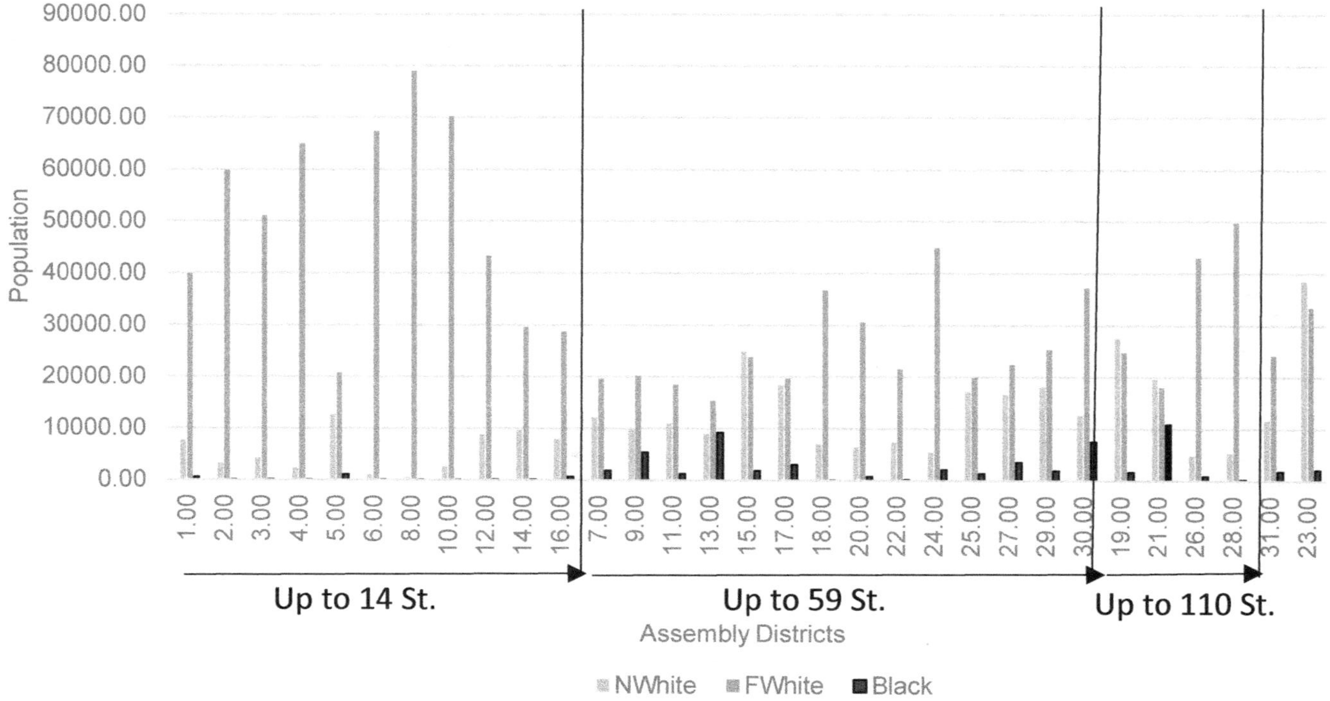

Figure 5.1. Native and foreign-born white and black population by Manhattan Assembly Districts, 1910. *Source:* US Census of Population, IPUMS National Historical Geographic Information System, 2014.

In figure 5.1, as in subsequent figures, there are three bars for each Manhattan district. The first bar is of native-born Whites; the second is of foreign-born Whites; and the third is of Blacks. Figure 5.1 reveals the dominance of European, foreign-born communities below 14th Street. Additional immigrant clusters by Assembly Districts ran up 3rd Avenue, and over to the East River, from 59th Street to 110th Street. Whites with both native-born parents (native Whites) were a minority on the island and lived in three main clusters. The first was in adjoining districts (5, 7, 9 and 11) running from West 4th Street up to 5th Avenue to 14th Street, and then, west of Broadway, up to West 42nd Street. The second cluster included districts 25, 27, and 29, running east and west off 5th Avenue, from 14th Street up to 59th Street, and then continuing along 5th Avenue and Park Avenue, up to 96th Street. Then, as now, these were the wealthiest residential areas on Manhattan Island, and in the city as a whole. The third cluster consisted of district 23, which ran from West 116th Street up the West Side, to the top of Manhattan Island: then semirural Washington Heights and Inwood.

In contrast, the Black presence (figure 5.1, black bars) that Mary White Ovington described in 1910 was hardly evident. Relatively small concentrations of Blacks lived in two areas already described: district 9, around West 34th Street, and district 13, San Juan Hill, near present-day Lincoln Center. Blacks in upper Manhattan were concentrated in district 30, or what is now known as Spanish Harlem, East 96th Street up to East 110th Street, and in district 21, currently labeled the Upper Westside, along Amsterdam Avenue, from 102nd to 116th Street, near Columbia University.

Blacks lived in the most northern, urban residential areas of Manhattan, farthest from the downtown. Center Harlem hardly existed at the time. Immigrants were spread throughout the island, seemingly served as a buffer between Native White and small Black populations. However, major events greatly changed the landscape. After the Great Depression, Prohibition, and the decline of European immigration, the three communities that existed in 1910, had shifted in residence on Manhattan Island by 1940. Census population figure 5.2 illustrates how.

In figure 5.2, 1910 Assembly Districts were replaced with geographically smaller and more numerous Health Districts in 1940. In order to show more districts, one bar, rather than three, illustrated the proportions of each primary population in each health district. The bold black top of each bar represented the Black Population; the narrow black bottom of each bar represented Native Whites; and the gray middle were foreign-born Whites. By 1940, native Whites were 60 to 70 percent of the population in 50 of 68 health districts and once again became the majority of Manhattan's population below

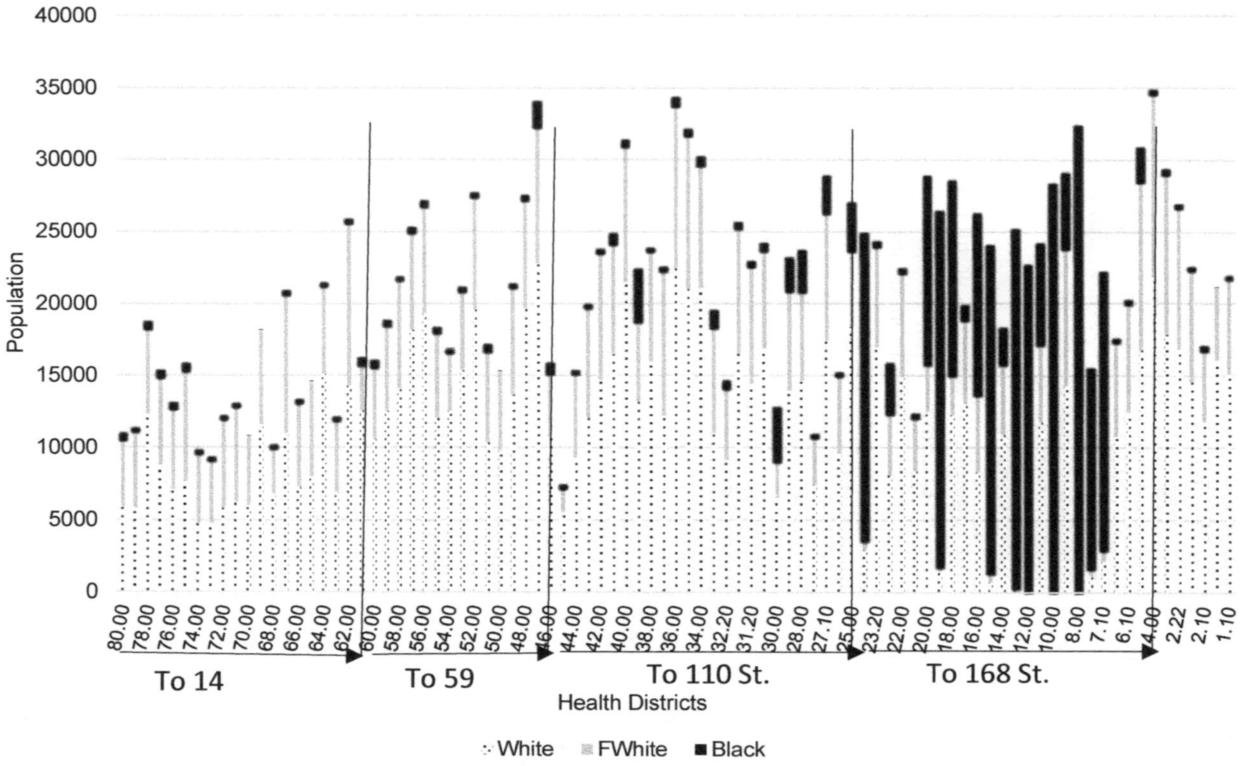

Figure 5.2. Native and foreign-born white and black population by Manhattan health districts, 1940. *Source:* US Census of Population, IPUMS National Historical Geographic Information System, 2014.

110th Street. Instead of clustering below 14th Street, as they had in 1910, both native and foreign-born Whites dominated all but eight health areas. European immigrants were much more widely dispersed in 1940 than they were in 1910. Communities, referred to as ethnic ghettos in 1910, were broken up. The only health areas that showed little population change between 1910 and 1940 were the wealthiest Manhattan residential areas along 5th Avenue, from 14th Street, up to 96th Street.[1]

The dramatic increase in native Whites was not due to White in-migration from other parts of the country. It is equally doubtful that native Whites suddenly accepted immigrants as neighbors. There are two explanations for immigrant barriers breaking down. First, European immigration dropped sharply during the Great Depression and ended altogether during World War II. In 1940, foreign-born immigrants were only 28 percent of their 1910 numbers (540,197/1,927,703). Second, it is more likely that, by 1940, many of the children and grandchildren of 1910 immigrants were considered now as native Whites. A broad intergenerational assimilation of European immigrants occurred, which is discussed in detail elsewhere (Alba & Nee, 2003).

Manhattan's Black population went from 60,534 in 1910, to 298,365 in 1940: a five-fold increase. Figure 5.2 shows that Black communities virtually disappeared from lower Manhattan (District 50, 34th Street), and San Juan Hill (District 47, West 50s)[2]—they are clustered as dots at the top of these districts in figure 5.2. Upper West Side Blacks almost disappeared from below West 114th Street. The pressure to house five times the Black population fell on upper Manhattan Health Areas (16, 20) that were 45 to 47.6 percent Black, bound by fifth and third avenues, from E. 112th Street up to the Harlem River. Also, six Health Areas (24, 15, 12, 10, 8, and 7) were 88.9 to 99.6 percent Black, starting at 110th Street, and then running between eighth and fifth avenues to 159th Street and the Harlem River. These areas mark the current boundaries of central Harlem.

1950–2010

Between World War II and 1960, Western European immigrants virtually disappeared from American shores. Puerto Ricans replaced them, joining Blacks at the bottom-rung of New York City's labor force. At that stage, the Servicemen's Adjustment Act (GI Bill) of 1944, in addition to federal funding of home mortgages, paid for racially segregated housing in the suburbs, which excluded Blacks (U.S. Congress, 2016). The 1956 National Interstate and Defense Highways Act authorized the construction of 41,000 miles of highways, connecting cities to suburbs where federally subsided segregated housing stood (U.S. Dept. Trans, 2016). Then, the 1965 Immigration and

Naturalization Act eliminated quotas based on national origin that favored European immigrants. Uniting families and attracting skilled labor were the new emphases, but the outcome was increased immigration from Asia, the Americas, Eastern Europe and Africa. Meanwhile, a major shift took place in New York City. Labor-intensive manufacturing, at the core of the city's economy for one hundred years, began moving overseas, to the new suburbs, and to the South, along all the new federal interstate highways (Bluestone & Harrison, 1982; Ehrenhalt, 1993). All these government acts had vast, unintended consequences for New York City.

By 1980, White flight was underway. At least 32 percent of the 1960-era White native and foreign-born Manhattan populations, the core of the White working-class, had moved, presumably to the suburbs. Nearly a half-million of more prosperous Blacks fled Harlem, as well. Harlem lost 25 percent of its 1960 population. Job losses and population flight took a toll on New York communities. Rapidly rising unemployment rates among Blacks and Puerto Ricans fueled heroin use and drug trafficking, which further undermined family and community life. In 1975, the declining tax base, and rising social service costs drove New York City to the edge of bankruptcy. The city's housing and general physical infrastructure went into rapid decline. Abandoned housing and factories in lower Manhattan, deterioration of port facilitates, and blighted blocks in greater Harlem and the Bronx indicated the collapse of the manufacturing and industrial-based working class in New York. Table 5.1 on page 126 provides an overview of the effects of these changes over a fifty-year period, to the last decennial census.

In Manhattan in 2010, the 1970 White population average (mean) had declined from 71 percent of all census tracts to 57 percent. The foreign-born population average increased from 19 percent of all tracts to 27 percent. In this same period, the Black population declined from 24 percent to 17 percent. The dispersal of foreign-born residents showed up in another way, too. In 1970, 43 percent of Manhattan census tracts were at least 90 percent White. By 2010, only four percent were. The 13 percent of census tracts that had been at least 90 percent Black in 1970, declined to zero percent by 2010. Meanwhile, the percent of 16-year-olds, and older, in the labor force, increased from 57 percent to 66 percent. The unemployment rate in the civilian labor force increased between 1970 and 2000 but declined in 2010. The ratio of Black-to-White household income declined as well, indicating a growing racial income disparity.

These statistics illustrate how Puerto Ricans and other new immigrants were dispersed widely, as were earlier European immigrants. They moved into the working-class housing left behind by White and Black flight. During this period, New York's manufacturing and industrial economy bottomed-out,

Table 5.1. Manhattan

	Mean % All Tracts			Mean % 90% Tracts		Mean % Labor Force		Mean Income Househould		Inc. Ratio Black/ White
	Wt.	ForB.	Blk.	Wt.	Blk.	/ Pop 16+	Unempl.	White	Black	
1970	71	19	24	42.6 (121)	12.8 (11)	57	5			
1980	59	22	25	25.0 (072)	11.0 (32)	60	8			
1990	56	23	26	19.4 (55)	8.2 (24)	64	10	71283	24533	0.34
2000	54	27	21	8.9 (025)	1.0 (03)	64	11	112625	37398	0.33
2010	57	27	17	4.3 (14)	0.0 (0)	66	9	155919	48354	0.31

Source: U.S. Census Bureau, IPUMS National Historical Geographic Information System, 2014; Social Explorer, 2005–2017.

thereby eliminating hundreds of thousands of manual labor jobs. Blacks and Latinos, being at the end of the job queue, were left with virtually no way to economically support themselves.

Meanwhile, a new economy was emerging, making it possible for New York to recover from its hard times. By 2010, unemployment rates had reversed, and labor-force participation and income levels had increased. As early as 1990, the White population showed signs of stabilizing, with increasing numbers. Every Manhattan tracts saw upsurges in White population (figure 5.3 on page 128). These increases were pronounced particularly in those tracts below 14th Street, and in the Upper West Side, to 110th Street. Except for the remaining concentration of Blacks in Harlem and West Harlem (lower Washington Heights), the Black proportion of each census tract becomes smaller and more distinct as one travels north on the island. The population between Blacks and Whites at the bottom of each column increases. This is indicative of the increase proportion of foreign-born residents as one goes north on Manhattan. For the first time in over a century, even central Harlem had White residents. These new comers to Harlem are not from the White working- and lower-middle classes. Instead, these Harlem newcomers are younger, better educated and work in the new mix of global, high-tech, banking, finance, management, and creative industries that comprise the city's new economy.

Foreign-born Asian and Latino residents increased in every decade since 1970, supplemented by Russians, other Eastern Europeans, and Africans. In contrast, Manhattan's Black population has declined in all but one decade since 1960. Between 1960 and 1980, drug use and trafficking blighted Harlem, followed by equally destructive crack cocaine and HIV epidemics. By 2010, there were fewer African Americans on Manhattan Island than there were in 1940, before the post-war migration. It is worth noting that figure 5.3 shows a new development, not evident in prior decades. There is a small Black population in virtually every tract, including the most expensive. Thirty-five percent of Black Manhattan residents do not live in Harlem and are dispersed across the entire island.

It is almost as if history has repeated itself. Native, White "gold coast" enclaves are right where they were in the previous century. Immigrants from the rest of the world have replaced Western European immigrants. The difference, however, is that there are fewer new immigrants. Work in the smaller service sector has replaced labor-intensive industrial work. Black working-class enclaves in lower Manhattan, and on the West Side and East Side, have been re-purposed or gentrified completely. Harlem became the new refuge. Now, even Harlem is being gentrified. If reducing racial inequality was ever a real goal, this is not what is happening. It is worth seeing whether this is the case for the other city boroughs, as well.

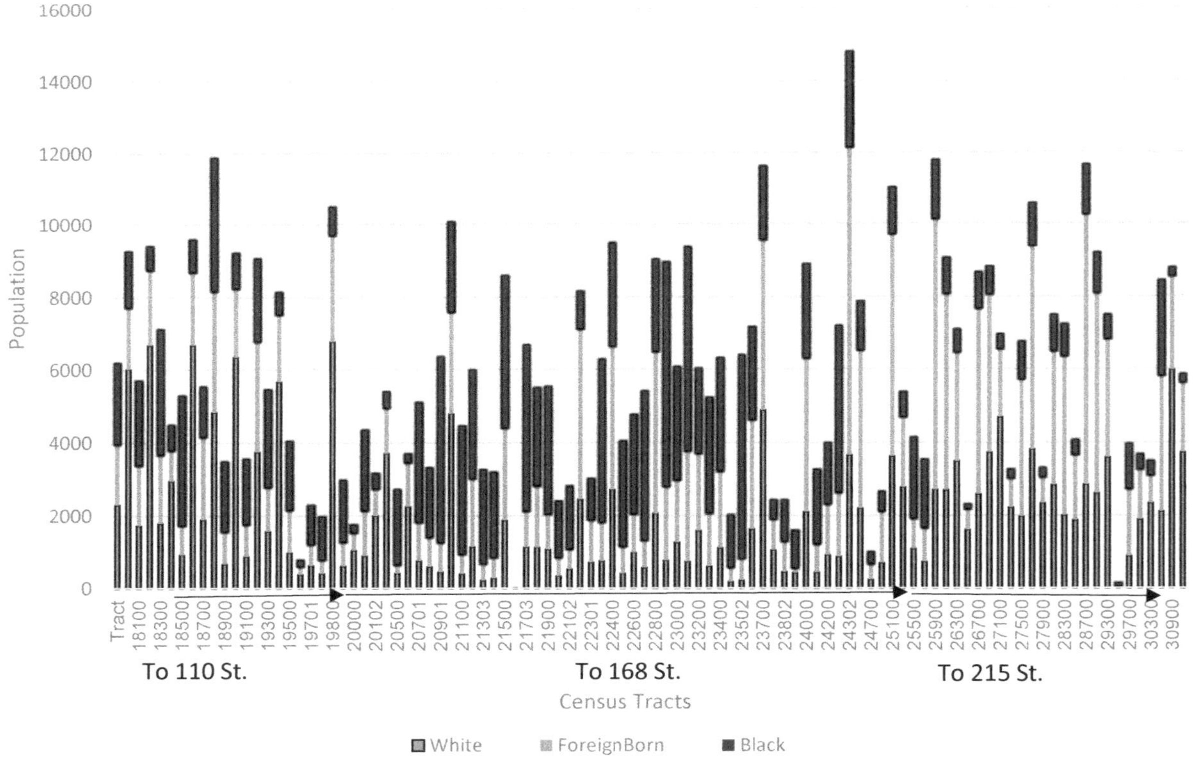

Figure 5.3. White, foreign-born, and black population by Manhattan census tracts, 2010. *Source:* US Census of Population, IPUMS, 2014.

The Other Boroughs

The Bronx

The Bronx began its development once it could be reached by bridge, rather than by ferries. Then in 1909, the subway was built from Manhattan into the Bronx. Brick apartment complexes were constructed along the elevated subway lines, forming city grid-blocks from the South Bronx, northward. The extensive apartment developments were designed to relieve overcrowding in Manhattan and to make the commute to Manhattan convenient. Thousands flooded into the Bronx. First, there were the Irish, followed by German, Italian and Jewish immigrant families. In 1930, after a generation, the Irish began to move to better suburban housing. Germans, Italians, and Jews closely followed them out to the suburbs in the subsequent decades. Before 1950, the census showed virtually no concentrations of Blacks in the Bronx.

However, by 1950, Puerto Ricans, Dominicans, and African Americans began concentrating in the South Bronx, across the East River from Harlem. See census tracts 121 to 145 in figure 5.4 on page 130.

Besides the south Bronx, there were small numbers of Blacks in virtually all Bronx tracts (note the large number of dots at the top of each tract in figure 5.4). The gray bottoms of each tract were the remaining White population, and the thin area between indicated foreign-born residents. Soon after Blacks and Puerto Ricans began succeeding White ethnic in route to the suburbs, Robert Moses ran the Cross-Bronx Expressway through the South Bronx. Whole communities were leveled, and the residents who remained nearest the highway were isolated from public transportation, from one another, and from parks. Those who could began to move out (Caro, 1975). Then a second, more devastating, "bomb" hit the Bronx. Industries that had employed hundreds of thousands of Bronx residents began to disappear. From the 1960s on, joblessness devastated the borough.

Over the next decade, stores and banks closed. Residents could not pay their rent, and insurance companies stopped insuring building owners. Apartment buildings were abandoned, while drug trafficking and use trapped many who could not flee. Buildings were burnt out, allegedly for insurance payments, just as city fire services were withdrawn in tandem with the city's fiscal crisis. Despite some redevelopment after 1990, the Bronx today has the highest average unemployment levels and crime rates, and the lowest income levels in the City of New York. When one compares figure 5.4 with figure 5.5, one can see the extent of Bronx depopulation. Figure 5.5 on page 131 also shows the extent to which the Black poor are now spread borough-wide. But

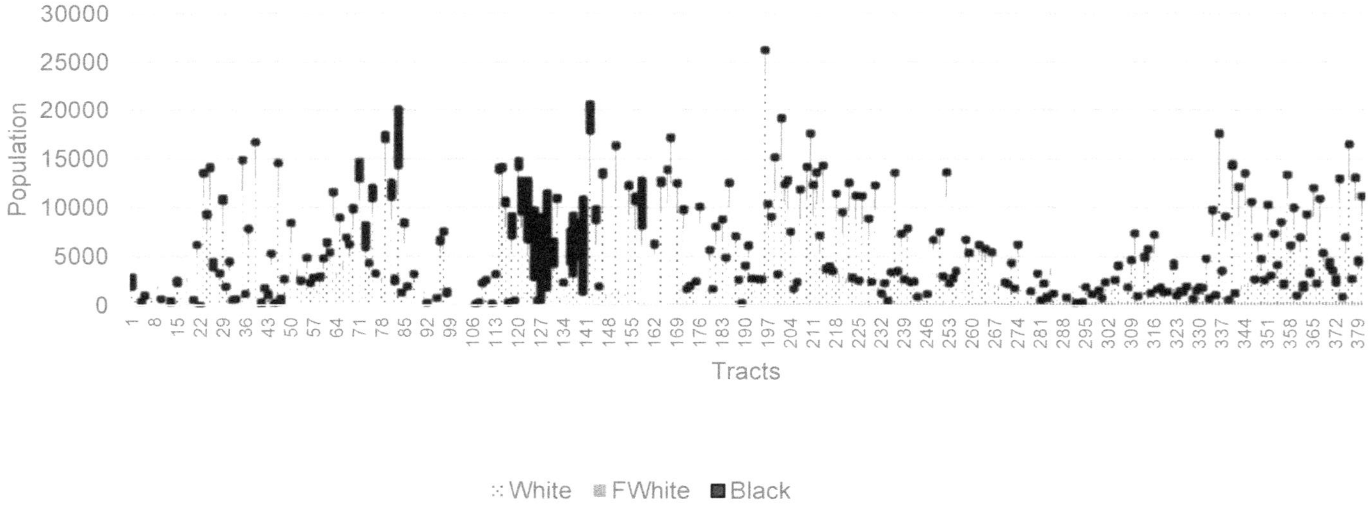

Figure 5.4. Native, foreign-born white and black population by Bronx census tracts, 1950. *Source:* US Census of Population, IPUMS National Historical Geographic Information System, 2014.

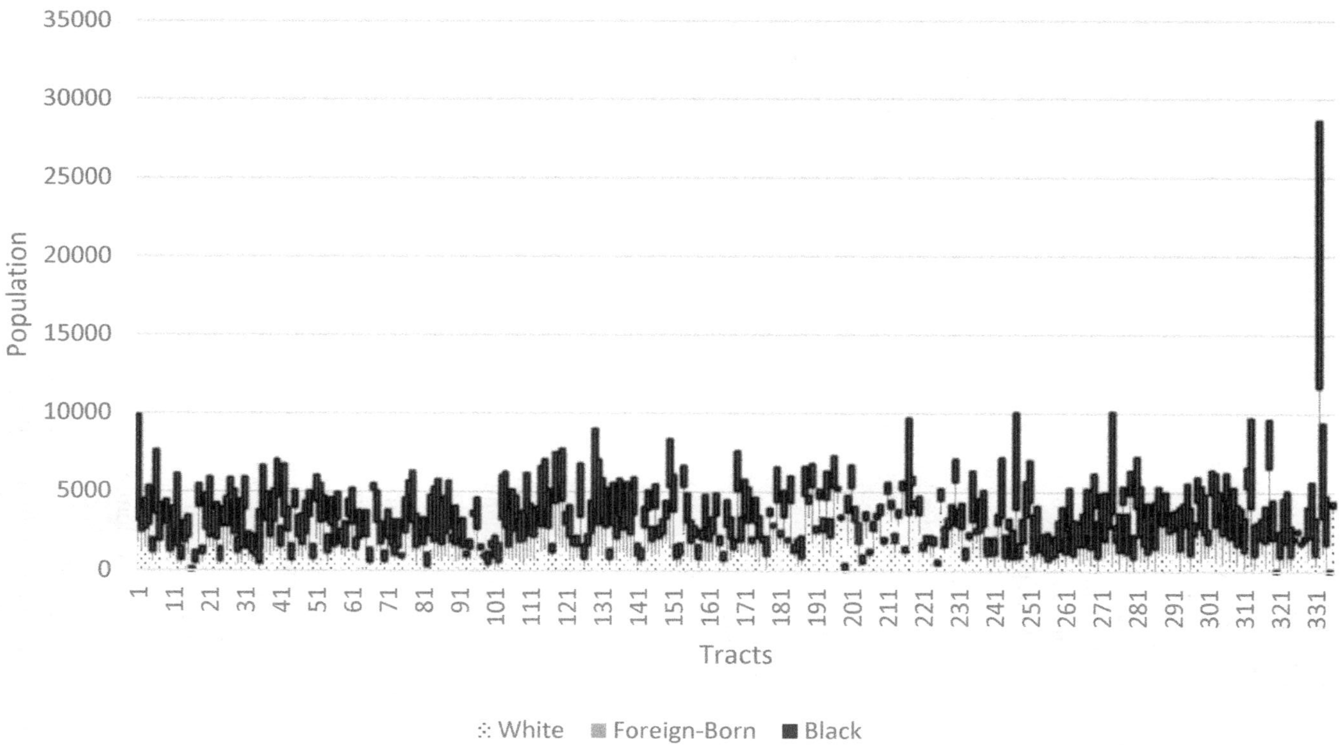

Figure 5.5. White, foreign-born, and black population by Bronx census tracts, 2010. *Source:* US Census of Population, IPUMS National Historical Geographic Information System, 2014.

even here, there is evidence of a returning White population. The contrast between census years is striking.

Statistics can reveal the social health of a borough. Table 5.2 shows that Whites were, on average, 78 percent of the population in Bronx census tracts in 1970. By 2010, their number had dropped to 30 percent, while the foreign-born and Black populations had increased substantially. Bronx tracts are now much more racially diverse. Forty-seven percent of Bronx tracts were at least 90 percent White in 1970. They were down to three percent in 2010. In 2010, the Bronx had one of only two census tracts in New York where 90-plus percent of the population was foreign-born. Despite the dispersal of Blacks throughout the Bronx, one more tract was 90 percent Black in 2010 as in 1970—from two to three. The proportion of residents 16 years or older in the workforce was unchanged, although unemployment rose to 15 percent by 2000, the highest of any borough in the city. The ratio of Black-to-White household incomes also shows increasing racial income disparity.

After a century, the center of racial inequality in New York is no longer Manhattan's Harlem, nor is it in Brooklyn, as we will see. Now it is the Bronx. No other borough has the same concentration of Black and foreign-born poor, nor higher unemployment. If racial inequality is to be addressed in New York, it will have to start in the Bronx.

Brooklyn

Unlike the Bronx, Brooklyn had its beginnings before 1900 with rural agricultural settlements. At that time, they included Brooklyn Village, Brooklyn, Bushwick, Flatbush, the Flatlands, Gravesend and New Utrecht. Well into the 1800s, slaves made up one-third of the population. Weeksville, a community of freed Black, was founded in 1838. It stood in what is now Bedford-Stuyvesant. Brooklyn developed as a borough in precisely the same way as did the Bronx. The Brooklyn Bridge opened in 1883, followed by the Williamsburg Bridge, in 1903. The subway came through the borough starting in 1908. With the bridges in place, housing development accelerated, especially along the subway lines. The borough soon was flooded with immigrant workers moving directly from the Lower East Side of Manhattan.

The 1950 census figures, summarized in figure 5.6 on page 134, show Blacks were concentrated in Bedford-Stuyvesant tracts 190 to 325. Black navy yard workers settled in predominantly Black middle-class tracts in the 1940s, both during and after the War. Like the Bronx, Brooklyn in 1950 had a large core Native White population, large concentrations of foreign-born residents and a small Black presence in most tracts.

In the next half-century, Brooklyn, like Manhattan and the Bronx, experienced its share of "white flight" to the suburbs, in addition to depopulation,

Table 5.2. The Bronx

	Mean % All Tracts			Mean % 90% Tracts			Mean % Labor Force		Mean Income Househould		Inc. Ratio Black/ White
	Wt.	ForB.	Blk.	Wt.	ForB.	Blk.	/ Pop 16+	Unempl.	White	Black	
1970	78	17	20	47.1 (153)		1.0 (2)	53	4			
1980	49	18	29	15.6 (51)		1.2 (4)	50	10			
1990	39	22	35	13.6 (46)		1.4 (5)	55	12	33597	28476	0.85
2000	33	28	34	3.3 (11)		0.9 (3)	51	15	44700	37415	0.84
2010	30	33	35	0.0 (0)	0.9 (1)	0.0 (0)	59	14	58913	46273	0.79

Source: US Census Bureau, IPUMS National Historical Geographic Information System, 2014; Social Explorer, 2005–2017.

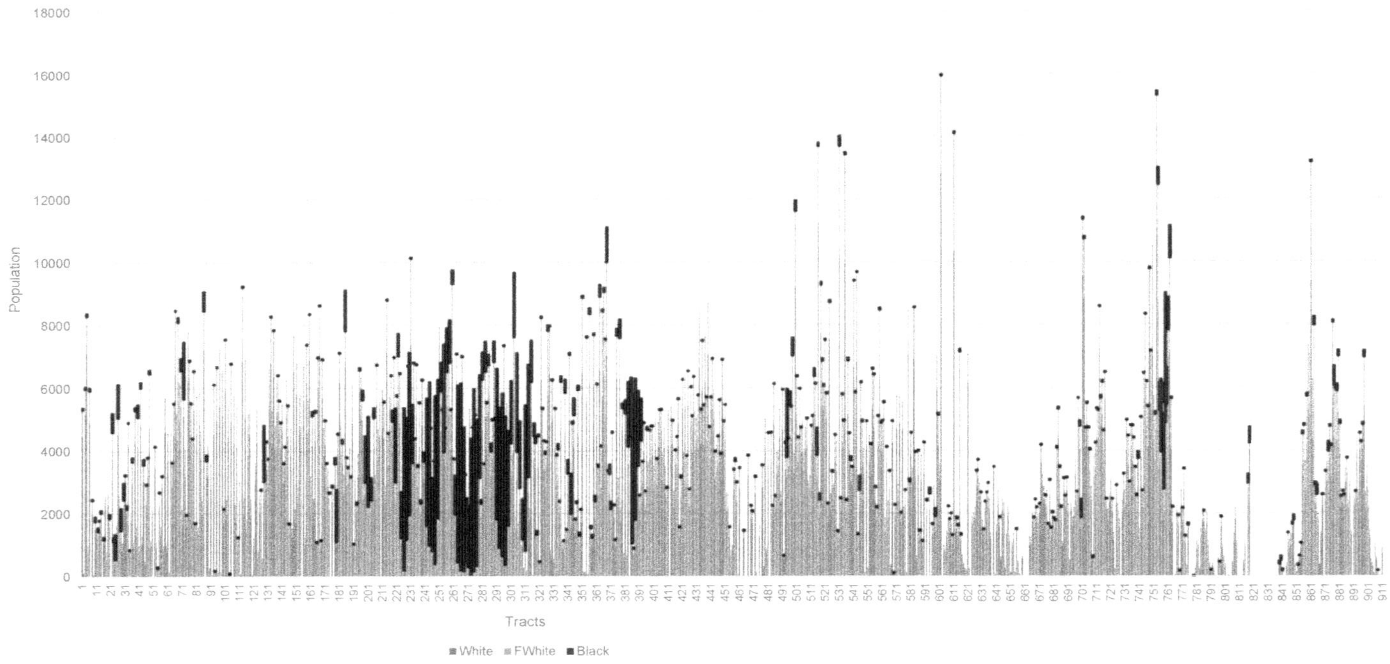

Figure 5.6. White, foreign-born, and black population by Brooklyn census tracts, 1950. *Source:* US Census of Population, IPUMS National Historical Geographic Information System, 2014.

and impoverishment of its industrial workforce. Housing was abandoned, and the oldest working-class communities were blighted in downtown Brooklyn and Bedford-Stuyvesant. Unlike the Bronx, older Jewish and Italian immigrant communities remained in place. Brooklyn became the borough-of-choice for post-1960 immigrants, especially from the Caribbean. Blacks moved into White flight neighborhoods surrounding Bedford-Stuyvesant, such as Crown Heights, Williamsburg, East New York and Brownsville. Compare figure 5.7 on page 136, 1950, with figure 5.6, 2010 for population changes.

When comparing figure 5.6 to figure 5.7, one can see the extent of White flight, and the degree of Black and immigrant resettlement in Brooklyn. The deep concentration and dispersal of Blacks throughout the borough is striking. Despite these changes, Brooklyn maintained its neighborhood characteristics in comparison to the Bronx. Brooklyn still has strong ethnic social networks, low population density, and high homeownership. Brooklyn's high rate of homeownership has been a strong incentive for the White, immigrant and Black middle classes to remain in the borough. Whites, immigrants, and Blacks now live near one another, with the accompanying tensions that are inherent in this mix. Despite gentrification in the older tracts closest to Manhattan, most tracts have a mix of Whites, immigrants, and Blacks. Immigrants seem to serve as buffers between the mostly White and Black tracts. Employment in service industries (work done primarily by new immigrants) has superseded Brooklyn's older, industrial workforce.

Table 5.3 on page 137 shows that Whites, on average, declined from 79 percent of the borough's population in 1970, to 44 percent by 2000. The foreign-born and Black populations increased substantially to 37 and 34 percent, respectively. The number of Brooklyn tracts that were 90-plus percent White declined from 64 percent to eight percent, while tracts that were 90-plus percent Black, hardly changed, increasing from five to seven percent by 2010. The proportion of the working population that was 16 years of age or older increased, while unemployment has remained at 10 percent since 1990. Like Manhattan and the Bronx, racial differences in household income have increased, showing greater disparity.

Queens

The Queensboro Bridge, originating in Manhattan, opened in 1909, extending Queens Boulevard across the borough. In 1915, a new subway line opened parallel to the boulevard. Farms and open space quickly disappeared, but Queens took a different turn from the other boroughs. In 1910, the Pennsylvania Railroad tunnel connected Queens and Long Island with Manhattan. This encouraged the construction of single-family suburban housing, rather than

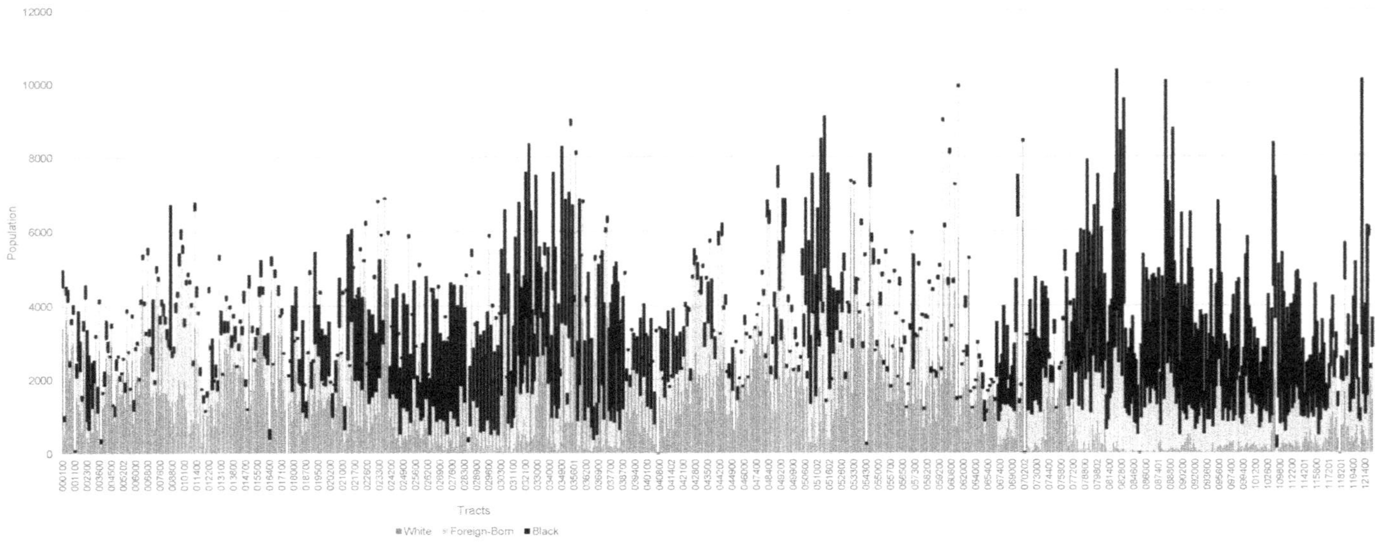

Figure 5.7. White, foreign-born, and black population by Brooklyn census tracts, 2010. *Source:* US Census of Population, IPUMS National Historical Geographic Information System, 2014.

Table 5.3. Brooklyn

	Mean % All Tracts			Mean % 90% Tracts		Mean % Labor Force		Mean Income Househould		Inc. Ratio Black/ White
	Wt.	ForB.	Blk.	Wt.	Blk.	/ Pop 16+	Unempl.	White	Black	
1970	79	17	20	63.5 (482)	5.3 (41)	54	5			
1980	61	23	28	35.9 (255)	8.9 (68)	53	9			
1990	52	27	32	24.4 (184)	13.3 (102)	58	10	38828	29041	0.75
2000	44	36	34	9.6 (71)	10.5 (79)	56	11	53454	40463	0.76
2010	44	37	34	7.5 (54)	7.4 (54)	62	10	73291	52711	0.72

Source: US Census of Population, IPUMS National Historical Geographic Information System, 2014; Social Explorer, 2005–2017.

tenements and apartment buildings. Queens developed mostly middle-class communities, such as Forest Hills (1906), South Ozone Park (1907), Howard Beach (1911) and Kew Gardens (1912). These were not just railroad stops on the way to Long Island. They became early suburbs and bedroom communities for Manhattan business owners and managers.

The new Queens communities had covenants that forbade residents from selling their properties to Blacks. Addisleigh Park, in St. Albans, was the exception. During the 1920s, famous Black entertainers moved into the Park, decades before 1948 when the U.S. Supreme Court outlawed racial covenants. By 1950, St. Albans had become the borough's only Black middle-class enclave and the only concentration of Blacks in the borough. This would be the only point of interest in illustrating 1950 Queen census tracts.

A great deal has changed in Queens (figure 5.8). Its White population is concentrated in tracts closest to Manhattan, and further out, near Hempstead. White residents have vacated vast areas of aging, single-family homes, especially near subway stops. This housing has been taken up by Black and foreign-born New Yorkers. In figure 5.8, the dots at the top of the tracts, indicate that the Black population is as dispersed as in the Bronx and Brooklyn, but it is much smaller. This suggests a much weaker Black presence in the borough.

The space between the black tops and bottoms of the columns indicate foreign-born residents. Chinese, Pakistanis, Mexicans, Latin Americans, and Russians have all aggregated to the borough's older housing. There are clusters of Chinese in Flushing and communities of East Indians in Jackson Heights. Social class further divides each ethnic group. It is interesting to note that in Queens, the relatively high concentrations of Blacks and Latinos live nearest the city's two major airports. In the decades since 1970, the airports have expanded, and air traffic has increased. Therefore, housing in the airport take-off and landing paths has become less attractive and has been passed on to Blacks and Latinos.

As in Brooklyn, Whites were 82 percent of Queens's population in 1970, but down to 40 percent by 2010. Foreign-born residents have more than doubled from 20 percent to 46 percent, while Blacks have increased in number from 17 percent to 22 percent. In 1970, 73 percent of Queens's tracts were 90-plus percent White. However, that number was down dramatically by 2010, to two percent. The second 90-plus percent foreign-born tract in New York is in Queens. The 90-plus percent Black tracts have hardly changed. Sixty-five percent of the 16-plus-year-olds are in the labor force. That is up from 59 percent. Unemployment has increased from three to ten percent, and the racial differences in household income indicate, again, an increasing disparity, as experienced in the other boroughs.

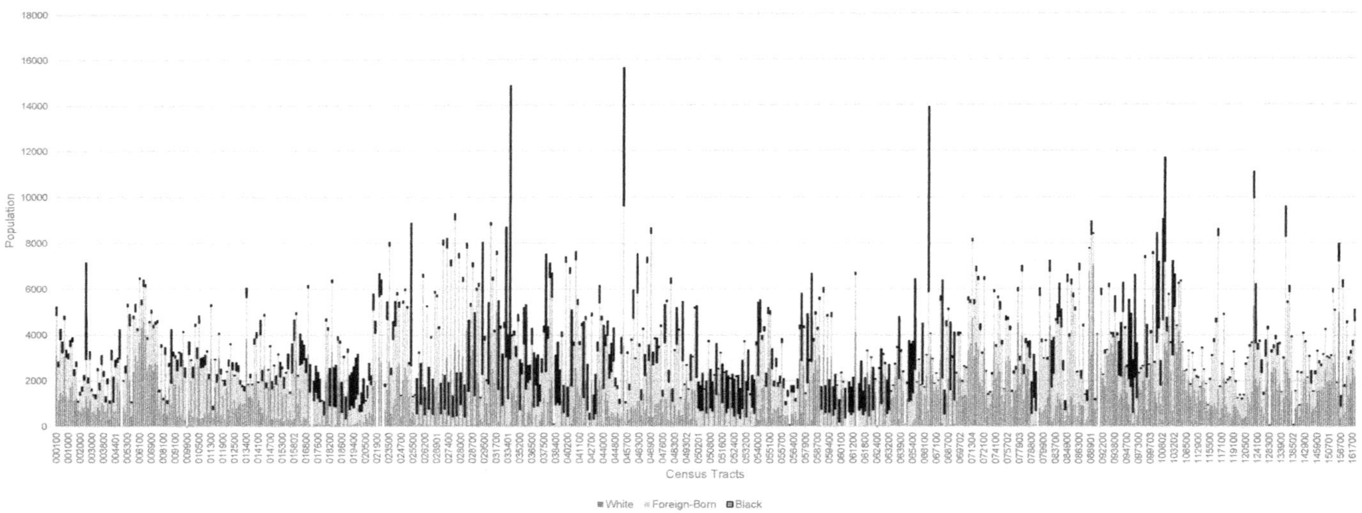

Figure 5.8. White, foreign-born, and black population by Queens census tracts, 2010. *Source:* US Census of Population, IPUMS National Historical Geographic Information System, 2014.

Table 5.4. Queens

	Mean % All Tracts			Mean % 90% Tracts			Mean % Labor Force		Mean Income Househould		Inc. Ratio Black/ White
	Wt.	ForB.	Blk.	Wt.	ForB.	Blk.	/ Pop 16+	Unempl.	White	Black	
1970	82	20	17	73.4 (475)		9.2 (60)	59	3			
1980	69	26	22	40.4 (245)		9.2 (59)	59	7			
1990	57	33	25	16.7 (107)		14.7 (097)	64	8	41904	40205	0.96
2000	43	43	23	4.5 (29)		11.1 (72)	58	8	56133	53136	0.95
2010	40	46	22	2.5 (16)	0.2 (01)	7.9 (51)	65	10	72275	68131	0.94

Source: US Census of Population, IPUMS National Historical Geographic Information System, 2014; Social Explorer, 2005–2017.

Staten Island

It was not until the Verrazano-Narrows Bridges opened in 1969 that Staten Island had a bridge connection to the rest of New York City. Before that, the only way to get to Staten Island was by ferry, at the foot of Manhattan, or by a long circular drive through New Jersey. The borough consisted of a series of small towns and remained largely undeveloped until the 1960s. Staten Island has the highest proportion of Italians of any county in the U.S.: 34 percent in 2000. Table 5.5 on page 142 shows that Staten Island has the lowest proportion of foreign-born residents of any borough, with their numbers increasing from 10 percent in 1970, to 20 percent by 2010.

The largest community of Sri Lankans in New York City is in the Tompkinville neighborhood of Staten Island. There has been no apparent White flight from Staten Island since the 1960s. The White population was 94 percent of all residents in 1970 and dropped to 71 percent by 2010. Even though the foreign-born population is not large, they have integrated all the historically White tracts. Seventy-seven percent of all tracts were 90 percent White in 1970. These virtually all-White tracts dropped to 29 percent by 2010. No Staten Island census tract has ever had 90-plus percent of either foreign-born or Black residents.

The proportion of 16-plus-year-olds in the labor force has increased from 56 percent to 60 percent, but over the last 40 years, unemployment has also increased from three to eight percent. Household income disparity declined in 2000 and then increased again in 2010. Staten Island could easily be a suburb of Westchester or Long Island. Despite the borough's long history of abolitionism and Underground Railroad activity during the nineteenth century, Blacks have had a minimal presence on the island. This is notable since Sandy Ground, the oldest freed Black community in New York City is located in this borough. Staten Island has the distinction of being the only New York borough to vote to secede from the city. In fact, 65 percent of the residents supported the 1993 measure, which was proposed during the mayoral term of the only Black mayor of New York, David Dinkins. The State Assembly turned down the measure.

Conclusion and Policy Implications

Until the Civil War, New York was the nation's premier center of import-export and mercantile trade. After the Civil War, the city added manufacturing and factory production to its portfolio. Millions of European immigrants entered the city near the bottom of the social and economic hierarchy, working in entry-level jobs. They did not remain there long. These immigrants were

Table 5.5. Staten Island

	Mean % All Tracts			Mean % 90% Tracts			Mean % Labor Force		Mean Income Househould		Inc. Ratio
	Wt.	ForB.	Blk.	Wt.	ForB.	Blk.	/ Pop 16+	Unempl.	White	Black	Black/ White
1970	94	10	6	77.1 (74)	0	0	56	3			
1980	88	11	9	65.9 (60)	0	0	57	5			
1990	82	12	11	50.5 (48)	0	0	63	7	52091	31271	0.60
2000	74	17	11	34.7 (101)	0	0	60	6	70274	43952	0.63
2010	71	20	12	29 (29)	0	0	60	8	91902	56068	0.61

Source: US Census of Population, IPUMS National Historical Geographic Information System, 2014; Social Explorer, 2005–2017.

assimilated, and in subsequent generations, experienced upward mobility. The fact that freed slaves were already in New York before them, and were overlooked as the logical labor supply, has never been acknowledged. It was at this stage that people of African ancestry were assigned a subordinate status. Their inferior position became ingrained in the nineteenth-century social fabric of the city, that is, if it had not already been there during slavery.

The four propositions listed at the end of part 1 foretold this historic subordination, based upon where and how long Blacks and immigrants resided in the city in the 1800s. It should be evident from studying the city's evolution in the past century, that immigrant and Black subordination continues. Immigrants are now a diverse array of people of color, and the city's African American population has been supplemented with African descendants from the Caribbean and Africa. However, Blacks continue to represent the bottom of the city's social hierarchy in housing, with new immigrants of color following close behind.

Gentrification

The gentrification of Harlem, and other immigrant communities on Manhattan perpetuates the historic pattern of dispersing racial and ethnic communities in favor of higher-status residential use. This confirms proposition four: as the city grows beyond its Black enclaves, these communities are forced to resettle or be re-purposed. The same applies to the Bronx after the Cross-Bronx Expressway was driven through it. After the repurposing and gentrification of Upper Manhattan, the entire Bronx is now the largest area in New York City with the potential for residential redevelopment and re-purposing. Likewise, for every block gentrified on Manhattan Island, Blacks and immigrants have had to resettle in aged housing in an estimated four other blocks in the Bronx, Brooklyn, and Queens.

We are witnessing the whitening of Manhattan, and the residential dispersion of people of color into the outer boroughs. When faced with this fact, some people suggest that the presence of relatively high-income Blacks in Cambria Heights, or Rosedale in Queens, or the "gold-coast" tracts of Manhattan, is evidence that racial inequality in housing has waned. This ignores the history of Black and immigrant settlements in New York. From the earliest settlements to today, there is a pattern. Freed Blacks, as now the Black middle class, pioneer new enclaves. In time, these communities gain progressively higher concentrations of poorer Blacks, and then immigrants, as Whites flee. This is Harlem's history, as well as St. Albans's, right next to Cambria Heights. This confirms proposition two: freed and middle-class Blacks pioneer new Black communities.

There is final confirmation. Native White communities enjoyed the least disruption in land use and the highest residential longevity in the periods studied in this chapter. Robert Moses, Henry Hudson, and Harlem River highways on Manhattan were notable exceptions when high-status Whites were dislocated (Caro 1975). However, the overall stability of these communities confirm proposition three: residential land use is racially stratified.

Conclusion

Taking this long view puts the short-term in perspective. First, when a group is defined as low-status, based on their work, or on their non-White race or ethnicity, it virtually guarantees they will reside in low-status communities. Second, lower-status communities do not last forever and never did. They last two to three generations (50–75 years) before the children and grandchildren of residents are either displaced or transformed. The city's poorest residents live in communities with the shortest community half-life. Third, gentrification is only one phase of community transition. When higher-valued residents, based on their race and occupation, displace lower-valued residents, it suggests that the older community is in decline, while a second is emerging in the same physical space.

Logically, gentrification has a flipside. Higher-value residents vacate older, timeworn housing and lower-valued residents take this housing over. This is happening currently in Brooklyn and Queens. Housing that is more than 60 years old, located in historically White ethnic neighborhoods, is now being populated by Blacks and foreign-born residents. Racialized housing has hastened the displacement of Whites (White flight), but it also has accelerated the re-purposing and displacement of Black and Latino communities (gentrification).

The long view yields some surprises. Today, New York City is remarkably integrated by race and social class, when compared to 1910. The poor and wealthy, Black and White, as well as other social groups, are increasingly dispersed throughout the boroughs, and now residing within walking distance of one another. Ethnic ghettos have been broken down and are now shadows of what they once were. The speed at which the city's population declined, and is now repopulating, is extraordinary. The transferring and exchange of living spaces throughout the city are unprecedented as well. Blacks and Latino immigrants are being displaced from Harlem and Upper Manhattan, appear to be dispersed across the Bronx, Brooklyn, and Queens. Staten Island is the exception.

Manhattan is on its way to becoming a majority middle-class city with significant cultural and artistic assets enjoyed by only a few other cities in the world, such as Paris or London. However, to date, this "gilding" has required physically transplanting the issue of racialized inequality to other boroughs and surrounding municipalities, with the city's poor being displaced as part of a national trend (Howell & Timberlake, 2014; Kneebone & Garr, 2010).

The long view also raises new questions. Racialized inequality has always been based on a now-defunct hierarchy in a labor-intensive manufacturing and industrial economy. One then has to ask, "Are structural inequalities going to be any different in the city's emerging global economy?" Manufacturing in 1910 Manhattan required the efforts of 1,103,819 foreign-born European immigrants, plus space to house them. Now, the service sector only needs 455,248 foreign-born, mostly non-European residents, to fill its jobs. With the advent of robots to perform many service roles, the future may see progressively fewer service jobs being done by humans and a further reduced need for unskilled labor.

Finally, the ethnic composition of foreign-born residents has changed. The vast majority of foreign-born residents are now people of color, and not of European ancestry. This adds a new dimension to the prospects of immigrant assimilation. Will those who cannot pass for White be assimilated into the American public in the same way Irish, German, Italian and other Western European immigrants were? One of the first things all immigrants learn in their socialization is the American color hierarchy (Brettell, 2011). Even African immigrants learn to be wary of African Americans and try to avoid their fate at all cost. Given the ease of travel and communication in the global village, many immigrants of color may opt to maintain ties to their old country and become bicultural and bi-national instead.

Policy Implications

Social policy recommendations to reduce racial inequality presume that non-government and government entities alike know what steps to take. Although racial inequality is grounded in our economy and culture, it can be reduced. Here are some ideas to consider.

> **Truth and Reconciliation:** Past efforts to address racial inequality have had limited success for a reason. Presuming White racial superiority, and conversely, Black racial inferiority has been at the root of racial inequality and conflict ever since the end of the American Civil War. By not addressing this legacy directly, each generation fails to end the nightmare of race. This is a national problem. However, if the nation's most important city would acknowledge the legacy of structural racism and its role in its own

development, this would be a significant start. Efforts to challenge racism effectively will require continued efforts to monitor and address racism's toxic effects in employment, housing, education, policing and social services: something this book is recommending.

Gentrification: This research suggests that gentrification is just one aspect of racialized population change. The displaced do not just disappear, and those who replace them do not come out of anywhere. The poor, immigrants and Blacks are dispersed into working-class residential belts in the outer boroughs, as well as into suburbs and smaller cities surrounding New York City. They include the counties north of New York City, in northern New Jersey, and as far away as eastern Pennsylvania. New residents are coming from the outer suburbs, and from other metropolitan areas all over the nation, and the world. If cities are truly interested in shaping this change, they must do regional planning on a scale that goes well beyond just one city such as New York. Toronto, Vancouver, and Hong Kong have all done excellent jobs of integrating their workforces and preserving mixed-income housing through regional planning. They all serve as positive examples of how to do effective regional planning (Newman & Thornley, 2005).

Mixed-Income Housing: If left to market forces, Manhattan will become predominantly upper middle class, having to look for people in other boroughs to provide functional, first-response, and other essential and commercial services. This is a strategic nightmare in the making for New York City. It will create critical vulnerabilities, and continue to push up the cost of all services. Increasing below-market-rate housing with strong eligibility and enforcement provisions is essential to retaining middle- and working-class residents in the city, and is key to reducing race and class ghettoization in outer boroughs.

Job Transformation and Preparation: Economic transitions do not happen overnight. They are decades in the making. To ignore a former economy's workforce is unconscionable and costly. Every day, we can see the consequences of abandoning an entire workforce. Large numbers of mostly Black men are on our streets, without homes, insane, in jail, and without the skills they need to hold contemporary jobs. Older White men are becoming an increasing part of this world of lost laborers as well. As traditional industries decline, worker retraining should become an essential function of modern governments. This training should occur well before workers are laid off. Germany has a very effective national model of worker retraining (Jacoby, 2014). There, layoffs and plant closings must be announced far enough in advance for workers to be transferred, compensated or retrained (Kremp, 2015). Such practices could be implemented on a smaller scale in New York City, and surrounding municipalities could be encouraged to do the same.

Notes

1. These changes are not due to a change in the census micro-geography from Assembly Districts to Health Districts. If anything, Health Districts should have revealed more ethnic clustering since they are smaller geographies and more numerous than Assembly Districts.

2. Numeration of Health Districts in 1940 was in reverse of the numeration of earlier Assembly Districts.

References

Adalberto Aguirre, J., & Baker, D. (Eds.). (2008). *Structured inequality in the United States: Critical discussions on the continuing significance of race, ethnicity, and gender* (2 ed.). Upper Saddle River, NJ: Pearson Prentice Hall.

Alba, R., & Nee, V. (2003). *Remaking the American mainstream: Assimilation and contemporary immigration*. Cambridge: Harvard University Press.

Berlin, I., & Harris, L. (2005). Uncovering, discovering, and recovering: Digging in New York's slave past beyond the African burial ground. In I. Berlin & L. Harris (Eds.), *Slavery in New York* (pp. 1–28). New York, NY: The New Press.

Bernstein, I. (2005). Securing freedom: The challenges of Black Life in Civil War New York. In I. Berlin & L. Harris (Eds.), *Slavery in New York* (pp. 289–324). New York, NY: The New Press.

Bluestone, B., & Harrison, B. (1982). *The deindustrialization of America: Plant closing, community abandonment and the dismantling of basic industry*. New York, NY: Basic Books.

Bowser, B. (2007). *The Black Middle Class: Social mobility—and vulnerability*. Boulder, CO: Lynne Rienner Publishers.

Brettell, C. B. (2011). Experiencing everyday discrimination: A comparison across five immigrant populations. *Race and Social Problems, 3*(4), 266–79.

Caro, R. (1975). *The power broker: Robert Moses and the fall of New York*. New York, NY: Vintage Books.

Ehrenhalt, S. (1993). Economic and demographic change: the case of New York City. *Monthly Labor Review*, 40–50.

Foner, P., & Lewis, R. (Eds.). (1989). *Black workers: A documentary history from colonial times to the present*. Philadelphia, PA: Temple University Press.

Howell, A. J., & Timberlake, J. (2014). Racial and ethnic trends in the suburbanization of poverty in U.S. metropolitan areas, 1980–2010. *Journal of Urban Affairs, 36*(1), 79–98.

Jacoby, T. (2014, October 16). Why Germany is so much better at training its workers. *The Atlantic*.

Johnson, J. W. (1968). *Black Manhattan* (3 ed.). New York, NY: Atheneum (originally published 1930).

Kneebone, E., & Garr, E. (2010). *The suburbanization of poverty: Trends in metropolitan America, 2000 to 2008*. Retrieved from Washington, DC: Suburbanization-of-Poverty-in-the-Bay-Area1.pdf

Kremp, P. (2015). Employment and employee benefits in Germany: overview. *Practical Law*. Retrieved from http://us.practicallaw.com/3-503-3433#a569511.

Lovejoy, P., & Bowser, B. (Eds.). (2013). *The transatlantic slave trade and slavery: New directions in teaching and learning*. Trenton, NJ: Africa World Press.

McKay, C. (1968). *Harlem: Negro metropolis*. New York, NY: Harcourt Brace Jovanovich, Inc.

Newman, P., & Thornley, A. (2005). *Planning world cities: Globalization and urban politics*. New York, NY: Palgrave Macmillan.

Ottley, R., & Weatherby, W. (Eds.). (1967). *The negro in New York, NY: An informal social history 1626–1940*. New York, NY: Praeger Publishers.

Ovington, M. W. (1971). Before Harlem: The black ghetto in New York City. In J. J. Bracey, A. Meier, & E. Rudwick (Eds.), *The Rise of the Ghetto* (pp. 32–39). Belmont, CA: Wadsworth Publishing Company. (Reprinted from: *Half a Man: The status of the Negro in New York*. New York, NY: Longmans, Green, 1911, pp. 18–26).

Quigley, D. (2005). Southern slavery in a free city: Economy, politics, and culture. In I. Berlin & L. Harris (Eds.), *Slavery in New York* (pp. 263–88). New York, NY: The New Press.

Richardson, H. C. (2001). *The death of reconstruction: Race, labor, and politics in the post-Civil War North, 1865–1901*. Cambridge, MA: Harvard University Press.

U.S. Census of Population and Housing. (2014). *The National Historical Geographic Information System (NHGIS)*. Minneapolis, MN: Minnesota Population Center, University of Minnesota.

U.S. Congress. (2016). Servicemen's Adjustment Act (G.I. Bill). Retrieved from https://www.ourdocuments.gov/doc.php?doc=76.

U.S. Department of Transportation. (2016, July 12). History of the Interstate Highway System. Retrieved from http://www.fhwa.dot.gov/interstate/history.cfm.

White, S. (2005). Black life in freedom: Creating a popular culture. In I. Berlin & L. Harris (Eds.), *Slavery in New York* (pp. 147–80). New York, NY: The New Press.

Chapter 6

Latino Americans

The Evolving Latino Population in New York City

HECTOR R. CORDERO-GUZMÁN

A Global, Transnational, Dual, and Increasingly Latino City

Historically, New York City has had several identities. It has been a point of entry, a center for commerce, a seat of exchange, and a gateway connecting the U.S. to the rest of the world. New York has been described as an immigrant city, a global city, a transnational city, a dual city and, most recently, as one of the nation's largest Hispanic\Latino cities.[1]

The Pew Hispanic Center estimates that the Los Angeles metropolitan area, which includes Los Angeles, Long Beach, and Anaheim, is 45.1 percent Hispanic. This region has a Latino population of 5,979,000 persons, the largest number in the United States. The New York metropolitan area, which includes Newark and Jersey City, is 23.9 percent Latino, with 4,780,000 Hispanics. The Miami region has 2,554,000 Latinos, or 43.3 percent Hispanic, and in the Houston area, 36.4 percent of the local population is Latino, comprised of 2,335,000 persons.[2]

In the decades between 1970 and 2015, the number of immigrants in New York increased substantially, occasioned in part by the 1965 changes in U.S. immigration laws, and by increased employment and social opportunities in the city (Foner, 2000). At the same time, economic globalization and geopolitical developments broadened ties between various countries and regions in the Caribbean, Latin America, Asia, and Africa. There was a steady growth in the foreign-born population in New York City. From the 1970s to 1980, the proportion of foreign-born grew by 23.6 percent. By 1990, it was 28.4 percent, up to 35.9 percent by 2000, and by 2011, up again to 37.2 percent.

This is close to the 40 percent historical peak at the turn of the twentieth century (City of New York, 2013).

While other foreign-born populations decreased in New York City between 1930 and 1970, Latinos increased. There was a significant influx of U.S. citizens from Puerto Rico, along with African Americans from the South (Waldinger, 1996). In the 1950s and 1960s, New York City experienced widening diversity due to large and consecutive migrations from the Caribbean, Latin America, and Africa (Torres, 1995). As a result, by 2011, over three million foreign-born persons were living in New York City. This included about five percent from Africa, 28.1 percent from Asia, and 16.2 percent from Europe. Close to one million people, or 32.8 percent of the city, were from Latin America and the Hispanic Caribbean, and 19.8 percent, or about 600,000 people, were from the non-Hispanic Caribbean (City of New York, 2013). Migrants had a distinct Andean (Ecuador, Colombia, and Peru), and Caribbean (Dominican and West Indian) flavor.

This chapter traces the transformation of the Latino population in New York City, starting in the 1970s when a majority of Latinos came from Puerto Rico and finishing in 2014, by which time the Latino population had grown much more diverse. Today, there are sizeable communities from the Dominican Republic, Mexico, Central America and the Andean region of South America, in particular, Ecuador, Colombia, and Peru.

In addition to examining the socioeconomic characteristics of the Latino population, as it compares to the overall rates for New York City, this chapter also explores similarities and differences between the various Latino subgroups. Specifically, I look at education and migration patterns, citizenship status, group connections to the labor market, and income and poverty rates.

This analysis reveals that many Latino groups are experiencing ongoing impediments in the city. The chapter concludes with public policy recommendations that focus on how increased investments in education, workforce development and training, fair jobs policies, and anti-poverty initiatives would make it possible for Latinos to reach their full potential.

Understanding the Latino Presence in New York City

Several authors have written about the history of Latinos in New York City. Torres (1995) covered the topic in detail. Haslip-Viera and Baver (1996) did an extensive study of the New York Hispanic community. In their volume, they organize Hispanic history into four periods. In the period before 1900, immigrants were considered pioneers. From 1900 to 1945, foundations were built in communities and industries. In the period between 1945 and 1970,

Puerto Rican and other Latino populations grew enormously. Finally, from 1965 to the present, the Hispanic communities diversified extensively. Smith (2006) studied transnational ties that were involved in the growing Mexican migration, while Torres-Saillant and Hernandez (1998) described the migration of Dominicans into New York, as well as this group's sustained connections to and significance for their homeland.

Haslip-Viera and Baver (1996) focused on the changing and growing Latino populations in New York City. Torres (1995) addressed the evolving relations between Latinos, African Americans, and related Afro-Caribbean populations. Torres's work tells a rich and detailed history of migration, demographic change, added contact, and neighborhood succession in New York City. It puts in context the growth, increasing importance, and visibility of Latino communities.

Before 1900, most Latino immigrants were involved in commerce and trade. Many were political exiles fleeing persecution. In the second phase, between 1900 and 1945, there was a definite "Antillean Orientation" to Latino immigrants in New York City. These newcomers maintained close political, commercial, economic and social ties between New York City and the Caribbean (Haslip-Viera & Baver, 1996). In fact, New York City served as an administrative and commercial hub for the Caribbean. The countless investments, commercial and personal ties facilitated and sustained the early migrations from Puerto Rico, Cuba, and the Dominican Republic.

Puerto Rican migration surged during the third phase of Hispanic growth in New York City. Soon, small settlements expanded into larger communities throughout the Bronx, Manhattan, and Brooklyn. The garment industry, manufacturing, and trade played a crucial role in absorbing large segments of the Puerto Rican population, which in turn, branched out into other sectors of the economy.

In the fourth phase of Latino settlement, starting around 1965, the Hispanic population continued to grow and to diversify. People from Latin America and the Caribbean, from the Dominican Republic, the Andean region of South America, as well as Ecuador, Colombia, Peru, Mexico and Honduras, all, created their own communities (City of New York, 2013).

International migration from Latin America and the Caribbean grew significantly between 1970 and 2011. In 1970, there were approximately 211,000 immigrants from Latin America and the Hispanic Caribbean and another 113,000 from the non-Hispanic Caribbean (City of New York 2013). By 1990, the number of immigrants from Latin America and Hispanic Caribbean countries rose to 574,151, with an additional 410,532 people coming from the non-Hispanic Caribbean. The Latino and Caribbean populations continued to grow to 984,722 persons born in Latin America and the Hispanic Caribbean, excluding Puerto Rico, and another 595,740 persons born in the non-Hispanic Caribbean (City of New York 2013).

Haslip-Viera and Baver (1996) divide the period from 1965 to the present, into two additional phases. The first phase, from 1965 to 2001, was a period of massive growth in the foreign-born population. Hispanics grew from 18.2 percent (1.4 million) of the City's population in 1970, to 35.9 percent (2.8 million) in 2001. That means 800,000 foreign-born Latinos arrived in the single decade between 1990 and 2000. In the second phase, from 2001 to the present, the total population of the city hovered at around 8.3 million persons, with the number of foreign-born being near 3 million, or 37.2 percent of the city's population.

In 1986, President Reagan signed a bill that made it possible for millions of immigrants to normalize their migrant status. These individuals and their families could now stay legally in the United States. This happened at a time when New York City's economy was recovering from the financial crisis of the 1970s. The local economic elites encouraged the city to refocus its economy on the finance, insurance, real estate and services industries, and to connect itself to the global market. Mollenkopf and Castells write:

> This largely white, disproportionately male stratum has benefited directly and disproportionately in the development of New York City's corporate economy. Clearly, the economic boom between 1977 and 1987 gave great impotence to this group, which, through 1989, provided the core constituency for the dominant electoral coalition. Much of what happens in arenas ranging from politics and the housing market, patterns of childbearing and even crime reflects the interests, values, and lifestyles of this stratum. (Mollenkopf & Castells, 1991, p. 17)

The 1989 election of Mayor David Dinkins marked a period when a majority-minority coalition worked to develop progressive policies that supported low-income populations and communities. However, social and racial pressures built up and, as Mollenkopf and Castells warned, local elites reasserted themselves by focusing on issues like "quality of life" and "crime." Their backlash was directed at native minority populations, African Americans and Puerto Ricans.

The backlash started in 1993, at the beginning of Rudolph Giuliani's mayoral term. Poor, minority and immigrant populations were held responsible for reducing the quality of life in the city, because of their dependence on government services and programs. The growing anti-immigrant dispute culminated in 1996 when new immigration and welfare reform laws were passed. These laws limited immigrant access to the social safety net and initiated the detention and deportation drives that persist to this day. The "White restoration," that occurred after the brief Dinkins mayoralty was a case of the dominant political and economic groups in New York City reasserting themselves. These groups retrenched the welfare state, cut social services and expanded the police state. After 2001, community policing was rejected, and more stringent stop-and-frisk policies were introduced. The 9/11 attack ushered in an era of national security for New York City. Efforts to achieve comprehensive immigration reform were slowed both locally and nationally. Despite these efforts, the Latino population continues to grow based on internal migration and a high birth rate.

The Giuliani anti-welfare and police state policies continued with the 2001 election of Mayor Michael Bloomberg. This technocratic mayor, with his significant wealth, global influence, and strong ties to the financial, real estate, and information industries was close to the elites of New York City. Throughout his 12 years in office, economic development strategies focused on attracting and retaining large corporations and employers. New York City became a playground for both American and international privileged classes.

New York, dubbed the "entertainment and services city," aligned itself with real estate, financial and corporate interests. Neighborhood-based, local developments were passed over in favor of exclusive, large retail spaces in the more selective areas of the city. As a result, the largest sectors of the economy, in order of size, became education and health services; professional and business services; trade, transportation, and utilities. The government sector is followed by financial activities, leisure and hospitality, accommodation and food services, information technologies and services, social assistance. Then, there are a range of other personal and professional services, construction and, lastly, a small specialized manufacturing sector (Milkman & Ott, 2014).

Changing Demographics

The Latino population in New York State is large and growing. As of mid-2017, the state's total population is nearly 19.1 million persons. Of this total, 2.7 million are Blacks\African Americans (14.2 percent), and 3.5 million are Hispanics\Latinos (18.5 percent). That is a combined total of 32.7 percent of the total state population or one in three residents. New York City itself has a total population of 8.3 million, with 1.8 million Blacks/African Americans, and 2.4 million Latinos. Taken together, the 4.3 million Blacks/African Americans and Latinos constitute close to 51.3 percent of the total population of New York City.

Puerto Ricans continue to be the largest group of Latinos, followed closely by Dominicans. Mexicans have quickly become the third largest Latino group in New York City, increasing at a faster pace than the Ecuadorian, Colombian,

Honduran, Salvadorian and Peruvian populations. There are also immigrants from Cuba, Guatemala, Panama, Spain, Argentina, Venezuela, Nicaragua, Chile, Costa Rica, Bolivia, Uruguay, Paraguay, plus smaller numbers of people from other Central and South American countries.

An analysis of population data for both the city and state of New York points to some notable trends. First, the Latino population is increasing overall in both localities. Second, the proportion of the population that is of Latino\Hispanic origin has changed. Third, the national origins of the Latino population are increasingly diverse. This is important because there are as many differences as there are similarities among Latino subgroups. Analysts have merged data for all Latino subgroups into one broad "Hispanic/Latino" category. However, this obscures relevant factors that define the differences between Latino subgroups. Fourth, over the last three decades, the socioeconomic characteristics that distinguish between Latinos and non-Hispanic White, Black and Asian populations have diverged. Data suggest there are now higher poverty levels among Latinos, with local labor market trends and external forces intensifying the inequality among Latinos.

In this chapter, the population of New York City is divided into eight groups, four of which are Latino (see figure 6.1). These include Puerto Ricans,

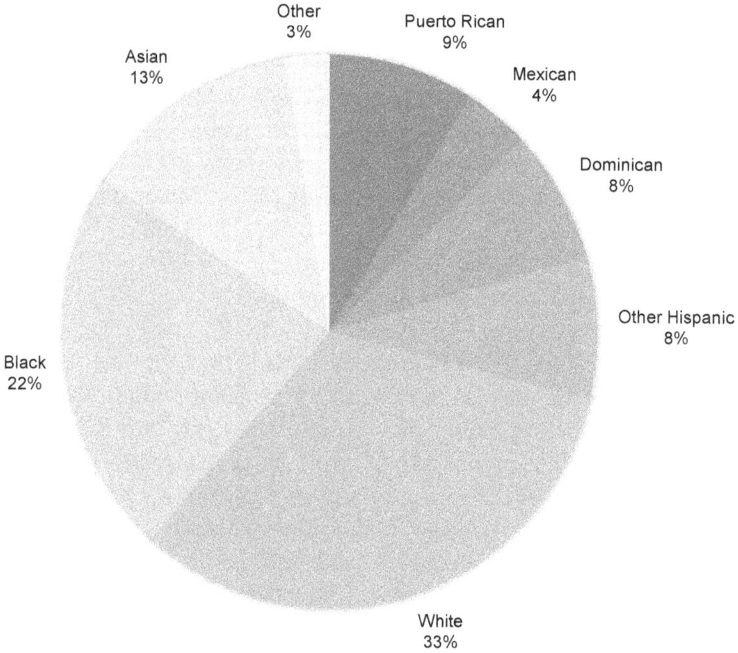

Figure 6.1. Population in New York City. *Source:* American Community Survey Public Use Microdata Sample, five-year file.

Mexicans, Dominicans, and all other groups of Hispanic origin. These four groups are then compared to non-Hispanic Whites, non-Hispanic Blacks, Asians, and a small category (three percent of the total) of others.

Geographically, Puerto Ricans are concentrated in the Bronx, and in Brooklyn. Mexicans are distributed evenly among the boroughs of Queens, Brooklyn, and the Bronx. Dominicans are also concentrated in the Bronx, with others living in Manhattan, Brooklyn, and Queens. Other Hispanics are based in Queens and Brooklyn, with smaller numbers in the Bronx and Manhattan.

There are distinct differences in the citizenship status of the various Latino subgroups. Puerto Ricans are U.S. citizens; 70 percent were born on the mainland, and 28 percent were born on the island. Only a small contingent has been born abroad. Almost 46 percent of Mexican New Yorkers are born in the United States. On the other hand, nearly the same percentage were not citizens as of 2015. Seven percent of this group has been naturalized. Thirty-nine percent of Dominicans are born in the United States, 29 percent are not citizens, and about 30 percent have been naturalized. For other Hispanics, about 39 percent were born in the United States; another 29 percent are not citizens, and the remaining 32 percent have been naturalized.

The Latino population in New York City is young: more than one-third of the people under 29 years of age are Latino (see figure 6.2). That means the

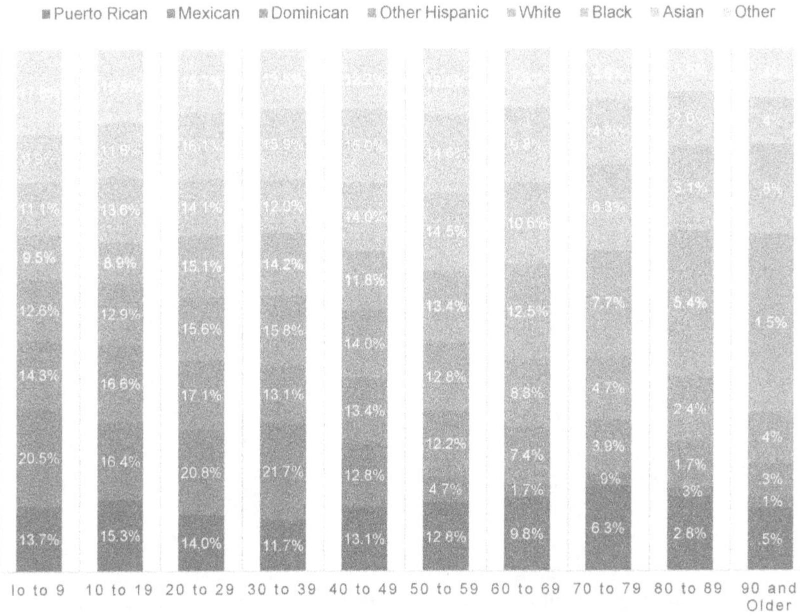

Figure 6.2. Age in New York City. *Source:* American Community Survey Public Use Microdata Sample, five-year file, 2014.

policies and programs NYC puts in place today can have a long-term impact on the advancement of the Latino population, as much as on the economic health of the city and the state.

Since so many Latinos are young, education is a critical issue. How much access these individuals have to quality education and its resources is key to understanding education outcomes. About 28 percent of Puerto Ricans in New York are enrolled in school, 34 percent of Mexicans, 32 percent of Dominicans, and 28 percent of other Hispanics. Latino school enrollment is slightly higher than White enrollment and is similar to other minorities. It is worth noting, however, that although Latinos enroll in school at rates similar to other segments, their educational outcomes and college attendance rates are significantly lower. Figure 6.3 provides comparative data on the levels of education achieved by different population groups, based on national origin.

Latinos achieve lower education levels than Whites, Blacks, and Asians. Recent data on high school graduation rates, by ethnic group, shows that Latinos have the lowest proportion of individuals with high school diplomas, or "some college or more." Only 38 percent of Puerto Ricans, 26 percent of Mexicans, 36 percent of Dominicans, and 42 percent of "Other Hispanics"

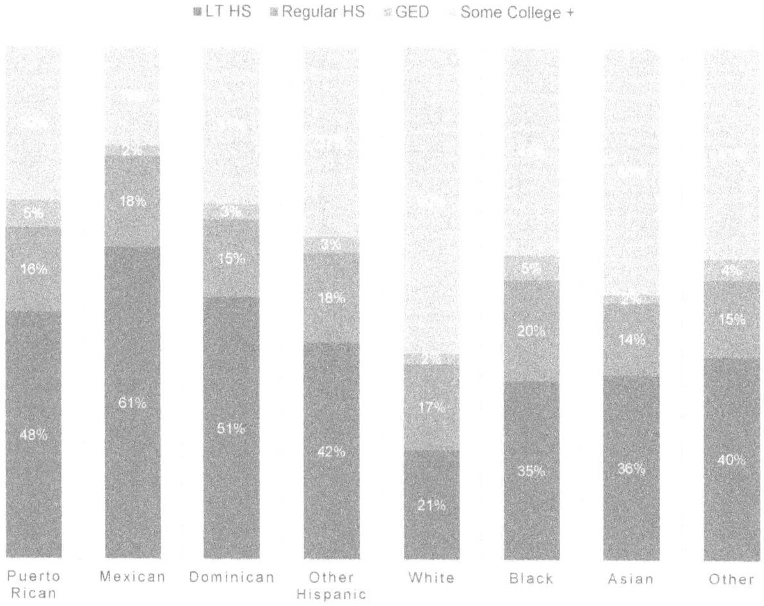

Figure 6.3. Completed education in New York City. *Source:* American Community Survey Public Use Microdata Sample, five-year file, 2014.

have high school diplomas. In contrast, nearly 63 percent of Whites have a high school diploma, 51 percent of Blacks, 47 percent of Asians, and 48 percent of "Others." The shares of Whites and Asians "in college" are much higher than for Latinos. Puerto Ricans and Mexicans have the lowest college enrollment rates. College access is the critical barrier (Banks & Oliveira, 2011; Levitan, 2005; Treschan, 2010). These differences in educational achievement affect employment rates, the occupations available, and income and poverty levels for all Latino groups in New York.

Employment, Poverty, and Income

The extent of employment or unemployment is very different among the various Latino subgroups. In New York City, Mexicans hold the highest proportion of the labor force, and Puerto Ricans the lowest. Figure 6.4 shows that 42 percent of Puerto Ricans are employed, 64 percent of Mexicans, 54 percent of Dominicans, and 58 percent of other Hispanics. African Americans are the exception with slightly lower labor force participation. Data indicate that about eight percent of both Puerto Ricans and Dominicans are unemployed,

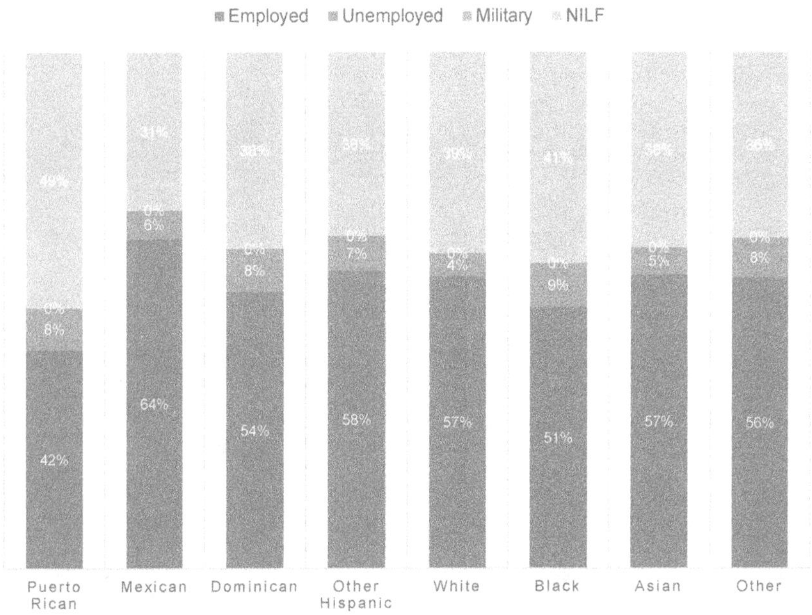

Figure 6.4. Employment status in New York City. *Source:* American Community Survey Public Use Microdata Sample, five-year file, 2014.

and about nine percent of Blacks. Mexicans and other Hispanics have an unemployment rate of six percent and seven percent, respectively. Whites and Asians have the lowest levels of unemployment in New York, at four percent and five percent each. The percentage of the population out of the labor force also varies by national origin. Forty-nine percent of Puerto Ricans, 41 percent of Blacks, 39 percent of Whites, 38 percent of Dominicans, 38 percent of Asians and 36 percent of other Hispanics are not in the labor force. At 31 percent, Mexicans have the highest rate of labor force participation of any group in the city.

Latinos experience much higher poverty rates than Whites, with additional disparities among Latino subgroups. Figure 6.5 illustrates this. Poverty rates range from *extreme poverty*, representing persons with family incomes below 50 percent of the poverty cut-off point, to *below poverty*, where individuals are between 51 and 100 percent of the federal poverty threshold. African Americans and Hispanics combined, comprise over half (51.3 percent) of the City's total population. However, these same groups constitute almost two-thirds (65.1 percent) of the city's poor: a total of 1.1 million persons. More than one in four Blacks and Hispanics live below the poverty level, and almost

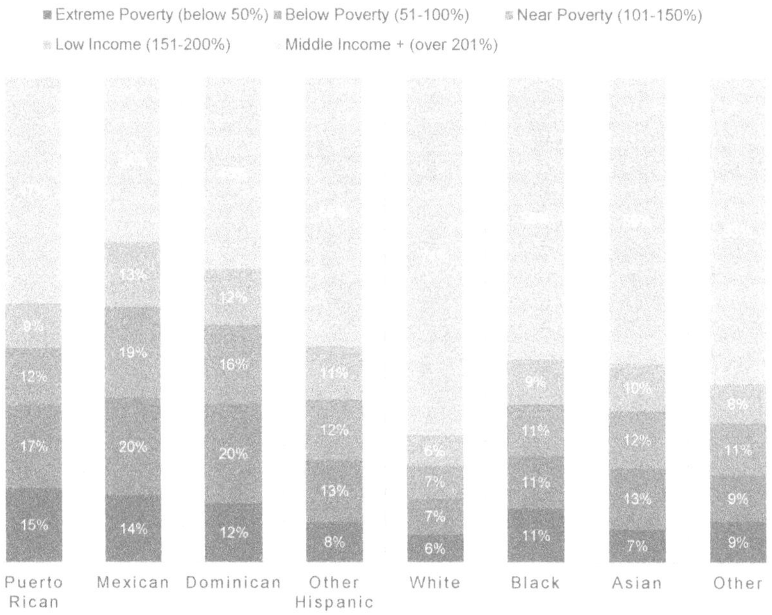

Figure 6.5. Poverty level in New York City. *Source:* American Community Survey Public Use Microdata Sample, five-year file, 2014.

one out of every two people (43.9 percent) have incomes near the poverty threshold, and below 150 percent of the poverty line.

The overall poverty rate in New York City is 20.6 percent. That is approximately 1.7 million persons, out of 8.3 million residents, who live below the federal poverty level. Serious as this figure is, it still obscures the significant differences that exist due to a person's race or national origin. For example, non-Hispanic Whites make up 32.4 percent of the City's total population but are only 19.5 percent of the poor. Their poverty rate is 12.4 percent or one in ten. Blacks are 22.3 percent of the population, and 24.1 percent of the poor. Slightly over one in five Blacks live in poverty (22.4 percent). Hispanics, on the other hand, make up only 29 percent of the city's population, yet 40.9 percent of them are poor, and have a poverty rate of 29.1 percent (more than one in four). About 33 percent of Puerto Ricans live in poverty, as do 34 percent of Mexicans in New York City. Thirty-three percent of Dominicans have family incomes below poverty, and 21 percent of the other Hispanics do as well.

Figure 6.6 shows the different income distribution patterns for the eight ethnic groups analyzed. Twenty-three percent of the total are Whites with

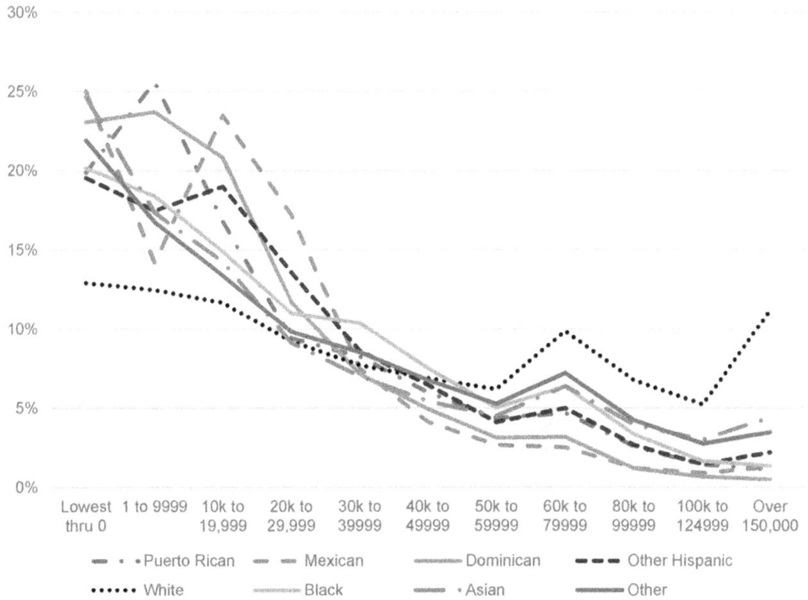

Figure 6.6. Income distribution by group in New York City. *Source:* American Community Survey Public Use Microdata Sample, five-year file, 2014.

median incomes over $80,000. That is the largest percentage of all groups in this income category. As the graph illustrates, Hispanics are concentrated in the lowest income categories: fewer than nine percent have incomes over $80,000.

When reviewing income distribution within populations in New York City, it becomes clear that, even though a racial group may claim a larger proportion of the population, they do not earn a greater proportion of overall income. Figure 6.7 highlights this. The data show that non-Hispanic Whites form 34 percent of the population, but earn more than half of the total income in New York City. Blacks comprise 22 percent of the city's population, yet bring in only 16 percent of the total income earned in the city. Asians are now 14 percent of the population, but they collect close to 12 percent of total income. Individuals classified as "Other" constitute nearly two percent of the population and draw about two percent of total income. Latinos, on the other hand, make up 27 percent of the population, yet realize only 15 percent of total income.

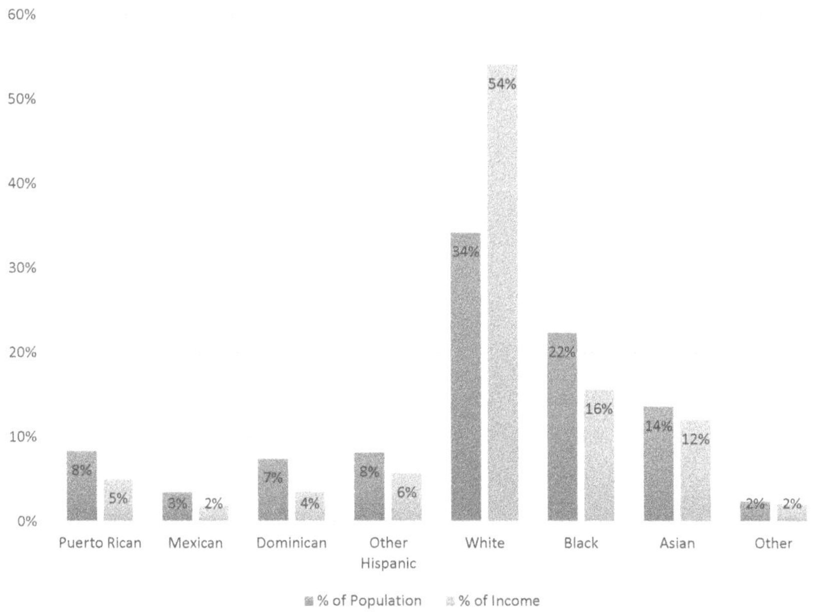

Figure 6.7. Distribution of income and population in New York City. American Community Survey Public Use Microdata Sample, five-year file, 2014.

The Future of Latinos in New York City

Over the last six decades, the Latino community in New York City has grown and diversified, both in numbers and in importance. Close to 29 percent of New Yorkers claim some Latino origin, and almost one in three New Yorkers under 19 years of age is of Hispanic origin. Latino influence is unmistakable in many neighborhoods, communities, restaurants, shops, and theaters that enhance the economic and cultural life of the city.

As a Latino city, New York has become very important throughout Latin America and the Caribbean. However, the city is also a challenging place, where immigrants must work long hours for low pay, and have to cope with exploitative employers and landlords. While New York offers opportunities for many, it also traps large numbers in poverty. Opportunities for advancement are limited often by a person's race, social class, or place of residence (Parrott, 2014).

Latino migrant communities operate in a more globalized context. Although they may live in New York City, they retain many transnational connections to their original countries and communities. Maintaining these ties is vital to the relationships immigrant communities want to have with their home countries and regions. New York City is a center of exchange, action, and struggle. Here, the global meets the local and the local must take into account global trends, forces and population dynamics that affect everyone.

There are notable differences in the composition, characteristics, concentrations, socioeconomic background and outcomes between various Latino subgroups. Moreover, the distinctions do not stop there. There are also disparities in socioeconomic and demographic characteristics between Latinos and other groups (Asians, Whites, African Americans, West Indians, and others). For instance, the Latino population has the highest poverty rate in New York City. As a poorer population, Latinos experience persistent disadvantages and socioeconomic inequality. They are more vulnerable to economic shocks, to changes in social and public policies, and to the reductions in social services.

Over the last decade, the contrast between being a citizen and being a non-citizen, particularly an undocumented one, has increased greatly. During this time, the processes and means for acquiring citizenship have become more restrictive. Because of this, the number of undocumented immigrants has risen, as have their vulnerabilities.

With changes in the structure and functioning of the economy and labor markets, new opportunities have arisen in the service sector. However, these same changes have polarized the labor market and concentrated many immigrants in low-wage jobs. Individuals have been locked into more insecure jobs, with fewer opportunities for socioeconomic and occupational mobility (Carlson, 2010; Milkman & Ott, 2014).

To reduce levels of poverty and inequality among Latinos, policies must be reviewed in several domains. Existing immigration policy and the failure to pass comprehensive immigration reform have trapped many Latinos in their undocumented status and limited their employment and labor market opportunities. Immigration policy is a federal issue, but New York City needs to continue to develop its own local policies aimed at protecting the rights of all residents, including immigrants. Community-based organizations offer some protection, but they too need to redouble their efforts to educate immigrants on their rights and to inform them of the paths that are open to them. Education policies and outcomes are critical. Increasing the quality of public education, expanding access to college, and improving graduation rates all impact Latinos directly (Treschan 2010).

Latino low-wage workers need assistance to protect their employment rights and to receive fair pay. That is why campaigns to increase wages, to reduce wage and hour law violations, to increase occupational safety and health are so essential. Latino workers also need to be better connected to workforce development, job training and mobility opportunities (Cordero-Guzman & Nunez, 2013; Milkman & Ott, 2014). Social welfare policies that erode worker benefits can limit people's access to necessary resources, and advancement opportunities. Restoring a realistic social safety net is critical, particularly for low-income Latinos. In addition to social policies and employment rights, criminal justice policies that target young African Americans and Latinos need to be replaced by productive investments in education, job training and work opportunities (Banks & Oliveira, 2011).

Some actions have been taken to reduce negative outcomes for out-of-school youth, but the long-term impact of existing programs have yet to be measured. Generic approaches directed unilaterally at all youth may have a broad appeal, but they do not address the specific needs and challenges faced by each ethnic community. There have been some attempts to address this shortcoming, such as the Young Men Initiative. More targeted efforts such as this work to reduce specific barriers that limit group opportunities. Programmatic efforts are vital because minority families and children need culturally sensitive assistance to elevate their education levels, to gain better access to training opportunities, to connect to the labor market, and to climb more advanced career ladders. It is only through individual growth and community economic development that minority groups can increase their incomes, and escape poverty (Banks & Oliveira, 2011).

Unfortunately, there is a programmatic disconnect that exists today. While the need for social services and anti-poverty programs continues to grow, city and state governments are cutting program funds. Latinos and other immigrants have responded by forming their own community organizations, and by engaging in social action. A vibrant civil movement and a Latino advocacy infrastructure are seeking to counteract the limitations and restrictions put in place by the neo-liberal state (Cordero-Guzman & Nunez, 2013).

Latino organizations strive to manage existing resources, to offer needed services and to represent the interests of their communities. Many groups engage in community-building activities and promote the ties between immigrant communities and their home countries. These are just some of the ways Latino and immigrant community-based organizations play a central role in evolving political structures in New York, and respond to the city's hardening class and racial lines (Cordero-Guzman, et al., 2013; Milkman & Ott, 2014).

In 2013, the current mayor of New York City, Bill de Blasio, campaigned with promises to reduce inequality, to invest in neighborhood initiatives, and to support marginalized populations. His election brought some cautious optimism to the Latino community. People hoped his administration might put forward policies that would address Latino issues. There is broad support for increasing the minimum wage, for offering a living wage in publicly funded projects, and for providing paid sick days (Cordero-Guzman, 2011). Despite the mayor's support, local elites continue to exert their power over New York City's development agendas and apply their influence over the distribution of investments and resources. As Andres Torres (2013) has argued, the existing class and ethnic division of labor and resources in New York have concrete repercussions for the Latino community and the prospects of Latino youth. He writes:

> We can summarize Latino socioeconomic patterns based on the experience of the past few decades. First generation Latinos work intensively in low wage jobs, while their native-born children split among three pathways: (1) those who move up into professional positions through higher education, (2) those who gain access to stable, often unionized, jobs providing somewhat decent incomes, and (3) those who get stuck in poverty jobs or are sidelined from the formal labor market altogether. The last group, some 25 percent to 30 percent of Latino households, represents the hardest hit by the wrenching economic difficulties of recent years. Latino and African American poverty is between double and three times the level of white New Yorkers. (Torres, 2013)

As the Latino population grows and diversifies, it is critical for city administrators to understand changes in population trends, evolving demographics, and changes in education, employment, labor, income and poverty levels. To date, mainstream policy development has not kept pace with the increased importance of the Latino community. Latinos are still invisible at the state and city levels of policy analyses and discussions. Before anyone can address the challenges and external forces that affect the Latino community, they need to analyze and understand them fully. It is equally crucial to understand how policy issues and challenges affect distinct subgroups in precise ways and to be clear on what can be done to address the express needs of Latino subgroups and populations.

Notes

1. Throughout this chapter, I will use the term Hispanic and Latino interchangeably.

2. See http://www.pewhispanic.org/interactives/hispanic-population-in-select-u-s-metropolitan-areas/.

References

Banks, D., & Oliveira, A. (2011). *Young men's initiative: Report to the mayor from the chairs*. New York, NY: Office of the Mayor.

Carlson, N. F. (2010). *Futures in the balance: Meeting the workforce development needs of Latinos in New York City*. New York, NY: Hispanic Federation.

City of New York. (2013). *The newest New Yorkers*. New York, NY: Department of City Planning.

Cordero-Guzman, H. R. (2011). *An analysis of the opinions of New York City residents on minimum wage, paid sick days, and living wages: Results from a survey of 1200 New Yorkers*. New York, NY: Baruch College School of Public Affairs, The City University of New York.

Cordero-Guzman, H. R., & Nunez, D. (2013). Immigrant labor in the U.S. Economy: A profile. *New Labor Forum, 22*(2), 16–27.

Foner, N. (2000). *From Ellis Island to JFK: New York's two great waves of immigration*. New York, NY: Russell Sage Foundation and Yale University Press.

Haslip-Viera, G., & Baver, S. L. (1996). *Latinos in New York: Communities in transition*. Notre Dame, IN: University of Notre Dame Press.

Levitan, M. (2005). *Out of school, out of work . . . out of luck? New York City's disconnected youth*. New York, NY: Community Service Society.

Milkman, R., & Ott, E. (2014). *New labor in New York: Precarious workers and the future of the labor movement*. Ithaca, NY: Cornell University Press.

Mollenkopf, J. H., & Castells, M. (Eds.). (1991). *Dual city: Restructuring New York*. New York, NY: Russel Sage Foundation.

Parrott, J. (2014). *Over one-third of New York City Employees are paid less than $14 an hour; workers of color are twice as likely to be low-wage*. New York, NY: Fiscal Policy Institute.

Smith, R. C. (2006). *Mexican New York: Transnational lives of new immigrants*. Berkeley, CA: University of California Press.

Torres, A. (1995). *Between the melting pot and the mosaic: African Americans and Puerto Ricans in the New York political economy*. Philadelphia: Temple University Press.

Torres, A. (2013). Latino New York: An introduction. *NACLA report on the Americas* (Winter issue).

Torres-Saillant, S., & Hernandez, R. (1998). *The Dominican Americans (New Americans)*. Westport, CT: Greenwood Publishing.

Treschan, L. (2010). *Latino Youth in New York City: School, work, and income trends for New York's largest group of young people*. New York, NY: Community Service Society.

Waldinger, R. (1996). *Still the PROMISED City? African-Americans and new immigrants in postindustrial New York*. Cambridge, MA: Harvard University Press.

Chapter 7

West Indian Americans

Select Socioeconomic Characteristics of West Indian Immigration in New York City

Calvin Holder and Aubrey W. Bonnett

The United States government's immigration policy was highly restrictive in the first six decades of the twentieth century. Its draconian Immigration Acts of 1921, 1924, and 1952 sharply curtailed immigration from Eastern and Southern Europe and virtually halted it from Africa, Asia, the Caribbean and Latin America. The policy reflected the prevailing view in American society that immigrants from the third world were less desirable than those from Western and Northern Europe, from which the majority of American immigrants came. Indeed, the policy in its application to Africa, Asia, the Caribbean and Latin America was glaringly racist. However, in 1965, Congress passed the Hart-Celler Immigration Act, which swept away the restrictive acts and ushered in a new and liberal immigration policy. The upshot of this change in policy has been an unprecedented wave of immigration to the United States from Africa, Asia, the Caribbean, and Latin America. Millions of brown and black immigrants have settled in the country since the enactment of the law some fifty-two years ago (Waters & Ueda, 2007). Among them have been millions from the English-speaking Caribbean, people who call themselves "West Indians" and are so identified by the U.S. government in its census records.

This chapter examines selective socio-economic characteristics of the post–1965 West Indian immigration to the United States and New York City. In so doing, it will at times compare them to similar characteristics of the majority population, non-Latino/Hispanic Whites, to assess the extent to which

West Indians have attained economic and social equity. In its assessment, we argue that many West Indian have made a successful adjustment to life in the U.S., becoming productive citizens, while others have found life in their new homeland extremely challenging, resulting in an existence fraught with social and economic problems. The essay draws heavily from U.S. Census Bureau records.[1] It also utilizes primary and secondary literature on immigrants. The authors, West Indian immigrants, have been students of West Indian immigration since the early 1970s and, in this capacity, have resided for decades in communities with large numbers of West Indians and have been members of West Indian organizations. In other words, we have been deeply engaged in the life of the community as scholars and residents. This chapter is informed by our experiences.

The Census put the number of West Indians in the country who self-identify as West Indians at 1,402,699 in 2011–13.[2] Jamaicans are the largest group, accounting for almost fifty percent of the movement's population. Their representation is not surprising. Of the nations of the English-speaking Caribbean, Jamaica is second in size only to Guyana. See table 7.1 below.

Moreover, Jamaicans have a history of emigrating in significant numbers. This is evidenced by their settlement in the tens of thousands in Panama and other Central American countries in the first two decades of the last century and the United Kingdom in the 1950s and 1960s (Glennie & Chappell, 2010, p. 1; Grant, 2009, pp. 23–33). However, the Census data do not accurately convey the full representation of individuals in the West Indian immigration. There are more West Indians in the country than are evident in the data.

Table 7.1. West Indian Population, 2011–2013

Country of Origin	Population (%)	Men	Women
Antigua and Barbuda	20,515 (1.4)	43.7%	56.3%
Bahamas	32,485 (2.3)	46.8%	53.2%
Barbados	51,544 (3.6)	43.5%	56.5%
Dominica	27,433 (1.9)	45.6%	54.4%
Grenada	31,902 (2.2)	40.9%	59.1%
Guyana	259,815 (18.5)	46.4%	53.6%
Jamaica	714,743 (50.6)	42.1%	57.9%
St. Lucia	21,754 (1.5)	40.5%	59.5%
Trinidad and Tobago	232,026 (16.4)	42.8%	57.2%
St. Vincent	22,827 (1.6)	41.3%	58.7%
Total West Indians	1,402,699 (100%)	43.4%	56.6%

Source: U.S. Census Bureau, 2016.

Tens of thousands came on visitors' visas, never returned to their countries of origin and were never able to acquire legal status. These "unauthorized" immigrants are concentrated overwhelmingly in New York City, and other metropolises along the Eastern Seaboard (Thomas, 2012, p. 6).

The composition of the West Indian Immigration reflects the multiracial character of West Indian societies. Black West Indians are its majority, but another racial group is also well represented: Indo-West Indians, descendants of East Indians who were brought to the West Indies as indentured servants in the nineteenth and early twentieth centuries. Numbering in the thousands, they are overwhelmingly from Trinidad and Guyana, with the latter country providing the majority. Significantly less well represented are Whites, Chinese, and individuals of Indian-Black, Black-Chinese, and Indian-Black-Chinese backgrounds. These individuals come almost exclusively from Trinidad, Guyana, and Jamaica, all countries with diverse racial and ethnic communities (Holder, 2007).

West Indians have settled throughout much of the United States, but the great majority of them have been domiciled along the Eastern Seaboard, especially in its Northeast corridor. New York City and its environs, as in the past, are at the center of this migration; more specifically the outer boroughs of Brooklyn, the Bronx, Queens, and Long Island and Westchester; few West Indians now reside in the Harlem, the historical locus of Black settlement in the city. Boston and its suburbs, and Cambridge are home to thousands of West Indians, as well as Hartford, Philadelphia, and Metropolitan Washington, D.C. West Indian immigrants have also established roots in Atlanta and its suburbs, especially Stone Mountain, Dallas, Houston, and Florida, notably the suburbs of Miami, Fort Lauderdale, and communities near Walt Disney World. Returning "home" is an integral part of West Indian acculturation, and Florida's geographical location best facilitates West Indians' visits. Moreover, Florida's subtropical climate approximates the climate to which they had been accustomed at home. West Indians have also taken up residence in California (Los Angeles) and Illinois (Chicago) (Holder, 2007).

The dynamic of American racial divisions manifests itself, to some extent, in the pattern of settlement of West Indians. For example, Afro-West Indians and Indo-West Indians live in separate communities in New York City. The former are concentrated overwhelmingly in the North Bronx, and in Flatbush, East Flatbush, Canarsie, Flatlands and Crown Heights in Brooklyn. Some Indo-West Indians are also residents of these communities, but the great majority of them live elsewhere in the city. Their stronghold is Richmond Hill, Queens. This heavy concentration in Richmond Hill has led to settlement in adjacent communities like Ozone Park and South Ozone Park, but still Richmond Hill, a thriving community, is their primary center (Holder, 2007).

At this juncture in West Indian immigration, it is evident that immigrants constitute an aging population. The median age of West Indians nationally is 47.9 compared to 42.6 for the White population (U.S. Bureau of the Census, 2016). The vast majority of West Indians arrived in the twentieth century when barriers to emigrating were not as formidable as they are. Indeed, until the passage of immigration legislation in 1986, it was relatively easy to enter the United States from the West Indies, either with permanent resident status or on a visitor's visa. Those with the latter status acquired permanent residency through marriage or under the amnesty provisions of the immigration legislation of the mid-1980s. In this century, visitors' visas have been much more difficult to acquire as the United States government has imposed more challenging barriers to entering the country. The result of these changes is that the flow of the West Indian immigration has declined significantly and is expressed acutely in the aging of its population. If the present low rate of entry continues unabated, it will be only a matter of time before the movement becomes a shadow of its former self.

Education

At present, nationally, West Indians have achieved a level of education that is not equal but close to that of White Americans. The data in table 7.2 on educational attainment for West Indians and White persons 25 years and older illustrate this point. West Indians of African descent from the islands above are compared with White Americans. There are proportionately more West Indians without high school diplomas, but there is a higher high school completion rate compared to Whites for all except Bahamians. West Indians have proportionately fewer with some college or who have attained an associate's degree. Interestingly, in this category, Bahamians have more. Fewer West Indians are college graduates, and fewer have attained graduate or professional degrees when compared to White Americans.

Public secondary education has been free and mandatory in the United States from the early decades of the past century. It was not free in many of the countries from which immigrants hail until these countries became independent starting in the early 1960s. Significant numbers of immigrants who arrived as adults in the 1970s had not completed high school. The data in table 7.2 regarding higher educational attainment contradicts part of the popular belief in West Indian exceptionalism. That is West Indians have high educational achievement levels and are virtually indistinguishable from Whites Americans, showing that White racism is somehow not a barrier for non-native-born Blacks (Sowell, 1975).

One might argue as well that the higher education statistics in table 7.2 for self-identified, mostly Black West Indians are only a few percentage points

Table 7.2. Educational Attainment of West Indian Immigrants and Whites (not Hispanics or Latinos) Twenty-Five Years and Over, 2011–2013

Country of Immigrants	Population	Less Than High School Diploma	High School Graduate	Some College or Associate	Bachelor's Degree	Graduate or Prof	Total Percent
Antigua & Barbuda	19,093	17.2%	32.5%	25.1%	14.2%	11.1%	100%
Bahamas	26,666	11.6%	24.1%	34.7%	17.5%	12.1%	100%
Barbados	49,343	14.3%	33.8%	28.9%	14.4%	8.7%	100%
Dominica	23,711	21.0%	31.4%	23.7%	15.5%	8.4%	100%
Grenada	29,394	15.4%	34.3%	27.0%	14.7%	8.5%	100%
Guyana	231,462	21.2%	33.1%	23.3%	13.8%	8.7%	100%
Jamaica	632,004	16.2%	32.4%	28.4%	14.7%	8.3%	100%
St. Lucia	18,674	17.7%	35.2%	26.5%	13.1%	7.5%	100%
Trinidad and Tobago	213,977	13.4%	31.8%	30.1%	14.8%	9.8%	100%
St. Vincent	20,836	22.7%	32.3%	24.8%	11.4%	8.8%	100%
West Indian	1,265,160	17.1%	32.1%	27.3%	14.4%	9.2%	100%
US Whites	140,911,329	8.6%	28.7%	30.1%	20.2%	12.3%	100%

Source: U.S. Census Bureau, 2016.

away from White Americans. In which case, several factors might explain the somewhat favorable comparisons. The West Indian movement has been, to a degree, a very selective one, containing ambitious individuals, many of whom arrived already with secondary or tertiary education (Holder, 2007, p. 678). Moreover, West Indians have attached a high premium to education, as it has been the primary accelerant for social mobility in their homeland. In addition, they have found in the United States ample opportunities to acquire a secondary and tertiary education (Bashi, Clarke, & Clarke, 2001; M. C. Waters, 1999, pp. 66, 253).

Since the 1960s, thousands of West Indians in New York City have graduated from colleges and universities in the United States. This has been most apparent at the City University of New York. Heavily concentrated in New York City, West Indians in the thousands have pursued an education at the University, where the tuition has been modest, and government loans have been readily available to defray tuition cost. Several hundred other West Indians have been educated at some of the nation's most selective colleges and universities. Many of these immigrants were educated at elite secondary schools in their homeland and excelled academically after their arrival in the United States. Some in New York City were beneficiaries of programs, such as Prep for Prep, which recruited Black students with academic promise for elite high schools in the city and preparatory schools in the Northeast. Upon graduation, they attended highly selective U.S. universities. Others graduated from universities and colleges like CUNY and pursued professional degrees at selective institutions (Brown, 2008; Massey, Mooney, Torres, & Charles, 2007).

While some West Indians have attained high levels of education and material success, others have failed to acquire a quality education that would adequately prepare them for productive participation in the marketplace. In her seminal study of West Indian immigrants in the 1990s, Mary Waters comprehensively documents the marginal academic performance of some public schools in New York City with a majority of West Indian immigrants and their children. In these schools, the immigrants with the poorest academic records were those who had had a minimal level of education in the West Indies; they were often from rural communities in their homeland, where educational facilities were substandard (Holder, 2007; M. C. Waters, 1999). In the almost two decades since Waters' study, the problem of poor academic achievement continues, but is less pronounced among women students.

Gender and Marriage

Nationally, West Indian immigration has been a movement primarily of adult women. Of the 1,415,044 West Indians, 43.4 percent were men, and 56.6

women (table 7.1). The highest representation of females, slightly more than 59 percent, was among St. Lucians and Grenadians, and the lowest among Bahamians and Guyanese. Why the preponderance of women?

Men were no less motivated to emigrate to the United States than their female counterparts, although both tended to view the United States through a somewhat paradisiacal lens: For both genders, the United States was the proverbial land where an omnipotent power guaranteed material success. However, the confluence of some factors during immigration facilitated the dominance of women.

Impressionistic evidence suggests that the changed status of women in the West Indies during immigration helped forge the gender disparity. Since their advent as national states, women in virtually all the West Indian countries made impressive gains in critically important areas of public life. This is obviously in banking and other commercial enterprises, government bureaucracies, the healthcare industry, and educational institutions. Women have dominated the teaching profession at the primary and secondary levels for years; and women have become a formidable presence among lawyers, physicians, nurses, accountants, business executives and government bureaucrats the past five decades. At the University of the West Indies, women are over-represented. Women of all socio-economic backgrounds have exhibited an entrepreneurial spirit that has resulted in establishing and maintaining viable and successful small businesses.[3] Women, irrespective of their material circumstances, have exhibited tremendous drive and ambition. Thus, often satisfying the criteria to emigrate, and attracted by the greater opportunities for professional growth and material success, some already ambitious women in the West Indies opted for a life in the United States.

The U.S. government's immigration policies also privileged certain categories of immigrants that worked to the advantage of women. Nurses and other healthcare professional were accorded preferential entry to satisfy the economy's demand for such workers. West Indian nurses availed themselves of this opportunity to emigrate. They found employment in private and public medical facilities in some American cities (Bashi et al., 2001, p. 219; Holder, 2007; McCabe, 2012, p. 4).

Emigrating in significantly higher numbers than nurses were domestic servants. American immigration policy permitted middle- and upper-middle-class American families to sponsor West Indians to work as domestics in their households. In the West Indies, the women sponsored had been mainly domestics, bank tellers, sales clerks, housewives, industrial workers, and white- and blue-collar government workers. Some of them came directly to the United States as domestics; others arrived on visitors' visas and entered domestic service. Their employers subsequently sponsored them.

American law stipulates that a citizen of another country is eligible for immigrant status who marries an American citizen. This law became a vehicle by which many West Indian women attained immigrant status and eventual citizenship. Cognizant of the law, some women entered the country on a visitor's visa, which entitled them to stay for a period. Some fell in love with American citizens. They got married, which made citizenship possible. Others entered into "arranged marriages"—that is marriages only in name, sometimes facilitated by attorneys who specialized in immigration law. They paid thousands of dollars to their sham "husbands" and lawyers. In the past several decades, this has not been an especially productive avenue to legal status, as the U.S. immigration authorities have developed effective methods to counter it. For example, when the women in these marriages apply for immigrant status, they and their prospective spouses are closely questioned about their personal lives. When major discrepancies emerge in the course of the questioning, these women are denied immigrant status and are sometimes prosecuted and deported. Their spouses can be prosecuted as well. Still, these marriages have made it possible for significant numbers of West Indian women (and men) to become legal residents of the United States.[4] Legal marriages have been an important characteristic feature of West Indian life in the United States, as the Census data illustrates in table 7.3.

There was a noticeably higher rate of marriage among Whites—6.7 percent higher—than West Indians. Whites were less likely than West Indians to have been separated or to never have been married; the difference for the former circumstance was 3.5 percent and the latter 3.4 percent respectively. There were no meaningful differences between the two constituencies for persons divorced and widowed.

West Indians marry mainly individuals from their homeland or another West Indian country. Many West Indians arrived in the United States already married; they and their spouses almost invariably are from the same country. In the United States, where immigrants from the various countries live near each other, marriages involving West Indians from different countries are quite common. It is only in the United States (and the United Kingdom) that such marriages occur with frequency (Holder, 2007, p. 677).

Interestingly, marriages involving individuals from the two principal immigrant constituencies—Afro-West Indians and Indo-West Indians—are not commonplace. They have occurred, especially among Trinidadians, and to a much lesser extent among Guyanese. However, marriage for the two constituencies has been essentially an intraracial affair. Religious traditions have often played a decisive role in precluding marriage between the two groups in the West Indies and the United States. Residing in separate neigh-

Table 7.3. Marital Status of West Indians* and Whites (not Hispanics or Latinos) Fifteen Years and Over, 2011–2013

Ethnicity	Population	Married	Widowed	Divorced	Separated	Never Married	Total Percent
West Indians*	1,381,967	45.7%	6.0%	12.5%	5.1%	30.7%	100%
Whites	165,403,603	52.4%	6.8%	11.9%	1.6%	27.3%	100%

*From ten selected nations, self-identifying as Caribbean. *Source:* U.S. Census Bureau, 2016.

borhoods in cities like New York City has been a contributing factor as well (Holder, 2007, p. 677).

In addition to marriages, the composition of West Indians households provides additional perspective on the immigrants' family life in the United States in comparison to Whites as the norm. The Census data once again are the most authoritative source here (table is not shown). For West Indians, the data indicate that an average of 72.0 percent of the 655,438 of Black West Indians, who identify as from Caribbean households, had family households compared to 64.3 percent for Whites. On average 37.8 percent of West Indian households were married couples compared to the average of 51.3 of White households. For female-headed households with children under 18 years old, the comparison was an average of 27.9 percent for West Indians households compared to an average of 9.2 percent for Whites. Whites had on average a higher percent of non-family households than West Indians, 35.7 percent compared to 28 percent respectively. These statistics reveal an outcome of an immigrant reliance on one another (endogamy) and of having high educational achievement on one end and low educational achievement—less than high school—on the other. The result is having on average higher rates of family households than the norm, but also there are higher rates of female-headed households with children than the norm.

West Indians and African Americans

Although West Indians and African Americans have lived in the same communities, marriages involving persons from the two groups have not occurred with any regularity. Many in both groups harbor negatives stereotypes of each other, a contributing factor to few intermarriages. Impressionistic evidence suggests the following: Indo-West Indians and Black West Indian women have been most resistant to marrying African Americans; African American men have evinced a strong inclination not to marry outside their ethnic group. Still, West Indians and African Americans have gotten married; most often these are unions between African American women and West Indian men (Holder, 2007, pp. 677, 680).

Poverty

Poverty is an issue in West Indian family life. Of the 468,770 West Indian families from the ten island nations focused on in this analysis, 14.7 percent lived in poverty. Nationally, poverty affects Whites families less so. Of White families, 7.3 percent were in poverty in 2011–13.

Table 7.4. Poverty Rate for West Indian and White Families (not Hispanics or Latinos), 2011–2013

Ethnicity	Population	All Families	Married Families	Female-Household, No Husband Present
West Indians	468,770	14.7%	6.8%	23.9%
Whites	51,933,743	7.3%	3.9%	24.3%

Source: U.S. Census Bureau, 2016.

Married-couple- and female-householder, no husband present, families accounted for 6.8 percent and 23.9 percent respectively of West Indian families in poverty. In contrast, the percentages for White families in these two categories were 3.9 percent and 24.3 percent respectively.[5] Poverty was more pronounced among married-couple West Indian families, almost twice the percentage of White married-couple families. Given the much greater prosperity of White communities, the data show anticipated results. However, what stands out in the data, in particular, are the virtually identical poverty rates for White and West Indian female-headed families. What these families share in common is the presence in them of significant numbers of children, many of them minors.

West Indians share a common view regarding the use of corporal punishment in childrearing. Its use is pervasive among many working-class West Indian parents, and it has brought a number of them in conflict with various state institutions: public schools, police departments, and child welfare agencies. It is less common among middle-class West Indians parents, who are professionals. However, there is little disagreement among West Indians, of both classes, that corporal punishment is a morally appropriate practice in childrearing, particularly for disruptive and disrespectful children. West Indians adhere to the view that sparing the rod corrupts the child and reserve a visceral contempt for parents of unruly children. The downside to this childrearing practice is that it provides some parents with validation for the brutalization of their children (M. C. Waters, 1999, pp. 226–36, 240–41).

Employment and Occupation

West Indians have been actively engaged in the American economy. The Census data show that 69.9 percent of West Indian immigrants 16 years and older were in the labor force compared with 63.3 percent among Whites. Among West

Indians, 7.6 percent are unemployed compared with 4.8 percent of Whites. West Indians participated in the labor force at a higher rate than Whites did, but they experienced a conspicuously higher level of unemployment.

Some of the comparative data are subject to multiple interpretations: The higher rate of participation of West Indians in the labor force could be the result of greater employment opportunities for them. Alternatively, unlike in the White population, more of them are required to work, to survive in their adopted homeland. The data on unemployment is consistent with the fact that, historically, Whites have had low levels of unemployment compared to other groups in the society.

In what occupations have West Indians secured employment? The census data highlight five areas. They pertain to civilians 16 years and over.

Of the 849,898 West Indian immigrants, 16 years and over, 31.5 percent were in management, business, science and arts occupations compared to 40.4 percent of Whites. In services, West Indians are 29.2 percent compared with 15.2 percent of Whites. In sales and office occupations, West Indians are 21.3 percent compared to 25 percent of Whites. Nine percent of employed West Indians are in natural resources, construction and maintenance compared to 8.6 percent of Whites. Finally, in production, transportation, and material moving, nine percent of the West Indians workforce are in these occupations compared to 10 percent of Whites. Most obvious is the inescapably higher representation of West Indians in service occupations—a difference of 14.0 percent. In New York City, Boston, and the environs of Tampa and Miami, West Indians, notably immigrant women, have been heavily concentrated in service occupations. Thousands of the women have been employed in these cities as nurses' aides and nannies and other service occupations (Model, 2001, p. 60). Most of them receive modest compensation—minimum wage or slightly above—for their labor. However, some are compensated well. The former has sometimes been hard-pressed to maintain the viability of their families and household.

West Indians number in the thousands in the healthcare industry; in New York, Florida, and Massachusetts, West Indians are represented well among Black professionals—nurses and physicians, lawyers, teachers, academics, and business executives. Some of these nurses, physicians, and academics acquired their training outside the United States, but the great majority of them were educated in the United States. They are often products of elite high schools in the West Indies and made their entry into the middle and upper middle classes by taking advantage of the economic opportunities American society offered them (Holder, 2007, p. 683).

Some West Indians have made inroads in skilled trades closed to Blacks in the past and have attained a modicum of success. In the West Indies,

Table 7.5. Occupations for West Indian and White (not Hispanic or Latino) Civilians Sixteen Years+

Ethnicity	Population	Man., Bus., Sci., and Arts	Service	Sales and and Office	Nat. Res., Const, and Maint.	Prod., Trans., and Materials	Total Percent
West Indians	849,898	31.5%	29.2%	21.3%	9.0%	9%	100%
Whites	94,719,984	40.4%	15.2%	25%	8.6%	10%	100%

Source: U.S. Census Bureau, 2016.

persons of color dominate the skilled trades and thousands from this group—carpenters, electricians, automobile mechanics, and masons—have been part of the West Indian immigration. They emigrated at a time when the efforts of African Americans helped coerce skilled trade unions into ending their most egregious discriminatory policies against Blacks. Consequently, skilled West Indians in cities like New York and Boston have secured membership in the unions and remunerative employment at large construction projects. Other skilled West Indians have earned their livelihood providing services to the Black community. A small number of them have established construction companies, automobile shops and hardware stores.

A small class of businesspersons has emerged in the immigrant movement, one that has provided special services for immigrants. They have catered to their compatriots' culinary needs and have provided shipping service to immigrants' homelands. Although they have been in the country for decades, West Indians have clung to their culinary habits, engendered at home, and have passed them on to their American-born children (Indeed, their cuisine has even acquired a measure of popularity among persons outside the West Indian community). To satisfy this appetite, West Indian entrepreneurs have established scores of restaurants and bakeries. They are found mainly in New York City, Boston, Fort Lauderdale, and Hartford in communities with significant West Indian populations. In New York City, for example, there are restaurants such as Sugar Cane, The Door, and Suede; there are Allan Bakery and Kingston Bakery, Tower Isles, and Golden Crust, purveyors of Jamaican patties. Tower Isles and Golden Crust patties are found in some supermarkets in Metropolitan New York, and Golden Crust has franchises throughout the Northeast, Florida, and Georgia. There is a plethora of shipping companies whose services West Indians utilize to send American products to friends and family in their homelands. Dennis Shipping Company is one of the largest and most successful of its kind (Moskin & Severson, 2005).

The presence of West Indian entrepreneurs must not obscure the fact that in communities in which West Indians reside Blacks do not own most of the businesses. In New York City, with few exceptions, Koreans own the produce stores, cleaners, and hair emporiums that proliferate in the West Indian community. There are arguably more Chinese restaurants than West Indian restaurants. In the main, Yemenis run the candy stores, often located near subway stations, and Palestinians own the supermarkets like Key Food, Associated, and C-Town. There is no doubt that West Indians own businesses in the communities in which they are the majority or constitute a significant numerical presence, but they are not the major entrepreneurs in these communities.[6]

Income and Housing

Employment data and business activities as well as household and family incomes, shed information on West Indians' economic adjustment from the ten island nations focused on in this analysis. About "Income in the Past 12 Months (in 2013 Inflation-Adjusted Dollars," the Census data reveal the following in table 7.6.

The median income for immigrant West Indian households was $49,238 and $72,260 for White households; the latter earned $15,663 more than the former. Even though West Indians reside in parts of the country where income is generally highest, White households have had glaringly higher incomes. In contrast, the difference in per capita incomes ($31,477 versus $33,144) is negligible compared to median household income.

Whereas West Indians' per capita income compares favorably to Whites', their housing tenure pales in comparison to that of Whites. The Census data indicate that 48.4 percent of West Indian occupied housing units were owner-occupied compared to 71.5 percent of White occupied housing units—a 23.1 percent difference. West Indians privilege the acquisition of family property. Why, then, is there a comparatively low representation among West Indian owners of housing units? A plausible explanation lies in where West Indians' reside in the United States. They are concentrated heavily in expensive cities such as New York City and Boston, where the price of housing is prohibitively high. Indeed, the homeownership that they have attained is a testament to the importance they place on it. Moreover, the prohibitively high price of housing in New York and Boston is a factor in why West Indians have settled increasingly in Florida, Georgia, and Texas, where the cost of housing is more affordable.

West Indians' homeownership does not approximate that of Whites by any stretch of the imagination. Nevertheless, the median value of West

Table 7.6. Median Household Income and Per Capita Income for West Indians and Whites (not Hispanic or Latino), 2011–2013

Ethnicity	Families	Median Household Income	Population	Per Capita Income
West Indians	468,770	$56,597	1,415,044	$31,477
Whites	51,933,743	$72,260	197,212,499	$33,144

Source: U.S. Census Bureau, 2016.

Indian owner-occupied housing units was greater by tens of thousands of dollars than the median value of White owner-occupied housing units. The Census shows that median value for owner-occupied housing by Whites was $177,200 compared with a median value of West Indian owner-occupied units of $254,950. The explanation for this major difference in the value of the housing units of the respective populations can be attributed again to the location of West Indian housing units: Many, if not most, are in cities where the housing prices are among the highest in the country.

Some West Indian homeowners in New York City, Boston, Miami, Fort Lauderdale, and Orlando are still feeling the deleterious effects of the Great Recession on their property values. Some own houses that are still underwater or valued only slightly more than their original cost. Moreover, the prospects that their properties will attain their original purchasing price or a meaningful increase in equity are not especially promising. The most important investment these immigrants are likely to make in their adopted homeland has become their albatross. More than a few of these homeowners purchased these houses at highly inflated prices; they were often aided and abetted by unscrupulous realtors, West Indians among them, who used unethical and sometimes illegal means to make their purchases possible.[7]

Crime, Drugs, and Gangs

West Indians have been engaged as well in business activities that do not show up in census reports that are an integral part of their informal economy. For decades, West Indians have run illicit lottery operations, the "numbers," in New York City. Residents would give their numbers runner a four-digit number and money to play their number at certain odds. All the numbers were collected, and the numbers organizers would select several winning numbers. Those with matching numbers would be paid at the odds they paid for by their runner. Therefore, two dollars at one hundred-to-one could earn $200 and so on. Numbers organizations were highly lucrative, employed hundreds of runners and were one of the largest part-time employers in Harlem and Bedford-Stuyvesant. Legal lotteries replaced numbers.

Some West Indians have been involved in importing, distributing, and retailing marijuana and cocaine since the 1960s. They have used American and Caribbean carriers to transport the drugs to the mainland for distribution and retail. Drug dealing has been immensely profitable for some West Indians as was numbers dealing before 1960. Money made from the sale of cocaine and marijuana has been laundered to establish businesses in New York, other American cities and in the West Indies (Treaster, 1988).

West Indians' involvement in drugs intensified in the mid-1980s with the advent of the crack cocaine epidemic in New York City's Black and Latino communities. West Indians became major dealers of cocaine in its powdered and crystal (crack) forms, as well as marijuana, which was imported primarily from Jamaica, where it was grown commercially. Most important among them were the dealers who had formed gangs or "posses"—criminal groups whose roots were in impoverished Kingston, Jamaica, neighborhoods. They exhibited an assertiveness and entrepreneurial skills frequently associated with Jamaicans. In doing so, the posses were a dominant presence in the distribution of cocaine and marijuana in New York City. They were also in communities across the country in which there was a demand for these drugs. They also extorted Black businesses. The posses were ruthless in their use of violence to achieve their business objectives; they brutally killed their competitors and wrought fear in the communities in which they plied their products. Their criminal conduct cast a shadow on the image of West Indians as law-abiding citizens. In time, the posses came under the scrutiny of the Federal government and various city and state authorities, which resulted in the arrest, prosecution, and incarceration of posse members. The intervention of state authorities and the end of crack epidemic have diminished the posses' footprint in the communities they once had such debilitating impact (Kasinitz, 1992, pp. 79–84). While greatly diminished, the posses are still a part of the fabric of West Indian life in the United States.

West Indians also have been involved in the Bloods and Crips gangs. Formed in California, the gangs have succeeded, primarily in this century by recruiting young West Indians in prison and high schools. As in the case of the posses, these West Indian Bloods and Crips deal crack cocaine, marijuana, and other drugs, as well as participate in other illegal activities. There have been deadly confrontations involving West Indian members of the Bloods and the Crips in Brooklyn. Their conflict has even marred the annual Labor Day West Indian Carnival in New York. However, these West Indian gang members have not acquired a reputation as fierce as that associated with posse members (McPhee, 2000).

For several decades now, West Indians have been caught up in the criminal justice system in cities where immigrants have been concentrated. At present, several thousand are in the system: The overwhelming majority of them are males and are incarcerated, on probation or parole. Convicted of serious felonies, they have daunting futures. For those who are citizens, their opportunities for meaningful and legal employment are seriously circumscribed, once they are no longer yoked to the criminal justice system. Those incarcerated and without citizenship will be deported to their country of origin immediately after serving their prison sentences. They will face a grim life, like others who preceded them, often living as strangers in the countries of their birth (Staff, 2016).

Conclusion

The picture that emerges of West Indian adjustment in the United States is one of both failure and success. Poverty, family instability, significant levels of incarceration, poor student performance seem to be increasing rather than diminishing in West Indian communities. However, these social ills are only part of West Indians' adjustment, and ultimately do not define their immigration. Some immigrants have done exceptionally well, attaining extraordinary material success and others have made it into the middle classes. Most are working class and living comparatively stable lives. What is unique about West Indians Americans is that they pay a heavy toll for their common racial identity with African Americans. Like millions of others in the country, West Indians are mostly hard-working, law-abiding, productive citizens who have yet to attain equity with White Americans despite their efforts to do so.

Notes

1. See *Selected Population Profile in the United States: 2011–2013 American Community Survey 3-Year Estimates*. Data was taken for Antigua and Barbuda, the Bahamas, Barbados, Dominica, Grenada, Guyana, St. Lucia, Jamaica, Trinidad and Tobago, and St. Vincent. In addition, *Selected Population in the United States, 2011–2013 American Community Survey 3-Year Estimates* was used for Blacks, White alone, not Hispanic or Latino. Both sets of statistics are accessible under ACS Public Use Microdata. See document S0201 for each group.

2. Our analyses are based upon our experience with immigrants from the geographic Caribbean. We selected immigrants from only ten island nations (recognizing that Guyana is part of South America). We do not use the U.S. Census pan-Caribbean geographic definition that would also include the French and Spanish Islands. We have selected only immigrants predominantly of African ancestry who self-identity as "Caribbean." For example, Haitians will correct you if you refer to them as "Caribbean."

3. In the Inaugural Dame Nita Barrow Lecture at the University of Toronto in December 1997, Dr. Violet E. Barriteau presented "Are Caribbean Women Taking Over? Contradictions for Women in Caribbean Societies" in which she acknowledged the significant social and economic progress women made in West Indian societies and the backlash it engendered. University of Toronto (Oise.utoronto.com).

4. Based on the authors' unpublished research; *The New York Times* in 2010 ran a long article on how the Federal government acted to prevent immigrants from

attaining permanent residency or citizenship through fraudulent marriages (*The New York Times*, July 11, 2010).

5. Table V11.
6. Based on authors' unpublished research.
7. Based on authors' unpublished research.

References

Bashi, V. F., Clarke, B., & Clarke, A. Y. (2001). Experiencing success: Structuring the perception of opportunities for West Indians. In N. Foner (Ed.), *Islands in the city: West Indian migration to New York City* (pp. 210–20). Berkeley, CA: University of California Press.

Brown, D. (2008, June 24). Prep for prep: A brilliant education idea realized. *Huffington Post*. Retrieved from https://www.huffingtonpost.com/dan-brown/prep-for-prep--a-brillian_b_108932.html.

Glennie, A., & Chappell, L. (2010). Jamaica from diverse beginnings to diaspora in the developed world. Washington, D.C., *Migration Policy Institute*, 1–14.

Grant, C. (2009). *The Negro with a hat: The rise and fall of Marcus Garvey*. London, England: Vintage Books.

Holder, C. B. (2007). West Indies. In M. Waters & R. Ueda (Eds.), *The new Americans: A guide to immigration since 1965* (pp. 675–76). Cambridge, MA: Harvard University Press.

Kasinitz, P. (1992). *Caribbean New York: Black immigrants and the politics of race*. Ithaca, NY: Cornell University Press.

Massey, D. S., Mooney, M., Torres, K. C., & Charles, C. Z. (2007). Black immigrants and Black natives attending selective colleges in the United States. *American Journal of Education, 113*, 243–71.

McCabe, K. (2012). Foreign-born healthcare workers in the United States. Washington, D.C., *Migration Policy Institute*, 1–9.

McPhee, M. (2000, November 26). Gangs waging war on streets: Crips and Bloods take their deadly battle to Brooklyn. *New York Daily News*.

Model, S. (2001). Where New York West Indians work. In N. Foner (Ed.), *Islands in the city: West Indian migration to New York City* (pp. 60). Berkeley, CA: University of California Press.

Moskin, J., & Severson, K. (2005, July 20). Jamaican passions. *The New York Times*. Retrieved from https://www.nytimes.com/2005/07/20/dining/arts/jamaican-passions.html.

Sowell, T. (1975). *Race and economics*. New York, NY: D. McKay Comp.

Staff. (2016, November 3). 20,000 Jamaicans deported from the United States. *Jamaica Star*. Retrieved from http://jamaica-star.com/article/20161103/20000-jamaicans-deported-united-states.

Thomas, K. J. A. (2012). A Demographic profile of Black Caribbean immigrants in the United States. Washington, D.C., *Migration Policy Institute*, 1–20.

Treaster, J. (1988, November 13). Jamaican gangs take root in U.S. *The New York Times*. Retrieved from https://www.nytimes.com/1988/11/13/world/jamaica-s-gangs-take-root-in-us.html.

U.S. Bureau of the Census. (2016). American community survey PUMS data. Retrieved from http://www.census.gov/programs-surveys/acs/data/pums.html.

Waters, M., & Ueda, R. (Eds.). (2007). *The New Americans: A guide to immigration since 1965*. Cambridge, MA: Harvard University Press.

Waters, M. C. (1999). *Black identities: West Indian immigrant dreams and realities*. Cambridge, MA: Harvard University Press.

Chapter 8

Asian Americans

Immigration, Diversity, and Disparity

Howard Shih

The 1965 Immigration Act opened the United States to immigrants from other parts of the world beyond Europe. Fifty years later, Asian immigrants are the fastest growing major race and ethnic group in the city. During this time, the Asian community in New York City has also become increasingly diverse, going from a largely Chinese population to one that contains 17 different Asian ethnicities. Concurrent with this rise of diversity has been an increase in income inequality among Asians in New York City. This chapter will examine various dimensions of income inequality in Asian New York communities. After summarizing the historical context of income inequality, immigration restrictions and racial discrimination against Asian Americans, we will examine the factors contributing to increasing income inequality within the Asian community. Brief profiles of Asian workers in poverty in contrast with high-income Asian workers will highlight the rapid growth at both ends of the economic spectrum contributing to the increased inequality. The chapter will also show the increasing burden of housing costs on the Asian community.

Historical Context

The misperception of Asians as the model minority[1] is a recent construct. Much of the impetus for the Chinese Exclusion Act of 1882 and subsequent acts that resulted in bans on almost all immigration from Asia in the late 19th and early 20th centuries stemmed from the exact same arguments that inform the current debate around Hispanic immigration. Similar to Hispanic immigrants today, Asians then were viewed as direct competitors to other low-skilled workers and were blamed for downward pressure on wages (Lee, 2015). Asians were viewed as well as unable to assimilate and as perpetual foreigners. Other laws restricted the rights of Asians to naturalize. In addition, restrictions on property rights were put in place to limit opportunities for Asian Americans. Preferential systems, thought to exclude Asians, were put in place to favor highly-skilled immigrants when immigration reforms were enacted. This included the 1952 McCarran-Walter Immigration and Naturalization Act, which allowed naturalization and the Immigration, and Nationality Act of 1965, which lifted restrictions on immigration from Asian. As a result, an unanticipated wave of highly-skilled, highly-educated Asian immigrants availed themselves of the opportunity to come to the United States. Mainstream portrayals emphasize these highly-skilled Asian immigrants and their accomplishments, despite the fact that Asian refugees and low-skilled immigrants continued to arrive and are the majority of immigrants from Asia after 1965.

With the lifting of immigration restrictions, the Asian population in New York City began to grow at a rapid pace, from just over 40,000 in 1960 to over 1.3 million in 2015. Changes in immigration laws also have increased the diversity in the Asian communities of New York City. In 1960, more than three-in-four Asians in New York City identified as Chinese. The only other two Asian categories in the 1960 Census were Japanese, who were 14 percent of the Asian New Yorker population, and Filipino, who were 10 percent. By 2015, less than half of Asians in the city identified as Chinese and over 30 percent of Asians identified as either Bangladeshi, Bhutanese, Indian, Nepalese, Pakistani or Sri Lankan. The diversity visa program started by the Immigration Act of 1990 helped to jump start immigration from Bangladesh, Nepal, and Pakistan in the 1990s. As a result, New York City now has the largest Bangladeshi and Pakistani communities in the United States.

One of the major challenges of working with historical data on the Asian community is that the definition of who is Asian has changed over time. For example, Asian Indians were classified as Hindu in the 1940 census and earlier. They were White in the 1970 census and Asian Indian from the 1980 census going forward. The 1980 Census was the first decennial census to use "a standard set of expanded race categories . . . for all states" (Gibson & Jung, 2005). This included expanded Asian ethnic group categories to include Chinese, Japanese, Filipino, Korean, Asian Indian, and Vietnamese. One of the goals of this chapter is to shed light on the increasing diversity of the Asian community in New York City and the impact that has had on income inequality among Asian Americans. Consequentially, this chapter will largely focus on the changes in income inequality from 1980 to the present, in order to present inequality among Asian ethnicities on a consistent basis.

Two papers in the last four years examine the impact of the changes in immigration laws on overall Asian income inequality relative to Whites and Blacks (Dunleep & Sanders, 2012; Hilger, 2016). Because of restrictive immigration laws before 1965, the wage gap between Asians and Whites before 1965 cannot be explained by immigration since most Asian residents were not born in the United States at the time (Dunleep & Sanders, 2012). Analyses in both papers show that substantial wage gaps between Asians and Whites existed in 1960 and earlier but were erased by the late 1960s. After controlling for factors such as education, English proficiency, self-employment, industry and occupation, work experience, regional differences in wages, and immigration, both papers conclude that the wage gap between Asians and Whites closed primarily due to a decline in anti-Asian discrimination in the labor market. The fact is educational attainment of native-born Asians was already higher than it was for Whites by 1960 (Dunleep & Sanders, 2012).[2] Asians had near parity with Whites in the Army General Classification Test scores in 1943 (Hilger, 2016). However, continuing inequality belies the myth that Asians were able to achieve economic parity with Whites purely through education and hard work. Even with the recent shift in anti-Asian discrimination in the labor market, Asians still face challenges in the labor market. A recent report from the U.S Department of Labor found that Asian workers had the second highest share of unemployed workers who were long-term unemployed and earned less than White workers who had similar characteristics and jobs (United States Department of Labor, 2016).

An analysis of 1960 Census data and the 2010–14 American Community Survey data/IPUMS-USA shows a similar trend in New York State. Asians were already highly educated by 1960. In 1960, for adults age 25 years and older, Asians in New York State were twice as likely to have college degrees as Whites, yet poverty rates for Asians in New York State was at 31 percent, compared to 26 percent for Blacks and 13 percent for Whites (Ruggles et al., 2015). By 2014, Asians and Whites in New York State had similar rates of college education among adults age 25 years and older (45 percent of Asians and 39 percent on Whites had college degrees). The poverty rate for Asians in the state had fallen dramatically to 16 percent, while that for Blacks only fell to 22 percent and for Whites to 9 percent. Part of this improvement was due to college-educated Asians in the state achieving wage parity with college-educated Whites. In 1960, the median wage for college-educated Asians in the state was only 75 percent of the median wage for their White peers. By 2014, the median wages for both groups were nearly equal ($60,982 for Asians and $63,160 for Whites) (Ruggles et al., 2015).

Asian Income Inequality in New York City

One impact of new immigration patterns was a shift in income inequality within Asian communities. An estimate of the Gini coefficients in New York City for Asian, Blacks, Hispanics, and Whites reveals that income inequality in the Asian community has been rising faster than all other groups since 1980 (figure 8.1). Income inequality has been increasing in the Asian community due to growth at both ends of the income spectrum. The number of Asians in New York City living in poverty has grown by 757 percent since 1980, much faster than the 446 percent overall growth rate of the total Asian population in the city.

At the top end of the income scale, the Asian households with the top 20 percent of incomes are earning larger shares of aggregate income for their racial group. In particular, the top 20 percent of Asian household earned only 46 percent of aggregate Asian household income in 1980, around the same level as the top 20 percent of Black and Hispanic households. In 2014, the top 20 percent of Asian households earned 54 percent of aggregate Asian

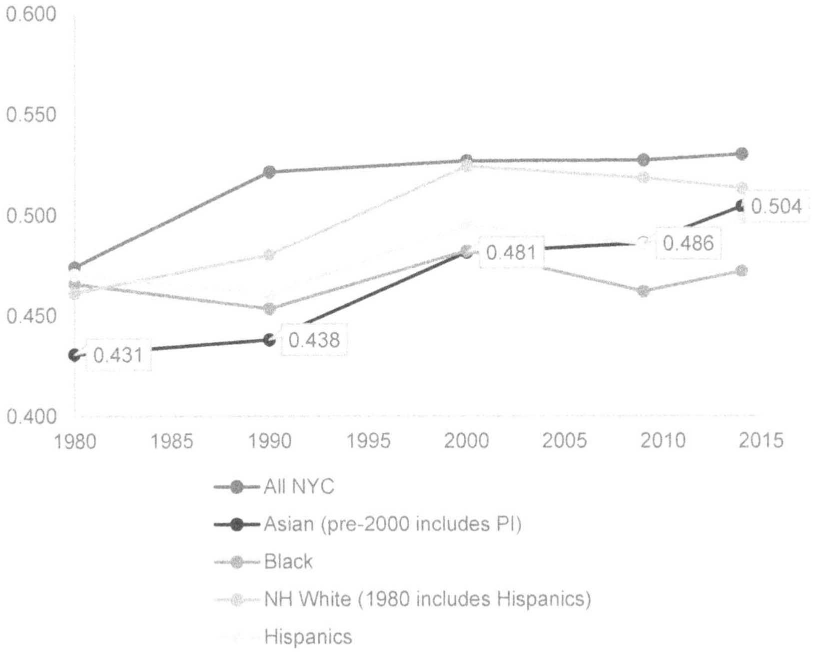

Figure 8.1. Gini coefficients for Asian household incomes in New York City. *Source:* Minnesota Population Center, 2016, and the US Census Bureau, 1993 and 2016.

household income, which approaches the same level as the top 20 percent of White households.

One result of the shifts in income inequality among Asian New Yorkers is that median incomes for Asian households have not kept pace with White households (Ruggles et al., 2015). Asian households had the lowest growth in real incomes between 1980 and 2014. A parity ratio analysis shows that Asian median household income fell further behind median White household income.

Asian Workers in Poverty

Poverty rates in the Asian community remain stubbornly high. The New York City Center for Economic Opportunity generates an alternative poverty measure for New York City that "includes the effect of income and payroll taxes, and the value of in-kind nutritional and housing assistance. Non-discretionary spending for commuting to work, childcare, and out-of-pocket medical care are accounted for as deductions from income" (New York City Center for Economic Opportunity, 2017). The high cost of housing is also accounted for. These poverty measures show that Asian residents in New York City have higher effect poverty rates than Blacks and Hispanics during the time from 2005 to 2014. The most recent data show that 26.6 percent of Asians were living in poverty, compared to 21.5 percent of Blacks, and 24 percent of Hispanics (New York City Center for Economic Opportunity, 2017).

Poverty remains persistent regardless of skill level. Anecdotal evidence of Asian professionals unable to find work in their field of expertise after immigrating to the United States is borne out in the increasing shares of Asian workers who were poor and have college educations. Figure 8.2 shows that

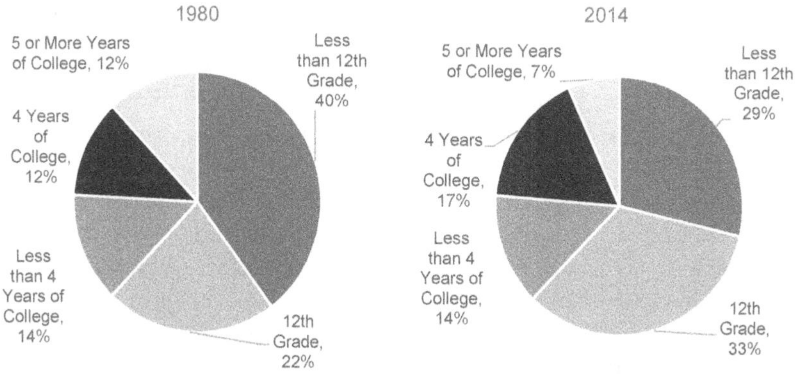

Figure 8.2. Years of education for Asians in the labor force living below poverty level. *Sources:* 5 percent sample, Asian workers in poverty, 1980; five-year American Community Survey Public Use Microdata Sample, Asian workers in poverty, 2014.

the shares of Asian workers living below the poverty level with high school diplomas and bachelor's degrees grew between 1980 and 2014.

Immigrant professionals have a difficult time transferring their credentials to the U.S. labor market in part due to the challenge of English proficiency. Those workers with limited English proficiency (defined as those responding that they speak English less than very well) saw their poverty rates increase between 1980 and 2014, while the poverty rates of those with strong English skills did not see a rise in poverty rates (data compiled from Ruggles et al., 2015). Asian immigrants as a whole are also having a harder time adapting to the U.S. labor market. In 1980, only the most recent Asian immigrants (those who had arrived in the last five years) had substantially higher poverty rates compare to native-born (data compiled from Ruggles et al., 2015). By 2014, higher poverty rates than native-born Asians persist even for Asian immigrants who had been in the country for up to 20 years.

In New York City, the decline of the garment industry over this period cut off a major source of jobs for low-skill immigrants. In 1980, approximately 14,000 Asian workers were employed as textile sewing machine operators. By 2014, only 6,000 Asians were employed in that occupation. This source of unionized jobs for new immigrants has given way to a more diverse range of occupations. Where seven occupations employed half of poor Asian workers in 1980, fourteen occupations employed just over half of poor Asian workers in 2014 (data compiled from Ruggles et al., 2015). While food service and entry-level retail occupations continue to provide job opportunities for low-skilled Asian workers, new sources of jobs have emerged as taxi drivers, hair stylists and cosmetologists, and health care aides. There are clear differences in employment opportunities for Asian men and women living in poverty. Only cashiers, waiters and janitors come anywhere close to gender parity. In a major shift, waiters were predominately male in 1980 and are now a predominately-female occupation among the Asian poor. Cooks and food prep workers, drivers of all sorts, sales clerks, construction workers, and supervisory sales jobs were predominately-male occupations among the Asian poor, while hairdressers and cosmetologists, nursing aides and attendants, child care workers, and textile workers were predominately female.

Another challenge for Asian households in poverty is the lack of access to government benefits (Ruggles et al., 2015). Asian households were the least likely to receive Supplemental Nutrition Assistance Program (SNAP) benefits among those households who potentially meet the income eligibility requirements for SNAP benefits (household income less than 125 percent of Federal Poverty Level). Asian households are less likely to receive food stamps for a variety of reasons. First, a large number of Asian immigrants are recent arrivals and are not eligible. Second, eligibility rules are complex and often Asians do not apply because of language barriers and the perception that applying for benefits impact their immigration status or their ability to sponsor family members' immigration visas. Finally, the sheer range of languages spoken as well as the lack of built up trust in the Asian community for non-Asian institutions makes it difficult for government and mainstream service providers to inform the community about potential eligibility.

Asian High Income Workers

At the opposite end of the economic spectrum, the growth in the number of high-income Asian workers has also increased income inequality in the Asian community. In this chapter, we define high-income workers as those who earn wages and salaries higher than 95 percent of all wage and salaried workers, i.e. the top 5 percent of all earners. Using the IPUMS data set, the wage and salary threshold was $29,645 in 1980 and $152,445 in 2014, all in nominal dollar values. In 1980, Asians represented four percent of the top five percentile of earners. By 2014, Asians represented 13 percent of those earners. Opportunities for those with limited English abilities to be among the top earners have decreased over time. In 1980, 29 percent of Asian top earners were limited English proficient, which fell to only 14 percent by 2014. As second generation Asians grew up, they became a higher share of top earners. In 1980, only 18 percent of Asians who were top earners were native born, becoming 32 percent by 2014.

Despite the increased share of Asians among the ranks of the top earners, a parity analysis of the industries and occupations that employ the top earners reveal the presence of a "bamboo ceiling."[3] The parity ratios in table 8.1 on page 194 were calculated based on the shares of workers who were top-earners for the top ten industries and occupations with the most top-earners.

For example, the parity ratio for lawyers in table 8.1 is calculated from the percentages of lawyers who were top-earners divided by the total number of lawyers for both Asian and non-Hispanic White lawyers. A parity ratio less than 100 means that Asian lawyers were less likely to reach top-earner status than non-Hispanic Whites, and a parity ratio greater than 100 means that Asian lawyers were more likely reach top-earner status than non-Hispanic Whites. Asians had a harder time reaching top-earner status for many of the occupations and industries typically associated with top-earning jobs. In table 8.1, only chief executives and financial services sales occupations saw parity among Asian workers with non-Hispanic White workers. None of the top ten industries had Asian workers achieving parity with non-Hispanic White workers.

Gender disparities also exist among the largest occupations for top earners (analysis not shown). Only among physicians, accountants and auditors was

Table 8.1. Ten Occupations and Industries with the Largest Number of Top Asian Earners, 2014

	Parity Ratio Asian to White
By Occupations	
Lawyers	80
Managers and Administrators, n.e.c.	79
Chief Executives and Public Administrators	91
Physicians	78
Other Financial Specialists	56
Financial Managers	58
Financial Services Sales Occupations	106
Accountants and Auditors	50
Managers and Specialists in Marketing, Advertising, and Public Relations	68
Supervisors and Proprietors of Sales Jobs	48
By Industries	
Security, Commodity Brokerage, and Investment Companies	78
Legal services	55
Banking	47
Hospitals	68
Credit Agencies, n.e.c.	64
Advertising	36
Management and Public Relations Services	77
Real Estate, Including Real Estate-Insurance Offices	34
Insurance	41
Computer and Data Processing Services	57

Source: Steven Ruggles, 2015.

gender parity close to being achieved. Even then, Asian males outnumber Asian females. Lawyers and managers in marketing, advertising and public relations were the only occupations where the majority of top earning Asians were women. The remaining occupations were overwhelmingly male among top earning Asians.

Inequality among Asian Ethnic Groups

While this chapter is primarily focused on the differences between Asians and the other major race and ethnic groups, it is also important to note that inequality within the Asian community has increased due to increasing diversity. The Gini coefficient for the largest Asian groups in New York City varied considerably, from a low of 0.38 for Filipinos to 0.51 for Taiwanese (table 8.2). The two fastest growing Asian groups in the City, Bangladeshis, and Pakistanis, were on the opposite ends of the Gini scale, while having similar poverty rates.

Poverty rates among Asian ethnic groups also varied widely. Based on the Federal poverty guidelines, the poverty rates calculated from the 2014 Five-Year American Community Survey Public Use Microdata shows that Bangladeshis, Pakistanis, and Chinese New Yorkers had higher poverty rates than the citywide rate of 20.8 percent. Koreans had a poverty rate close to that of the citywide rate, and the remaining four largest Asian groups in New York City had lower poverty rates. The poverty rates for each of the eight Asian groups track closely with education levels.

The statistics in table 8.2 indicate more complex stories within each community, each worthy of a full chapter or book. However, a few notes on each community in this chapter will be illustrative. With one in three Filipino workers employed in the healthcare industry, many as registered nurse and doctors, income equality seems to be low in the Filipino community. However, our work with Damayan, a workers' rights group organizing low-wage Filipino workers, has found that community to be especially hard to count in the Census and other government surveys. The Taiwanese community has low poverty rates yet has the highest income inequality among the Asian groups. Among Taiwanese New Yorkers age 18 and older living in poverty, half were enrolled in school, indicating the income inequality is more a function of a

Table 8.2. Gini Coefficient of Income for Largest Asian Groups in New York City

Asian Group	GINI Coefficient	Poverty Rate	Percent College Educated for Population Age 25 and Older	Limited English Proficiency Rate
Filipino	0.38	11.3%	63%	22%
Taiwanese	0.51	14.6%	66%	47%
Japanese	0.48	15.4%	68%	42%
Indian	0.47	18.0%	46%	26%
Korean	0.49	20.4%	54%	52%
Chinese	0.50	21.8%	32%	65%
Pakistani	0.50	30.9%	33%	49%
Bangladeshi	0.42	31.4%	35%	60%

Sources: U.S. Census Bureau, 2016; Steven Ruggles, 2015.

high population of college students living off savings or student loans. The Japanese community also has a high rate of school enrollment among adults similar to the Taiwanese. The Indian population in New York City is a mix of Indo-Caribbeans who are part of the Indian diaspora that emerged from the colonial period and new immigrants arriving as educated professionals directly from India. The Korean community is strongly entrepreneurial driven by a combination of high education levels and the lack of mainstream economic opportunities due to the lack of English skills. Both the Chinese and Pakistani communities have large percentages of the adult population age 25 and older who never completed high school, 31 percent in the case of Chinese and 45 percent for Pakistanis. Taxi drivers were the most common occupation for Bangladeshi and Pakistani workers, with 12 percent of Bangladeshi and 20 percent of Pakistani workers employed in the taxi industry. In the end, immigrants share similar experiences; those with both the credentials, such as a college degree from an internationally recognized institution, and the English language skills, will do well in this economy and those lacking one or both will have to find their way through the ethnic enclave economy (Ruggles et al., 2015).

Housing

Asian households in New York City have significant issues in securing affordable housing. Key housing measures such as rent burden, mortgage burden, and overcrowding point to a population that must devote a burdensome portion of household income to housing and have to fit more people into housing units. A majority of both Asian households with mortgages and Asian households renting had to spend more than 30 percent of household income on housing costs (U.S. Census Bureau, 2016). Aggregate Asian data also hides the wide differences in housing burden among the Asian ethnic groups in the city. Newer communities such as Bangladeshis and Pakistanis have a much harder time finding affordable housing. Between 60 to 78 percent of households are housing burdened (U.S. Census Bureau, 2016). Japanese and Filipino households were more like non-Hispanic White households, with fewer than 40 percent of households identified as housing burdened. For the remaining four groups, a little over half of households were housing burdened.

Asian households were also more likely to be overcrowded than other race and ethnic groups. Hispanic and Asian households were similar in overcrowding. A large variation in overcrowding exists among Asian ethnic groups. Around two-in-five Bangladeshi and Pakistani households were living in overcrowded conditions. At the other end of the scale, Japanese and

Korean households were about as likely at non-Hispanic White households to be overcrowded.

New immigrants tend to congregate together and the Asian communities of New York City are no exception. Asian ethnic neighborhoods have spread throughout the city. Bangladeshis were spread throughout the city in neighborhoods such as Norwood and Parkchester in the Bronx; Kensington and Midwood in Brooklyn; Astoria, Sunnyside, Jackson Heights, City Line and Jamaica in Queens. Neighborhoods with large Chinese populations include Chinatown in Manhattan; Bayside, Elmhurst and Flushing in Queens; and Bensonhurst, Sheepshead Bay, and Sunset Park in Brooklyn. The neighborhoods with the largest Filipino populations include Woodside, Elmhurst, Fresh Meadows, Jamaica Estates, and Queens Village in the Queens Borough. The largest concentration of the Indian population in the city is in eastern Queens in the neighborhoods of Jackson Heights, Ozone Park, Richmond Hill, Jamaica, and Bellerose. The Japanese community is spread throughout the neighborhoods of Manhattan particularly around Midtown and in Long Island City and Astoria in Queens. Neighborhoods with higher concentrations of Koreans include Bayside, Douglaston, Elmhurst, Flushing, and Murray Hill in Queens; and Koreatown in Midtown Manhattan. The largest Pakistani neighborhood in the city was located in the Midwood-Kensington area of Brooklyn, with growing populations in Fresh Meadows, Queens, and Bensonhurst, Brooklyn. Neighborhoods with large Taiwanese populations include Bayside, Flushing and Murray Hill in Queens.

Inevitably, these communities will overlap. In Bensonhurst, Brooklyn, Chinese and Pakistani neighborhoods adjoin. In Kensington and Midwood, Brooklyn, Bangladeshi and Pakistani communities are more intertwined. In Sunnyside, Woodside, and Jackson Heights, Queens, Bangladeshi, Filipino, and Indian communities share a residential and commercial corridor along the No. 7 subway line. Finally, in Bayside, Flushing, Murray Hill, Queens, the Chinese, Korean, and Taiwanese communities overlap.

Asian neighborhoods also exist in close proximity to other communities of color, the most prominent of which are Sunset Park, Brooklyn, and Jackson Heights, Queens, where Asians and Hispanics adjoin, and Jamaica, Ozone Park, and Richmond Hill in Queens, where the large Indo-Caribbean community neighbors the Black communities of Southeast Queens.

Conclusion and Future Research

The model minority myth that Asian New Yorkers are economically successful ignores the fact that the Asian community in New York City is heterogeneous and has growing income inequality. In addition, the story that Asians in New York City were able to improve their economic standing solely through hard work and education is also false. Given that Asians in New York State were already better educated than non-Hispanic Whites in 1960. Yet, they were poorer than even Blacks in New York State were at the time. Recent scholarship suggests that the prime reason for Asian Americans reaching income parity with non-Hispanic Whites was a reduction in anti-Asian discrimination in the labor market.

Income inequality has also increased within the Asian community. Growth in both the number of poor and high-income populations in the Asian community has created increased income inequality. Among the Asian poor, strong English language skills are becoming increasingly important to increase economic opportunity. Opportunities for workers in the ethnic enclave economies are fewer, especially since the loss of textile jobs. For high-income Asians, despite their economic success, a parity analysis shows that Asians in occupations and industries typically associated with high incomes were less likely to reach the highest pay in those industries and occupations.

While the end results of labor market discrimination on Asian New Yorkers differs from other communities of color, the root causes of the challenges and barriers for Asians are the same as for other communities of color. Opportunities to engage other communities of color around the issues surrounding income inequality, such as the Stafford Symposium, are vital for building bridges, sharing experiences, and participating in discussions around race and inequality. It is only then can we begin to address the mutual challenges faced by all communities of color.

As a leadership organization, the Asian American Federation relies on partnerships with academia to develop innovative research methods to examine the policy challenges facing Asian Americans. New research is needed to explore fully income inequality among Asian New Yorkers. First, research into poverty needs to focus on disaggregating data to account for the diversity within Asian community. Second, research into how housing costs affects Asian New Yorkers at all income levels will increase our understanding of the impact of gentrification on Asian neighborhoods, cost of living on Asian living standards, and the ability to build wealth. Another area of study is wealth and wealth accumulation among Asians. Recent studies suggest that Asian households have wider wealth inequality than non-Hispanic Whites nationally (Weller & Thompson, 2016). Another report on wealth among various race and ethnic groups in Los Angeles reveals the wide wealth gaps among Asian ethnic groups, highlighting the need for further studies that disaggregate data for Asian ethnicities (De la Cruz-Viesca, et al., 2016).

Notes

1. The model minority myth seeks to portray a particular minority as more successful socioeconomically than the mainstream and often in contrast to other minorities.

2. All references to Whites are to non-Hispanic Whites as defined in the American Community Survey.

3. The term, "bamboo ceiling," refers to institutional or cultural barriers that prevent Asian employees from reaching senior management roles, as evidenced by the underrepresentation of Asians at those levels.

References

De la Cruz-Viesca, M., Chen, Z., Ong, P., Hamilton, D., & William A., Darity Jr., W. A. (2016). *The color of wealth in Los Angeles.* Federal Reserve Bank of San Francisco Report, Los Angeles: Duke University Research Network on Racial and Ethnic Inequality, The Milano School of International Affairs, Management and Urban Policy at The New School, and UCLA Asian American Studies Center.

Duleep, H. O. & Sanders, S. (2012). *The economic status of Asian Americans before and after the civil rights act.* Discussion Paper Series, Bonn, Germany: Institute for the Study of Labor (IZA).

Gibson, C. & Jung, K. (2005). *Historical census statistics on population totals by race, 1790 to 1990, and by hispanic origin, 1970 to 1990, for large cities and other urban places in the united states.* Population Division Work Paper No. 76, Washington, DC: U.S. Census Bureau.

Hilger, N. (2016). *Upward mobility and discrimination: The case of Asian Americans.* NBER Working Paper Series, Cambridge, MA: National Bureau of Economic Research.

Lee, E. (2015). *The making of Asian America: A history.* New York: Simon & Schuster.

Minnesota Population Center. (2016). National historical geographic information system: version 11.0 [database]. Accessed September 13, 2016. http://www.nhgis.org.

New York City Center for Economic Opportunity. (2017). *Poverty data tool.* Accessed February 20, 2017. http://www.nyc.gov/html/ceo/html/poverty/lookup.shtml.

Ruggles, S., Genadek, K., Goeken, R., Grover, J., & Sobek, M. (2015). *Integrated public use microdata series: Version 6.0 [dataset].* Accessed August 1–31, 2016. http://doi.org/10.18128/D010.V6.0.

U.S. Census Bureau. (1993). *1990 census of population: Social and economic characteristics.* Washington DC: GPO.

U.S. Census Bureau. (2016). *American community survey PUMS Data.* Accessed 2016. http://www.census.gov/programs-surveys/acs/data/pums.html.

U.S. Census Bureau. (2016). *American factfinder.* Accessed 2016. http://factfinder.census.gov.

United States Department of Labor. (2016). *The economic status of Asian Americans and Pacific Islanders.* Special Report, Washington, DC: United State Department of Labor.

Weller, C., & Thompson, J. (2016). *Wealth inequality among Asian Americans greater than among Whites.* December 20. Accessed February 26, 2017. https://www.americanprogress.org/issues/race/reports/2016/12/20/295359/wealth-inequality-among-asian-americans-greater-than-among-whites/.

Chapter 9

Ethnic Conflict

How Much Exists in New York City?

Benjamin P. Bowser, John Flateau,
Hector R. Cordero-Guzmán, Howard Shih,
Calvin Holder, and Aubrey W. Bonnett

In this volume, we focus on the following question: In the 50 years between 1965 and 2015, did racial inequalities increase, decrease, remain the same, or transform in some way? Part 1 of this book explores these inequalities by measuring the disparities between White Americans and other racial groups in the areas of employment, education, income, residential segregation, and political engagement. It is clear that changes in the global, national, and city economies have transformed the playing field during the half-century we examined. African, Latino, Asian, and West Indian New Yorkers have all experienced disparities in varying degrees, when compared with White New Yorkers. There was a high point. We found that when members of each non-white group achieve a higher level of education, their racial disparities decrease. For example, Asian Americans achieved educational parity by 1965. Since then, their level of racial disparity shrank the most, followed by West Indians and Latinos. African Americans have progressed the least. Today, those who did not received a higher education find themselves exactly where they were in 1965, or perhaps even further behind.

We need to ask a second key question. Were there conflicts associated with such disparities? In the last half-century, were there conflicts between and within Whites, Blacks, Latinos, Caribbean, and Asian New Yorkers? It would not be the first time discord arose among the city's residents. In the nineteenth and early-20th centuries, serious friction existed between native White New Yorkers and European immigrants. There was literal warfare between Irish, Italian, Jewish, German, Greek and Eastern European immigrant New Yorkers (Bayor, 1988; Delaney, 2006). Street encounters generated serious clashes, as did job competition, housing shortages, and efforts to control neighborhood streets. Multi-generational gangs, popularly called the "gangs of New York," were the agent provocateurs. As one reviews the past half century, one wonders what part ethnic conflicts and rivalries played in the experiences of Blacks and new immigrants.

In the prior four chapters that addressed specific racial and ethnic disparities, no author concentrated on the inter- and intra-group conflicts that may have occurred in New York City. This chapter corrects that omission. Everyone agrees that conflicts between groups exist. In fact, every author independently asserts that, historically, White Americans' relationships with each group led to their specific racial disparity in employment, housing, etc. Conflicts between non-White ethnic groups were not the causes of racial social and economic disparities. We have done an extensive literature search of racial and ethnic conflict in New York City in the past 50 years. There are a number of surprises.

A Never-Ending Threat

During World War II, youth crime skyrocketed in the United States, particularly in large cities. In the summer of 1945, New York newspaper headlines were dominated by reports of vandalism, robberies, rampaging, and massive gang "rumbles," where large groups of youth battled one another in public (Woodsworth, 2013, p. 37). They beat each other with car radio antennas, baseball bats, chains, brass knuckles, curtain rods, blocks of wood, and trashcans. Switchblade knives and zip guns were particularly lethal. The violence was not random. It was ethnic-specific, and occurred, more often, on the boundaries of ethnic neighborhoods. In upper Manhattan, the "Irish Dukes" fought the "Negro Sabres." In Bedford-Stuyvesant, the Black "Nits" fought the Black "Greene Street Stompers," and Italian gangs calling themselves the "Brewery Boys," joined forces in ethnic solidarity to take on Blacks, and anyone else, who eyed their neighborhoods.

In his 1958 testimony before Congress, New York City Mayor Robert Wagner, Jr., said the city might "explode in an orgy of racially motivated youth violence." So anti-delinquency efforts should be the "number one project for the city" (Woodsworth, 2013, p. 72). During these post-war years, Blacks and Puerto Ricans were pouring into the city, escaping the poverty and oppression in the South, and in their native Puerto Rico. Ever-increasing levels of racialized street violence appeared inevitable. However, it was different than in the 1800s, when it was young European immigrants killing each other and Blacks. Now, the mayor's nightmare centered on the growing numbers of Black and Latino youth who were at war with young Irish and Italians youth, as well as with each other. However, Wagner's nightmare did not occur as he anticipated, partly because White ethnic neighborhood borders in every borough, excluding Staten Island, gave way to Blacks and Latinos.

The next mayor, John Lindsay was overtaken by unexpected events. On July 18, 1964, a White, off-duty police officer, Thomas Gilligan, killed James Powell, a 15-year-old Black teen wielding a knife. Riots erupted soon afterward in Harlem, Bedford-Stuyvesant, Brownsville and South Jamaica, Queens (Flamm, 2017). Here began the first of the nation's long-hot summers of progressively violent and costly race riots. Harlem had rioted before, in 1935 and in 1943, following incidents where police beat and killed Blacks. The 1964 riots, however, were more frightening and consequential. Stores were looted and property was destroyed as in prior riots, but this time, people were willing also to confront the police head on. Plus, the riots spread beyond Harlem to other Black communities in New York City.

There were a number of anomalies in the 1964 Harlem Riot. First, James Powell was not shot in Harlem, but rather on East 70th Street. Second, police had regularly beat and shot unarmed Blacks in Harlem and other Black communities, but riots had not ensued. Third, the riot was not in the Jim Crow South, but occurred in New York where there was mounting anger over racial discrimination in employment, housing, and education. Finally, the riots took place several weeks after the 1964 Civil Rights Act was passed in Congress. Ironically, the Act did not address the racial economic inequality that was at the heart of the Harlem riots.

In the decade that followed, there were 143 race riots nationally (Kerner et al., 1968). Newark, Detroit, and Los Angeles were each brought to a halt, and the riots cost these cities billions of dollars in damages. Local police departments could not control them, so the National Guard and Army paratroopers were mobilized to bring them under control (Locke, 2017). If Black riots on the scale of Newark's or Detroit's, had taken place in New York City, they would have sparked secondary riots, and defensive violence by other ethnic groups, as well as against Blacks. Riots would have been far more costly in America's most densely populated city.

A near miss occurred in 1968, when the Reverend Martin Luther King, Jr. was assassinated. Mayor Lindsey personally walked the streets, joining forces with his Youth Services Agency, which worked with New York's street youth (Woodsworth, 2013). These youth workers alerted the city to pending violence. From then until 1993, the potential for spontaneous Black civil disorder hung over the heads of the next three Democratic mayors of New

York: Abraham Beame, Ed Koch, and David Dinkins. In fact, the 1991 Crown Heights disorders between Blacks and Hasidicbrookl Jews in Brooklyn ended Dinkins' chance for re-election.

Ethnic Conflict in New York City

Conflicts between Blacks and the police have always been about more than law enforcement. In truth, they are more accurately characterized as ethnic/racial conflicts (Johnson, 2003). Over the past century, the Irish have dominated law enforcement in New York City. They still do, albeit to a lesser extent. It was rare to find even Italian police officers, until after World War II. In effect, the Irish have made a good living enforcing racial discrimination, and the exclusion of Blacks and Latinos from neighborhoods, businesses, services, and public spaces. The Irish have defined the city's police culture right down to the NYPD's ceremonial (Scottish) bagpipes. To this day, the very presence of Irish police officers in Black communities provokes anger.

There were a series of direct ethnic conflicts in New York City since the 1964 Harlem race riots. We refer to these as "direct conflicts," because they involve face-to-face, public action between opponents with different racial-ethnic identities. The following is a list of these events:

1. In the 1960s, Black parents in East Harlem Elementary School 201 attempted to improve the education of their children through community control of the curriculum. They came into direct conflict with predominantly White Jewish teachers in the United Federation of Teachers. Parents had problems with the few Black teachers in the school as well, suggesting that this was both a racial and social class clash (Lee, 2014, p. 211).

2. During the same decade of the 1960s, Puerto Rican parents advocated bilingual education for their children, to improve their academic performance. New York City's predominantly Jewish, United Federation of Teachers opposed bilingual education as well (Lee, 2014, p. 212).

3. The Union Federation President, Albert Shanker, convinced the New York State legislature to pass the Decentralization Act of 1969, which ended community control of schools and the introduction of bilingual education (Lee, 2014, p. 213).

4. In the summer of 1977, a citywide electrical blackout occurred. Sixteen hundred stores were looted, in 32 mostly poor Black and Latino neighborhoods. There were also 1,040 fires, generally caused by arson. This overnight violence was not against any specific ethnic group, but it was racial to the extent that race and ethnic hierarchy overlaps social class hierarchy (Halle & Rafter, 2005, p. 354).

5. Throughout the 1980s, the predominantly Italian and Jewish Bensonhurst section of Brooklyn was well known for its hostility toward Blacks. In 1989, a young Black man, Yusef Hawkins, and some friends came into one of its neighborhoods to view a used Pontiac he was interested in buying. They were chased by neighborhood youths for being in Bensonhurst and Yusef was killed (Halle, Gedeon, & Beveridge, 2005, p. 169).

6. Until the 1990s, the New York City Sanitation Department used river barges to remove garbage from four of its five boroughs, then disposed of the garbage in a city-run dump on Staten Island. In the 1990s, predominantly White Staten Island residents successfully pressured the city to close the Staten Island dump, ending barge transfers. The city subsequently collected garbage at 54 private waste transfer stations and trucked it to landfills as far away as Virginia. Environmental opponents pointed out that 56 percent of the transfer stations were in two predominantly Black and Latino residential areas: Williamsburg/Greenpoint and the South Bronx. They contend that the station's negative health effects and environmental impacts on these neighborhoods were ignored, because of who lived in the neighborhoods (Sze, 2003).

7. By the 1990s, Italians, and increasing numbers of Blacks, Puerto Ricans, Dominicans, Jamaicans and Albanians populated the North Bronx's Pelham Parkway communities. As the Black and Latino student populations grew, the Albanian dominance of Christopher Columbus High School's culture waned, and serious turf conflicts arose (Pinderhughes, 1991).

8. In 1991, a Black youth was shot and killed in a Korean-owned grocery store in Elmhurst, Queens. There was an effort to

boycott Korean grocery stores citywide. Black boycott organizers asserted that these stores over-priced, refused to hire Blacks, and disrespected Black customers (New York State Advisory Committee, 1994).

9. Also in 1991, a Hasidic Jewish driver killed a Black youth in a hit-and-run accident in the Crown Heights section of Brooklyn. This served to aggravate the tensions that had been building for some time between Blacks and Jews in the area. Young Blacks were enraged at the police department's initial failure to arrest the driver. This lead to four days of riots in which a young Hasidic man was killed as well (Shapiro, 2006).

10. In the summer of 1992, the police in the Washington Heights section of Manhattan killed a young, unarmed Dominican youth. This happened at a time when tensions were rising between police and Dominicans, many of whom were dark skinned. Rioting went on for ten days (Halle, 2005, p. 42).

11. In April of 2016, Police Officer Peter Liang stood in the darkened stairwell of a Brooklyn public housing building, with his gun drawn. Two young people entered the stairwell, surprising Liang and his partner. Liang shot one of the youths, who died soon afterward. Liang, an Asian-American, is one of the few New York City Police officers ever prosecuted for murder. Blacks called for his conviction, while Asian-Americans demanded his exoneration. Both sides admitted, however, that if the officer had been White, he would never have been prosecuted in the first place (Yee, 2015).

In Retrospect

In 50 years, there were three occasions when New York City was close to repeating the 1964 Harlem Race riots. They were the 1977 Blackout looting, the 1991 Crown Heights riot, and the 1992 Washington Heights riot. Five of the ten direct conflicts we have described here involved the police. Police shootings and violence against unarmed Black and Latino youth still have the potential to ignite civil unrest. However, none of these historic incidents resulted in the horror Mayors Wagner and Lindsay feared, or that any of their successors dreaded. New York City did not experience out-of-control, city-crippling race riots and counter riots. David Dinkins, the first Black mayor, was the only mayor whose career was ended by a riot (Crown Heights).

By 1994, when Rudy Giuliani became mayor, it was clear that Blacks no longer had the capacity to mount rebellions that threatened the entire city. It was not because the underlying causes of the 1964 Harlem race riots had been addressed successfully. Rather, it was because decades of drug abuse and trafficking in Black and Latino communities, casualties from the war in Vietnam, and the police "war on drugs" (aimed directly at Black people), had killed and incarcerated enough young Black men to neutralize their capacity to wage citywide riots (Flateau, 1996).

Riot potential and crime figures were reduced by another under-recognized factor: the decline in the number of young city residents, aged 13 to 29 years (Latzer, 2017). New York City is an expensive place to live in, and the high cost of rearing and housing young people translates into fewer low-income families with riot-age youth. It is no coincidence; the only race riot to occur since the 1960s was in Washington Heights, among Dominican immigrants with relatively young, large families.

It is also worth noting that, by 1994, the New York Police department had increased its numbers, discipline, tactics and weapons sufficiently to meet any threat. Even before SWAT, New York had tactical, riot police, all standing over six feet tall, carrying steel-lined, extra-long clubs. Department policy was if public disorder was suspected, hundreds of these officers were bused to the neighborhood or event. These officers then patrol in intimidating groups of three to five, sometimes more, and were backed by special-weapons teams. They are well prepared to do mass beat-downs and arrests.

Of the five remaining conflicts we described, the incident involving officer Peter Liang was the only other episode of a police shooting. The remaining four events were cases where White New Yorkers took advantage of their connections to city and state government, to disadvantage Black and Latino residents. Their efforts ended community control of schools, blocked bilingual education, and concentrated garbage transfer stations in Black and Latino communities.

In fact, since 1965, Whites have turned increasingly to conservative national politics, and Republican-controlled state governments to protect their privileges and to disadvantage people of color. Who needs ugly, face-to-face confrontations on the streets and in the neighborhoods, when you have direct access to the state capitol or city hall.

The two remaining conflicts we described are neighborhood-based. Bensonhurst and Pelham Parkway are by no means the only New York communities where youth of different racial-ethnic backgrounds have tense relationships with one another. We know from chapter 2 that New York is the most racially segregated large city in the United States. Chapter 5 shows us that the boundaries of the city's ethnic communities are fluid and ever-changing. When Irish, Italians and other White ethnics move from their older, working-class areas, or choose to defend them as enclaves, they develop tense relationships with the youth of the new groups moving near or into their communities. This is happening mostly in Brooklyn, Bronx, and Queens. The tension, and potential for violence among young New Yorkers is symptomatic of the negative attitudes parents and friends have toward their new or fleeing neighbors. The good news is there has not been a return to 1940s-scale racialized violence. Mayor Wagner's nightmare of ethnic gangs engaged in mass rumbles against one another has not been realized. However, the potential for smaller-scale violence still exists on the boundaries of communities going through demographic changes.

Other Conflicts

Another kind of racial-ethnic conflict does not make the headlines nor generally involves the police. Conflict in employment and job succession produced ethnic stratification. In the prior two centuries, the order of ethnic stratification was established (Dinnerstein & Reimers, 1975; Shibutani & Kwan, 1965). Early German and Irish immigrants monopolized higher-paying jobs in emerging industries. Italian, Jewish, Polish, and Eastern European immigrants, who came later, took the lower-paying jobs in older, more dangerous and dirtier industries. Those on the bottom could not move up until those above them made room for them or moved on. The people on the top rungs resisted any attempts by people on the lower rungs to bypass them. Employers used this inherent competition to keep demands for higher wages and benefits under control. Managers only needed to threaten to bring in lower-status laborers, at lower wages, to convince workers to accept their lot. Blacks, who held the lowest positions, were used as a reserve labor force to rein in wage demands of higher-status workers, and to break strikes, as well.

To date, the research literature and newspaper accounts have not assessed how much ethnic-racial stratification and competition exists in New York job markets over the past half-century. There is one exception: a dissertation on racial/ethnic conflict in the New York City garment industry, 1933–80 (Laurentz, 1980). Black, Puerto Rican, and Jewish business owners, union organizers and labor leaders alternated between being allies and enemies in zero-sum struggles. They fought with one another, and occasionally resorted to violence. They struggled with one another until their industry died, due to obsolescence or overseas competition.

We cannot answer the following questions. To what extent does the current rainbow of racial-ethnic groups compete with one another in low-paying service industries? Are there implicit racial hierarchies in current industries such as fast food, retail, or childcare? If there are, how are these hierarchies enforced? It may be employers who determine which groups get jobs, and which groups are rejected in each industry.

There are other emerging conflicts between contemporary racial-ethnic groups in New York. Blacks just recently gained political representation with Puerto Ricans as supporters. Today, Latinos from Mexico, Central and South America are the fastest growing racial-ethnic group in the U.S. They are an emerging political block in their own right as the African American population decreases and disperses (Lee, 2014). One must look at the end of the Charles Rangel era in Harlem, and the emergence of the Dominican, Adriano Espaillat, in Rangel's place to know there is a new source of conflict between Blacks and Latinos in the making.

Another source for potential conflict exists in the city's elite high schools where Asian American students vastly outnumber Black and Latino students (Spenceroct, 2012). If Black and Latino enrollments increase, it follows that openings for Asian American would decrease. Asian Americans are also starting to rise to the top of public housing waiting lists, a place African Americans have held for decades. Now, Black New Yorkers are sharing buildings with Asian Americans, as well as Latinos. There is growing potential for racial conflict in public housing.

Gentrification poses the greatest threat for generating conflict. To date, White trailblazers have initiated neighborhood gentrification. Remarkably, there has been little violence between this group and long-term Black and Latino residents. These groups appear to live in peaceful coexistence, even when they live in the same building. One wonders, though, whether this peace can last.

One final category of racial-ethnic tension does get sufficient attention. Often there are individual acts of violence, where a member of one ethnic group attacks others, whether it is on the streets of New York, or in the subway system. Such individual acts of violence are widely reported in the news, with police going to great lengths to find the perpetrator. Generally, these offenders acts alone, and suffer from some form of mental illness.

An Explanation for the Lack of Group Conflict

Perhaps, the New York media exaggerates conflict between races and ethnic groups. Certainly, the city is too small and densely populated to ignore incidents of public violence. However, it would help to understand how so many different people, existing in varied social strata, can successfully share public spaces without generating more group conflict than we have seen.

New York is the most densely populated city in the United States. It has twice the population it had in 1940, but not twice the conflict. It has three times as many people as it did in 1900, but not three times the public conflict. In addition, there are at least three times as many ethnic groups in New York City as there were in 1900. Numbers such as these suggest a greater probability for ethnic conflict.

Consider the following. Residents from different countries have historic enmities with one another. In a city such as New York, they are bound to encounter one another on the streets, or on public transportation. Yet despite this daily exposure to one another, their historic rivalries do not continue. Perhaps expanded employment opportunities have made the difference. Residents of different ethnic groups do not have to compete for low-paying, entry-level jobs offered by a few large employers as in the 1800s. Instead, today, there are hundreds of employment options available.

In the post-war years, Whites used labor unions to protect their employment and higher wages, and to serve as barriers against competing workers of color. Perhaps, non-unionized citizens and immigrants alike who work in the new service industries do not expect higher wages and better benefits. Consequently, they rarely resort to marches, demonstrations, or strikes. For instance, the recent restaurant workers campaign for living wages might have been expected decades ago. In a more unionized environment, workers at the bottom of the economic scale might compete with one another, and along ethnic lines. Today, however, it is possible that there is less conflict, because the work immigrants do is considered too poorly paid by citizens to compete for the same jobs. Citizen laborers might still believe that only immigrants do the lowest-paid, least-desirable work.

In addition, ethnic community leaders and residents are less likely to demonize others as they might have in the past. In a very crowded city like New York, groups, by necessity, must live close together. Residents must find ways to communicate with one another, and learn to bargain informally for access to, and common use of public spaces. The difference between the past and present is that everyone benefits by working through the political process (Mollenkopf, Olson, & Ross, 2001). Today, there are no external barriers to any ethnic group's participation. Ethnic leaders find that commonalities among groups far outnumber differences, so they are more apt to defuse racial and ethnic conflicts, than they are to inflame them.

A social services infrastructure helps to alleviate neighborhood conflicts, too. New York City councilpersons have allotted funds to support community organizations and projects (Jones-Correa, 2001). There are numerous citywide and community-based social service organizations dedicated to the needs of every racial-ethnic group in the city. The number of such organizations did not exist in the 1800s and early 1900s. Broad access to city-sponsored social services and resources can result in local and citywide political competition for offices. Therefore, frustration over unmet neighborhood needs do not have to be resolved through violence and direct conflict with neighbors. One observer said it best regarding Elmhurst-Corona:

> In Elmhurst-Corona, people of all races want effective policy to control drug trafficking, prostitution, gambling, and illegal dumping; and they want livable neighborhoods where parking, public transportation, schools, recreation facilities, access to hospitals, and a safe, decent housing supply are in balance. (Sanjek, 2000, p. 370)

The struggle to have common needs met is no longer seen as a zero-sum game, where Black, Latino, Asian, Italian and Irish New Yorkers must all compete for limited resources. Instead, meeting community needs are viewed as the government's responsibility, whether city, state or federal. Perhaps, most New Yorkers, regardless of their race, ethnicity, or social class, may believe in equitable solutions to social problems, whether these beliefs are actualized or not. In this environment, many agree that the unequal level of services communities receive is based more on governmental favoritism or neglect, rather than on the inherent ill will or monopoly by other ethnic neighbors.

The lack of ethnic conflict in New York among current immigrants might be explained ultimately by a shared immigrant experience. However, European ethnics entering New York in the 1800s shared a common immigrant experience as well, but they still engaged in their famous ethnic gang conflicts. That may be because, prior to the World War II, European ethnic immigrants saw their ethnicity as an either-or proposition. You were either in their group, or you were not. People certainly did not think about mixed ethnicity, and, if so, were probably against it. In contrast, ethnic identities have become more fluid since 1965, spurred by powerful media exposures, and more one-on-one contact between people of different ethnicities in school and at work.

Theory and Identity

This 50-year review of ethnic conflict implies that the theories underlie ethnic identity and inter-group relations in New York City did not go far enough.

In the 1960s, Glazer and Moynihan made it clear that the idea of New York as a melting pot was more of a wish than fact (1963). African Americans, Puerto Ricans, Jews, Italians, and the Irish have not entirely given up their Southern, Island and European cultural roots. They may have assimilated into American life, but their ethnicity still exists, and remains an important part of their social identities.

Milton Gordon conceptualized just how ethnic groups simultaneously assimilated into American life and maintained their ethnicity (1964). Structural divisions exist in every group. Some members choose to be more "Anglo-conformed." Others choose to remain more ethnic. These internal divisions become "subcultures." Therefore, members of different ethnic groups may share subcultures across their ethnic boundaries; one cannot assume there is a single experience that defines any ethnic identity.

Based upon Moynihan, Gazer, and Gordon, we hypothesize that, within each ethnicity, there are multiple subcultures with flexible and permeable boundaries. In effect, individual members of a particular ethnic group are in fact part of more than one subculture within their ethnicity (Butterfield, 2004). In addition, boundaries between ethnic groups can be flexible and permeable. Individuals in one group can have close cultural contact with other ethnic groups. In New York City, individuals may be identified initially by their parents' ethnicity, but by the time they are young adults, the multiethnic environment in which they live makes it possible for them to assume, "visit," and try out identities in other ethnicities as well.

For example, U.S.-born West Indians of African ancestry might identify as West Indians, based on their island heritage (Trinidadian, etc.), or as Black Americans (Waters, 1999). Puerto Ricans, Dominicans, Cubans and others Latinos may affiliate as White, Latino or Black, depending on their color, their behavior, and the language they choose to speak (Spanish or English) (Navarro, 2012; Tafoya, 2004). East Indians can be White, Hindus or "people of color." On Saint Patrick's Day, Italians can become Irish, and on Columbus Day, Irish can become Italian.

In New York City today, it is possible, maybe even preferable, to maintain contact with one's roots in the old country, via convenient travel and worldwide cell phone networks. However, one is simultaneously American. In effect, it is the norm to be dual- and tri-cultural. With the decline of single identities, it is more difficult to mobilize oppositional conflict based on only ethnicity.

We posit that the maintenance of ethnicity creates the need within each group for a political class which in turn results in electoral competition and differing policymaking agendas (Lee, 2014, p. 214). At the same time, it is necessary to build and expand multiracial, multiethnic, and multicultural voting blocs as a fundamental prerequisite for electoral victory. We need to ask two empirical questions. First, how much flexibility and permeability exist within and between ethnic groups? Second, who can cross ethnic identity boundaries; who cannot, and under what circumstances? We contend that the answers to these questions vary by group.

Latinos

The public may not find it easy to distinguish between Latino ethnicities. Latinos come from Puerto Rico, Cuba, the Dominican Republic, Panama, Mexico, El Salvador, or Honduras. Within each ethnicity, there are variations based on region, social class, education, occupation, urban-rural experience, and and a mixture of European, Amerindian, and African ancestry. Some Latinos speak fluent Spanish, while others speak versions of Indian and regional dialects, and very little Spanish. Some come to the United States as refugees fleeing drug and ideological wars, political oppression, land theft, rape, gangs, and murder. Others come strictly as economic refugees. Some come with material and human resources; others come with none. This diversity among Latino immigrants produces a web of social networks, and boundaries within the group. Beyond the Spanish speaker looms a multi-cultural person, possessing multiple identities within a single ethnicity. Over time, young second and third generation Latinos learn to navigate this diversity, become fluent in the differences, and can claim multiple identities as a result. To the outer world, these individuals are simply Latinos or Hispanics. The inner cultural complexities among Central and South Americans make Pan-Latino unity, and political mobilization, much more difficult, and make the prospect of conflict with others ethnic groups difficult.

Blacks

As we have pointed out before, West Indians born and reared in the United States find it relatively easy to move back and forth between island-specific nationalities such as Trinidadian, Jamaican, Grenadian, Panamanian, plus other identities such as West Indian, African-American, Black, and Pan African (Butterfield, 2004). In addition, there are differences based on agricultural versus urban backgrounds, educational levels, and social class. Haitians are a distinct ethnicity among West Indians, not simply because they speak primarily French and Creole rather than English, but also because they have a unique history of both political independence, economic and social isolation, and environmental trauma.

It is important to acknowledge the unexplored cultural divisions among African Americans. There are Southern rural and urban subcultures distinct from Northern and Midwestern subcultures. There is a social division between African Americans from the Upper South (Virginia and Carolinas), and the Low South (Alabama, Louisiana, and Mississippi). The latter divide evolved from distinct regional histories that evolved during slavery, in addition to the different African cultural-ethnic backgrounds that slaves brought to each region. There are still social divisions based on skin color, hair texture and physical characteristics, as well as potential new identities among those who are biracial (Desantis & Williams, 2016).

Asians

The Asian designation is extremely diverse. This mega-label encompasses Chinese, Vietnamese, Laotians, Cambodians, Koreans, Mongolians, Filipinos, Bangladeshi, East Indians, Pakistanis, Iranians, and Indonesians. None of these cultures shares a common language, culture, history, or color. Like Latinos and Blacks, each has multiple, inner sub-cultural divisions. Despite the lack of permeability between cultures, there are social bonds develop across even Asian ethnicities. There are members in each ethnicity who are bi- and tricultural across ethnic boundaries. Then, there are social bridges in the second and third generations among Asians reared in New York and educated in the New York City public schools.

Since the American public does not grasp such complexity, the interior subcultures and identities among Asians go unrecognized. People of vastly different national and cultural origins are reduced to one identity: Asian American. It is an imposed identity, by default, but it is also one defined, redefined, negotiated and shaped by Asian Americans as well. Because of these formidable inner differences among Asian Americans, it is difficult to get more than, perhaps, Chinese Americans (the largest of Asian ethnicities in New York) to engage in conflict with other ethnic groups, or to be mobilized politically.

Role of Color and Race in Ethnic Identity

European immigrants in 19th century New York did not want to be viewed on the same social level as Blacks. The threat of such a fate motivated many to learn English, and to adopt the American culture. They knew that as long as they spoke no English, or expressed their foreign culture, they would remain near the bottom of the social hierarchy with Blacks. As long as they remained ethnic Irish, they were expected to live in the same neighborhoods as Blacks, and to compete for the same miserable jobs. The same motivation exists for post–1965 immigrants, the vast majority of whom are people of color. Americanization begins with recognizing that White Americans considers Black Americans lazy and innately inferior. Individual Blacks may be successful, but the group as a whole is to be avoided (Okome, 2004, p. 187). The worst fate is to be considered Black.

Anti-Black socialization poses a special dilemma for immigrants of color who cannot pass for White (McClain & Tauber, 2001). This hits African immigrants particularly hard (Okome, 2004). No matter how successful they become, and how much they assimilate as Americans, they are indistinguishable from African Americans. It is important to not lose their accents or stop wearing African clothes. They have strong incentive to remain African for as long as possible so they can enjoy temporary advantages. If they stay in the United States, it is unavoidable that their children or grandchildren will be exposed to African Americans and the contempt Whites hold for them. They too will become African American as far as White Americans are concerned and experience the disadvantages that come with that identity.

Puerto Ricans and Cubans, in their third and fourth generations, have already gone through the color sorting process. Children, who can pass for white, have done so. Like the Irish, Italians, and Jews before them, they have been able to succeed, to join the middle class, and to move to the suburbs. They are virtually indistinguishable from any other White American. Latinos whose children and grandchildren show any African or Amerindian ancestry, remain Puerto Rican, Cuban, Panamanian, et cetera. The darkest of them are destined in time to become African Americans of Puerto Rican, Cuban or Panamanian heritage. Dark-skinned East Indians, Pakistanis, etc., have the same long-term dilemma. In a nation still intent on maintaining White racial purity and Black inferiority, one can only wonder how their grandchildren and great-grandchildren will be classified. What will be their eventual "racial" fate?

Conclusion

New York City is a perfect setting for ethnic competition, and enduring racial conflict. Since 1965, immigrants from all over the world have come to New York City. If they have financial resources like Taiwanese Chinese, they can go right to the suburbs and immediately enjoy middle class status (Zhou & Kim, 2003, p. 137). They can support themselves by starting small businesses that employ members of their own ethnic group who do not have the linguistic and cultural skills to work in the larger economy. Immigrants who do not have adequate financial, linguistic, or human resources at their disposal, must enter at the bottom of the economy. However, once their children have been educated and assimilated into the culture, they can expect to enjoy higher income, wider opportunities, and greater success relative to their parents or grandparents. If they can pass for White, so much the better, they can move toward parity with White Americans.

However, since 1965, the majority of immigrants have been people of color. This has complicated the historic function of ethnicity in New York City. Those who can pass for White will do so and will follow the traditional path into White America. Those who cannot pass will experience different outcomes. American society will continue to identify these individuals as African, Caribbean, Latino, and Asian. It is certainly possible for African and Caribbean Americans to retain their distinct identities, as long as they preserve their ethnic enclaves in New York City. It is unlikely that members of either of these two ethnic groups will be able to maintain their distinct identity for more than two generations if they leave New York for cities and states without African and Caribbean immigrant enclaves. Ironically, as their children and grandchildren achieve educational and economic success in New York and take advantage of opportunities nationally, over time, they will be identified as African Americans.

Ethnic conflicts in New York City have had two distinct periods. There was widespread violence in the 1800s. In contrast, there has been comparatively little violence in the 20th and 21st centuries, despite its continuing threat. The public violence and rioting that has taken place since 1965 has been racial conflict between Blacks and police (Irish), or between Blacks and Italians, Jews, or Koreans. There has been no public group violence between Asian, Latino, and Caribbean immigrants. Because many Dominicans are dark complected, the 1991 riot between Dominicans and police in Washington Heights, can be considered a race riot. Overall lack of violence does not mean there has been no ethnic conflict among new immigrants. It is just that we have not looked in the right places to find the conflicts, which likely occurs in workplaces, or on the borders of ethnic enclaves. New York City has become, in the words of Gordon Lewis, a "multilayered pigmentocracy" like that in Puerto Rico and the Caribbean (1963). Whites are at the top; Blacks are at the bottom, and everyone else is in the middle.

Any conflict going forward will continue to be generated by dynamics within and among ethnic groups. The potential for ethnic and racial conflict also remains a function of unregulated growth in New York City. When Whites gentrify central city Black and Latino neighborhoods there is a back-end. Displaced Blacks and Latinos are pushed to formerly White working-class neighborhoods away from the downtown and in the inner suburbs. Blacks, people of color, who immigrate to the U.S. without financial, and human resources, are now restricted to the least-desirable housing, located on the edge of the Bronx, Brooklyn, and Queens. The flipside of gentrification is the formation of unacknowledged "Bantustan" communities on the edge of the city.

As in the past, racial discrimination in housing, and in mortgage and loan financing, help to delineate racial housing boundaries. In the 1960s, end-of-market enclaves were referred to as "ghettos," and displacing residents called it "Negro removal." Now, ghettos are not repurposed for public housing and highways, but instead for housing a new class of White middle-class urbanites. Low-income people of color are pushed to specific new locations by the same lack of mortgages and loans and real estate steering that created the prior ghettos (Brown, 2005, p. 45). Displacing people of color, uprooting their communities, and confining them in new locations will create fresh incentives for racial and ethnic conflict, far into the future.

For a time, race seemed to decline in importance in the midst of the post–1965 wave of immigration. However, we may be in for some surprises in the future. New York City has depended on a succession of immigrants to fill its lowest-paid and least-desirable jobs. As one ethnic group advances, another one moves in behind it. The outcome is the city's ethnic social hierarchy. The children and grandchildren of European immigrants sit at the top of the hierarchy, having moved into the middle class. They have become White Americans, while maintaining elements of their ethnicity.

Finally, this chapter asks, "Will people of color in the post–1965 wave of immigrants experience the same outcome as prior European immigrants?" New immigrants are building racially diverse political classes. However, will their eventual political representation be able to solve the problem of racial-ethnic inequality and reduce the prospects for conflict? No one knows. It is possible to have political representation, and still not have the power to reshape gentrification, employment, and the quality of city schools. Black representatives can testify to this (see chapter 14).

In light of the dramatic changes that are looming in federal immigration policy, we cannot anticipate whether there will be new immigrants coming to New York City. Are there people from any part of the world who are not already here? Will people of color on the bottom of the city's economic and social hierarchy achieve upward mobility, and not be replaced, displaced, deported or gentrified out of New York City? If new immigrants cannot become White, they might form a semi-permanent underclass, and continue in successive generations to do the least-desirable work.

It will take effective and creative racial job and housing discrimination interventions. It will also require effective reform of the city's K–12 schools, and renewed support for public higher education. These institutions must be reinvigorated to serve the function they did for European immigrants in the last century. Otherwise, the efforts of immigrants from all over the world to enter the American middle class will be frustrated and continue to be a potential source of conflict well into the future.[1]

Note

1. All of these differences play subtle roles in the creation and definition of African American social networks, ethnic boundaries, and affiliations as well as the group's willingness and ability to mobilize.

References

Bayor, R. H. (1988). *Neighbors in conflict: the Irish, Germans, Jews, and Italians of New York City, 1929–1941.* Urbana, IL: University of Illinois Press.

Brown, E. (2005). *Fried Chicken or Ox Tail: An Examination of Afro-Caribbean and African-American Conflict in New York City.* (Doctoral dissertation). State University of New York, Albany, Albany, NY.

Butterfield, S.-A. (2004). Being racialized ethnics: second generation West Indian immigrants in New York City. In J. Krase & R. Hutchinson (Eds.), *Race and ethnicity in New York City* (pp. 107–36). Amsterdam, Netherlands: Elsevier.

Delaney, T. (2006). *American street gangs.* Upper Saddle River, NJ: Prentice Hall.

Desantis, A., & Williams, J. (2016, September 15). I, too, sing America: The National Museum of African American History and Culture. *The New York Times Magazine.*

Dinnerstein, L., & Reimers, D. (1975). *Ethnic Americans: A history of immigration and assimilation.* New York, NY: Dodd, Mead and Company.

Flamm, M. W. (2017). *In the heat of the summer: The New York riots of 1964 and the war on crime.* Philadelphia, PA: University of Pennsylvania Press.

Flateau, J. L. (1996). *The prison industrial complex: Race, crime and justice in New York.* Brooklyn, NY: Medgar Evers College Press.

Glazer, N., & Moynihan, D. P. (1963). *Beyond the melting pot: The Negroes, Puerto Ricans, Jews, Italians and Irish of New York City.* Cambridge, MA: The MIT Press.

Gordon, M. (1964). *Assimilation in American Life: The role of race, religion, and national origins.* New York, NY: Oxford University Press.

Halle, D. (2005). The New York and Los Angeles Schools. In D. Halle (Ed.), *New York and Los Angeles: Politics, society and culture, a comparative view* (pp. 1–48). Chicago, IL: University of Chicago Press.

Halle, D., Gedeon, R., & Beveridge, A. A. (2005). Residential separation and segregation, racial and Latino identity, and the racial composition of each city. In D. Halle (Ed.), *New York and Los Angeles: Politics, Society and Culture, a Comparative View* (pp. 150–94). Chicago, IL: University of Chicago Press.

Halle, D., & Rafter, K. (2005). Riots in New York and Los Angeles. In D. Halle (Ed.), *New York and Los Angeles: Politics, society and culture, a comparative view* (pp. 341–66). Chicago, IL: University of Chicago Press.

Johnson, M. S. (2003). *Street justice: A history of police violence in New York City.* Boston, MA: Beacon Press.

Jones-Correa, M. (2001). Structural shifts and institutional capacity: Possibilities for ethnic cooperation and conflict in urban settings. In M. Jones-Correa (Ed.), *Governing American Cities Inter-Ethnic Coalitions, Competition, and Conflict* (pp. 183–209). New York, NY: Russell Sage Foundation.

Kerner, O., et al. (1968). *Report of the National Advisory Commission on Civil Disorders.* Washington, DC: U.S. Government Printing Office.

Latzer, B. (2017). *The rise and fall of violent crime in America.* New York, NY: Encounter Books.

Laurentz, R. (1980). *Racial/ethnic conflict in the New York City garment industry, 1933–1980.* (Doctoral dissertation). State University of New York at Binghamton, Binghamton, NY.

Lee, S. S.-H. (2014). *Building a Latino civil rights movement: Puerto Ricans, African Americans, and the pursuit of racial justice in New York City.* Chapel Hill, NC: The University of North Carolina Press.

Lewis, G. K. (1963). *Puerto Rico: Freedom and power in the Caribbean.* New York, NY: Monthly Review Press.

Locke, H. G. (2017). *The Detroit riot of 1967.* Detroit, MI: Wayne State University Press.

McClain, P., & Tauber, S. (2001). Racial minority group relations in a multiracial society. In M. Jones-Correa (Ed.), *Governing American cities inter-ethnic coalitions, competition, and conflict* (pp. 111–36). New York, NY: Russell Sage Foundation.

Mollenkopf, J., Olson, D., & Ross, T. (2001). Immigrant political participation in New York and Los Angeles. In M. Jones-Correa (Ed.), *Governing American cities inter-ethnic coalitions, competition, and conflict* (pp. 17–70). New York, NY: Russell Sage Foundation.

Navarro, M. (2012, January 13). For many Latinos, racial identity is more culture than color. *The New York Times.*

New York State Advisory Committee. (1994). *Resolving intergroup conflicts in New York City.* New York, NY: United States Commission on Civil Rights.

Okome, M. O. (2004). Emmergent African immigrant philanthropy in New York City. In J. Krase & R. Hutchinson (Eds.), *Race and ethnicity in New York City* (pp. 179–92). Amsterdam, Netherlands: Elsevier.

Pinderhughes, H. L. (1991). *Ethnic and racial attitudes among youth and the rise in racial conflict in New York City.* (Doctoral dissertation). University of California Berkeley, Berkeley.

Sanjek, R. (2000). *The future of us all: Race and neighborhood politics in New York City.* Ithaca, NY: Cornell University Press.

Shapiro, E. S. (2006). *Crown Heights: Blacks, Jews, and the 1991 Brooklyn riot.* Hanover, NH: University Press of New England.

Shibutani, T., & Kwan, K. (1965). *Ethnic stratification: A comparative approach.* New York, NY: Macmillan Company.

Spenceroct, K. (2012, October 26). For Asians, school tests are vital steppingstones. *The New York Times.*

Sze, J. (2003). *The racial politics of urban health and environmental justice.* (Doctoral dissertation). New York University, New York.

Tafoya, S. (2004). *Shades of belonging.* Washington: Pew Hispanic Center.

Waters, M. C. (1999). *Black identities: West Indian immigrant dreams and realities.* Cambridge, MA: Harvard University Press.

Woodsworth, M. (2013). *The forgotten war: Waging war on poverty in New York City, 1945–1980.* (Doctoral dissertation). Columbia University, New York.

Yee, V. (2015, February 22). Indictment of New York officer divides Chinese-Americans. *The New York Times.*

Zhou, M., & Kim, R. (2003). New immigrant Chinese Communities in New York and Los Angeles. In D. Halle (Ed.), *New York and Los Angeles: Politics, society and culture, a comparative view* (pp. 124–50). Chicago, IL: University of Chicago Press.

PART 3

Practice and Policy

Introduction to Part 3

Barriers to racial equity have never been fixed. As old barriers are challenged and become less effective, new ones replace them. Then, the process of understanding how the barriers work and then challenging them starts over again. We have witnessed such a transition in racial oppression in New York since 1970. As racial discrimination in employment and housing were challenged with relative success, criminal justice, drug trafficking, drug addiction, HIV/AIDS, and government divestment have become the new barriers. At the same time, the barriers to racial equality have never been received passively. People of color have acted invariably to resist the barriers in both an unorganized and organized fashion. They do not choose to be hapless victims of the discriminatory forces affecting their lives. They act, find ways to overcome the new barriers, and to eventually improve their plight. In part 3, we examine the new barriers—criminal justice, drug trafficking and abuse, HIV/AIDS, government divestment and the efforts of those who experience racial barriers to struggle against them.

Chapter 10

Policing

Stop and Frisk

Continuity of Racial Control and Reconstructed Blackness

Natalie P. Byfield

At 11:30 p.m., on March 9, 2013, 10th-grader Kimani Gray was on the street in East Flatbush, Brooklyn. It was there that he lost his life at the hands of police. Fifty-one percent of the people living in East Flatbush, known as a Caribbean enclave, are foreign-born, with 76 percent hailing from Jamaica, Haiti, Trinidad and Tobago, Guyana and Grenada (Lobo, Lobo, & Salvo, 2013). The street presents a mix of small-sized, brick-faced apartment buildings, plus one- and two-family houses that embody the American dream for its foreign-born residents. Officially known as East Flatbush-Farragut (Lobo et al., 2013), most of the boundaries of East Flatbush correspond with the borders of the New York Police Department's 67th Precinct, an area they have labeled a high-crime zone.

Gray and six or seven of his friends returned home from a birthday party that March night and stopped for a while to laugh and chat. It was a Saturday night, with whispers of spring in the air so that one can imagine the celebratory mood of the teens. A snowstorm had hit the area during the two preceding days, leaving behind up to four inches of snow. However, on that Saturday, midday temperatures had climbed to the mid-50s. The group of friends gathered under a street lamp on East 52nd Street, their laughter and chatter growing loud enough to be heard by Tishana King, who lived just a few driveways down from where Gray and his friends stood. Curious about the loud voices, King peered out of her third-story window. She recognized several faces, including that of 16-year-old Kimani, known as "Kiki" to his friends (Devereaux, 2013, March 18). Gray frequently visited kids who lived on her block.

Gray and his friends also caught the attention of two NYPD police officers, Mourad Mourad, an anti-crime sergeant of Egyptian descent, and Jovaniel Cordova, a Latino officer. That night, they were working as plainclothes police and driving around the East Flatbush precinct in an unmarked car. The police practice is known as "Stop, Question, and Frisk," authorized them to interdict any crime in the making or prevent a crime before it happened.

Press reports noted that Kimani Gray, who came from a family of Guyanese and Jamaican migrants, drew the officers' attention because he "adjusted his waistband in a 'suspicious manner' " (Rivas, 2013, March 12). Police patrolling the streets are taught to judge waistband adjustment as a signal that someone may be carrying a weapon. Seeing this telltale sign was all the police needed to justify their approaching Kimani. Law and society researchers refer to this as a "Terry stop,"[1] which in this case, led police to fire 11 rounds into the boy (Devereaux, 2013, March 18). The bullets hit Kimani "seven times, including three in his back" (Marzulli, 2016, March 18).

Since the shooting, conflicting reports have emerged in the press about whether Gray was carrying a gun that night, and about how the interaction between police and Kimani unfolded. The police claimed Gray had brandished a .38-caliber revolver, pointing it at them. Members of his family said otherwise. Tishana King's account, based on what she saw from her third-floor window, differs from the police version in four crucial ways (Devereaux 2013). She insists that: (1) she could see what transpired from her vantage point; (2) the officers did not have their badges displayed; (3) the only thing they told Kimani was, "Don't move," and (4) the only guns she saw were the ones held by police (Devereaux 2013).

In the days following Gray's death, protests broke out in the community, some even turning violent. Numerous press reports suggested that the officers involved in the shootings had a history of abuse, for which the city had paid out $215,000 in legal settlements (Devereaux 2013). The police officials remained steadfast in their version of events. They said Kimani had threatened police with a gun that night. The Brooklyn District Attorney's office decided not to pursue criminal charges against the officers.

The question remains: why would a seemingly innocuous police stop result in the shooting death of Kimani? This young man's state-sanctioned killing was not an isolated event or a random incident. It was the consequence of the existing "Stop and Frisk" public policy that singles out Black communities in general, and young Black men in particular.

Stop and frisk is the latest rendering of a long history of explicit and implicit American policies whose objectives are to rigidly control Black people, whether they have committed a crime or not. Within the premise of White superiority and Black inferiority (racism), there is a white stereotypic belief that Black people are dangerous, unpredictable, violent, and incapable of self-control. Chapter 10 explains how the White social construction of blackness, both past, and present, has informed policing policies toward Black people. Until racism and its stereotypes are challenged effectively, Stop and frisk will continue to evolve into new forms and new titles, and the state will kill more Kimani Grays.

Stop and Frisk

Policing policies in Kimani Gray's neighborhood are a living example of the NYPD's Stop, Question, and Frisk (SQF) program, more often referred to as stop and frisk. SQF is the approved method police officers use to stop and question people whose activities appear suspicious, and who are congregating in high-crime areas. When the police stop someone, they will analyze the situation and determine what they consider is an appropriate response or combination of responses for the existing circumstances. They may choose to release a person, frisk them, ticket them, or arrest them on the spot.

In keeping with the historical pattern of labeling Black communities high-crime areas, at least 76 men and women have been killed in New York City since 1999, while in police custody (Staff, 2014).[2] In 2011 alone, proportionally more Black men were stopped because of this policy than the absolute number of Black males in the city's population (New York Civil Liberties Union, 2012, p. 2). If a person is Black and male, they are automatically under suspicion, and very likely guilty of a crime. The police make no distinction between the majority of individuals who commit no crimes and those who do.

The 67th precinct, where Kimani Gray was killed, is predominantly Black and is among the top ten precincts for police interventions designed to prevent or control crime. Black neighborhoods in the borough of Brooklyn are among the most heavily patrolled neighborhoods in the city's 75 precincts. The following chart shows how many Stop and Frisks occurred in some of the most-heavily policed precincts in Brooklyn, in the 2003 to 2013 timeframe.[3]

Interestingly, the 67th precinct in East Flatbush is not the precinct with the most Stop and Frisks. Figure 10.1 on page 228 shows that there are four other Brooklyn precincts with consistently higher numbers: they are the 70th, 73rd, 75th, and 83rd. In 2013, nine other precincts in the City of New York had more Stop and Frisks than the 67th. In fact, the 73rd Precinct in Brownsville had the largest number, as reflected in table 10.1 (page 228) statistics.

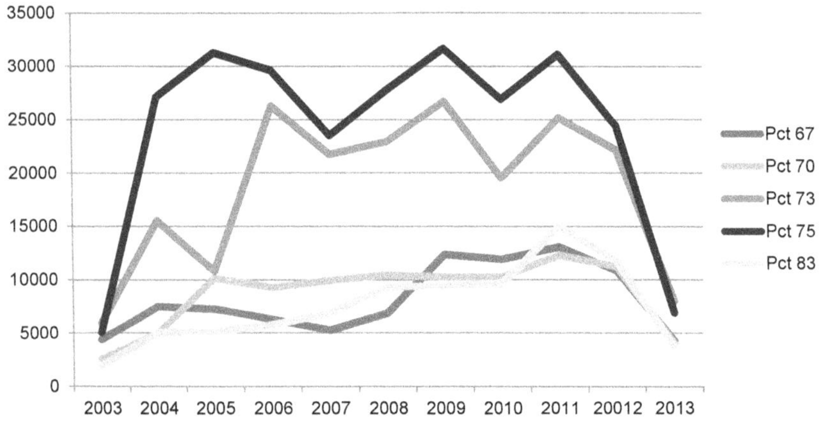

Figure 10.1. Police stops by precinct by year. Precinct 67: East Flatbush; Precinct 70: Flatbush; Precinct 73: Brownsville; Precinct 75: East New York; Precinct 83: Bushwick. *Source:* Byfield, 2019.

Table 10.1. Most Heavily Policed Precincts in New York City in 2013

	Precincts	Stop, Question, and Frisk 2013
1	73-Brooklyn	8001
2	75-Brooklyn	6928
3	101-Queens	6528
4	79-Brooklyn	5481
5	105-Queens	5163
6	103- Queens	4944
7	40-Bronx	4592
8	120-Staten Island	4536
9	60-Brooklyn	4478
10	67-Brooklyn	4317

Source: Byfield, 2019.

The media, whether mainstream or otherwise, framed Kimani's killing as just one more example of police killing a Black male. After all, these types of killings have been going on for more than a century, and the debate over them continues. There is a historical relationship in the United States between race and crime. This relationship affects policing agencies and their interactions with Blacks and other communities of color. When a community is labeled a high-crime zone, it receives more police attention. Increased policing leads to more crime being logged on the books, particularly street crime. This skews crime figures, but it does not follow that the people in these areas commit more crimes than people in other areas.

The criminal justice system positioned its response to Kimani Gray's killing as crime control and used this point of view to justify their approach to police/public interactions (Manning, 2001, pp. 315–21). There is an underlying logic to this explanation of "crime-control." At its foundation, the state is the only agency that can declare specific acts as transgressions or crimes. It judges who is and who is not a criminal, and then decides what to do with someone (Hinton, 2016). However, what happens if the system starts to interpret Blackness as inherently criminal? At that point, racial identity and criminality become one in the same. The state and its agents use this identity to decide how they will punish criminals: through fines, incarceration, or on-the-spot execution.

Critical social theory would challenge the crime control explanation by suggesting that Gray's killing, and the ensuing response from the criminal justice system, are tied instead to much broader social phenomena such as capitalism, globalism, demographics, or even digitization of the economy.[4]

Stop, and Frisk is Not New

Stop, and Frisk is not the first method adopted to control Black people. Related techniques have been used since the end of slavery. Emancipation removed traditional controls, so Whites immediately found new ways to control Blacks, in masse. The Black Codes set up an anti-vagrancy law that ensured Blacks could be incarcerated easily, and then leased out as unpaid labor. Through the convict-lease system, Southern states earned money from this labor pool (Du Bois, 2003). After the Civil War, "about seventy percent of all prisoners in the South are black; this, however, is in part explained by the fact that accused Negroes are still easily convicted and get long sentences, while whites still continue to escape the penalty of many crimes even among themselves" (Du Bois 2003, pp. 86). The convict-lease system not only increased the post-slavery Black incarceration rate, it also ensured white supremacy, and subordinated Blacks through the continued devaluation of their labor.

Blacks in the North were controlled in different ways. For one, they were denied the right to vote. Second, Blacks faced rapid incarceration. Du Bois described the situation in Pennsylvania this way: "the Negro . . . was arrested for less cause and given longer sentences than whites" (2003, p. 43). As Blacks moved north in the Great Migration, crime increased in response to the increased complexity and poverty of life in new cities, and as a "symptom of countless wrong social conditions" (2003, p. 44).

Regardless of what caused the uptick in crime, Du Bois's study of Blacks in Philadelphia showed a tremendous increase in the number of Blacks being incarcerated during the 1890s. This was when scientists who believed in White race dominance began to use social statistics to "measure the behavior and characteristics of black people" (Muhammad 2010, p. 19). "Out of the new methods and data sources, black criminality would emerge, alongside disease and intelligence, as a fundamental measure of black inferiority" (Muhammad, 2010, p. 20). Criminality was seen as a trait encoded in Black people and became part of the definition of blackness. Muhammad (2010) notes:

> With the ascendance of "Statistical Anglo-Saxonism" at the 'fore of the human sciences' and the reform in the 1890s, abstract ideas of universal suffrage and abstract principles of equality, which had proven false and dangerous in the catastrophe that was Reconstruction, would no longer shape the future of race relations. Statistical data on the absolute and relative growth of the black prison population in the 1890 census, for example, would now be analyzed and interpreted as definitive proof of blacks's true criminal nature. (pp. 33–34)

The White social scientists of this period linked the concept of criminality to being ex-slave African descendants, or Black people. They would not accept that racial oppression could explain the crimes Blacks committed and denied the possibility that racism could be behind the crime-fighting techniques used by the state and other dominant White institutions. The legacy of this historical work plagues Black communities to this day. Since slavery began in the United States, Blacks have grown accustomed to prejudicial law enforcement and police scrutinizing Blacks more closely than Whites. Little has changed since the post-slavery and Reconstruction periods. Although Blacks may commit the same infractions as Whites, a White person will suffer fewer consequences than a Black person, or more probably, be excused altogether. For instance, nationally, there is a great disparity in arrest and incarceration rates for illegal drug use by Blacks or Whites. In New York City, NYPD is far less likely to deploy the stop, question, and frisk tactic in a White community than they are in a Black community.

Throughout the country, there are numerous contemporary examples of racial disparity in policing. For example, in a 2013–14 focus group conducted in a Southern low-crime area, participants noted, "the harshest police scrutiny and actions were reserved for Black males" (Wilder-Bonner, 2014, p. 139). Participants said they perceived a race and gender hierarchy in the way police treated different groups, with White women receiving the most preferential treatment (Wilder-Bonner 2014, p. 139).

Where there are concentrations of African Americans in the United States, in either large or small urban areas, there is a long history of the abuse of police power, and acts of violence against Blacks. In cases like these, the judicial system does not charge the police with any crime. Contemporary cases like those of Freddie Gray in Baltimore, Michael Brown in Ferguson, and Eric Garner in New York City repeat a familiar pattern that can be traced to recent events.

In the 1970s and early 1980s, well before today's highly publicized shootings, there was a series of "controversial shooting cases involving white police officers and young [B]lack males" in New York City (Johnson, 2003, p. 282). In 1983, Congress held hearings on the subject of police brutality in the city. The House Judiciary Subcommittee on Criminal Justice, chaired by U.S. Representative John Conyers, highlighted 98 cases, mostly involving Blacks, Latinos, and Asians, that had occurred over the previous 25 years. Fifty-two of those cases, beginning in 1978, had transpired during the administration of Mayor Edward Koch (Roberts, 1983, October 27).

Some very dramatic changes in criminal justice policies took place at the time Conyers's committee was working. Politically conservative interests seized the discourse around "law and order" (Alexander, 2010; Hinton, 2016; Murakawa, 2014; Parenti, 2008). Critical race theory and law and society scholars have depicted their actions as pushback from the racial justice campaigns of the 1960s. More recent scholarship (Murakawa, 2014) indicates that the "law and order" campaigns had a progressive wing that existed two decades earlier. In their own way, they contributed to building the system of mass incarceration that we see today.

The Johnson administration passed the Civil Rights Act of 1964, and the Voting Rights Act of 1965, with a major federal crime-fighting bill being passed at the same time. In post-Johnson Washington, when conservative elements took control of the federal government, other crime-fighting bills were passed, as well. For conservatives, crime fighting and racial justice were interchangeable (Hinton, 2016). From the Nixon administration on, crime fighting would be a major federal concern, with federal funds being allocated to states to address their own crime problems (Parenti, 2008; Alexander, 2010; Murakawa, 2014; Hinton, 2016). The funds were used to professionalize local police forces, and to target the people legislators perceived to be committing the most crimes, namely, Blacks. Data from the U.S. Department of Justice shows that the uptick in Black incarceration began in the late 1970s, in large part at the state level (Langan, 1991, p. 5).

Since the Reagan Administration, the war on drugs has transformed federal, state, and local law enforcement priorities. The lion's share of the money appropriated for the drug wars went to law enforcement and criminal prosecution. Funds were cut from agencies that focused on education, prevention, and treatment (Alexander 2010, p. 49). Around the country, poor Black and Latino communities became the primary sites for drug interdiction programs. The result was a tremendous increase in arrest and incarceration rates, often disproportionate to the number of Blacks in the general population (Human Rights Watch, 2000).

Policing in New York City

In New York State, the growing incarceration rates reflected more aggressive local policing, from forces such as the NYPD. Increased levels of police abuse accompanied the crime-fighting stance of the criminal justice system. Historian Marilynn Johnson's (2003) documentation of police violence in New York City notes that Black communities developed a strong distrust of the police during the 1970s and early-1980s. When documenting the controversial police shootings that occurred during this time, Johnson points out that even Black police did not trust their White counterparts:

> As in past investigations, hundreds of Black citizens turned out to recount their stories of police abuse, expressing bitter disappointment with the ineffectiveness of the CCRB (the Civilian Complaint Review Board) and the police disciplinary system. Some of the most persuasive testimony came from members of the Guardians Association [an organization of Black officers] who recounted recent cases of the shooting of Black plainclothes and off-duty officers by their White colleagues. When the House Subcommittee issued its report the following year, it concluded, "Racism appears to be a major factor in alleged police misconduct." (Johnson, 2003, pp. 282–83)

The Civilian Complaint Review Board (CCRB) was created in 1953, in large part because of New York City police abusing their power against African Americans and Puerto Ricans. It was an official way to respond to complaints from these two communities.[5] The CCRB initially consisted of three deputy police commissioners, whose purview was to investigate civilian complaints. There was a long history of minority communities criticizing the board for its biased assessments of police brutality cases. Political leaders from communities of color regularly called for civilian representation on the board. This demand was fulfilled for a short time during the 1966–73 administration of Mayor John Lindsay. However, the police union, the Police Benevolent Association (PBA), vigorously opposed civilian representation. They challenged Lindsay's board and won. After that, the configuration of the board did not change again until 1987.

A 1988 incident at Tompkins Square Park pushed public opinion in the direction of an all-civilian board. What started as a rally ended up a riot where police officers assaulted Blacks and hurled epithets at Black politicians? The police-dominated board exonerated all police officers involved. The public uproar led to the appointment of civilian board members, who worked alongside police to investigate abuse cases. Unfortunately, even with the addition of civilians to the board, racial profiling and racism in policing have not abated. As a watchdog agency, New York City's complaint review board has a reputation for weakness, at best.

Every new Police Commissioner arrives with their own program designed to address the crime problem. However, they never have a plan for eliminating racism or eradicating police abuse of power. The year after Representative Conyers's hearings, Mayor Koch appointed Benjamin Ward to be the first Black police commissioner in New York City. Ward served for one of Koch's three terms. Of the 98 cases of police violence heard during the Conyers hearings, 52 occurred during the Koch administration. Twenty-five of them resulting in a death: "prosecutors and grand juries found criminality in 1 of the 25, and, in that case, the officers were acquitted by a judge" (Roberts, 1983, October 27). Ward's tenure ended several months before Koch's final term was over. It was at this time the infamous sexual assault of the Central Park jogger occurred. Powerful forces in the city reacted with horror over the assault and sought revenge for the victim. Because of public pressure, police and prosecutors charged and convicted five Black and Latino teens with the rape and assault of the jogger. After the incident, the city's power structure labeled Black and Latino communities ungovernable, therefore requiring even more rigorous policing. It turned out that all five were innocent.

Policing Black People

David Dinkins, the first and only African American mayor of New York City, succeeded Koch as mayor from 1990 to 1993. Dinkins appointed Lee Brown, an African American, as police commissioner. Brown served for three years and ushered in the "Community Policing" model. His concept required police to build relationships with the people they serve. Officers should get out of their cars, walk the streets, talk with residents, and get to know them and their concerns, firsthand. By patrolling the same areas each day, police can familiarize themselves with a neighborhood, at the same time residents are getting to know them. Taken together, these actions put a human face on policing and help to create relationships that are based on trust and mutual helpfulness. The goal is for residents to start to work with the police and to use police services to improve their communities.

Many believed that, by appointing Brown, Dinkins was sending a message to the Black community, his core supporters, that the city's chief administrator shared their concerns. Dinkins also installed the first all-civilian, Civilian Complaint Review Board. Two years later, when Brown resigned abruptly due to his wife's illness, Raymond Kelly was appointed to fill the opening. He claimed he would continue with community policing during his tenure.

David Dinkins served only one term as mayor. Rudolph Giuliani, who appointed William Bratton as police commissioner, succeeded him. Bratton's preferred method of policing was based on a crime control model called "Broken Windows," a criminological theory first introduced by James Q. Wilson in a 1982 article (Kelling & Wilson, 1982). The idea is that major crimes are first preceded by minor crimes such as vandalism, public drinking, auto break-ins and toll jumping. If criminals can get away with minor crimes, they move on to more serious ones such as drug dealing, gun violence, rape, and auto theft. In effect, broken windows in a community indicates a lack of strong social norms and a high degree of secrecy. Broken windows signal that a neighborhood is vulnerable to more serious violations of social norms. Residents will take neither notice of, nor report crimes to the police.

As an adjunct to Broken Windows, Commissioner Bratton implemented CompStat, a management tool using computer generated statistics. It is a compiling of up-to-the-day crime data and deployment information from each police precinct. In using CompStat, the commissioner was able to identify where crime was increasing, and what crimes were being committed. Additional police and specialized units would then be redeployed to the identified hot spots so they could head off additional or more serious crimes. Police would also employ an aggressive policy of stop, question, and frisk. The rationale was as follows. When young men, who sell drugs, and use guns in violent offenses, know their community is being heavily policed, and find out that police will stop and frisk them for drugs and weapons, they will stop carrying drugs and guns. Therefore, both drug sales and gun violence will drop in the more heavily patrolled communities.

However, there is a problem with CompStat. Individual precincts generate their own CompStat data, which could bias their interpretation. It is well known that the harder one looks for crime, the more crime one finds, and some precincts looked harder than others, especially if their residents are Black.

Mayor Giuliani was vehement in his claims that the overall decline in New York City crime rates during his time in office was due to the deployment of CompStat, and Stop and Frisk. He went on to say that withdrawing either tactic would result in a resurgence of crime. However, there was another way of looking at things. The mayor and his police supporters ignored critics at the time who pointed out that there were other factors present. They more logically accounted for the rapid decline in New York crime. The city economy was growing rapidly, overall unemployment was down, and the proportion of the population that was under 29 years of age had rapidly declined. That means the factors that contribute to increases or decreases in crime, leaned toward a decline, and the pool of people who were committing the crimes had decreased. Giuliani and company were fixated on the idea that blackness is a crime, and that Black men need to be controlled.

Giuliani did not acknowledge another important factor. When criminals see more police in an area, they just move to another place that is not as heavily patrolled. In addition, a person can own a gun without always carrying it. They can stash it somewhere that is easily accessible in the neighborhood, or just go back home to get it. From the perspective of the police patrolling the streets of Black communities, the real problem with CompStat, and stop and frisk, is that neither can help them make an important real-time distinction. When on patrol, how do they distinguish between the vast majority of law-abiding citizens and those who have already committed a crime, or are about to commit a crime? White police officers who are unfamiliar with a neighborhood, and the people who live there, cannot tell one Black person from the other. Faces and demeanors all seem the same. To them, everyone fits the description of a suspect they might be looking for. Therefore, the police end up suspecting and fearing everyone. "They" are all criminals, and potentially dangerous to the officers.

Amadou Diallo, a 23-year-old immigrant from Guinea, is a case in point. On February 4, 1999, Diallo was walking toward the entryway to his apartment building in the Bronx. The police, who were following him, mistook him for a rape suspect. They shot at him 41 times, killing him with 19 bullets. Diallo was unarmed, and not wanted for any crimes. The police officers were charged with second-degree murder, yet were acquitted by a jury in Albany, New York.

On March 15, 2000, an undercover police officer approached Patrick Dorismond and attempted to buy drugs from him as part of an anti-drug-dealing sting operation, called Operation Condor. A struggle ensued, and

Dorismond was shot dead. The undercover officers never identified themselves as police. On May 16, 2000, the police stopped Father Smith, a black Catholic priest, as he was driving home from services at his Brooklyn church. He was unarmed, yet shot dead after objecting to his treatment. On June 4, 2000, undercover police followed William Baga, 22, into his Lenox Avenue apartment building. When Baga attempted to close his first-floor apartment door, he was shot six times and died. Baga was the fifth unarmed Black man, killed by the police in a 13-month period. Not one of these individuals had committed a crime (Chou, 2000, April 1). Mayor Giuliani defended the police in all of these shootings and argued that all of them were justified.

Michael Bloomberg's mayoral administration (2002–13) continued the aggressive policies Giuliani had initiated in Black communities. Police Commissioner Raymond Kelly added another way to gather information during stop and frisk stops. Form UF-250 is used to collect data on every aspect of an individual who is stopped: demographics, place of the stop, and physical characteristics such as tattoos or birthmarks. The number of stop and frisk stops increased during the Bloomberg administration.

Barbara Fields (1990) pointed out that the criminal justice system, whether the state's or in this case New York City's, equates being Black with being a criminal. If someone would ask the question, "Who or what are Black people?" the answer would be, "They are criminals." The perception of Black people in New York, in 2017, is the same as it was in the post-slavery, Jim Crow South of 1900. The war on drugs played a particularly important role in nationalizing the initially Southern definition of Black people as criminals.

After examining Stop, Question, and Frisk data, it becomes clear that there are extensive racial disparities in how these investigatory stops are used to patrol and to control Black neighborhoods. The objectives of Stop and Frisk practices appear intentional, given the disproportionate number of Black and Latino males affected by them. A 2012 *The New York Times* short documentary film illustrates the impact this process has on the lives of young men of color. It notes the following:

> The practice of stop-and-frisk has become increasingly controversial, but what is often absent from the debate are the voices of young people affected by such aggressive policing on a daily basis. To better understand the human impact of this practice, we made this film about Tyquan Brehon, a young man who lives in one of the most heavily policed neighborhoods in Brooklyn.
>
> By his count, before his 18th birthday, he had been unjustifiably stopped by the police more than 60 times. On several occasions, merely because he asked why he had been stopped, he

> was handcuffed, placed in a cell and detained for hours before being released without charges. These experiences were scarring; Mr. Brehon did whatever he could to avoid the police, often feeling as if he were a prisoner in his home. (Dressner & Martinez, 2012)

Brehon could have been killed during any of these stops. He could have been arrested for whatever charges the police wanted to register. Following the standard practice, his case could then have been adjudicated by plea-bargaining so he would avoid serious penalties. Despite being innocent of any crime, there were 60 opportunities for Tyquan to have served jail time for no other reason than the fact that he was Black and poor. Stop, and frisk suggests that establishment boundary enforcers have classified significant aspects of Black masculinity as suspicious and criminal. This makes Black males, in general, unfit for mainstream participation. An October 2012 article about the city's Stop and Frisk program noted the following facts about the practice: "more young Black men were stopped by the NYPD in 2011 than there are young Black men in New York City; . . . nine out of 10 of those stopped in 2011 were neither arrested nor given summonses; . . . (yet) Whites are almost twice as likely to be found with a weapon" (New York Civil Liberties Union, 2012, p. 2).

There are two other unexplored dimensions of stop and frisk. Experts have failed to examine the Stop and Frisk data for evidence of racial disparity between patrols in White communities and patrols in Black neighborhoods. Blacks are stopped more frequently overall, but also, they are stopped more frequently when they are traveling in White communities. Therefore, these stops are not about reducing crime in Black communities. What is so suspicious about a young Black man being in a White community that it warrants searching them for drugs and weapons? Perhaps stop and frisk in White communities is more about harassment and maintaining racial boundaries than it is about maintaining safety.

A second unexamined fact is that Blacks in immigrant communities are stopped less frequently than Blacks in precincts where the population is largely native-born. Since policing in New York has more to do with race than crime, why does this discrepancy exist? Also, if the police have trouble detecting differences among Blacks, how is it that they end up stopping more native-born residents than foreign-born ones? There are some theories to consider. Perhaps more minor crimes occur in predominantly native-born, Black communities, which attract more intense police patrolling. There are differences in unemployment rates between the two populations. If more native-born Black men are on the streets because they are unemployed, then there is a greater likelihood they will be stopped and frisked. Foreign-born Black men are employed more often, so they are not on the streets. Another possibility is that there may be a larger number of younger, native-born Black men than there are foreign-born residents, who tend to be older. There is a larger demographic pool of young Black men for police to stop.

Conclusion

Rates of Stop and Frisk in New York City's majority-Black communities, escalated tremendously while Michael Bloomberg was mayor. These neighborhoods grew to be like incarceration zones. Vitale and Jefferson (2016) note the following:

> Unlike other major cities, (that rely on incarceration), New York City has relied on intensive and invasive policing to a much greater extent than mass incarceration in order to contain disjuncture. . . .(T)he NYPD's core policing strategies represent a shift: from an emphasis on using extensive imprisonment as the primary tool of punitive social control towards the intense regulation of low-income communities of color as prisonlike spaces themselves. (pp. 157–58)

After a series of successful lawsuits, the NYPD has had to stop doing Stop and Frisks in buildings where landlords have permitted them to do so (Mueller, 2017, February 2). This is an important restriction, especially in the Bronx and Brooklyn, where stop and frisks have been pervasive. During the de Blasio administration, the number of stop and frisk searches has dramatically dropped citywide, along with crime rates. The city administration has withdrawn its free pass that previously allowed police to search whenever they wanted to. Has stop and frisk ended? Perhaps it has. However, future administrations may choose to return to the stop and frisk model, especially if crime rates reverse and rise again.

Taking the long view, Stop and Frisk did not start racially biased policing in New York City, nor will it end it. Rather, Stop and Frisk is a modern, formal expression of an administrative policy that goes back to a historic bias against African descendants. In one form or another, Stop and Frisk date back to 1919 when police brutality triggered the first Black riot in New York City. Since then, Blacks have been carefully watched, held under suspicion as lawbreakers, and perceived as individuals who need to be controlled. All early ethnic immigrants were subjected to police harassment, but only Blacks have been harassed consistently throughout the city's history. The irony is that native-born, White officers harassed Irish and Italian immigrants. Now, the great-grandchildren of the very same immigrants are harassing Blacks. In the past century, when Blacks have rioted, the confrontation was sparked by an incident of police brutality.

Unless something is done to address this underlying historical racial bias, it is safe to assume that stop and frisk will evolve into new policy and practices that will continue to criminalize Black people. Ending stop and frisk does not eliminate the motivation to criminalize and control Black people. In fact, it is very likely that stop and frisk is a crude antecedent of much more effective and potentially oppressive systems now made possible by advances in data gathering, electronic storage, analyses, and accessibility. In time, and with improvements to CompStat, anyone who is stopped and questioned by the police will have a permanent record of all their encounters with police, and everything about them will be accessible immediately to the officer and the courts.

Police can give electronic bracelets to anyone they ticket or warn. Anyone on parole, or with a court date, can be implanted with a microchip. Both the bracelet and chip will have the capacity to remind them of their court date, warn them about an imminent violation, or track them so they can conveniently be picked up and rearrested once again. It can be argued that these more sophisticated versions of stop and frisk are race-neutral, and finally get at the individuals who commit the crimes. Some claim it is a coincidence that the vast majority of these people continue to be Black.

For the near future, it is likely that the majority of New Yorkers will be people of color: Latino, Asian, Black, and mixtures of all three, plus Whites. Therefore, it will be critically important to know who will be defined as Black, or dark enough to warrant police attention. If there is no change in the historical belief that Black people should occupy the bottom of the social hierarchy, and that they are by definition criminal, then a person's perceived color will have grave consequences. As sociologist Clara Rodriguez argues, inasmuch as color has been an important race marker for Latinos in the United States, a person's color might be perceived differently depending on where they are located in the city.

Writing in the first person, Rodriguez muses about one shared experience among Latinos, the continually shifting perception of their skin color. She writes:

> A natural "tan" in my South Bronx neighborhood was attractive, whereas downtown, in the business area, it was "otherizing." I also recall that the same color was perceived differently in differ-

> ent areas. Even in Latino contexts, I saw some people as lighter or darker, depending on certain factors such as their clothes, occupation, and families. I suspect that others saw me similarly, so that in some contexts, I was very light, in others darker, and in still others about the same as everyone else. Even though my color stayed the same, the perception and sometimes its valuation changed. (Rodriguez, 2000, pp. 3–4)

It is clear that some immigrants experience racialization through whatever classification they receive in the U.S. system of racial dichotomy: White versus all others. Place may serve as a criterion for establishing one's race. Richard Ford points to the importance of "space" or "place" in establishing race in the United States. He argues, as Jim Crow segregation became illegal, and race as a biological concept lost credibility, separation of the races continued through economics and self-imposed segregation (Ford, 1992, p. 127). In the post–Civil Rights era, spatial segregation in urban areas has been intense. If residential space continues to be racially segregated in New York and police continue to use CompStat and stop and frisk in communities of color, then color becomes the signifier of social status in these neighborhoods.

In New York City, residential demarcation by color is profound. The Bronx, Queens, and Brooklyn have the largest foreign-born populations of color. In 2000, the Dominican Republic, China, Jamaica, Guyana, and Mexico were large sources of immigration to New York City. One only needs to look at a map of Brooklyn, where so many immigrants live. Some of the most darkly colored areas of foreign-born residents are in Canarsie, East Flatbush, Flatbush, Midwood, and Bay Ridge-Benson Hurst. In the Bronx, those neighborhoods are Belmont, University Heights, Norwood, Morris Heights, High Bridge, Williams Bridge, and Wakefield. For Manhattan, areas with the largest number of immigrants are Washington Heights, and in Queens, they are Flushing, Astoria, and Elmhurst.

Police may argue that they patrol areas based only on crime, but there are no dramatic differences in the number of felonies in precincts populated by foreign-born residents. If low-level crime, broken windows, goes up in any of them, they can become the target of intense police patrolling, and Stop and frisk criminalization. Residents, young men, in particular, might find themselves marked as new and augmented Black people and criminals. The tragedy that cost Kimani Gray his life occurred because of the NYPD's excessive use of crime control strategies and tactics. Many recognize this, but overlook the fact that something much greater is unfolding, with long-term consequences.

Notes

1. The term "*Terry* stop" is a reference to the 1968 U.S. Supreme Court decision from the case, *Terry v. Ohio*, in which the Court ruled that police do not violate the Fourth Amendment protection against unlawful search and seizure when they stop and search people on the street in an "investigatory" manner to discover concealed contraband materials and to prevent the execution of a crime. See *Terry v. Ohio*, 392 U.S. 1. See also U.S. Commission on Civil Rights Report (1999), *Police Practices and Civil Rights in New York City*. Washington, DC. New York's Criminal Procedure Law (CPL) essentially codifies the United States Supreme Court's holding in *Terry*, authorizing police officers to make limited intrusions upon the liberty of persons in public places for investigative purposes, when the attendant circumstances provide an articulable basis to suspect involvement in criminal activity. Section 140.50 of the CPL authorizes a police officer "to stop a person in a public place . . . when he reasonably suspects that such person is committing, has committed or is about to commit either (a) a felony or (b) a misdemeanor." Once such a stop has been made, New York law authorizes a frisk of the person only if the officer "reasonably suspects that he is in danger of physical injury." These provisions form the core of what is popularly referred to as New York's "Stop and Frisk Act." (chapter 5, p. 4)

2. Beginning in 2015, *The Washington Post* began keeping a database of fatal police shootings. In 2015 and 2016, *The Washington Post* found that 43 and 41 percent, respectively, of the people police across the country shot and killed were Black and Latino. So far, in 2017, 37 percent of those shot and killed by police were Black and Latino.

3. This chart was first published in *Social Identities* (Byfield, 2018). The main distinction between these precincts is that some are more heavily populated by immigrants than others. The 67th Precinct in East Flatbush and the 70th Precinct in Flatbush are populated predominantly by immigrants from the Caribbean. Over the 10-year period of this data, the 83rd Precinct grew tremendously in foreign-born population. Chart 1 shows that three precincts heavily populated by immigrants have far fewer stops than the 73rd and the 75th Precincts which are populated primarily by native-born Blacks. This may be a reflection of the process of racialization.

4. Similar forces were described by Du Bois in *The Philadelphia Negro* as shaping the lives of Blacks in late 19th century Philadelphia. Loughran (2015) highlights these features of Du Bois' study to point out the implicit urban theories in his work.

5. All information about the Civilian Complaint Review Board is from the board's website: http://www.nyc.gov/html/ccrb/html/history.html.

References

Alexander, M. (2010). *The New Jim Crow: Mass incarceration in the age of colorblindness*. New York, NY: The New Press.

Byfield, N. P. (2019). Race science and surveillance: Police as the new race scientists, *Social Identities: Journal for the Study of Race, Nation and Culture*, vol. 25: 76–90.

Chou, J. (2000, April 1). Operation Condor. *GothamGazette*. Retrieved from http://www.gothamgazette.com/criminal-justice/1633-operation-condor.

Devereaux, R. (2013, March 18). Eyewitness: Police shot Kimani Gray while the 16-year-old was on the ground. *The Village Voice*. Retrieved from http://www.villagevoice.com/news/eyewitness-police-shot-kimani-gray-while-the-16-year-old-was-on-the-ground-6708923.

Dressner, J., & Martinez, E. (2012, June 12). The scars of stop-and-frisk. *The New York Times*. Retrieved from http://www.nytimes.com/2012/06/12/opinion/the-scars-of-stop-and-frisk.html.

Du Bois, W. E. B. (2003). Spawn of slavery. In S. L. Babbidon et al. (Eds.), *African American classics in criminology and criminal justice*. Thousand Oaks, CA: Sage Publications.

Fields, B. J. (1990). Slavery, race and ideology in the United States of America. *New Left Review*, 181, 95–118.

Ford, R. T. (1992). Urban space and the color line: The consequences of demarcation and disorientation in the postmodern metropolis. *Harvard Blackletter Journal, 9*, 117–47.

Hinton, E. (2016). *From the war on poverty to the war on crime: The making of mass incarceration in America*. Cambridge, MA: Harvard University Press.

Human Rights Watch. (2000). Punishment and prejudice: Racial disparities in the war on drugs. *HRW Reports, 12*(2).

Johnson, M. (2003). *Street justice: A history of police violence in New York City*. Boston, MA: Beacon Press.

Kelling, G., & Wilson, J. Q. (1982, March). Broken windows: The police and neighborhood safety. *The Atlantic*.

Langan, P. A. (1991). *Race of prisoners admitted to state and federal institutions, 1926–86*. Washington, DC: U.S. Department of Justice National Institute of Justice.

Lobo, A., Lobo, P., & Salvo, J. J. (2013). *The newest New Yorkers: Characteristics of the city's foreign-born population* (2013 ed.). New York: Department of City Planning, City of New York.

Manning, P. K. (2001). Theorizing policing: The drama and myth of crime control in the NYPD. *Theoretical Criminology, 5*, 315–44.

Marzulli, J. (2016, March 18). Witness says teen killed by cops in Brooklyn had hands up. *New York Daily News*. Retrieved from http://www.nydailynews.com/new-york/nyc-crime/witness-teen-killed-cops-brooklyn-hands-article-1.2579528.

Mueller, B. (2017, February 2). New York police dept. agrees to curb stop-and-frisk tactics. *The New York Times*. Retrieved from https://www.nytimes.com/2017/02/02/nyregion/new-york-police-dept-stop-and-frisk.html.

Muhammad, K. G. (2010). *The condemnation of blackness: Race, crime, and the making of modern urban America*. Cambridge, MA: Harvard University Press.

Murakawa, N. (2014). *The first civil right: How liberals built prison America*. Oxford, UK: Oxford University Press.

New York Civil Liberties Union. (2012). Stop-and-frisk 2011. *New York Civil Liberties Union*. Retrieved from https://www.nyclu.org/sites/default/files/publications/NYCLU_2011_Stop-and-Frisk_Report.pdf.

Parenti, C. (2008). *Lockdown America: Police and prisons in the age of crisis*. New York, NY: Verso Books.

Rivas, J. (2013, March 12). NYPD kills teen who witness says was just adjusting belt. *Colorlines*.

Roberts, S. (1983, October 27). When police are accused of brutality. *The New York Times*. Retrieved from http://www.nytimes.com/1983/10/27/nyregion/when-police-are-accused-of-brutality.html?

Rodriguez, C. E. (2000). *Changing race: Latinos, the census, and the history of ethnicity in the United States*. New York, NY and London, UK: New York University Press.

Staff. (2014, December 8). Unarmed people of color killed by police, 1999–2014. *HuffPost*. Retrieved from http://www.huffingtonpost.com/2014/12/08/unarmed-people-of-color-k_n_6290398.html.

Vitale, A. S., & Jefferson, B. J. (2016). The emergence of command and control policing in neoliberal New York. In J. T. Camp & C. Heatherton (Eds.), *Policing the planet: Why the policing crisis led to Black Lives Matter*. London and New York, NY: Verso Press.

Wilder-Bonner, K. M. (2014). Race, space, and being policed: A qualitative analysis of residents: Experiences with Southern patrols. *Race and Justice, 4*(2), 124–51.

— POLICING ADDENDUM —

Race-Based Discrimination in Expert Witness Testimony

George W. Woods and Stephen Greenspan

Within our legal system, there exists a form of race-based discrimination with substantial consequences for people of color and impaired abilities. It is called "cultural shadowing." Forensic mental health professionals use it when they testify about persons of color in criminal or civil cases. Cultural shadowing presents itself in two different situations. First, there is *cultural-overshadowing*, which occurs when culture or race is used to minimize or ignore important person-based qualities, such as brain damage, mental illness, or physical illness. Second, there is *cultural under-shadowing*, which ensues when testimony relies excessively on alleged personal qualities, but without sufficient attention given to the explanatory role of pertinent cultural and environmental factors.

We explored New York City legal cases for examples of cultural shadowing by expert witnesses, and found it in situations when consultants were: (1) predicting future dangerousness; (2) diagnosing medical or neuro-developmental disorders; (3) determining possible malingering; (4) identifying sexually violent offenders for post-sentence civil commitment, and; (5) making recommendations in child custody and parental termination cases. Many experts exhibited cultural overshadowing when they assumed that minority men, especially Blacks, are inherently more dangerous. They tended to overlook signs of brain impairment in minority defendants, attributing their limitations to family factors, even when siblings were competent, and signs of brain impairment, such as Fetal Alcohol Spectrum Disorder, were evident. Minority defendants were accused of manufacturing symptoms or faking cognitive limitations much more often, as well.

Cultural under-shadowing, the failure to appreciate contextual factors and strengths, can have a distorting effect as well. For instance, authorities are sometimes reluctant to restore parental rights, because they fail to appreciate attachment strengths in minority families. Experts also tend to apply White middle-class standards of sexual normalcy to all situations, thus introducing the sexual predation concept inappropriately.

Expert witnesses who practice cultural shadowing in criminal or civil proceedings, can profoundly and unfairly affect the rights of minority individuals who are targets of their opinions. The experts in question are typically trained; doctoral-level psychologists or psychiatrists who have chosen to specialize in a forensic mental health practice. Frequently, their expertise is based on divergent training about the role of race, culture, class, neighborhood, and social context. Generally, these topics are not part of mainstream studies in medical and psychological graduate programs.

Cultural shadowing often results in defendants being treated in an inequitable and racist way, by individuals who may themselves have minority backgrounds, and are not consciously racist. Cultural literacy has received little attention in the forensic mental health field, but it is something that requires greater consideration over time.

Chapter 11

Public Health

Public Policy, HIV/AIDS, and the Destruction of Community in New York City

Robert Fullilove

In 2015, New York City was home to almost 10 percent of the people living with HIV disease in the United States (CDC, 2016). This unusually heavy burden of disease and disability is not a mere function of the city's size and position as the largest urban center in the U.S. Nor is the rate of infection somehow a consequence of the city's significant population of Black and Hispanic residents, who in both New York City and the broader U.S., are the two groups that constitute the majority of those living with HIV/AIDS (CDC, 2016; NYCDOH, 2015). As this chapter will argue, the burden of HIV infections can be traced to three disastrous public policy crises that have led to the destruction of low-income Black and Latino communities.

First, during the 1970s and 1980s, widespread fire disasters occurred, resulting in a massive loss of housing in the city (D. Wallace & Wallace, 1998; R. Wallace, 1988; R. Wallace, Fullilove, & Wallace, 1992). These fires, in turn, caused several drug-using networks to scatter throughout the city, leading to a significant increase in the levels of HIV infection among those who injected drugs (Des Jarlais, Friedman, Sotheran, Wenston, & Marmor, 1994; Hahn, Onorao, Jones, & Dougherty, 1989). Second, a series of laws were passed aimed at criminalizing the possession of drug injection paraphernalia. These laws drove people to share injection equipment in so-called shooting galleries (Beletsky, Davis, Anderson, & Burns, 2008; Hahn et al., 1989). This underground needle-sharing further intensified the spread of HIV. Third, an era of mass incarceration began in the 1970s and 1980s, popularly called the War on Drugs. This so-called war had a substantial impact on those who were caught, arrested, tried and convicted for drug-related crimes (Golembeski & Fullilove, 2005).

Taken together, these three developments generated disastrous changes in the behavior of those at risk for HIV. This amplified the city's dubious distinction as an epicenter of the HIV/AIDS epidemic in the United States. These policies prompted the utter destruction of low-income Black and Latino communities where the war was fought, and where drug abuse and HIV were concentrated. They also provoked several other serious consequences. They include the collapse of neighborhood ties; the untying of community bonds; the exhaustion of social capital, and; the dispersal of residents from low-income Black and Latino communities. In turn, these policies set the stage for the gentrification of many of these communities by the year 2000.

Burning the South Bronx

In their landmark text, *A Plague on Your Houses: How New York Was Burned Down and the National Public Health Crumbled*, Deborah and Roderick Wallace (1998) argue that the policies New York City instituted from the 1960s through the 1970s, in fact, promoted what the authors call "planned shrinkage." The city did this by withdrawing essential municipal services from selected low-income neighborhoods. The city cited different reasons for its decision. For instance, they said they wanted to extend industry and industrial plants into New York City neighborhoods. They also had plans to reduce municipal spending on neighborhoods with substantial levels of poverty.

Non-white neighborhoods were targeted because policymakers were struggling with the sequelae of the civil rights movement in this era. City administrators were fascinated by the proposal made by Daniel Patrick Moynihan, President Nixon's domestic policy advisor. Moynihan suggested that the racial tensions of the 1960s might be reduced by adopting a set of policies that he described as "benign neglect." In truth, this meant the government would reduce its support of pro-Negro, pro-civil rights policies and programs. In 1970, Moynihan asserted that racial progress was being made nationally, so a cooling-off period should be instituted by the federal government to reduce the hysteria and histrionics of "extremists of either race" (Moynihan, 1970).

> "Planned shrinkage" was the New York City expression of Moynihan's "benign neglect." A form of triage, it dictated the withdrawal of essential services from sick neighborhoods, which were seen as unable to survive or undeserving of survival. These services

> ranged from libraries to fire service to public transportation. Of course, the neighborhoods diagnosed as "sick" were all poor and nonwhite. (Wallace and Wallace, 1998, p. 24)

As part of the strategy of planned shrinkage, the city reduced the fire services available to poor communities. Based on operations research models created by the New York City Rand Institute, 50 New York City firefighting units serving densely populated neighborhoods in West Bronx, Central and East Harlem, Bushwick/Brownsville/East New York and South Jamaica were either reduced, disbanded or removed altogether. The results were catastrophic: "From 1972 to 1976, coincident with fire service reductions, engine company structural fire worktime (a composite of building fire number and seriousness) rose from 44,000 to 63,000, an increase of some 45 percent. The increase was concentrated in areas that already had high fire rates (Kolesar & Walker, 1972), such as Brownsville, East New York, and the South Bronx . . ." (Wallace, 1988, p. 3).

Wallace concludes that these reductions triggered "a highly contagious form of urban decay" in which a continuous rash of building fires rapidly created an entire block of deserted, abandoned buildings. The destroyed blocks and buildings multiplied in number, and soon entire neighborhoods were blighted. The tabloids in the 1970s and 1980s described this disaster as the "burned out South Bronx" (Wallace, 1988). Block after block, one saw only ruins of formerly sturdy brick apartment buildings. This became increasingly common in other low-income Black and Latino communities in New York City.

Structures that had previously been overcrowded fell victim to this contagious destruction, creating a massive displacement of residents. With its domino effect, this increased the overcrowding that already existed in relatively intact neighborhoods. Residents fleeing this ruination could only afford to settle in other impoverished areas. The result, Wallace concludes, was a *synergism of plagues* in which drug abuse, tuberculosis and HIV/AIDS, all scourges of the poor, fed on each other (Wallace, 1988; Wallace and Wallace, 1998).

The impact of the city's policies on the HIV/AIDS epidemic was particularly significant. During the 1970s, HIV existed in many of these communities but went completely unrecognized. It is worth remembering that 1981 was the year people first became aware of HIV in the U.S. when a group of young men with Pneumocystis Pneumonia presented themselves for treatment in Los Angeles. Their cases were reported in a landmark article that appeared in the CDC's Morbidity and Mortality Weekly Report (CDC, 1981). This has been historically marked as the beginning of HIV/AIDS in America. It is worth noting that Pneumocystis is an AIDS-defining condition, which means these were men in the end stages of HIV disease, and not at the asymptomatic stage that is characteristic of an early HIV infection. Therefore, the actual beginning of the HIV/AIDS epidemic in the U.S. occurred sometime in the 1970s, or even earlier, when many individuals were infected but showed no signs of their illness (Fullilove, 2012). This is the same time that the South Bronx and many other poor communities were burning down in New York City.

Networks of injection drug users were among those displaced by these fires. Wallace hypothesizes that each successive displacement broke up networks of syringe sharers. This forced them to relocate, and reorganize their networks in other neighborhoods, frequently with new partners. No one could have imagined a more efficient way to transmit HIV, and to destroy entire communities. Wallace concludes, "In fact, the city's planned shrinkage program seems to have significantly spread AIDS in the Bronx, by driving intravenous drug abuse from a relatively well-defined center in the South Central Bronx to an almost borough-wide phenomenon" (Wallace, 1988, p. 18). Injectors were driven into other parts of the city, and beyond. The challenge of controlling the epidemic magnified. For more than a decade, high-risk populations scattered and then reconstituted. HIV prevention efforts taking place in neighborhood care centers were outpaced by constantly changing neighborhood social networks (Wallace, 1988; Wallace, Fullilove, and Wallace, 1992; Wallace and Wallace, 1998).

Needle Sharing, the Law, Shooting Galleries, and HIV/AIDS

Des Jarlais and colleagues examined the HIV epidemic among injecting drug users, from the years 1984 to 1992. They wrote, "The HIV epidemic among injecting drug users (IDUs) in New York City was the first and has been the largest of all known HIV epidemics among IDUs" (Des Jarlais et al., 1994, p. 192). The practice of sharing injecting drug equipment most readily explains the high rate of infection, even more than does the use of illicit drugs, alone. In one of the earliest efforts to summarize the impact of intravenous drug use on the U.S. epidemic, Hahn and colleagues reviewed 92 published and unpublished studies of HIV in this population. In a 1989 article, they concluded, "Sharing of drug-injection equipment is common, ranging from 70 percent to 100 percent in different regions of the country. So-called shooting galleries, where intravenous injection paraphernalia are rented and shared, are reported to be more common in the Northeast . . ." (Hahn et al., 1989, p. 2680).

In large part, shooting galleries owe their existence to anti-drug policies that make it illegal to possess drug-injecting equipment without a prescription. According to *New York Consolidated Laws, Public Health Law—PBH § 3381., Sale and possession of hypodermic syringes and hypodermic needles* say the following. "It shall be unlawful for any person to obtain or possess a hypodermic syringe or hypodermic needle unless such possession has been authorized by the commissioner or is pursuant to a prescription" (New York Consolidated Laws, 2017). Moreover, "While it is against the law to possess, manufacture or sell illegal drugs, under New York Penal Code § 220.45, it is also against the law to possess a hypodermic needle that could be used to inject such drugs."

To avoid the possibility of arrest and incarceration for possessing injection equipment, IDUs increasingly resorted to using hidden shooting galleries. In the early years of the HIV/AIDS epidemic, more and more people grew to understand that addicts could avoid an HIV infection if they had access to over-the-counter (OTC) syringes available at pharmacies. Illegal syringe exchange programs began operating where and when IDUs congregate. Such programs could dramatically reduce the burden of infection in this population. Advocates of effective prevention struggled then, as they do now, to get lawmakers to accept the idea of syringe exchanges (Anderson, 1991; Beletsky et al., 2008).

In 2001, Friedman, Perlis, and Des Jarlais (2001) examined the impact of failing to enact such programs. Their cross-sectional study focused on HIV prevalence and incidence in 96 U.S. metropolitan areas, comparing areas that had OTC laws, with those that had anti-OTC laws.

> Mean HIV prevalence was 13.8 percent in metropolitan areas with anti-OTC laws and 6.7 percent in other metropolitan areas (pseudo-P<.001). Median HIV prevalence was also greater in cities with anti-OTC laws than in cities without them. In linear regression controlling for distance from New York City and HIV prevalence among men who have sex with men (MSM), seroprevalence among IDUs was greater by 5.8 percent in metropolitan areas with anti-OTC laws (pseudo-P<.001). (Friedman, Perlis, & Des Jarlais, 2001)

In essence, two public policy challenges, how to control illicit drug use and how to manage municipal services in poor communities of color, generated policies, laws, regulations, and resource management decisions that contributed significantly to the propagation of HIV in New York City. The war on drugs was a third. This policy only further exacerbated the circulation of HIV/AIDS in the 1970s and 1980s.

The War on Drugs, Mass Incarceration, and HIV/AIDS

President Richard Nixon appeared on national television in 1970, and declared, "Drugs are public enemy number one." With this one statement, he triggered the introduction of laws and policies that targeted the one segment of the population that was at an elevated risk for exposure to HIV: those caught up in illicit drug use (Fullilove, 2012). By the end of the 1960s, controlling the increase in drug use was already a challenge to the nation's health care establishment. Addiction rates and crime rates associated with drug use were on the rise. Drug treatment advocates prescribed expanding access to treatment and proposed engaging in local and national efforts to educate the public about the prevention and treatment of drug abuse (Anderson, 1991).

However, the war on drugs took a different direction. The nation instead invested heavily in arresting, trying, and incarcerating those with drug-related offenses. It was no coincidence that the vast majority of these drug users were Blacks and Latinos in large cities, such as New York. The aftermath has been grim: by 2015, almost one-half million people were serving time in U.S. state and federal prison facilities, and more than five million were on probation or parole by that date (The Sentencing Project, 2017).

> Sentencing policies of the War on Drugs era resulted in dramatic growth in incarceration for drug offenses. Since its official beginning in the 1980s, the number of Americans incarcerated for drug offenses has skyrocketed from 40,900 in 1980 to 469,545 in 2015. At the federal level, people incarcerated on a drug conviction make up just under half the prison population. At the state level, the number of people in prison for drug offenses has increased tenfold since 1980. Most of these people are not high-level actors in the drug trade, and most have no prior criminal record for a violent offense. (Sentencing Project, 2017, p. 3)

Not surprisingly, rates of HIV/AIDS in prison have skyrocketed, as revealed in periodic reports from the Justice Department, all chronicling the impact of the epidemic that began in 1991. Lawrence Greenfeld, the acting director of the Bureau of Justice Statistics, wrote the first report documenting HIV in U.S. prisons and jails. He wrote, "Because of their comparatively high rates of drug abuse, jail and prison inmates are at greater risk of contracting AIDS . . . During their lives, nearly 1 in 5 prisoners had used a needle to inject illegal drugs" (Bureau of Justice Statistics, 1993).

Incarcerating members of this HIV/AIDS risk group created a key source for spreading HIV in jails and prisons. For example, at a time when the CDC reported the HIV/AIDS national seroprevalence using a rate-per-100,000 persons metric, prisons were holding one of the largest, if not the largest, pool of HIV/AIDS cases, measured and reported as a *percent* of the total population in custody.

According to the Bureau of Justice Statistics, in 1991, the national percent of HIV/AIDS cases in state and federal prisons, as a percent of the total custody population, was 2.2 percent. Inmates in New York State represented 13.8 percent of the total national population in custody that year. With almost 75 percent of the New York State prison population originating from seven neighborhoods in New York City (Ellis, 1990), the prison pool of HIV/AIDS cases was, in reality, a reflection of the epidemic in New York City. The seven neighborhoods in question were precisely those neighborhoods that have historically reported the highest background HIV seroprevalence rates in New York State, if not in the U.S. (Fullilove, 2012).

Cycling inmates in and out of New York State prison facilities, and in and out of their original neighborhoods, contributed greatly to the spread of HIV/AIDS in New York City. This circulation also explains why New York is one of the major epicenters of the national HIV/AIDS epidemic. More importantly, the New York City epidemic has its origins in three sets of policies. The first were policies that destabilized the housing in the poor communities that report high rates of HIV infection. The second were policies that outlawed the purchase of syringes, which then drove many users to go to shooting galleries where they frequently shared injection equipment. Finally, there were national policies that punished drug addiction with arrests and lengthy prison terms, instead of opportunities for treatment and rehabilitation.

American HIV/AIDS research in the 1980s and early 1990s, rarely acknowledged that prisons were a pivotal source of HIV. Studies, that assessed the role of injection drug users, focused largely on IDUs who were in treatment. Hahn and colleagues noted in 1989, "Surveys of HIV seroprevalence have been conducted almost exclusively among IVDUs in drug treatment programs. Rates of HIV infection among IVDUs not in treatment have been measured in only a few studies" (Hahn et al., 1989, p. 2683).

In the early years of the epidemic, many researchers did not study the prison population. At that time, AIDS research generally focused on the people at risk, and on the behaviors that put them at risk of infection. What mattered to most AIDS researchers early on was the "who" and the "what" of the disease: who is engaged in HIV-risk behavior and what are the behaviors they are engaging in that put them at risk. At the outset of the epidemic, few researchers paid much attention to the structural factors that created *risk environments*. Instead, they concentrated on risk behaviors, such as sharing needles or syringes, which occurred in non-structural settings and were, in fact, secondary to widening the epidemic.

It is crucial to note. At the beginning of the epidemic, it seemed easier to fix people, than to fix the social and economic structures that created the risk environment in the first place, and that promoted high exposure and death rates (Rhodes, Singer, Bourgois, Friedman, & Strathdee, 2005).

Risk-group members engaging in risk-taking behaviors were not the only reason for the HIV epidemic in New York. Public policies, laws, and regulations, both nationally and in New York City, were equally responsible for the HIV epidemic in the 1960s, 1970s and 1980s. Their impact on the HIV/AIDS crisis strongly suggests that HIV risk at the outset of the epidemic was "socially produced."

> If HIV risk is socially produced then so too are public health solutions . . . An understanding of social determinants and an embracement of social change in HIV prevention also seeks to connect HIV risk reduction within the context of human rights and vulnerability more broadly, thereby encouraging a shift in understanding responsibility for harm and the focus for change as a product of individuals to a product of the social situations and structures in which individuals find themselves. (Rhodes et al., 2005, p. 1036)

The public policies that were officially responsible for expanding drug abuse and the HIV/AIDS epidemic were separate from those that caused the rapid social and physical decline of low-income Black and Latino communities in New York City. These communities were affected strongly by four developments: the withdrawal of municipal services as a form of benign neglect; externally provoked drug abuse, HIV/AIDS, and incarceration. Taken together these forces dislodged residents, destroyed their housing, and set the stage for gentrification. After thirty years of destruction in low-income communities, residents find it hard to resist gentrification, which they would have fought fiercely in the 1960s and 1970s.

Conclusions and Recommendations

It has been argued here that HIV/AIDS in New York City is the result of more than drug users and sexually active individuals participating in high-risk behaviors. Rather, it was public policy decisions that prompted changes in housing, neighborhood social networks and individual risk-taking, which drastically altered the options available to residents of communities of color. Apartment fires that raged in the South Bronx, and in other poor neighborhoods in the city, destroyed both the homes and the social networks that residents relied on for their health and safety. The displacement associated with the fire epidemics during the 1970s and 1980s ripped familiar networks apart, as well as the social fabric of neighborhoods. The social capital that residents previously had available had made it possible for people to live in and raise children in impoverished conditions (Fullilove, Green, & Fullilove, 2000). When the fires displaced these individuals, and scattered them to the four winds, so to speak, they lost the essential elements of resident-based, neighborhood-based public interventions that would have prevented drug abuse and HIV risk behaviors.

Mindy Fullilove has written extensively about the problems of urban America. As a psychiatrist, she has generated an extensive body of work describing how urban segregation, policies of urban renewal and planned shrinkage have been at the core of the problems that are categorized in public health parlance under the rubric of *health disparities*. She has argued that in segregated urban settings, more than a problem-specific or even community-specific set of solutions is required. HIV/AIDS represents one of many challenges facing poor communities, in a nation that is beset with problems of racism, poverty, exclusion, and segregation.

If HIV is a neighborhood-based problem, then neighborhood-based solutions are needed to solve it. Fullilove suggests, however, by taking this approach one fails to acknowledge that urban centers are part of an ecological system. The only way to correct a system-wide problem is to develop policies, programs, and interventions that work at the full system level. Neighborhood-based solutions, in effect, are insufficient (Fullilove, 2013).

She notes that, in New York, HIV/AIDS is concentrated in neighborhoods dealing with poverty, and a host of health disparities. The temptation, then, is to direct our time, our attention and our resources to places that reveal these symptoms. Fullilove believes drug abuse, HIV/AIDS and other health disparities are simply symptoms of a system-level problem.

> *We can't just treat the neighborhoods* . . . In the medical model of disease, we know that symptoms arise from disorder in the organ, like the heart. The symptoms alert us to trouble, but what we treat is the problem in the organ. Arguing by analogy, the neighborhoods had the symptoms of disorder, *but the city was the organ with the defect of fracture* . . . Indeed the policies of segregation,

> redlining, urban renewal, and planned shrinkage, which caused the problems, *were policies of the city, not the neighborhood.* (Fullilove, 2013, pp. 21–22)

What cities or government entities do regarding public policies will drive and define structural outcomes in neighborhoods. Neighborhood-based efforts to provide treatment, HIV services, and community enhancements must be joined and connected to other, system-wide efforts. They must confront problems as diverse as homelessness, mass incarceration, and lack of access to medical services, improvements in public education, unemployment, violence, and drug abuse.

Ironically, this recommended focus correlates with the principles the U.S. Public Health Service espoused in *Healthy People 2020* (HP2020). This is a report that outlines the health goals and objectives they established for the U.S. HP2020 recognizes that population health is a function of individual health-seeking behaviors, as well as a larger set of social determinants essential to health. In this regard, the following social determinants can and should be addressed:

> **Drug Abuse:** The most effective way to reduce drug abuse in Black and Latino communities is to promote drug abuse prevention and treatment, and to foster job opportunities, rather than take the failed course adopted by the War on Drugs: an excessive dependence on incarceration. Drug trafficking is a crime, but drug addiction is not. It is a medical problem with medical solutions. Trafficking is also an economic problem that arises when young people have no viable options for earning a legitimate living wage. Instead, they seek ways to survive in the underground economy by drug trafficking and dealing.
>
> **HIV/AIDS:** The most effective way to reduce HIV rates is through risk-reduction practices. Injection drug users must not be driven underground and forced into needle sharing that virtually guarantees HIV infection. This could be accomplished by withdrawing needle and injection paraphernalia possession laws and replacing them with needle exchanges, prescription opioid substitutes, and HIV/AIDS treatment and prevention plans.
>
> **Community Destruction:** Withdrawing municipal services, especially fire services, from the most vulnerable New York City communities was the 1960s and 1970s equivalent to the more

> recent pumping of contaminated water into Flint, Michigan's water supply. It was a racially motivated act of genocide, and clearly a criminal offense. The outcome has been devastating to low-income Black and Latino New Yorkers and has set the stage for the gentrification of these areas. As an act of restitution, and of practical necessity, the City of New York needs to devise public policies to preserve rather than destroy low-income and below-market-rate housing, and racially diverse communities. Low-income workers are vital to the city and to stable, equitably resourced communities are essential for effective education, public health, and drug abuse and HIV prevention.

New York City is positioned uniquely to embrace solutions to its public health dilemmas. It can do this by supporting neighborhood- and system-wide interventions that promote health and prevent disease. It is hard to imagine a more fitting way to achieve the goals of HP2020 than by eliminating the structural barriers to healthy communities, and by reversing the destruction of communities.

References

Anderson, W. (1991). The New York needle trial: The politics of public health in the age of AIDS. *American Journal of Public Health, 81*, 1506–17.

Beletsky, L., Davis, C., Anderson, E., & Burns, S. (2008). The law (and politics) of safe injection facilities in the United States. *American Journal of Public Health, 98*, 231–37.

Bureau of Justice Statistics. (1993). *HIV in US jails and prisons*. Washington, DC: US Department of Justice.

CDC. (1981). Pneumocystis Pneumonia. *Los Angeles. MMWR, 30/21*.

CDC. (2016). HIV surveillance report, diagnoses of HIV infection in the United States and dependent areas, 2015. *27*.

Des Jarlais, D., Friedman, S., Sotheran, J., Wenston, J., & Marmor, M. (1994). Continuity and change within an HIV epidemic: Injecting drug users in New York City, 1984 through 1992. *Journal of the American Medical Association, 271*, 121–27.

Ellis, E. (1990). *85% of prisoners Black or Latino; 75% of state's entire prison population comes from just seven neighborhoods in New York City*. Paper presented at the Caribbean/African Unity Conference, Greenhaven State Correctional Facility.

Friedman, S., Perlis, T., & Des Jarlais, D. (2001). Laws prohibiting over-the-counter syringe sales to injection drug users; relations to population density, HIV prevalence, and HIV incidence. *American Journal of Public Health, 91*, 791–93.

Fullilove, M. (2013). *Urban alchemy: Restoring joy in America's sorted-out cities*. New York, NY: New Villages Press.

Fullilove, R. (2012). Mass incarceration in the United States and HIV/AIDS: Cause and effect? *Ohio State Journal of Criminal Law, 9*, 353–61.

Fullilove, R., Green, L., & Fullilove, M. (2000). Family to family program: A Structural intervention with implications for the prevention of HIV/AIDS and Other Community Epidemics. *AIDS, 14*(suppl 1), S63–S67.

Golembeski, C., & Fullilove, R. (2005). Criminal [in]justice in the city and its associated health consequences. *American Journal of Public Health, 95*, 1701–06.

Hahn, R., Onorao, I., Jones, T., & Dougherty, J. (1989). Prevalence of HIV infection among intravenous drug users in the United States. *Journal of the American Medical Association, 261*, 2677–84.

Kolesar, P., & Walker, W. E. (1972). *An algorithm for the dynamic relocation of fire companies*. New York, NY: The New York City Rand Institute.

Moynihan, D. P. (1970). *Toward a national urban policy*. New York, NY: Basic Books.

New York Consolidated Laws. (2017). Public health law—PBH § 3381. Retrieved from http://codes.findlaw.com/ny/public-health-law/pbh-sect-3381.html#sthash.k3uCw3Jg.dpuf.

NYCDOH. (2015). *HIV surveillance annual report, 2015*. New York, NY: HIV Epidemiology and Field Services Program.

Rhodes, T., Singer, M., Bourgois, P., Friedman, S., & Strathdee, S. (2005). The social structural production of HIV risk among injecting drug users. *Social Science in Medicine, 61*, 1026–44.

The Sentencing Project. (2017). Trends in US corrections: US state and federal prison population, 1925–2015: Fact Sheet. Retrieved from http://www.sentencingproject.org/publications/trends-in-u-s-corrections/.

Wallace, D., & Wallace, R. (1998). *A Plague on your houses: How New York was burned down and national public health crumbled*. New York, NY: Verso.

Wallace, R. (1988). A synergism of plagues: "Planned shrinkage," contagious housing destruction, and AIDS in the Bronx. *Environmental Research, 47*, 1–33.

Wallace, R., Fullilove, M., & Wallace, D. (1992). Family systems and deurbanization: implications for substance abuse. In Lowinson, Ruiz, Millman, & Langrod (Eds.), *Subtance abuse: A comprehensive textbook* (pp. 944–55). Baltimore,MD: Wilkins & Wilkins.

— PUBLIC HEALTH ADDENDUM —

Inequalities in Health and Access to Health Services in New York City: Change and Continuity

Michael K. Gusmano and Victor G. Rodwin

Introduction

Since 2000, there have been remarkable gains in New York City's health status, and access to health care services. Despite increases in the prevalence of obesity, high blood pressure, diabetes, and asthma, as well as poorer self-reported health status, life expectancy at birth has increased. Infant mortality has decreased, and the percentage of people who report having a regular source of care has increased (NYC Dept. Health and Mental Hygiene, 2013). Former Mayor Bloomberg's administration emphasized the importance of improving NYC's population health status, and it endorsed reducing disparities in access to health services. Bloomberg's successor, Mayor Bill de Blasio, continued this focus. Despite these efforts, however, we have found that inequalities in racial, ethnic, and neighborhood-level access to health care services persist (Gusmano, Rodwin, & Weisz, 2017).

One dimension of health system performance is particularly important in New York City. In the 12-year period between 2000 and 2012, access to community-based ambulatory care, as measured by hospital discharge rates for avoidable hospital conditions (AHC rates) fell by nearly 50 percent in Manhattan. Racial, ethnic, and neighborhood-level inequalities hardly declined. Our research shows how difficult it is to address health care inequalities at the local level when national policies prompt large and growing income and wealth inequalities.

Racial, Ethnic and Spatial Inequalities in NYC

In our analysis of population health, and of access to health care in Manhattan (Gusmano et al., 2010), we discovered a significant correlation between the neighborhood of residence, infant mortality, and "amenable mortality," that is, deaths that could be avoided if access to care is assured. Looking at these measures, we find that people living in Manhattan's lowest-income neighborhoods have notably higher mortality rates than the rest of the borough (Rodwin & Neuberg, 2005; Weisz, Gusmano, Rodwin, & Neuberg, 2008).

We also determined that there are significant neighborhood effects in access to heart disease treatment (Gusmano, Rodwin, & Weisz, 2010; Weisz, Gusmano, & Rodwin, 2004), and in lower-extremity joint replacement. Lack of access also affects treatment of breast cancer (Gusmano, Weisz, & Rodwin, 2009) and access to community-based ambulatory care. Differences between Manhattan and the urban core of other global cities are clear, even after controlling for patient age, co-morbidities, gender, and insurance status. When comparing Manhattan to other global cities, it appears that a person's neighborhood has an independent effect on access to health care services.

The National Context and Beyond

New York City, like the rest of the country, enjoyed economic growth from the beginning of the 1990s until the Great Recession of 2008. Yet, concurrent with this aggregate gain in wealth, was an uninterrupted increase in economic inequality. Although Mayor Bloomberg had several positive public health achievements during his 12-year term, income inequality and homelessness grew even so. NYC's economy still centers on its role as a global financial center, with large shares of revenue generated by its bankers, corporate managers, and specialized attorneys. Nevertheless, NYC is the most economically polarized large city in the United States (Chicago, Los Angeles, and Houston) (Fiscal Policy Institute 2016).

Change and Continuity

Over the course of Bloomberg's time in office, there were distinct improvements in the AHC rate in Manhattan, compared to figures at the end of the Giuliani administration. When correlating the periods 1999 to 2001, and 2011 to 2013, the AHC rate decreased by nearly 50 percent in all neighborhoods (Gusmano et al., 2017). However, while overall health status had improved, infant mortality and life expectancy at birth, obesity and obesity-related illnesses, diabetes and high blood pressure increased in Manhattan (table 11.1a).

Table 11.1a. Changes in Health and Access to Care, New York City, 2002–2010

Self-Reported Health Status (% Reporting Fair or Poor Health)	19.5%	20.9%
Life Expectancy at Birth	77.9 (2001)	80.9 (2010)
Infant mortality	5.83/1000 Live Births	4.48/1000 Live Births (2012)
Do You Have One Person or More Than One Person You Think of As Your Personal Doctor or Health Care Provider?	73.6%	83.7% (2014)
Obesity (CI)	18.2% (17.2–19.2)	24.2% (22.8–25.5)
High Blood Pressure Ever	25.9 % (24.9–26.9)	27.8% (26.6–29.0)
Diabetes Ever	8.0% (7.4–8.7)	10.7% (9.9–11.9)
Asthma Ever	12.1% (11.3–12.9)	12.5% (11.5–13.7)

Sources: Life expectancy: New York City Department of Health and Mental Hygiene; Infant mortality: Wang et al., 2013; Personal doctor or health care provider: New York City Community Health Survey, 2002 and 2014.

Despite the decline in Manhattan's avoidable hospital conditions rate, the disparities among the AHC rates, based on insurance status, race, ethnicity, and neighborhood, did not change over this period (Gusmano et al., 2017). The New York Community Health Survey reinforces this finding. Disparities data for Manhattanites show that racial and ethnic differences in self-reported health, and the incidence of most acute and chronic illnesses, were largely the same in 2014 as they were in 2002 when the survey was launched. This stagnation reflects inadequate investment in social programs that address broader social and economic determinants of health. In comparison to other wealthy nations, the U.S. spends a lower share of its GDP on social programs that affect population health, as shown by Bradley and colleagues (2011).

Cities in the United States share many common "urban problems," such as the geographic concentration of poverty, income inequality, and the persistent inequalities in population health and health care. Yet other wealthy nations have proven these conditions are not inevitable in modern cities (Dreier, Mollenkopf, & Swanstrom, 2001). Instead, the disparities in wealth and income in America have been heightened by our country's national policies and political decisions, which do not protect our population from racial and ethnic injustice.

References

Dreier, P., Mollenkopf, J., & Swanstrom, T. (2001). *Place matters: Metropolitics for the twenty-first century* (3 ed.). Lawrence, KS: University Press of Kansas.

Fennell, M. L., Pallas, S. W., Berman, P., Shortell, S. M., Curry, L. (2011). *Health Services Research 46*(6, pt. 2), 2019–2028.

Gusmano, M. K., Rodwin, V. G., & Weisz, D. (2010). *Health care in world cities.* Baltimore: Johns Hopkins University Press.

Gusmano, M. K., Rodwin, V. G., & Weisz, D. (2017). World medical and health policy. doi:101002/wmh3.226.

Gusmano, M. K., Weisz, D., & Rodwin, V. G. (2009). Achieving horizontal equity: must we have a single-payer health system? *Journal of Health Politics, Policy and Law, 34*(4), 617–33.

NYC Dept. Health and Mental Hygiene. (2013). *Increased life expectancy in New York City: What accounts for the gains? Epi Research Report.*

Rodwin, V. G., & Neuberg, L. G. (2005). Infant mortality and income in 4 world cities: New York, London, Paris, and Tokyo. *American Journal of Public Health, 95*(1), 86–90.

Weisz, D., Gusmano, M. K., & Rodwin, V. G. (2004). Gender and the treatment of heart disease in older persons in the United States, France, and England: A comparative, population-based view of a clinical phenomenon. *Gender medicine, 1*(1), 29–40.

Weisz, D., Gusmano, M. K., Rodwin, V. G., & Neuberg, L. G. (2008). Population health and the health system: A comparative analysis of avoidable mortality in three nations and their world cities. *The European Journal of Public Health, 18*(2), 166–72.

Chapter 12

Human Development Index

The Five New Yorks

Understanding Inequality by Place and Race in New York City

Kristen Lewis and Sarah Burd-Sharps

Introduction

New York City is a place of economic extremes: home to the super-rich and the truly destitute. That is why terms such as the "two New Yorks" and "the one percent" hit home with so many. However, it is more than just money that separates New Yorkers. The binary narrative of the haves and the have-nots, of personal well-being and equal access to opportunity, is far more complicated than that. In NYC, the numbers tell their own story (Measure of America, 2016):

- A baby born today in Manhattan's Murray Hill, Gramercy, and Stuyvesant Town can expect to live 85.3 years. That is longer than a baby born today in any country in the world except one: tiny, ultra-rich Monaco. However, a baby born today in Brooklyn's Brownsville and Ocean Hill can expect to live only 74.1 years, about the same as a baby born today in Armenia or El Salvador.
- In Battery Park City, Greenwich Village, and Soho, an astonishing eight in every ten adults hold bachelor's degrees, and nearly everyone aged 25 and up has a high school diploma. On the other hand, in Hunt's Point, Longwood, and Melrose, less than 1 in 10 adults holds a bachelor's degree, and nearly 45 percent of those aged 25 and older did not complete high school.

- Although money is not the only metric for gauging progress, it remains an important one. Median personal earnings (the point at which half the population earns more and half earns less) is just $18,264 for workers living in Morris Heights, Fordham South, and Mount Hope. This is less than one-quarter of what the typical worker living in downtown Manhattan brings home, which is well over $80,000. In today's dollars, this median personal earnings figure is about the same as median personal earnings in the United States in 1960.

This chapter focuses on two things. First, we look at whether the human development approach and the index to understanding well-being, apply to an affluent democracy, in this case, New York City. We draw on the views the late Walter Stafford, a professor at New York University, expressed in an unpublished paper he wrote in late-2007, early-2008. Second, we present the results of the American Human Development Index for New York City and highlight their similarities to the findings Professor Stafford revealed using his own adaptation of the United Nations Development Programme's (UNDP) human development index.

The Human Development Approach and Index

The human development concept optimistically believes that women and men should have the freedom to decide for themselves what to do with, and how to live, their own lives. The theory focuses on the everyday experiences of ordinary people, and the degree to which individuals are practicably able to access resources, seize opportunities, invest in themselves and their families, and realize both their human rights and their full potential (Measure of America, 2015a). The Human Development Index (HDI) is a tool used to measure this broad concept.

The HDI is the brainchild of the late economist, Mahbub ul Haq. During the 1970s and 1980s, Haq came to believe that existing measures of progress, such as the Gross Domestic Product (GDP), failed to account for the true purpose of development: making people's lives better. Building upon Nobel laureate and Harvard professor, Amartya Sen's capability approach, Haq was concerned with "the freedom that a person has to do this or be that—things that he or she may value doing or being" (Sen, 2009).

Haq developed the HDI as an alternative to GDP. It is a composite measure that brings together indicators of three basic dimensions of well-being: health, access to knowledge, and material living standards. The measure, which ranks the well-being of all countries in the world, debuted in the first Human Development Report in 1990. It has been the cornerstone of the Human Development Reports published by the United Nations every year since then (United Nations Development Programme, 1990).

The UNDP has supported scores of countries in producing their own national human development reports, adapting the global model to their different national contexts. Since 1992, universities, research institutes, and governmental agencies in 135 developing countries have produced more than 700 such national reports (Measure of America, 2015a).

The global Human Development Report and Index, and its abundant national offshoots are widely known throughout the world. The United States, however, is a notable exception. Mainstream Americans, with their widely held views of exceptionalism, seldom greet global goals, approaches, and comparisons with much enthusiasm. It is no different with the HDI (Walt, 2011). Measure of America, a nonprofit project of the Social Science Research Council, has created some domestic awareness of the development approach through its various national- and state-level reports. Despite this, the HDI has not achieved the same status in the United States that it has in countries such as Brazil, India, or the Philippines.

Despite this, Walter Stafford was struck by the explanatory power of the HDI approach and considered it a relevant way of explaining inequality in the United States. This was well before Occupy Wall Street had propelled the topic into mainstream consciousness. Stafford argued that a "North–South divide [existed] in the United States," a divide that is similar to the one that separates rich countries from developing countries. The meager level of well-being that some Americans, African Americans in particular, experience is akin to that found in low-income countries.

Stafford created a modified human development index for New York City, based on indicators of inequality he collected in the city's community districts. He summarized his findings in a paper he wrote during the fall of 2007, and the spring of 2008, titled "The Global North and South in New York City: In the Shadow of the UN." In this work, he analyzed the divisions in New York City, using the modified version of UNDP's human development approach. By ranking neighborhoods, he demonstrated that in New York, as elsewhere in the country, "race and ethnicity ground the U.S. disparities."

We first met Stafford in April 2007, when he invited us to his office to discuss his work and to talk about his preliminary research. At that meeting, we reviewed our own experience at the United Nations, especially Measure of America Co-Director Sarah Burd-Sharps' work at the UNDP Human Development Report Office. In a later meeting, he updated us on how his analysis was progressing, and we shared a draft of our first human development report for the U.S., *The Measure of America 2008–2009*, which was released by Columbia University Press in July 2008. We were all extremely enthusiastic about joining forces to apply the human development approach and index concept to New York City neighborhoods. We talked about how we could blend his initial data collection and analysis, with our work at the national level, and develop a report that focused strictly on New York City.

Stafford's tragic, premature death put an end to our burgeoning collaboration. In the subsequent eight years, we pursued the idea of doing a full-fledged human development report for New York City but were unable to raise funds needed to do this work, that is, until quite recently.

Stafford's study features a human development index that covers New York City's 59 community districts (Stafford, 2008),[1] which roughly align with neighborhoods or groups of neighborhoods. His iteration of the index uses the same basic domains as the standard UNDP index, namely, longevity, knowledge, and income, but it measures the domains using different proxy variables, based on data availability. Table 12.1 shows the indicators Stafford used, in contrast to the standard HDI and the Measure of America HDI.

The standard HDI uses life expectancy at birth as a proxy for health combined gross enrollment ratio for primary, secondary, and tertiary schools as a proxy for access to knowledge, and Gross National Income per capita as a stand-in for decent living standards. Stafford's index uses the age-adjusted death rate, the share of the population aged 25 and older with bachelor's degrees, and per capita income. At the time of his study, New York City did

Table 12.1. United Nations Development Programme (UNDP), Stafford, New York City, and Measure of Human Development Index Indicators

	UNDP	Stafford New York City	Measure of America
Longevity	Life Expectancy at Birth	Age-Adjusted Death Rate	Life Expectancy at Birth
Knowledge	Combined Gross Enrollment Ratio for Primary, Secondary, and Tertiary Schools	Percent of Population 25 and Older with Bachelor's or Higher Degree	School Enrollment Rate Ages 3–24; Highest Degree Attained, all Adults Age 25 and Older
Decent Standard of Living	Gross National Income Per Capita	Per Capita Income	Median Personal Earnings (All Earners Age 16 and Above, Full and Part-Time)
Scale	0–1	0–1	0–10

not make available life expectancy at birth, or the underlying mortality data required to calculate it. Therefore, Stafford decided to use age-adjusted death rate. He then calculated an index for each district, and divided the districts into three groups: high-, medium-, and low-development communities.

Like the UNDP and the Stafford indexes, Measure of America's (MOA), American Human Development Index combines the basic building blocks of a good life, health, education, and living standards, into a single number. MOA's index falls on a scale between 0 and 10, with 10 being the highest score possible. The 0–10 scale eliminates the possibility of direct comparisons with the UNDP index, which uses different indicators and a 0–1 scale. We also chose a 10-point scale, because we believed it would be easier to grasp, and thus more effective as an advocacy tool.

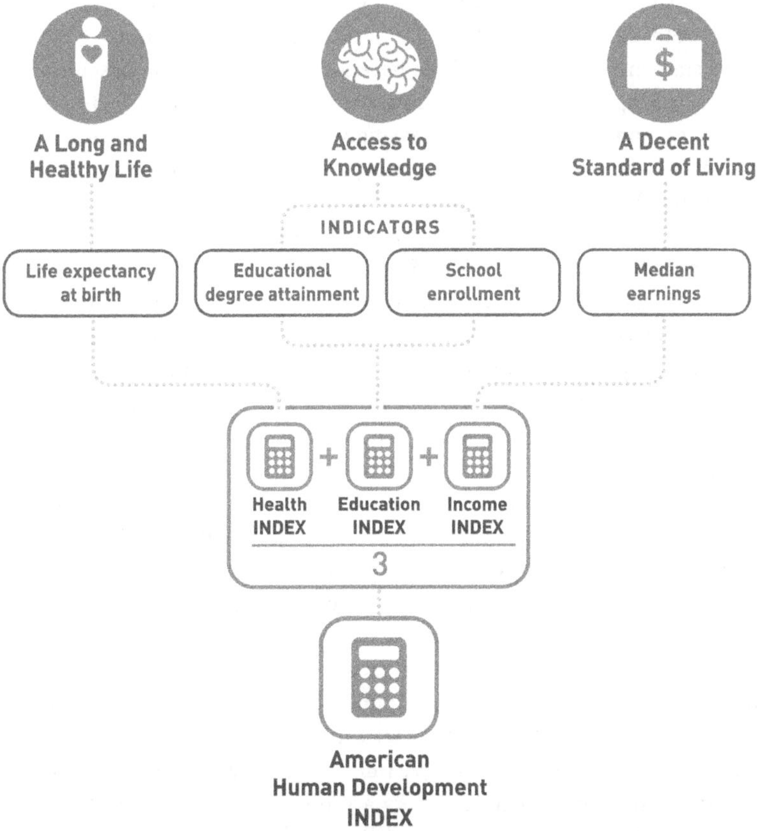

Figure 12.1. Measure of America's human development index. *Source:* Measure of America, 2008. Data2Go.NYC.

In the index, health is measured by life expectancy at birth, using data from the Department of Vital Statistics of the New York City Department of Health and Mental Hygiene. As we considered how the index would reflect the range of health outcomes in an affluent democracy, we assumed we might have to use a more complicated measure, such as Disability Adjusted Life Years (DALYs), or another gauge of years of healthy life. Instead, we stuck with the UNDP indicator, coupled with the explanatory simplicity of life expectancy. This is because there is such an astonishing range in life expectancy values across the U.S. For example, we found there are gaps of as much as a dozen years in some small counties, and a 25-year gap between Native Americans in South Dakota and Asian Americans in New Jersey.

To measure access to knowledge for adults 25 and up, we look at educational degree attainment, and for children and young adults ages three to 24, we look at school enrollment. The data we use comes from the annual American Community Survey of the U.S. Census Bureau. These two measures capture both the stock and flow of education in the population. It is critical that we start measuring at age three because this captures the preschool years, which have long-term impacts on education, earnings, and more. In addition, the post-secondary years are increasingly important in a knowledge-based economy where a high school diploma is no longer sufficient for economic security or jobs that afford agency and respect.

The median personal earnings data comes from the American Community Survey of the U.S. Census Bureau, and measures living standards for all workers ages 16 and up. Median personal earnings signify the control the typical worker has over their monetary resources. The measure includes both full- and part-time workers since many part-time employees would like to work full-time, but have to make do with lower wages. We use personal rather than household earnings so we can calculate scores for women and men separately.

The American Human Development Index uses a continuum to measure the well-being of all Americans. It goes beyond just income to gauge what expands or constrains a person's opportunities. To be sure, income is vital. However, a person needs a full "toolbox" of resources, from good health, to quality education, to some measure of economic security, to be able to realize his or her full potential. We need a broader assessment of well-being if we want to understand more fully why public policies succeed or fail. We need to foster conditions that allow all Americans to invest in themselves and their families, and to become productive, fulfilled members of society.

The American HD Index offers a more nuanced picture of American society than, for instance, the Federal Poverty Measure, which calculates the number of people living in poverty by using cash income as its basis. They use this same measure for determining who is eligible for certain social assistance programs. The income threshold, or poverty line, set by the Federal Poverty Measure, designates a level below which households are considered poor. This threshold, which uses the cost of food as its basis, is grounded in a formula developed in the mid–1960s. The measure creates a poor/non-poor binary. It contributes to us/them mindset and can alienate people living in poverty.

The American HD Index is far from perfect. After all, human development is an expansive concept that embraces everything that shapes the choices and opportunities available to a person. These include not only health, education, and income, but also political power, the built and natural environments one lives in, as well as the social bonds, religious beliefs, family ties, agency, and empowerment we may have.

No one index can completely reflect such a broad notion. Nonetheless, the American HD Index indicator set succeeds because it measures fundamental and non-contentious factors that most people value, such as living a long life, getting a good education, and enjoying a decent living standard. These are all essential outcomes that individuals on both the political left and right agree are desirable. Also, good proxy indicators exist for each area, which can be calculated at very low levels of disaggregation. Analysts can do a meaningful disaggregation in places as small as census tracts, or by race and ethnicity, gender or nativity. This makes it possible to do well-being rankings of social groups.

What Does the Index Reveal?

In New York City, community districts correspond to community planning boards and combine several neighborhoods. Measure of America calculated American Human Development Index scores for all 59-community districts in the city. In the discussion that follows, we use the data from the sources we described in the previous section, along with New York City data from 260 indicators included in a new mapping and data analysis Web site that Measure of America created in 2015, called Data2Go.NYC.

The top single district score, 8.83 out of 10, goes to Community District 7, the Upper West Side (Gilded New York). This district stretches from 59th Street to Cathedral Parkway, with the Hudson River to the west and Central Park to the east. It is home to landmarks such as Lincoln Center and the American Museum of Natural History. There, life expectancy is an impressive 83.8 years, and median personal earnings (the wages and salaries of the typical worker) in this principally White district are $67,428 per year. The district soars in education: three-fourths of adults have bachelor's degrees, and more than 4 in 10 have graduate degrees. It has the second-highest rate of three- and four-year-olds in preschool, 87 percent, and the lowest youth disconnection rate, at under four percent. Disconnected youth are young people, ages 16 to 24, who are neither working nor in school. Stafford's index had the Upper East Side in the top spot. The Upper West Side was fifth in his ranking. About 7 in 10 residents are White.

The bottom score, 2.58, goes to Bronx Community Districts 1 and 2, Hunts Point, Longwood, and Melrose. Each of these two adjacent districts has a small population, so they were combined to create a sufficiently large population to be included in this analysis. Located at the southern-most tip of the Bronx, Districts 1 and 2 are among NYC's most impoverished neighborhoods, by a variety of measures. Median personal earnings are just $19,525. Life expectancy is 76.6 years: five years fewer than the New York City average. One in three young people between the ages of 16 and 24 is disconnected: a rate that is eight times higher than in the Upper West Side. The area has the highest rate of single-mother families in the city, almost 27 percent, and the lowest share of adults 25 or older with high school diplomas, 55 percent. Although Hunt's Point is home to one of the largest produce markets in the world, yet its residents report the lowest levels of fruit and vegetable consumption in the city. Roughly, 7 in 10 residents are Latino.

The highs and lows of human development can be very revealing, especially when they overlap with race and ethnicity. However, most people do not live at either extreme. Rather, they live their lives somewhere else along the continuum. To analyze the situation in New York City, we used an approach we had featured in Measure of America's California. There we divided California's 265 Public Use Microdata Areas into "Five Californias," based on their index score. Similarly, we divided NYC's 59 community districts into "Five New Yorks" (see table 12.2) (America, 2011; Measure of America, 2015b). The groups were formed using cluster analysis.[2]

The scores range from 8.78 in top-scoring "Gilded NYC," home to the doyens of our new gilded age, to 3.07 in bottom-scoring "Precarious NYC." In the Precarious district, the residents' levels of well-being are more typical of the United States in the 1960s or 1970s, than they are of present-day America. To put the range of index scores in a national context, Connecticut, the best-performing state on the American Human Development Index, scores 6.71: the state with the lowest well-being score, Mississippi, scores 3.81 (Measure of America, 2014). The top congressional district in the country, regarding human well-being, is California District 18, which includes the Silicon Valley cities of San Jose, Palo Alto, Mountain View, and Los Gatos. This district scores 8.18. The worst-performer is California District 21, which comprises

Table 12.2. Five New Yorks

New York	American Human Develop. Index	Life Expect. at Birth (Years)	No High School Diploma (% Adults 25+)	At Least Bachelor's Degree (% Adults 25+)	Graduate Degree (% Adults 25+)	Median Household Income ($)
Gilded New York City	8.78	84.6	4.4	79.5	39.1	109,950
Opportunity-Rich New York City	7.49	82.5	8.5	58.1	26.4	81,924
Main Street New York City	5.68	81.2	18.6	32.1	12.1	52,634
Struggling New York City	4.55	79.6	26.0	23.4	8.6	40,707
Precarious New York City	3.07	77.0	37.7	12.6	3.5	26,019

Source: Measure of America, 2016. Data2Go.NYC.

Kings County and parts of Fresno, Kern, and Tulare Counties (Measure of America, 2015a). They score 3.04 out of 10 (America, 2011).

Grouping community districts by levels of well-being paint a striking picture of reality based on race and ethnicity (see table 12.3). Whites move in lockstep with the level of well-being found in each New York: the higher the level of well-being, the greater the share of Whites. The opposite is true for Blacks and, to an even greater degree, for Latinos. Asian Americans are found disproportionately in Opportunity-rich NYC and Main Street NYC. Also noteworthy is that life in these sectors is not only a bit better in one or two ways, but it is better across a wide range of indicators, as you move from one New York to the next. Traveling up the well-being scale from Precarious New York to Gilded New York, commute times get shorter. Fruits and vegetable consumption increases, teenage pregnancy and diabetes rates decline, and foreclosure rates drop, to name just a few gauges (Measure of America, 2016).

There are just four community districts in Gilded NYC (see table 12.4), which are all in Manhattan (Districts 1 and 2 have been combined). This sector encompasses the Upper West Side and West Side, the downtown neighborhoods of Battery Park City, Greenwich Village, SoHo, and the Upper East Side.

The score for this slice of the city is 8.78, an exceptionally high mark on the American Human Development Index, though not quite as high as the

Table 12.3. Five New Yorks by Race and Ethnicity

	American HD Index	Asian American (%)	Black (%)	Latino (%)	White (%)
New York City		13.4	22.4	28.9	32.6
Gilded New York City	8.78	11.8	03.3	09.0	73.0
Opportunity-Rich New York City	7.49	17.4	07.0	14.4	58.2
Main Street New York City	5.68	16.0	20.6	22.3	38.0
Struggling New York City	4.55	09.8	34.3	35.9	17.7
Precarious New York City	3.07	02.1	31.4	60.8	04.3

Source: Measure of America, 2016. Data2Go.NYC.

Table 12.4. Gilded New York City

Community District	Neighborhoods	HD Index
Manhattan Community District 7	Upper West Side and West Side	8.83
Manhattan Community Districts 1 and 2	Battery Park City, Greenwich Village and Soho	8.77
Manhattan Community District 8	Upper East Side	8.74

Source: Measure of America, 2016. Data2Go.NYC.

score for towns like Mountain View, Palo Alto, and Cupertino in California's Silicon Valley, which scored 9.26.

- A baby born today in Gilded NYC can expect to live 84.6 years: a life expectancy that is five and a half years longer than that of the average American, and nearly three years longer than that of the average New Yorker.
- Eight in 10 adults have bachelor's degrees, and 4 in 10 have earned graduate degrees.
- Median household income is over $100,000.
- Children and young adults are doing extremely well overall. Eight in 10 three- and four-year-olds attend preschool. There is only 6.85 percent of children live in poverty, just 5.4 percent of young people aged 16 to 24 are "disconnected youth" (young people neither working nor in school), and the rate of births to teenage girls is one-sixth the citywide rate.
- In addition to their economic resources and educational credentials, these New Yorkers have something every city resident craves: a short commute. The average commute time is just 27 minutes.
- Overall, residents of Gilded NYC tend to practice good health behaviors. They exercise more, eat more fruits and vegetables, and drink fewer sugary drinks than residents of the other New Yorks. However, they binge drink at a significantly higher rate, 32.3 percent. This coincides with research showing that upper-income college graduates drink more than other groups (Jones, 2017).

Three in four residents of Gilded NYC are White, and the next largest group is Asian American: about one in nine residents. Nine percent of residents are Latino, and just 3.3 percent are Black. The share of Whites in Gilded NYC is more than double their share in the city as a whole. All other groups are disproportionately under-represented—Blacks most of all. They are 22.4 percent of the city population but make up just 3.3 percent of the Gilded NYC residents.

Opportunity-rich NYC also has a very high score: 7.49. Opportunity-rich NYC encompasses nine community districts: three districts in Manhattan, three in Queens, two in Brooklyn, and one on Staten Island.

- A baby born today in Opportunity-rich NYC can expect to live 82.5 years.
- Six in 10 adults have bachelor's degrees, and one in four has earned a graduate degree.
- Median household income is $82,000.
- Young people are doing well, but most of their indicators fall quite short of those in Gilded NYC. Seven in 10 of three- and four-year-olds attend preschool, 15.2 percent of children live in poverty, and 11.2 percent of young people 16 to 24 are disconnected youth. The rate of births to teenage girls aged 15 to 19 is eight births per 1,000, which is lower than the citywide rate, but twice the rate found in Gilded NYC.
- Commute time is 35 minutes. That is less than the city average but higher than Gilded NYC's commutes time.

Opportunity-rich NYC, like Gilded NYC, is predominantly and disproportionately White, 58.2 percent. Asian Americans are highly likely to live in Opportunity-rich NYC. They make up 17.4 percent of the population there, compared to 13.4 citywide. Latinos are about half as likely to live in Opportunity-rich NYC, as they are to live in the city as a whole, while Blacks are about a third as likely.

Main Street NYC scores 5.68 on the index. This sector comprises 22 districts: nine in Brooklyn, seven in Queens, and two each in the Bronx, Manhattan, and Staten Island. Life expectancy is 81.2 years, longer than the U.S. average, but 1.3 years less than in Opportunity-rich NYC.

- Regarding educational attainment, 32 percent of adults over 25 have earned bachelor's degrees, and 12 percent hold a graduate degree. This is a big drop from Opportunity-rich New York.
- The median household income of this group, about $52,600 as of 2013, puts them slightly above the national median. The high cost of living, particularly for housing, means these Main Street dwellers have a lot in common with people living in Struggling NYC. Thirty percent of renters spend more than half their income on rent.
- Six in 10 of the three- and four-year-olds attend preschool. One in four children lives in poverty, and 15.8 percent of young people aged 16 to 24 are disconnected. The rate of births to teenage girls aged 15 to 19 is 18 births per 1,000. That is more

than double the Opportunity-rich NYC rate, and more than four times the Gilded NYC rate.

Of the five New Yorks, Main Street NYC looks most like New York City as a whole, though Whites and Asian Americans are slightly over-represented, and Blacks and Latinos are somewhat under-represented. No group has a majority: Whites are a plurality. Multi-ethnic Main Street NYC is 40 percent foreign-born, the largest share among the five NYCs. The sector is a mosaic of neighborhoods dominated by Asian, Latin American, and Caribbean immigrants, along with native-born Black and White middle- and working-class households.[3]

Struggling NYC scores 4.55. It encompasses 15 districts: five in Brooklyn, four in Queens, and three each in the Bronx and Manhattan.

- Life expectancy in Struggling NYC is 79.6 years, five years shorter than the life expectancy in Gilded NYC.
- Educational attainment for adults age 25 and older starts to show worrisome trends in this New York. One in four adults lacks a high school diploma, the bare-bones minimum in today's increasingly knowledge-based economy; 23.4 percent of adults have bachelor's degrees.
- Child well-being begins to falter seriously in Struggling NYC. Births to teenagers increase sharply to 30 per 1,000 girls aged 15 to 19, and the youth disconnection rate increases to nearly one in four young people aged 16 to 24. The child poverty rate is 35 percent.
- Economic anxiety is a constant companion for many, if not most, in Struggling NYC, where the median household income is $40,700. Housing costs are perhaps the chief reason. A third of renters pay more than half their incomes on rent and one in eight lives in overcrowded housing.

Blacks and Latinos make up the largest share of Struggling NYC, 34.3 percent, and 35.9 percent, respectively. Both are represented disproportionately. The share of Whites in Struggling NYC is roughly half what it is in NYC as a whole. Asian Americans are under-represented as well.

Precarious NYC (see table 12.5) scores 3.07 on the index. Precarious NYC has 11 districts, concentrated largely in the Bronx. It includes seven Bronx districts and two Brooklyn districts. Ongoing disadvantages have eroded the resilience in these neighborhoods. Residents are one fender bender, minor injury, or childcare breakdown from financial ruin. In Gilded and Opportunity-rich NYC, residents are far less vulnerable to the vicissitudes of life than they are in Precarious NYC. They work jobs that provide sick days and health insurance. They have credentials and contacts to draw upon should they lose their jobs. They can afford childcare, and often have sufficient flexibility in their jobs to manage their caregiving responsibilities without losing pay or their job. None of this is true in Precarious New York.

- Life expectancy in Precarious NYC is 77.0 years. Here, 30.7 percent of residents are obese, 13.3 percent are disabled, and 12.8 percent have diabetes. That is compared to only 3.7 percent in Gilded NYC, and 6.71 in Opportunity-rich NYC.
- A large share of adults aged 25 and older (37.7 percent) lack a high school diploma, and only 12.6 percent hold bachelor's degrees.
- The financial foundations of life in Precarious NYC are built on sand. Household income is only $26,000. Nearly four in ten residents live in poverty. The foreclosure rate, at 36.6 per 1,000, affects one in four family properties. That is over two and a half times the rate in Main Street NYC, and 13 times the rate in Gilded NYC. Thirty-six percent of renters spend more than half their incomes on rent. Residents have the longest average commute to work: 42 minutes.
- Only about half of all three- and four-year-olds in Precarious NYC attend preschool. Child poverty is alarmingly high, at 50.9 percent. One in four 16- to 24-year-olds are neither working nor in school, and the teen birthrate is 40 per 1,000. That is ten times the rate in Gilded NYC.

Precarious New York is predominantly Latino, 60.8 percent of the population, in fact. This is roughly double that of the city as a whole. Blacks make up 31.4 percent of the residents in Precarious NYC, as compared to 22.4 percent citywide. The share of Whites in Precarious NYC is eight times smaller than their share of NYC as a whole: just 4.3 percent. Just 2.1 percent of residents are Asian American.

Conclusion

This concept of five New Yorks adds contour and specificity to today's "inequality" conversation, and it confirms some widely held assumptions about the city's haves and have-nots. The premise also raises some new questions

Table 12.5. Precarious New York City

Community District	Neighborhood	HDI Index
Bronx Community Districts 3, 6	Belmont, Crotona Park East, and East Tremont	2.86
Bronx Community District 4	Concourse, Highbridge, and Mount Eden	3.08
Bronx Community District 5	Morris Heights, Fordham South, and Mount Hope	3.10
Brooklyn Community District 16	Brownsville and Ocean Hill	3.32
Bronx Community District 7	Bedford Park, Fordham North, and Norwood	3.59
Brooklyn Community District 4	Bushwick	3.68
Bronx Community District 9	Castle Hill, Clason Point, and Parkchester	3.96
Brooklyn Community District 5	East New York and Starrett City	4.04

Source: Measure of America, 2016. Data2GoNYC.

and challenges. For example, the makeup of Main Street NYC, which is 40 percent immigrants, offers a compelling counter-narrative to the reductionist debate about immigration that dominates the airways today. The Main Street NYC of today, and of the country as a whole tomorrow, is enriched by the dynamism of newcomers.

The five New Yorks theory also tells us a lot about segregation. One striking feature at the two ends of the spectrum—gilded on one end and precarious on the other—is the extent of residential segregation based on race and ethnicity. In Precarious New York's Brownsville and Ocean Hill, Brooklyn, 75.8 percent of the residents are Black, and 19.7 percent are Latino. In the other eight of the nine districts that make up Precarious NYC, between 62.1 and 70.4 percent of residents are Latino: the balance are Blacks. In Gilded New York, however, Whites are segregated. They make up between 68.9 and 79.3 percent of the population in the four community districts at the top of the well-being scale. In short, the mostly White parts of town have scores that are among the highest in the country, and those that are almost entirely Black and brown have some of the lowest.

Looking at the relationship between race and ethnicity, residential segregation, and well-being through a human development lens shifts the dialogue beyond the important-but-incomplete framing of income inequality. Inequality in America is about more than money. Professor Stafford wrote that "income is important to overall well-being, but so is the ability to use or convert income into well-being free of institutional barriers" (Stafford, 2008).

Inequality hinges on whether people can live freely chosen lives of value or not. Does someone have the freedom to walk outside to exercise without fear of being victimized by crime or the police? Does a person have the freedom to get a high-quality education in a nearby school? Does an individual have the freedom to influence the decisions that affect their life, and to chart a course for their future with the confidence that their capabilities can get them where they want to go? Achieving this kind of freedom for all New Yorkers requires an investment in people and neighborhoods, as well as a dismantling of barriers that cut communities of color off from many of life's most rewarding pathways.

Notes

1. New York City's community districts, established by local law in 1975, divide the city into 59 administrative districts each served by a community board.

2. The groups were formed by calculating the AHDI z score of each community district, then distributing each community district into one of the five NYCs.

3. More analysis to unpack the make-up of main street NYC is underway.

References

Jones, Jeffrey M. (2017). Drinking highest among educated, upper-income Americans. *Gallup*. https://news.gallup.com/poll/184358/drinking-highest-among-educated-upper-income-americans.aspx.

Measure of America. (2011). "A portrait of California." Lewis, Kristen, and Sarah Burd-Sharps. A Portrait of California. New York: Measure of America, Social Science Research Council, 2011.

Measure of America. (2014). "Measure of America 2013–2014." Lewis, Kristen, and Sarah Burd-Sharps. Measure of America, 2013–2014. New York: Measure of America, Social Science Research Council, 2014.

Measure of America. (2015a). "Geographies of opportunity." New York. Lewis, Kristen, and Sarah Burd-Sharps. Geographies of Opportunity. New York: Measure of America, Social Science Research Council, 2015.

Measure of America. (2015b). "A portrait of California 2014–2015." Lewis, Kristen, and Sarah Burd-Sharps. A Portrait of California 2015–2015. New York: Measure of America, Social Science Research Council, 2015.

Measure of America. (2016). "Data2Go.NYC." Measure of America, Social Science Research Council, 2018. Data2Go.NYC.

Sen, Amartya. (2009). *Idea of justice*. Cambridge, MA: Harvard University Press.

Stafford, Walter. (2008). "The global North and South in New York City: In the shadow of the UN." New York: Unpublished.

United Nations Development Programme. (1990). *Human development report*. Oxford, UK: Oxford University Press.

Walt, Stephen M. (2011). "The myth of American exceptionalism." *Foreign Policy*. https://foreignpolicy.com/2011/10/11/the-myth-of-american-exceptionalism/.

Chapter 13

Public Housing

New York City's Third City[1]

Victor Bach

New York is often referred to as two cities in one. First, there is the city of the "haves," people who have what it takes to thrive, such as Wall Street-types, corporate attorneys, real estate pros, celebrities, and recently arrived professional emigrants. Then there is the city of the "have-nots," comprised of lower-income wage earners, largely Black or Latino, many of them immigrants, who struggle to keep a toehold in the city's economy and strive to meet its high living costs while providing for their families.

In many ways, public housing forms a third city, very different from the other two. Physically, the 334 developments across five boroughs stand apart from the rest of their urban surround. They consist of massive residential complexes, prototypically made of red brick, with apartment towers rising over large tracts of open space that include green areas, playgrounds, and parking lots.[2] In this dense city, where high-rise apartment buildings are common, the distinctive configuration of these public housing developments often interrupts the local street pattern. The sheer size of the city's public housing is daunting. The New York City Housing Authority (NYCHA), its owner and manager, is the city's largest landlord, and the only public one. Its 178,000 apartments represent one out of twelve rentals in the city, housing a half-million residents: a population larger than Atlanta or Minneapolis.

These tracts primarily serve a have-not population, and from a housing perspective, they present a clear conundrum for the authority and the residents of this third city. Residents have the advantage of affordable rents, but they must live under abysmal conditions that some consider third world in nature. The conditions are far worse than those experienced by comparable tenants in the city's competitive, often cutthroat, low-end rental market. Public housing residents also experience higher crime rates than other communities, stemming from the stresses of poverty and the extent to which the projects exacerbate poverty.[3]

Institutionally, New York's public housing is under severe threat, with the authority struggling for survival as it faces financial strain and physical decline. The NYCHA is weighed down by an annual structural operating deficit,[4] and an enormous backlog of much-needed capital improvements. Experts estimate that it will take $17 billion over the next 15 years to fix the aging infrastructure. This is conspicuous in a city where virtually all other rental housing is thriving, and where rents have soared despite tenants having lived through the worst recession in recent history.

Public housing residents experience housing inequities that stem largely from their substandard living conditions. Each day, they must cope with accelerating deterioration: leaking roofs, failing elevators, fragile plumbing, crumbling facades, toxic mold, and more. Unlike lower-income tenants in the private rental market, theirs is not a crisis of affordability. Rather, it is a question of whether they can survive the deterioration of their buildings and their homes and withstand the authority's institutional failure to curb the decline.

Although the authority is clearly trying to take steps, no one has accepted full responsibility for the frequent failures. Ultimately, the residents bear the cumulative costs of decades of government disinvestment and neglect. Even after all the years of putting up with unresponsive management and mounting physical deterioration, many resident leaders acknowledge the de Blasio administration's recent attempts to address the situation. However, residents remain angry, distrustful, and fearful that, in the end, they will still lose their homes.

Public housing is a third city because, most importantly, political leaders consider it disconnected from other housing agendas. Unlike other locales, NYCHA exists in a city and state known for its housing activism (Schwartz 1999).[5] For example, in recent years, both Mayor Bloomberg and Mayor de Blasio have launched ambitious, multi-billion dollar plans for affordable housing that call for preservation as well as new construction. However, NYCHA was not included in these plans, despite its desperate situation. This year, in his State of the State message, Governor Andrew Cuomo announced a $5 billion, five-year affordable housing initiative, but with no mention of public housing. The irony here is that, for most of its eight decades,[6] NYCHA has been considered a national model for large-city housing authorities. The authority is perceived to be a high-performer, running the largest program in the nation, with Chicago running a distant second (Bloom, 2009).

This chapter examines the current state of the city's public housing, along with what has caused its marginalization and decline. It also reviews what is being done currently to address public housing's preservation problems, and what remains to be done. First, the chapter summarizes the recent history of government defunding and disinvestment in NYCHA's public housing. Second, it analyzes housing condition trends from 2002 to 2014. Third, it profiles NYCHA's resident population, in part as a way to dispel some of the misconceptions about who the residents are.[7] Fourth, the chapter assesses recent government efforts to address the inequities public housing residents endure and outlines near-future policy directions and strategies that might increase the success rate for these efforts.

A Perfect Storm of Government Disinvestment

From the turn of the millennium to the present, NYCHA has been weathering what some call a perfect storm of government disinvestment, as chronicled in a 2014 CSS report (Bach & Waters, 2014). Every level of government has been implicated, chief among them, the federal government. Chronically inadequate capital and operating funding started in the Reagan administration and evolved into starvation funding during the George W. Bush terms. The early Obama administration provided some short-term relief. The 2009 federal budget provided full funding for the public housing program. Additional capital funds of $423 million, were allocated to NYCHA under Obama's economic stimulus bill (ARRA).[8] However, as Congress moved toward deficit reduction and sequestration, the federal budget was tightened again. NYCHA estimates that the federal operating shortfall between 2000 and now is $1.4 billion (New York City Housing Authority, 2015).

New York State also played a significant role in defunding NYCHA. In 1998, Governor George Pataki ended operating subsidies to state-financed public housing. That left NYCHA holding 15 state developments that received no operating subsidies from any level of government. The agency estimated their operating shortfall to be $60 million per year. This added up to $720 million by 2010, when the developments were federalized finally under ARRA.

The city did its share of damage, too. During the post-9/11 fiscal crisis, Mayor Michael Bloomberg terminated operating subsidies to the six city-financed developments, leaving NYCHA with an annual operating shortfall of $30 million, and a cumulative shortfall of $240 million by 2010, when the developments were federalized. The city also passed on its share of NYCHA's community center programs. Although the city recovered and began to generate unprecedented surpluses, it did not resume the former operating subsidies. Despite NYCHA recording extraordinary operating deficits, $235 million in 2006 alone, the mayor continued to extract over $100 million in required annual payments from NYCHA to pay for police services and PILOT payments in lieu of property taxes. This practice persisted until 2014, when Mayor de Blasio relieved NYCHA of the payments.

NYCHA found it profoundly difficult to manage its housing because of this persistent privation. Instead, it had to use its federal capital subsidies to cover its major infrastructure improvements. It had to tap its operating reserves, as well. Because NYCHA had to take such actions, HUD demoted NYCHA in 2007 from its position as a "high-performing authority." The authority moved what it could from capital subsidies to cover the gap in operations,[9] but this left NYCHA with even less capacity to make major improvements. NYCHA's workforce headcount was reduced from 15,000 in 2002, to 11,000 today. It had hoped paring administrative positions would save enough, but unfortunately, front-line management and caretaking staff at the developments were affected, as well.

NYCHA and its residents were devastated by this barrage of government disinvestment, along with the authority's rising internal utility costs, and outlays for employee health and pension benefits. Tightened resources meant poorer management and fewer repairs or improvements to the aging buildings. Resident complaints had been mounting for some time, but by 2008, the cumulative impact on living conditions was unavoidable.

Another Kind of Housing Crisis—Affordable, but Deteriorating Housing

In American cities as a whole, low-income tenants[10] are experiencing a "rent affordability crisis" of mounting proportions, with soaring rents outpacing static incomes and subsuming a growing, disproportionate share of household income (Harvard Joint Center for Housing Studies, 2015; National Low Income Housing Coalition, 2016). In New York City, there are roughly 600,000 low-income households reliant on the private rental market. They do so without the benefit of any government assistance to assure affordable rents in relation to income. These households face enormous financial stresses in the city's tight, high-cost rental market. In 2014, they carried a median rent burden of 49 percent of household income (Waters and Bach, 2016). For nearly half of these households, at least half of their income must go toward paying rent.

Public housing residents, unlike their low-income counterparts in the private rental market, are shielded from the affordability crisis. That is because federal law requires their rents to be capped at 30 percent of house-

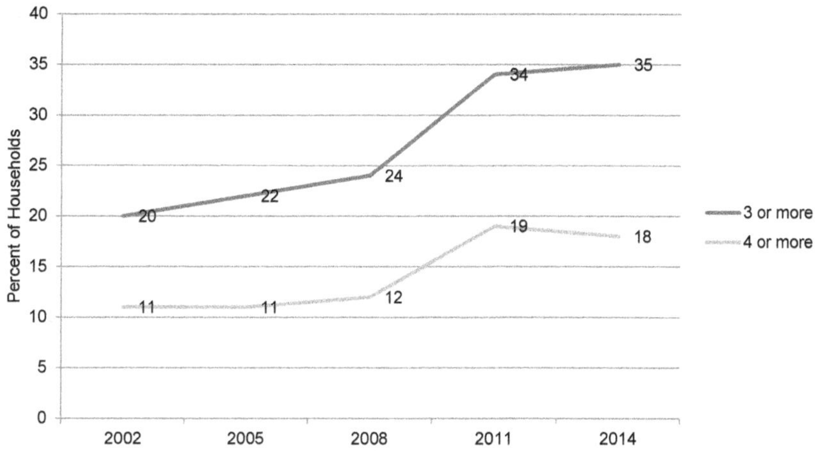

Figure 13.1. New York City Housing Authority households reporting at least three deficiencies, 2002–2014 HVS. *Source:* Victor Bach, Community Service Society of New York, March 2017.

hold income, the prevailing affordability standard.[11] However, they do face an infrastructure crisis, marked by a steady and accelerating decline in living conditions (see figure 13.1).

The NYC Housing and Vacancy Survey (HVS), conducted every three years by the U.S. Bureau of the Census, asks respondents to report on seven specific deficiencies in their apartments.[12] As of 2014, the most recent HVS, over a third (35 percent) of NYCHA residents reported three or more apartment deficiencies, and over a sixth (18 percent) reported at least four deficiencies. Deficiencies began to spike in 2008, no doubt as the cumulative consequence of an unprecedented period of government defunding at all levels.

Of course, low-income tenants in the private rental market are not immune to these types of deficiencies in their apartments, too. However, they did not experience a similar decline in living conditions, nor did they live through an infrastructure crisis comparable to their public housing neighbors (see figure 13.2 on page 284).

As of 2002, the dereliction found in NYCHA apartments roughly paralleled that in unassisted private rentals, and in other subsidized housing.[13] However, over the next twelve years, and through 2014, NYCHA deficiencies increased substantially, while those in the other rental sectors remained relatively stable.

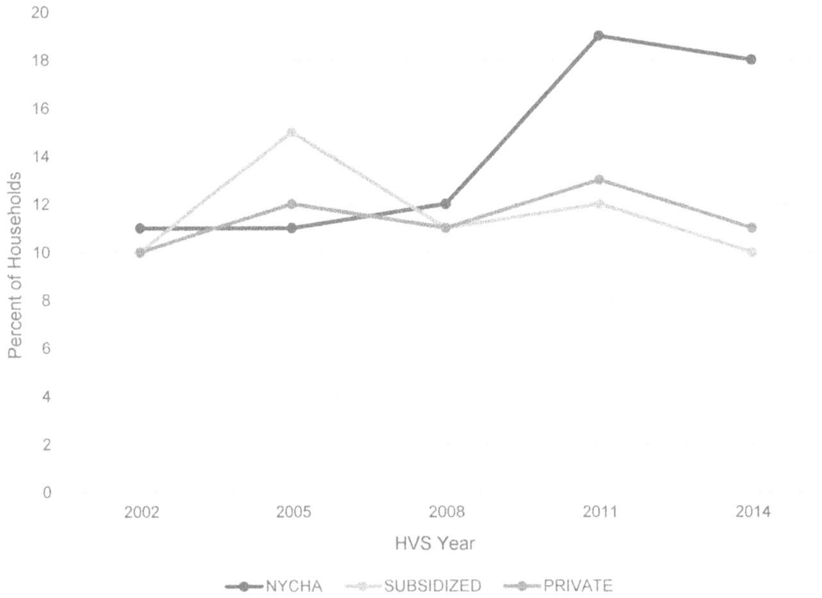

Figure 13.2. Households reporting four or more deficiencies, by rental sector, 2002–2014 HVS. *Source:* Victor Bach, Community Service Society of New York, March 2017.

The Residents

The media, and even some social policy professionals hold some misconceptions about who lives in New York's public housing. The common images, of course, reinforce the prevailing stigma attached to the projects, and make it more difficult for anyone to garner support for what residents need.

Residents are sensitive to the defaming of public housing, and they reject the term "project" when outsiders use it. Instead, they prefer the term "development." They have a certain misplaced pride in being called "residents," rather than "tenants." At meetings, resident leaders tend to address each other formally, as Mr., Mrs., or Ms., rather than using the more familiar first names. The length of time a person has lived in a development provides them with a certain rank among residents. In fact, at meetings or hearings, people often affirm their credentials by underscoring how many decades they have lived in that location.

This section provides a condensed profile of New York's public housing residents, based on characteristics provided in the HVS. The goal is to dispel stereotypes people have of residents: typecasting that hampers efforts to deal with their housing inequities.

Many low-income New Yorkers place a premium on living in public housing, despite the substandard conditions that prevail. Among current residents, the turnover rate for apartments is relatively low, 2.6 percent for 2015, with a vacancy rate of 0.5 percent (NYCHA, 2016a). No doubt, it is because the alternative, finding a suitable, near-affordable apartment in the city's housing market, is virtually impossible. In 2014, the median length of stay for public housing residents was 15 years. In that same year, the waiting list for NYCHA apartments reached an unprecedented high, now at 259,000 households (NYCHA, 2016b). Public housing may be stigmatized, and conditions may be poor, but that does not seem to matter to low-income New Yorkers who seek the affordability and potential economic security this housing offers.

Racial/Ethnic Composition

Public housing has maintained a consistent resident profile in recent decades, no doubt because of its low turnover rate. The developments primarily serve people of color. In 2014, Blacks and Latinos accounted for 90 percent of households in total, in roughly equal proportions. In earlier decades, African-Americans were in the majority, but more recently, Latinos have taken a slight lead, at 46 percent of households, with Blacks at 44 percent. In 2014, only five percent of households identified themselves as White, and four percent as Asian or Pacific Islander.

Income and Employment

Residents are chiefly low-income, with 45 percent of households falling within the federal poverty level. In 2014, that was $18,552 for a family of three. Another third (32 percent) are "near-poor," with above-poverty incomes up to twice poverty. As a result of NYCHA's admission policies, and its resistance to evicting over-income families, there is a relatively wide income range in the developments. Consequently, NYC has avoided the high-poverty concentrations found in other large-city housing authorities.

Figure 13.3 on page 286 depicts the 2014 income distribution of NYCHA households. Middle income ranges from two to four times poverty (maximum $74,000 for a three-person household), and high income is any income above that level. About a quarter (24 percent) of resident households are in the middle- or high-income category.

Although NYCHA households support themselves from a variety of sources, the principal source is from what they earn at work (see table 13.1 on page 286). A majority of households (60 percent) have at least one working member, and a substantial portion (39 percent) rely exclusively on those

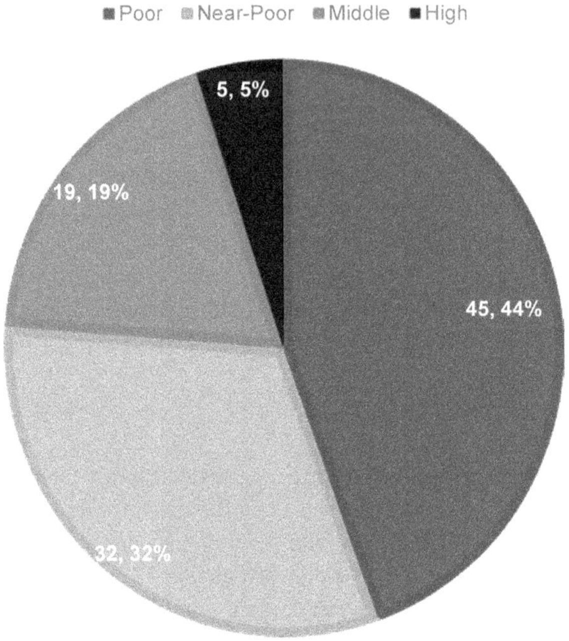

Figure 13.3. Income distribution, New York City Housing Authority households, 2014 HVS. *Source:* Victor Bach, Community Service Society of New York, March 2017.

earnings. Over one third (34 percent) of households receive retirement income from previous employment, but few (16 percent) rely on that exclusively. Public assistance, that is, Temporary Assistance to Needy Families (TANF), Safety

Table 13.1. Income Sources, New York City Housing Authority Households, 2014 HVS (Each Statistic Based Upon 100 Percent of Residents)

Source	At Least One Income from:	Sole Income Source
Work	60%	39%
Retirement	34%	16%
Public Assistance	32%	11%
SSI	25%	7%
TANF	9%	2%
SafetyNet		2%

Source: NYCH Housing and Vacancy Survey, US Bureau of the Census, 2014.

Net Assistance, and Supplemental Security Income (SSI), support fewer than a third (32 percent) of NYCHA families. Contrary to what many people think, welfare is not the dominant form of public assistance for residents. Instead, it is SSI for the elderly and disabled who are ineligible to receive social security. In other words, the work ethic is alive and well in public housing.

Not surprisingly, unemployment rates among NYCHA residents between the ages of 18 and 65, tend to be consistently higher than citywide unemployment rates (see figure 13.4). NYCHA residents have lower levels of the kind of education, training, and work experience that would qualify them for more secure, higher-paying jobs. About 30 percent of working-age adults do not have a high school diploma, and only 10 percent have a college degree. As a result, they are more vulnerable to downturns in the local economy.

Interestingly, the resident workforce is responsive to upswings in the economy. In the years 2002 to 2008, between the post-9/11 recession and the economic surge that preceded the Great Recession, resident unemployment plummeted from 20.9 to 9.5 percent: just four points above the citywide rate. Nonetheless, the NYCHA workforce, which was less resilient than the citywide labor force, was hit hard by the post–2008 recession. By 2014, its unemployment rate rose to 21.7 percent, close to what it was in 2002.

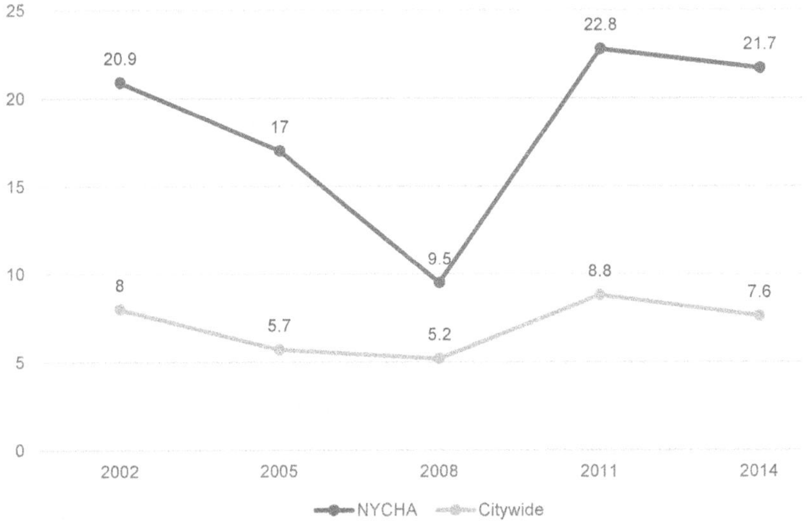

Figure 13.4. Unemployment rates, New York City Housing Authority, working-age residents and citywide, 2002–2014. *Source*: Victor Bach, Community Service Society of New York, March 2017.

At any one time, a substantial portion of NYCHA working-age residents are not seeking work. Between 2002 and 2014, the average was nearly 44 percent. One out of six residents finds it harder to seek work because of health and disability issues. NYCHA has a large population of elderly and disabled. This is due in part to the aging of its family population, as well as to the special accommodations it provides. Fifty-five of the developments, equaling around 10,000 units, are designated specifically for the elderly and disabled. On average, another 12 percent of working-age adults are in school or training, and six percent have family or child responsibilities that preclude their working. Another 10 percent are not seeking work because they have retired, or have other reasons. Actually, NYCHA residents do not differ greatly from other low-income, working-age residents in the city (see table 13.2).

When employed, nearly all of the NYCHA workforce are engaged in the service industries. The largest single employment source (20 percent) is the health sector, with retail services running second (14 percent). Other major employment sectors include accommodation/food-related services (9 percent), education services (8 percent), transportation/warehousing (8 percent), and public administration (5 percent).

Taken as a whole, this data paints a very different picture from the traditional portrait of public housing residents as a "dependent" population. The fact that the projects are physically separated from neighboring locales should not be mistaken for social isolation. Through its admission policies, NYCHA has created residential communities that, despite their clusters of minority and low-income households, have a significant number of employed and retired individuals who are connected to the world of work.

Table 13.2. Labor Force Participation, New York City Housing Authority vs. Low-Income, Working-Age Residents, 2014

	NYCHA (%)	Low-Income (%)
Working	46	51
Seeking Work	13	10
Not Seeking		
Health-Disability	15	10
In School/Training	11	12
Family Responsibilities	5	8
Retired or Other	10	9
Total	100%	100%

Source: NYCH Housing and Vacancy Survey, US Bureau of the Census, 2014.

Resident Power: "The Sleeping Giant"

Among the city's political insiders, NYCHA residents are sometimes referred to as the "sleeping giant." Although voter participation is low, many wonder what might happen if this sizable population would be sufficiently aroused to participate in the political process.

In 2011, some demonstrations took place to protest building conditions. At that time, several advocacy organizations issued a report card on NYCHA, based on a resident survey they had administered. The report concluded:

> Widespread disinvestment and mismanagement of the public housing stock is negatively impacting the residents' quality of life. Repairs take too long . . . and public spaces are crumbling . . . Building managers are allowed to operate unchecked and are not held responsible . . . Residents need to lead the push for change and work with advocates and public housing officials to pull New York City out of its ongoing crisis. (Community Voices Heard CAAAV, 2011)

There is a persistent call for resident leadership, coming from both advocates and residents themselves. NYCHA has a formal structure in place for organizing and leading residents. Every day, hard-working leaders must oversee issues that confront their neighbors, and communities at large. These include getting management to order necessary repairs, dealing with local incidents, mediating resident grievances, and securing programs for their community centers. The president of a resident association is, in effect, the "mayor" of his or her development. Despite their commitment, these leaders have not gained the political power to demand what they have the right to expect from the government: a decent home for everyone. A perplexing question remains. Why has not the giant been stirred enough to address the crisis that exists in its midst? There are no simple answers.

Under long-standing federal regulations, public housing residents have the right to organize. The HUD 964 regulations, sometimes called the resident bill of rights, guarantee individuals the right to form resident associations at each development, and these regulations specify the conditions that must be met to be recognized as such (HUD, 1994). Once an association is formed, and its officers elected, the housing authority must recognize it as the sole representative of the community as a whole and consult the association about all decisions that may affect the development. This kind of organization parallels labor's right to collective bargaining.

NYCHA also has a complex citywide resident governance structure which divides the city into nine geographical districts. These districts include two each in Manhattan and the Bronx, three in Brooklyn, and one each in Queens and Staten Island. Within each district, resident association presidents join to form a district council that elects a chair and meets regularly. The nine elected district chairs make up the Citywide Council of Presidents (CCOP), the jurisdiction-wide resident body. HUD 964 regulations require that NYCHA must consult with CCOP about all policies and plans for public housing.

In the best of all possible worlds, this elaborate structure would serve as a dynamic framework for resident mobilization and action. However, serious functional weaknesses exist. To begin with, one out of three NYCHA developments do not have a resident association, and there is no consistent effort to organize them. Some resident associations are strong, well-attended and closely linked to outside community leaders. Generally, they are led by a small circle of dedicated, long-term resident leaders who arrive at meetings, only to find them poorly attended by the resident constituency at large (Alinsky, 1971). It is a chronic challenge to find ways to increase resident participation in the associations.

There are several reasons for poor attendance. Most residents are too busy with work and raising a family, to get involved in association meetings. The only time they do make an appearance is when an immediate crisis is at hand. Then attendance increases. In the past, an institutional paternalism prevailed: what was good for NYCHA would be good for residents. Problems would be worked out in the NYCHA family. Residents did not feel they needed a strong community organization.

Nowadays, the level of trust in NYCHA is dissolving fast because of the serious infrastructure crisis. Despite this, resident leaders still choose to address their problems within the NYCHA family and do not seek support from additional resources such as elected officials, community organizers, and advocacy organizations. This insular approach generates a constant stream of complaints about, and to, NYCHA: complaints that are not shared elsewhere. This approach also reflects a distrust of outsiders. The more experienced resident leaders know better and link themselves with external support mechanisms, but as a rule, the leaders tend to work within NYCHA, rather than widen the engagement.

Even when leaders are frustrated by a lack of progress, and they complain loudly to NYCHA, they seldom take their problems outside the family. Many leaders believe they can handle their problems on their own as if working with outside resources means they are weak, rather than empowered. This parochial attitude focuses resident efforts almost exclusively on mothership NYCHA, rather than establishing a more inclusive, comprehensive approach that allows them to be heard at City Hall, in Albany, and in Washington.

The growing anger in the developments could be tapped to mobilize residents and give the sleeping giant a stature that could not be ignored. The problem is the lack of leadership initiative within the resident ranks. CCOP seems to be the most logical platform from which to act. It could coordinate resources, articulate policy positions, design campaigns, develop advocacy strategies, and mobilize residents. Yet that does not seem to be happening, despite CCOP's new openness to outsiders.

CCOP members rise through the ranks as resident association presidents, where they function as mayors of their developments. By nature, they are not policy makers, campaign developers, or organizers. Their full-time job is handling the immediate problems of their communities. Their responsibilities as district chair tap further into their personal resources, leaving little energy to attend CCOP meetings two afternoons each month.

These issues could be resolved if the Citywide Council of Presidents had sufficient staff resources. The council has no personnel to keep its records, and no agents to represent it at critical meetings where advocates and others are debating policies, formulating positions, and developing strategies. This shortfall is an acute problem.

Resident leaders, and the hundreds of resident association presidents expect more of CCOP than it can provide. Its image as a leader is weak, and because it is absent from critical discussions where advocates are debating issues and taking positions, it is excluded or ignored by them. The CCOP has become superfluous to the NYCHA, an organization the authority can easily bypass when making its major decisions, despite the 964 regulations.

Public housing infrastructure, and the capital needed to build it must be central to any long-term resident campaign. But before such goals could be met, there would have to be a presence strong enough to press demands at all levels of government. At two recent rallies in Albany, it appeared that some people were mobilizing for change. However, the motivation behind these events came largely from Community Voices Heard and its advocates. Although many resident leaders participated, CCOP was not directly involved.

What Is Being Done?

Mayoral Commitments to Affordable and Public Housing: the "Firewall"

With the election of Mayor Bill de Blasio in 2013, the city demonstrated a renewed interest in addressing NYCHA's financial and physical problems. By early 2014, the mayor fulfilled a campaign promise he had made: to suspend the required annual payment the authority had to make to the city for police services. With this single action, the NYCHA had over $70 million a year restored to its operating resources. Shola Olatoye, a fresh face in public housing, was appointed NYCHA chair and chief executive officer. Olatoye came from the New York office of Enterprise Community Partners, a national organization that plays an intermediary role in affordable housing development. Might these changes imply that housing development on available NYCHA land could become a higher priority, a continuation of Bloomberg's stalled Infill Program?[14] It also begged the question whether the authority might initiate the housing management reforms that were needed to address the mounting backlog of repair work orders and outstanding major improvements.

In the spring of 2014, the mayor announced his ambitious Housing New York Plan. His stated goal was to add 200,000 affordable housing units over ten years: 80,000 from new construction, and 120,000 from preserved stock (New York City Government, 2014). Nearly $8 billion was committed from the city's capital budget. Notably, the plan barely mentioned NYCHA, despite the plan's emphasis on preservation. Instead, a parallel effort, dubbed the Next-Generation NYCHA Plan, was scheduled for release early the following year.

The mayor's hallmark affordable housing program had three focal points: the private sector, producing affordable housing, and preserving affordability in privately-owned properties. Affordability is a serious issue. Federal subsidies could expire for some developments, and subsidized housing might be sold, as exemplified by the controversial pending sales of Stuyvesant Town and Peter Cooper Village. Notwithstanding the mayor's overt commitment to NYCHA, from the start his housing plan created a separation, a firewall, if you will, between its drive for affordable housing and the preservation of public housing.

At the same time, there was a mounting call among advocates at both the city and state levels, for a long-term capital investment in the authority, "a Marshall Plan for NYCHA." In September 2014, City Comptroller Scott Stringer entered the fray by proposing that the Battery Park City Authority (BPCA) dedicate any excess revenues over the upcoming decade[15] to NYCHA capital improvements. BPCA was expected to generate $40 million a year in excess revenues: that is $400 million over the decade. To date, both the comptroller and Governor Andrew Cuomo have agreed to commit the funds, but the mayor has demurred, possibly because it would impact city revenues. All three political leaders must sign off on the plan before it can happen.

In early 2015, the mayor continued his generosity toward NYCHA. His budget permanently relieved NYCHA of over $30 million annually in PILOT payments, in lieu of property taxes, in addition to the $70 million suspended for police payments. NYCHA's popular community center programs, at risk for years because the authority could no longer afford them, would be taken over by the city's Department for the Aging and the Division of Youth and

Community Development. Most importantly, the mayor's capital budget included an allocation of $300 million over three years for 27 NYCHA roof replacements. Roof replacements are a costly, system-wide NYCHA problem, and critical for stemming the water leaks and toxic molds that affect multiple apartments down the line. In a bold gesture, the mayor put the state on notice, challenging Governor Andrew Cuomo to match the city's capital commitment.

The Governor's Commitment to NYCHA Preservation

To draw state as well as city support for the Marshall Plan, advocates and resident leaders focused their attention on Albany. In March 2015, over 600 residents rallied in Albany, in an unusual show of strength, expertly organized by Community Voices Heard. They demanded a significant state commitment of $100 million a year for over ten years, totaling $1 billion for NYCHA improvements. That figure was close to the operating shortfall that had resulted from years of state disinvestment. With support from key legislators, the residents and advocates scored a victory. The Governor's 2016 budget included a commitment of $100 million for the year.

In April 2015, NYCHA submitted a proposal to HCR for the $100 million, requesting 123 roof replacements in the 18 developments that needed them most urgently. The governor did not respond directly to NYCHA's proposal but rather distributed $2 million to each legislative district containing public housing. Legislators were asked to submit their own proposals for using the funds, following HCR guidelines. Oddly, the guidelines prohibited major improvements like roof replacement and encouraged less urgent quality-of-life improvements, such as security devices, landscaping and playground improvements, new appliances, and the like. Apparently, the governor did not intend to address NYCHA's profound infrastrucure problems, preferring instead to spread the funds as political capital at the district level.

The NYCHA NextGeneration Plan

In May 2015, the NextGeneration NYCHA plan was released. This comprehensive analysis concentrated on the authority's most pressing issues: its financial difficulties, reforms needed in housing management, and how to reset resident engagement (NYCHA, 2015). About capital generation and reducing the existing backlog, the plan proposed two major housing changeovers: first, to lease available NYCHA land for private residential development and, second, to convert selected developments to privately-owned affordable housing.

The NYCHA plan called for the construction of 17,500 apartments: 10,000 units in 100-percent affordable developments, and 7,500 in mixed-income (50 percent affordable) developments.[16] Roughly 13,750 units (80 percent) would be affordable housing, which reversed the Bloomberg Infill 80/20 proposal, and the rest would be market-rate rentals. NYCHA estimated that fifty to sixty developments would be affected. Essentially, NYCHA land would cancel out one-sixth of the construction goals in the mayor's housing plan. NYCHA predicted that the mixed-income developments located in the stronger rental markets would become its largest revenue generator, yielding an estimated $300 million to $600 million in developer and leasing fees over the decade. These then would be allocated to major improvements.

The NextGeneration plan detailed another housing transition in NYCHA communities: shedding developments that were more costly to manage, including an estimated 15,000 units in scattered-site developments, and obsolete tower-in-the-park developments.[17] They hoped these estates would be converted under the HUD Rental Assistance Demonstration (RAD) Program, and transferred to private, nonprofit ownership as permanently affordable housing.

Under RAD, a development's public housing capital and operating subsidies are combined and converted into long-term rent assistance contracts,[18] thus making it possible for the new owner to draw investment capital to rehabilitate to a higher standard.[19] Permanent affordability is assured because the law requires HUD and the owner to renew contracts once they expire. RAD is the only program Washington is offering to housing authorities to recapitalize and preserve existing public housing developments, albeit as privately-owned Section 8 housing, not public housing. However, based on federal law, this program is currently capped at 185,000 units nationwide. Several large-city authorities, as in San Francisco and Baltimore, are already using it to convert most, if not all, of their inventories. In New York City, the limit had already been reached for HUD applications. So the question remained, how could NYCHA qualify for the HUD program?

It was during the Bloomberg administration that NYCHA made its first and only attempt at RAD conversion. The authority gained HUD approval for the conversion of Ocean Bay Apartments (Bayside), a 1,400 unit development located in Far Rockaway.[20] In late 2015, after a period of intense resident engagement, NYCHA issued a request for proposals (RFPs), and a development team was selected during July 2016.

The downside of RAD is that conversion requires privatization of the developments. Converted developments exit the public housing program (Section 9), and become part of HUD's program for private, multi-family housing (Section 8). Many people disagreed with the NextGeneration plan, because it called for privatizing close to a tenth of NYCHA's inventory. The authority pointed out that under its plan, the converted developments would be permanently affordable, and since they would be leased for 60 years rather than sold, the NYCHA would continue to play a role in the new ownership entity. In addition, the development would be rehabilitated to a higher standard. If HUD agrees with the plan, NYCHA estimates that the RAD conversions would reduce its capital backlog by a considerable $3 billion over the decade because of the private takeover and restoration investment (Wetzler, 2016). The operational savings would be significant, as well.

The NYCHA housing plan raised several questions. How affordable would the newly developed housing be? Would it be accessible to current, on-site residents? Would the revenues it generates be used for on-site capital improvements or allocated elsewhere? Should NYCHA land actually be used to develop market-rate housing? Should public housing be privatized? Resident leaders and housing advocates did not universally endorse the NextGeneration plan, but the opposition was not vocal enough to make a difference. People recognized that the housing measures were necessary for NYCHA to raise the capital it needs, and for it to achieve critical operational savings. So despite debates about many of its provisions, the plan gained acceptance without any discernable, united opposition.

From the perspective of a capital-starved housing authority, the NYCHA plan was, in effect, a bootstrap operation. The planners had found ingenious ways within their means to cut operating costs and to raise the capital they needed to reduce a portion of the authority's sizeable backlog. The city, however, was not providing any significant capital support, beyond the $300 million it had already committed to roof replacement. Although the NYCHA land would fulfill a major portion of the mayor's Housing New York construction goals, there would be no further capital commitment from the city. The firewall separating the mayor's plan and the NextGeneration plan, remained in place.

Further City and State Commitments by 2016

In early 2016, Mayor de Blasio expanded his commitment to NYCHA by allocating over $70 million in the city expense budget for façade work. Many of NYCHA's aging buildings have crumbling facades that need to be shored up. Because HUD regulations categorize façade work as repairs rather than eligible capital expenditures, NYCHA would find it difficult to allot limited operating resources to that project.

In March 2016, with a new FY 2017 state budget pending, hundreds of NYCHA residents again traveled to Albany to press for new capital commitments, this time specifically for infrastructure improvements. Prospects were good. In his State of the State Message, the governor had announced a $5 billion, five-year affordable housing initiative. Residents and advocates called for an appropriate, parallel five-year commitment to NYCHA preservation. The budget, released in April, did include $2 billion over the year for affordable housing but contained no specific allocations. Specifics would be decided later and arrived at jointly by the governor, the senate, and the assembly, and reflected in a Memorandum of Understanding. The assembly and some committed state senators pressed for $500 million for NYCHA capital improvements, but no agreement has been reached to date. At present, there is no clear indication of how, or whether, the funds will be dispersed.

NYCHA Management Reforms

Early in the de Blasio administration, and well before the NYCHA plan was released, several notable housing management reforms were initiated. The reforms were intended to make management more efficient, and more responsive to resident grievances. At the start of 2013, during the Bloomberg administration, 420,000 repair work orders were outstanding. These were addressed using the $70 million NYCHA would have had to pay for police services. By 2016, open work orders had been reduced to an average level of about 140,000 each month. Over 80 percent of non-emergency work orders are now handled within 15 days, and 80 percent of emergency work orders are completed within 24 hours (NYCHA, 2016).

In 2015, an innovative service called OPMOM was launched. Now called NextGen Operations, this department was created to decentralize on-site management and make it more flexible and responsive. In 18 of the developments, front-line management no longer had to go through tiers of borough management for budgeting or carrying out repairs.

In early 2016, NYCHA launched the FlexOps service in selected developments, which instituted staggered management shifts, from 6:00 a.m. to 8:00 p.m. This stirred up a great deal of controversy with the unions. Before this, on-site management worked only a single shift, from 8:00 a.m. to 4:30 p.m., which meant they were not around to make repairs in the evenings when residents were more likely to be home from work. The wider coverage, albeit still with limited staff, means residents will no longer have to lose workdays to get repairs.

NYCHA Moves Forward With its Housing Development Plan

NYCHA moved forward quickly on its housing development agenda, even before the NextGeneration plan was released. By late 2014, the authority had begun to enroll residents at three developments targeted for 100 percent affordable housing: Mill Brook Houses in the South Bronx, Van Dyke Houses in Brownsville, and Ingersoll Houses in Fort Greene. Though the process was not free of conflict, by 2016, NYCHA had selected developers for 156 senior units at Mill Brook, 188 family units at Van Dyke, and 145 senior units at Ingersoll. Project-based vouchers were used for the senior units, to enable existing residents to access the housing. At Van Dyke, there will be HPD subsidies and a tiered-income distribution of apartments. Regarding lottery applications, residents will be given a 25 percent preference, and there will be a 50 percent community preference.

These construction projects are not expected to generate revenues to be applied to capital investment in the existing buildings. This is an ongoing source of frustration for residents, many of whom expected to benefit from repairs and improvements. Rather than getting the maintenance they need to improve their living conditions, residents will have to stand by and watch while new housing and amenities are constructed on-site, and NYCHA land is being leased for a token one dollar.[21] As of July 2016, three additional 100 percent affordable developments have been slated for Betances V (senior housing) and Betances VI (family housing) in the Bronx, and Sumner Houses (senior housing) in Brooklyn.

In 2015, two developments were targeted by NYCHA for mixed-income housing: Wyckoff Gardens in Boerum Hill, and Brooklyn and Holmes Towers on the Upper East Side of Manhattan. The long engagement period was a contentious one. Residents bemoaned the possibility that new housing could accelerate gentrification pressures in the neighborhood: pressures many residents believe will ultimately displace them, despite the authority's assurances to the contrary. NYCHA argues that these communities are already experiencing substantial gentrification. The resident opposition was particularly strenuous at Holmes, because of the potential loss of a popular children's playground. This triggered a protest demonstration at nearby Gracie Mansion during a mayoral event. When council hearings were held at the development, Chair Olatoye stood firm in her stance that "NYCHA will move forward." It was manifestly clear that resident engagement does not convey veto power over development plans. Once NYCHA designates a development for construction or conversion, the only option residents have is to negotiate, as best they can, how to maximize community benefits, and how to minimize the difficulties that flow from redevelopment.

To maximize community benefits, residents could work to influence design considerations, petition for generated revenues to be applied to improving existing buildings, canvass for needed retail and commercial facilities, seek a commitment from developers to hire local residents for construction and permanent jobs, and so on.

The requests for proposals (RFPs) issued in April 2016, called for constructing 300 to 400 units at Wyckoff Gardens, and 350 to 400 units at Holmes. Undoubtedly, it will not be long before the NYCHA announces plans for additional developments designated for mixed-income housing. It is impressive how NYCHA is moving forward with its housing development agenda despite the resident resistance it has encountered.

The RAD Conversion Plan

In July 2016, the first wave of RAD conversions was officially announced, with NYCHA filing applications with HUD for 5,200 units in 40 developments. In the months before the announcement, NYCHA encouraged the Community Service Society and Enterprise Community Partners to form a RAD Stakeholder Roundtable on Resident Rights and Protections. NYCHA recognized that residents faced certain risks and uncertainties, because they would be tranferring to a new ownership entity. In addition, the new HUD program had different rules and regulations.

The roundtable began meeting in March 2016, assembling a range of stakeholders: resident leaders, advocates, community organizations that work with residents, and concerned housing organizations. The group was to develop guideline principles that would govern resident rights during and after conversion, and which NYCHA and the prospective owners/managers must comply with. The roundtable had issued its initial list of guideline principles by July, and NYCHA concurred. The roundtable will continue to meet to monitor the RAD conversion process, to identify and resolve any unexpected issues that emerge, and to provide independent information and assistance to residents targeted for conversion.

Summary of Progress So Far

Resident resistance to NextGeneration's plan for housing transformations has, not surprisingly, been concentrated in the communities where sites have been designated. NYCHA has invested many hours trying to gain resident buy-in. Where they have not won them over completely, they have managed to get a grudging acceptance of, or resignation to, the inevitable. Some advocacy organizations are conflicted over two issues: the use of NYCHA land for market-rate housing, and the privatization of NYCHA communities. However, most groups are pragmatic by nature. They understand the situation NYCHA is in, and how it needs to use every means available to reduce operating costs and raise enough capital to survive.

While the NextGeneration plan does not address the $17 billion outstanding capital requirement, it will significantly reduce the backlog, which will total at least $7 billion in ten years. About $3 billion is expected to come from RAD conversions as private capital takes on restoration close to $3 billion in ongoing federal capital subsidies at current levels. Another half-billion in revenues will be generated by mixed-income housing development, in addition to current and future capital commitments made by the state and the city.

One has to wonder whether NYCHA and its residents can survive the current infrastructure problems. Given the sheer scale of the problems, progress can only be slow and, at best, incremental. Residents continue to endure impossible conditions. The media is full of stories about households living with perpetual leaks, or elderly and disabled residents being forced to climb multiple stories because the elevator does not work. For them, it is either the stairs, or complete isolation in their apartments. So the question remains: can a Marshall Plan really be mounted, and will the government actually respond to resident needs?

The Way Forward?

This is not a time to count on Washington, given the stalemate of the last eight years, and the uncertainties under a new administration. It seems that, for the near future, New York City and New York State will have to manage this Marshall Plan for low-income New Yorkers. They will need to find the resources to meet the capital requirements of their largest, single, affordable housing provider.

It is hard to be sanguine about the current housing situation after reviewing the recent history of state reinvestment in NYCHA and its residents. Pressure from concerned legislators, residents, and the broader housing advocacy community has not motivated the governor to address the authority's basic infrastructure needs, even when there is $100 million in the budget set aside for that purpose. It is still unclear whether NYCHA will receive a portion of the pending $5 billion, five-year affordable housing initiative, either. On the positive side, the governor will dedicate $400 million in excess Battery Park City revenues to NYCHA improvements over the next decade. Unfortunately, the mayor appears to be the major obstacle in this case, no doubt because of the possible impact on the city budget.

Under Mayor de Blasio, the city has provided some significant support to NYCHA. It relieved over $100 million in required annual payments to the city, it allocated $300 million in the capital budget for roof replacement, and it designated $70 million for façade improvements. Nevertheless, this generosity pales when compared to the multi-billion capital commitment the mayor has made to his signature Housing New York plan. City Hall is where housing priority decisions are made, and where NYCHA learns what it can and cannot demand from Albany and Washington. No doubt the city will continue to support public housing, but without significant pressure from the outside, NYCHA will remain in a secondary position.

For NYCHA to receive its fair share of capital resources from the city and state, several things need to happen. First, the firewall now separating affordable housing initiatives from public housing preservation needs to be brought down. A parallel commitment is needed to NYCHA. The government may do that of its own accord, because of the critical importance of public housing in the city's housing infrastructure, and because it would serve a good purpose. Realistically, that will not happen on its own.

The best way for NYCHA to get what it needs is for someone to stir the sleeping giant into action. Someone needs to exert the kind of grass-roots political pressure that will compel government leaders to respond. The effort requires a concerted and persistent campaign that focuses on NYCHA's failing infrastructure and its capital requirements.

It would not be hard to capture the voices of dissatisfied residents, weary of impossible living conditions. You can hear them anytime you meet a resident. However, the voices need to be heard often, in the right places, in large numbers, and at a volume that cannot be ignored. Residents can always count on policy guidance and strategic planning specialists, as well as experts with organizing experience, and an expert at the grass-roots level.

The missing piece is knowing how to mount such a campaign. Leaders need to know where the resident initiative will come from, and who can channel resident anger and their deep-felt distrust, into a unified and organized crusade. CCOP is the natural seat for such an initiative, possibly in concert with the Resident Advisory Board (RAB).[22] Both organizations have been known to confront NYCHA with their concerns and complaints, but their voices are heard largely within the "NYCHA family." That energy needs to be channeled outward in a sustained, organized, strategic campaign, supported by outside advocates. That can happen only if the prevailing resident distrust of outsiders can be overcome. A collaboration such as this may be the only way to address the firewall that now separates major city and state affordable housing initiatives from the preservation of public housing.

The prospects for public housing are dismal without a dramatic change in government priorities. Policies must begin to restore public housing, rather than marginalize it, and they must cease exploiting public housing's land assets. Without such changes, NYCHA and its developments will continue to face physical decline. The authority may, at some point, have to take drastic measures, as other large-city housing authorities have done. It will have to privatize its inventory to assure its restoration and survival, or it will have to undertake the massive demolition and redevelopment of its real estate assets.

Among large-city housing authorities, NYCHA has been the standard-bearer for preservation efforts for generations. When you compare it to other authorities, such as Atlanta, Chicago, and Newark, NYCHA has been steadfast in retaining its inventory. However, the next generation brand implies that it will attempt to do otherwise in the future. NYCHA will need major capital support from government if it is to survive as an institution, and if it expects to do more than manage properties in decline and withstand the growing anger of residents.

Government's failure to deal with public housing at the level and scale required will doom New York's third city to continuing deterioration, and the impending loss of critically needed low-income housing. In the midst of a period of economic and population growth, and an otherwise vital housing market, the rotting core of public housing would not only be incongruous: it would be tragic.

Notes

1. This chapter was prepared in honor of Walter Stafford, a former CSS colleague, as part of the Walter Stafford Symposium on the Structure of Race and Inequality in New York City, held at New York University, October 13–14, 2016. It is closely related to an earlier report issued by the Community Service Society: Victor Bach & Tom Waters, *Strengthening New York City's Public Housing: Directions for Change* (July 2014). www.cssny.org.

2. Often referred to as the "towers-in-the-park" model given currency by the French architect, Le Corbusier, in the 1920s.

3. This paper focuses on housing and related policy issues facing NYCHA and its residents, rather than on the significant safety and security issues experienced in public housing communities.

4. In 2006, the operating deficit reached a peak of $235 million. It is now estimated at $22 million.

5. Historically, the state has been innovative in developing affordable housing policies, including public housing: The 1955 Mitchell-Lama program became a national model for federally subsidized housing programs by the 1960s. At the city level, the Bloomberg and de Blasio initiatives were preceded by Mayor Edward Koch's massive program to restore housing in neighborhoods of abandonment.

6. NYCHA was created under Mayor Fiorello LaGuardia in 1934, and developed the first public housing in the country, First Houses, in the Lower East Side.

7. Unless otherwise stated, the analyses in this chapter were drawn from the 2014 New York City Housing and Vacancy Survey (HVS). HVS is a triennial survey of the city's housing and resident population, based on a random sample of about 18,000 households, conducted by the U.S. Bureau of the Census.

8. Under the American Reinvestment and Recovery Act ARRA of 2009, NYCHA received $423 million in capital funds for "shovel-ready" projects. ARRA also allowed for the federalization of state- and city-financed developments, making them eligible for federal operating and capital subsidies.

9. Federal law and HUD regulations permit housing authorities to transfer up to 20 percent of their capital subsidies each year to operations.

10. As used here, "low-income" refers to household income levels at or below twice the federal poverty level. In 2016, that would mean an income up to $40,180 for a three-person household.

11. The Brooke Amendment, enacted in 1969.

12. It should be noted these deficiencies refer only to conditions within apartments. They do not include building deficiencies, such as elevator breakdowns, broken front-door locks, problems in common spaces. Reported deficiencies include: Water leaks; broken plaster/peeling paint (larger than 8.5 x 11 in.); cracks/holes in walls, ceilings, or floors; toilet breakdowns; heating breakdowns; additional heating needed; and rodents.

13. Other subsidized housing includes Mitchell-Lama rentals, federal Section 236 and project-based Section 8 developments, and private rentals where the tenant holds a Section 8 Housing Choice Voucher.

14. In 2013, during the Bloomberg administration, NYCHA proposed building private residential developments on available land in strong market areas. Twenty percent of the units were to be "affordable," eighty percent at market rent levels. Eight developments were targeted in East Harlem, the Lower East Side, and the Upper West Side.

15. In 1979, Mayor Ed Koch and Governor Hugh Carey approved the Battery Park City development plan as an upscale residential and commercial development. It was agreed that any excess revenues generated would be allocated to affordable housing needs in other communities.

16. Original affordability targets were households at 60 percent of AMI, above $47,000 for a family of three, an income level well about most NYCHA residents.

17. Scattered-site developments (about 6,500 units) are buildings that NYCHA agreed to take over when their original private owners defaulted. They are costly to manage because they are not built to conventional public housing standards and require customized repair and replacements. HUD considers a public housing development "obsolete" if it would cost less to construct than to rehabilitate.

18. Under RAD, the development becomes part of HUD's Multifamily Housing Program as project-based Section 8 and is transferred out of its Section 9 Public Housing Program.

19. RAD requires the new owner to meet the 25-year capital need.

20. One of the major reasons given for selecting Ocean Bay was the availability of Superstorm Sandy recovery funds to help make a conversion deal feasible.

21. The rate was a standing agreement between HPD and NYCHA in order to reduce development costs and promote affordability.

22. The creation of a Resident Advisory Board (RAB) is required each year under the 1998 Quality Housing and Work Responsibility Act to consult with the authority in the development of its annual plan. The NYCHA RAB has 51 members, including CCOP.

References

Alinsky, Saul. (1971). *Rules for radicals: A pragmatic primer for realistic radicals.* New York, NY: Random House.

Bach, Victor, and Tom Waters. (2014). "Strengthening New York City's Public Housing: Directions for Change." Community Service Society, July, 2014.

Bloom, Nicholas Dagen. (2009). *Public housing that worked, New York in the twentieth century.* Philadelphia, PA: University of Pennsylvania Press.

Community Voices Heard CAAAV. (2011). A report card for the New York City Housing Authority: Residents' evaluation of NYCHA and recommendations for improvement."

Harvard Joint Center for Housing Studies. (2015). *America's rental housing: Expanding options for diverse and growing demand.* Cambridge, MA: Harvard Joint Center for Housing Studies.

HUD. 1994. "HUD 24 CFR Part 964." in *Federal Register.* August 24, 1994. National Low Income Housing Coalition. (2016). *Out of reach, 2016: No refuge for low income renters.* Washington, DC: National Low Income Housing Coalition.

New York City Government. (2014). "Housing New York: A five-borough, ten year housing plan, April, 2014."

New York City Housing Authority. (2015). "Adopted budget for FY 2016 and the four year financial plan for FY 2017–2020." (p. 18).

NYCHA. (2015). The NextGeneration NYCHA Plan.

NYCHA (2016). NYCHA Metrics.

NYCHA. (2016a). Data from Office of Performance Management and Analytics. New York City Housing Authority.

NYCHA. (2016b). Draft—PHA Agency Plan; Annual Agency Plan for Fiscal Year 2017. (p. 161). New York City Housing Authority.

Schwartz, Alex. (1999). New York City and subsidized housing: Impacts and lessons of the city's $5 billion capital budget housing plan. *Housing Policy Debate 10*(4).

Waters, Tom, and Victor Bach. (2016). *Making the rent 2016: Tenant conditions in New York City's changing neighborhoods.* New York, NY: Community Service Society.

Wetzler, Libby. (2016). "Visit to Bronxchester shows NYCHA in transition." in *Gotham Gazette.* August 26, 2016.

Chapter 14

Political Participation

Black New Yorkers

Fifty Years of Closing the Political Inequality Gap, 1965–2016

John Flateau

A vital question needs to be asked. Over the past 50 years, how have Black New Yorkers exercised their power to challenge racial inequality in the city's political and social systems? This chapter reviews the evolution of Black political inequality in New York City in the last half-century and discusses many of the present challenges and prospects Blacks face.

New York City's Black body politic is not a monolith. Rather, distinct nuances exist based on the borough, political geography, party politics, ethnic and racial diversity, political alliances and coalitions. All of these reach far beyond local power bases, at all levels of government, and even have international influences. Black political New York *is intertwined* with cultural, religious, racial, ethnic, linguistic, demographic, and nationalist interests, all simmering and sometimes boiling over, in the global caldron called New York City.

By most measures, Black New Yorkers have achieved ethnic political ascendancy, as did European ethnic groups before them. They have won a trifecta of citywide offices, including the one-term mayoralty of David Dinkins, beginning in 1989; Bill Thompson's eight years as city comptroller, starting in 2001, and; the office of Public Advocate, held since 2013 by Letitia James. Black New Yorkers have also achieved several borough and state offices. These consist of presidencies in Manhattan, Queens, and Brooklyn, and district attorney positions in the Bronx and Brooklyn. Statewide political offices comprise governor (briefly due to a resignation), lieutenant governor, the state comptrollership for eight years, president of the state senate; and presently, speaker of the state assembly. The political path Blacks have traveled *is* worth noting.

Colonial Origins, a New Nation and Civil War

Starting in 1626, the Dutch West India Company began to bring people of African descent to New York City as slaves and as indentured servants. They built and maintained the New Amsterdam colony that is today's lower Manhattan. In 1664, the British took New Amsterdam from the Dutch, and the British monarch, King Charles II granted its charter to his brother James, the Duke of York. Slavery was expanded, and slaves became a large part of the city's labor force. British involvement in slavery continued until their defeat at the end of the America Revolutionary War. From the city's founding, Dutch, British, and American city legislatures were concerned about slave plots and insurrections, so they passed Black Codes to control their slaves.

In the newly independent United States, Federalists and Anti-Federalists fiercely competed for control of New York City's government. Because of heavy agitation by Black and White abolitionists, New York State passed the gradual Slavery Emancipation Act of 1799. Free Black males, progressively made eligible to vote, were a small but growing voting bloc in New York City politics. At this time, Andrew Jackson, the next president of the United States (1832–36), worked alongside Martin Van Buren, soon to be Andrew Jackson's Vice President. Van Buren became head of New York's powerful Regency political machine and a founder of the New York and national Democratic Party. At the New York State Constitutional Convention of 1821, Van Buren and allies engineered a new provision in the constitution requiring a $250 property ownership requirement, *only* for free Black males. This was their way of suppressing Black voter participation (Hayduk, 1996).

Throughout the 19th century, leading up to the Civil War, both Blacks and Whites in New York City agitated for the abolition of slavery, and for the right to vote. Their efforts helped in getting the 13th, 14th, and 15th amendments to the U.S. Constitution (1865–1870) passed. The abolition of slavery granted nearly four million African slaves freedom, made them U.S. citizens, and gave only males the right to vote. With newly empowered Blacks now voting, the first Black U.S. congressmen, plus state and local public officials were elected, with others holding numerous public offices in the years from 1868 to 1901. This included having the majority-control of the lower house of the South Carolina state legislature.

The main public policy mandate of Black reconstruction was to defeat the legacy of slavery and the scourge of racial inequality. Mandatory public education aimed at abolishing legalized illiteracy for Black slaves and Whites alike was one of many progressive measures advanced during this period, and a measure that has endured to this day. However, despite the existence of congressional reconstruction and post-Civil War martial law in the South, there was a rising tide of Southern White retaliation against Black progress, which became a flood of White rage. As a result, the new Black voters in the South were virtually re-enslaved.

Blacks bore the brunt of political assassinations, voter disenfranchisement, and economic re-enslavement through sharecropping, tenant farming, vagrancy laws, convict leasing and prison labor schemes (Du Bois, 1998; Franklin, 2004). The U.S. Supreme Court was complicit in all this, by ignoring lawsuits that challenged state and local government-sponsored terrorism, and the depriving of Black civil rights. One has to ask how all this could happen.

The 1876 Compromise: Betrayal and Repercussions

The year 1876 was a watershed year in American jurisprudence. In two U.S. Supreme Court decisions, *United States v. Cruikshank,*[1] and *United States v. Reese,*[2] the court overruled and rebuffed local federal prosecutors trying to enforce federal laws to protect the voting and civil rights of Black and White Republicans elected to office in the South. The U.S. Supreme Court tacitly approved of the murders of legitimately elected Black and White Southern Republican public officials. This ended all efforts to challenge racial inequality. The Court ruled that it was not in their jurisdiction to interfere with individual and states' rights, even if they were complicit in violating black human and civil rights.

In another incident, New York Democratic Governor Samuel Tilden and Ohio Republican Governor Rutherford Hayes contested the 1876 presidential election. The election was controversial and extremely close, foretelling a downward spiral of democracy for Black Americans. To break the deadlock over disputed Electoral College votes, the two major political parties struck an infamous political deal. The Democrats would concede the presidency to the Republicans, and in return, President Hayes would withdraw all remaining federal troops from the South.

This bureaucratic bargain ended Black reconstruction in the South by eliminating federal protective laws, and by removing military and judicial protection of Southern Black voters. This agreement also encouraged former Confederate White redeemers to re-establish their White, one-party Democratic control of state and local governments throughout the South. This, in turn, guaranteed Southern domination of the U.S. Congress, through the seniority system, and the U.S. Senate filibuster rule well into the twentieth century. Now, there were no prospects for passing progressive reforms to improve the quality of life for Black Americans.

Fleeing oppressive conditions in the South, in addition to fleeing from European colonialism in the Caribbean, Blacks fled to America's urban centers. Millions migrated to the Northeast, and to cities such as Chicago, Detroit, and Cleveland in the industrial Midwest. They also moved westward to Los Angeles, San Francisco, and Oakland. In her book, *The Warmth of Other Suns,* Isabelle Wilkerson estimates that, from 1910 to 1970, six million Blacks escaped the South. This was one of the largest mass migrations in U.S. history. Elsewhere in the Northeast and Midwest, and on the West Coast, Blacks were keen to gain greater economic opportunity and political representation as a means of advancing themselves (Wilkerson, 2011).

New York's Black Legislators

Harlem

Black Manhattan, centered in Harlem, has a storied history of political empowerment in New York City, including efforts to address racial inequality. New York City's first Black elected official was Edward A. Johnson. He was a lawyer and educator from North Carolina, who was elected in 1917 to the New York State Legislature as a Republican Harlem Assemblyman. There were earlier examples of Black political party operatives, both Democrat and Republican, who served the main party machine bosses in the late-19th and early 20th centuries (Irish & Riviere, 1990). One party patronage position went to Reverend Philip White, Rector of St. Phillips Episcopal Church. Then Brooklyn Mayor Seth Low, later Mayor of New York City and President of Columbia University appointed him to the Brooklyn Board of Education.

After Harlem's Johnson came a string of other firsts. Adam Clayton Powell, Jr. was the city's first Black Alderman/City Councilman, in 1937, and the first Black U.S. Congressman, in 1944. The first Black borough president was elected in 1954; the first Black elected judge was Harold Stevens in 1950 and J. Raymond Jones, was the first Black county leader for the Manhattan Democratic Party (Tammany Hall). These firsts paved the way for the already mentioned Black mayor, Dinkins, and State governor and lieutenant governor, Paterson. Also, in a crowded Democratic primary, Dominican Republic-born, New York State Senator Adriano Espaillat won the Northern Manhattan–South Bronx congressional seat held by Charles Rangel since 1970. This reduced New York City's four Black Congress members to three seats: two in Brooklyn (Yvette Clarke and Hakeem Jeffries) and one in southeast Queens (Gregory Meeks).

Brooklyn and Other Boroughs

From 1834 to 1896, Brooklyn moved from being a separate town to a village, and then to a city. It merged with Manhattan in 1897 in a citywide referendum on city consolidation. Black Brooklyn began rising in population. It was a distant second to Black Manhattan until the 1970 Census. In 1970, Brooklyn became the largest Black population-center in New York City's five boroughs, because of Southern and Caribbean immigration, and the ghettoization spurred by banking and real estate redlining. This laid the demographic foundation for Brooklyn's political expansion. The 1965 Voting Rights Act advanced Black political empowerment, and the Hart-Celler Immigration Act Of 1965 increased population with Caribbean immigration. This built upon a long history of Black insurgency born of Garveyism, the Civil Rights, and Black Power movements.

Brooklyn elected its first Black state legislator, Bertram Baker in 1948, and its first Black member of Congress, Shirley Chisholm, in 1968, both of Caribbean descent. Queens elected its first Black legislators in the 1960s. These included Kenneth Browne, Guy Brewer, Archie Spigner, and Helen Marshall. Queens's first Black Congressman was Alton Waldon, elected in 1986, followed by Reverend Floyd Flake, and currently Gregory Meeks. The Bronx elected its first Black legislators in the 1950s. They were Ivan Warner, Dennis Coleman, Joe Galiber, Gloria Davis, plus others. Staten Island elected its first Black city council member, Debra Rose, in 2009. Black New Yorkers have made sure that their efforts to reduce racial inequality through the political process have been represented well in local, state and federal governments.

Growing Political Representation, 1965–2016

Multiple factors have contributed to the evolution of Black political representation. As Table 14.1 on page 310 indicates, in the last 50 years, the number of Black elected officials in New York City has increased fourfold, or *more than 300 percent*, from 10 individuals in 1965 to 45 people in 2016 representing Blacks at city, state and federal levels.

During this time, the dramatic increase in state and city legislators has reduced Black political inequality in New York City. Here are some of the factors that both advanced and retarded this progress:

Table 14.1. New York City Black Elected Officials, Fifty Years of Growth, 1965–2016

	Man.		Brooklyn		Bronx		Queens		Staten Is.		Total	
	1965	2016	1965	2016	1965	2013	1965	2016	1965	2016	1965	2016
Borough President and County Dist. Attorneys	1	0	0	2	0	1	0	0	0	0	1	3
US Congressional Reps.	1	0	0	2	0	0	0	1	0	0	1	3
State Senators and Assembly Members	2	3	3	12	0	4	0	6	0	0	5	25
City Council Members	1	1	1	6	0	2	0	3	0	1	2	13
Citywide Elected/Home Borough	0	0	0	1	0	0	0	0	0	0	0	1
Total	5	4	4	23	0	9	0	10	0	0	9	45

Source: New York State Black, Puerto Rican, Hispanic, and Asian Legislative Caucus, *1917–2014: A Look at the History of the Legislators of Color*; New York State Black, Hispanic, Asian Legislative Caucus website, 2016; League of Women Voters, "They Represent You," 2016; John Flateau, *Black Brooklyn: The Politics of Ethnicity, Class and Gender*, 2016.

1. Party, borough, racial and ethnic political negotiations; campaigns and elections.
2. Class, racial and ethnic in-migration, white out-migration, changing demographics.
3. Foreclosures, lack of affordable housing, forced residential mobility and gentrification.
4. Structural changes in legislative bodies, (e.g., city charter revisions, etc.).
5. Immigration status; increasing citizenship, voter registration and voter turnout r.ates
6. The Census and Black population undercount, which in turn affects redistricting.
7. Legislative reapportionment and redistricting politics, processes and outcomes.

Table 14.1 shows that in 1965, the New York City Council had only two Black members, citywide. That is two out of 35 seats or only six percent of available seats—one from Central Harlem and one from Bedford-Stuyvesant. Fifty years later, there are 13 Black members on the now 51 member city council or 26 percent of that body. The city council expanded to 51 seats, because of concerted minority advocacy for city charter revisions. This same voting rights advocacy led to greater minority representation on the redistricting commission.

In 2016, Brooklyn had 23 Black elected officials: half of the total number for New York City. This includes the only Black elected official in a citywide position, Letitia James. Before this, City Comptroller, Bill Thompson (2001–09), was from Brooklyn. Manhattan claims the only other citywide Black elected official, Mayor David Dinkins (1989–93).

Diverse, Dispersed, and Politically Balkanized

According to the U.S. Census Bureau, New York State has the largest Black population of any state in the nation: approximately 3.6 million (U.S. Census Bureau, 2015). New York City itself contains approximately 2.2 million diverse, Black New Yorkers comprised of four ethnic groups: African Americans (1.2 million), Caribbean Americans (600,000), Continental Africans (200,000) and Afro-Latinos (200,000). These groups are dispersed geographically across the five boroughs. Black Brooklyn's population in 2015 was approximately one million, the highest ever, and nearly half the citywide Black population. Central Brooklyn is the epicenter of the Caribbean American population, whether in New York City, New York State, or nationally. Only the number of Caribbean Americans in South Florida rivals this population of some 400,000. The largest concentration of Continental Africans is in the Bronx.

There is a challenge to this representational achievement. Mortgage and tax lien foreclosures and subprime lending are still devastating the sizeable, home-owning Black neighborhoods of Central Brooklyn and Southeast Queens. These displacement forces, along with the lack of affordable housing, are causing New York City's Black population to disperse and migrate out of the city. This loss of population is critically undermining political representation of Blacks and is reviving the issue of racial political inequality. Persistent institutional racism and discrimination destabilize Black New York City's progress, and threatens to reverse its political gains of the last 50 years.

Several challenges exist within New York City's Black population, as well. Collective political action, political communication, consultation and coordination need to be improved. Black ethnic, cultural, and language differences need to be acknowledged and managed better. There also is the issue of political balkanization within boroughs, expressed through party loyalties, and loyalty to one's institutional leadership and legislative organizations (i.e., assembly, senate, city council, Congress).

Other challenges need to be recognized. Political leaders must define their priorities and muster the political will to stand and deliver on promises. A preoccupation with multiple agendas keeps people from moving forward. Also, despite an aging leadership, there has been no serious succession planning for ushering in new leaders. In cultivating new political leaders, Blacks need mentoring, knowledge transfer, and intergenerational dialogue. Add to this a growing diversity in attitude, age, race, class, ethnicity, and gender among Black elected officials, and the constituencies they represent.

Voting Rights Litigation

Passing the 1965 Voting Rights Act (VRA) was critically important. At the time, there was only one Black congressional district in New York, held by Reverend Adam Clayton Powell, Jr. Formerly, he had been the city's first Black alderman, as well as pastor of the largest Black faith congregation in New York City, the Abyssinian Baptist Church. Beginning in the 1930s, Charles Hamilton Houston, and his understudies at Howard University Law School that included Thurgood Marshall had been using the U.S. Constitution to defeat institutional racism in education and other policy arenas. They could be credited with the VRA as one of their victories. A direct outcome was the increase in Black political representation for New York's communities of color.

New York City's *Cooper v. Powers*[3] was one of the nation's first VRA lawsuits in the 1960s. Andrew Cooper of Brooklyn, later publisher of the *City Sun* Black newspaper, brought the case. The lawsuit played a crucial role in highlighting racial gerrymandering, and helped to bring about redistricting of Brooklyn's first Black congressional district, won in 1968 by Assemblywoman Shirley Chisholm. In the 1970s, *UJO of Williamsburg v. Carey*[4] was a key VRA lawsuit that upheld the creation of minority state legislative districts in Brooklyn, and beyond. In the 1980s, lawsuits including *Andrews v. Koch* (1981)[5] successfully challenged New York City to draw additional city council districts for Black and Latino communities.

In 1982, there was *Flateau v. Anderson.*[6] This case successfully challenged the governor and state legislature to draw additional congressional and state legislative seats for Blacks and Latinos, throughout New York State. In 1988, *Ashe v. NYC Board of Elections*[7] imposed a federal consent decree that required New York City to improve its election administration policies and procedures. This suit was necessary after discriminatory patterns were documented in minority communities that voted for Jesse Jackson in the presidential primary.

In 1989, *Morris v. NYC Board of Estimate*[8] abolished the at-large voting system in the city charter, which discriminated against Black and Latino voters. In the 1990s, *PRLDEF v. Gantt*[9] endeavored to abolish Congressman Rangel's Black congressional seat. That challenge was successfully defeated. Also in 1997, *Diaz v. Silver*[10] attempted to abolish Congresswoman Nydia Velazquez' congressional seat. That lawsuit was successfully defeated, as well. In 2012, *Favors v. Cuomo*[11] challenged New York's congressional redistricting and resulted in a third New York City Latino congressional seat, won by Adriano Espaillat, in 2016.

Over the decades, a fluid yet a durable coalition of legislative, civil rights and good-government groups participated in this array of voting rights litigation. Participants included the NYS Black, Hispanic and Asian Legislative Caucus, chaired by The Honorable Al Vann, with John Flateau, the executive director. Two principal attorneys were Esmeralda Simmons, Esquire, and then attorney, now the Honorable Paul Wooten, Justice, NYS. Supreme Court. There were many other contributors, including the Justice/ Puerto Rican Legal Defense and Education Fund, the Asian American Legal Defense and Education Fund, and the NAACP Legal Defense Fund.

Gender Inequality and the Path Forward

Table 14.2 addresses the challenges of gender inequality in the political arena and illustrates the progress made within the Black body politic over the past 50 years. The first Black woman elected in New York was Bessie Buchanan, a Harlem assemblywoman, elected in 1954. Ten years later, in 1964, Shirley Chisholm was elected as a Brooklyn assemblywoman, and in 1968, she became America's first Black congresswoman. In their day, Buchanan and Chisholm were nearly the only female elected officials in the White male-dominated legislative arena. Whether in local, state or federal elective office, this pattern of gender inequality persisted throughout the nation, regardless of race.

However, in 2016, half of New York's 45 Black elected officials were Black women: a majority of state assembly members. Black women were also a majority of Brooklyn's Black legislators. The only citywide Black elected official was Public Advocate Tish James, of Brooklyn. Brooklyn had two borough-wide elected officials, Borough President Eric Adams and District Attorney Ken Thompson, who was elected in 2013 but passed away in 2016. Brooklyn also has two Black U.S. representatives, Yvette Clarke and Hakim Jeffries, 12 Black state legislators, and six city council members.

Given a preliminary assessment of their ethnic ancestry, Brooklyn has the largest concentration of Caribbean American elected officials in New York City. These individuals include Congresswoman Yvette Clarke, State

Table 14.2. Black Male and Female, Caribbean, and African American Elected Officials, 2016

	Black Males	Black Females	Total	Caribbean American	African American	Total
Citywide	0	1	1	0	1	1
Borough Wide	2	1	3	0	3	3
US Congress	2	1	3	1	2	3
State Senate	5	3	8	2	6	8
State Assembly	8	10	18	6	12	18
City Council	7	6	13	2	11	13
Total	24	22	46	11	35	46

Source: New York Legislative Manuals and Red Books; League of Women Voters, "They Represent You," respective yearly publications; New York State Black, Puerto Rican, Hispanic and Asian Legislative Caucus, 2014, *1917–2014: A Look at the History of the Legislators of Color.*

Senator Roxanne Persaud, state assembly members Diana Richardson, Rodneyse Bichotte, Jamie Williams and Nick Perry, and City Council Members Jumaane Williams and Mathieu Eugene. The eight Caribbean American elected officials make up nearly three-quarters of the citywide total. The Brooklyn neighborhoods of Crown Heights, Flatbush, East Flatbush, and Canarsie, are the national epicenter of the Caribbean American population, estimated at 400,000 in Brooklyn, and 700,000 in New York City. It should be noted that Brooklyn's first Black Caribbean American elected official was Assemblyman Bertram Baker, who took office in 1948. Some other New York Black elected officials were Caribbean American, as well.

The ethnic diversity of the Caribbean American/African American dynamic has played an important role in the mobilization and demobilization of these two Black subelectorates. They both are active participants in the Black struggle to reduce the political inequality gap. These two electorates united to vote for Mario Cuomo against Ed Koch in the 1982 gubernatorial primary. They again voted as one bloc for Jesse Jackson in his 1984 and 1988 presidential primary campaigns. They joined forces for the third time in the 1989 and 1993 mayoral campaigns by David Dinkins. However, these same Black voting blocs split their support in the 1985 mayoral primary, with Caribbean American voters going for Ed Koch. They also voted in large numbers for Republican Governor George Pataki, in the 1994 gubernatorial general election, and they voted for Republican Michael Bloomberg in 2001, 2005, and 2009 mayoral elections (Flateau, 2016).

The two powerful Caribbean American and African American voting blocs have divergent political leadership styles, agendas, and strategies. They also have different political demands, resources, messaging, and voter mobilization efforts around key issues such as immigration reform. However, aligning with the "linked fate theory" of Michael Dawson (1994) and others, these two voting blocs unified again in the 2008 and 2012 presidential elections, voting both times in overwhelming numbers for Barack Obama, and then again in and 2016, they voted for Hillary Clinton.

Transcending Tribalism

Calvin Holder (1990), in his seminal article entitled the "The Rise and Fall of West Indian Politicians . . . ," offers a thesis for an interethnic form of tribalism within New York's Black body politic. He and others note that, in the 19th and early-20th centuries, generations of African Americans politically aligned themselves with the Republican Party. For them, it was the party of President

Abraham Lincoln, the party of the abolition of slavery, of reconstruction, and of the early civil rights movement.

West Indians who came to America in the early 20th century did not share this same historical frame of reference. They were more inclined to political alliances and deal-making with the Democratic Party. This was despite the fact that this party was a primary advocate of black racial oppression and segregation, particularly in the Southern states where the majority of Blacks still reside today. Such deviations in political orientation were part of the reason early fissures formed between NYC's two main Black political, ethnic groups: majority African Americans and minority West Indians. West Indian politicians were circumspect towards African Americans and did not promote their own West Indian ethnic identity in the broader Black community. Instead, they focused inward on their own circles. Beginning in the 1930s, most Blacks shifted from the Republican Party to the New Deal Democratic Party, following President Franklin Roosevelt's Depression-era relief programs. Unfortunately, to appease the Southern Democrats, these relief programs were racially discriminatory, eliminating coverage for Southern Black agricultural and domestic workers. Fortunately, Blacks had better access to these programs in urban centers.

Tribalism was based as well on political geography and residents, leading to political rivalry and competition. Brooklyn provides a case study, with NYC's largest Black population of nearly one million. Caribbean Americans were the majority of immigrants driven to Brooklyn by the post–1965 immigration laws. This influx of Blacks, aided by a manipulative real estate market, created neighborhoods that transitioned from White to Black in Bedford–Stuyvesant, Crown Heights, Flatbush, East Flatbush, and Canarsie. Similar shifts were underway in Springfield Gardens, Cambria Heights, Rosedale, and other parts of Southeast Queens.

Once the Caribbean immigrants in these neighborhoods achieved a critical mass, gained citizenship and registered to vote, they began to organize politically and started running for local political office. At this point, they were competing against White and African American incumbents. Initially, the result was that they helped ensure the reelection of incumbents by crowding the field with Caribbean American candidates. "Island nationalism" has its own political dynamic. A Pan Caribbean or Pan African political perspective does not exist. The four largest Caribbean groups in Brooklyn (Jamaicans, Trinidadians, Haitians, and Guyanese) sometimes view Caribbeans from other islands as political rivals and competitors. However, this perspective seems to be changing with successive generations, prompted by intermarriage and greater cross-cultural understanding.

Other Factors

Legislative redistricting can also be a political and structural barrier that spurs tribalism. Through redistricting, groups are often excluded from positions of power, which can retard political development, and impede ascendant immigrant groups from achieving symbolic political representation. For example, a political district may be drawn through "packing" (overcrowding) and "cracking" (divide and conquer) techniques. Often, this is done to protect a White or African American incumbent, but it is done at the expense of other Black groups who are seeking their own empowerment in a district. Immigrant groups may sponsor their own candidates, and seek to vote for individuals of their choice. However, the system may seem rigged against them.

Also, political tribalism can be based on specific locations or institutions. New York City consists of five boroughs, coterminous with five counties. Within these locales, multiple, semiautonomous political party structures exist, with rules governing each borough, and at times even rules differ for each party within a borough. For example, there are Brooklyn Democrats, Bronx Democrats, Manhattan Democrats, Queens Democrats, and so on. These are not political monoliths.

Black political solidarity has to supersede the gravitational pull of county parties, geographic borough interests, constituent and special interest demands, and institutional loyalties. Numerous other forces pressurize the decision making of local politicians. The linked fate theory describes this phenomenon (Dawson 1994). Internal gravitational pulls can be overcome, when an election has an overwhelming and compelling force for Black political solidarity. This was the case in the Jesse Jackson, David Dinkins, and Barack Obama elections. Ethnicity, class, and gender differences were overridden. Flateau (2016) affirms this observation.

Has Black Political Representation Made a Difference?

There are some fundamental questions. Has increased Black political representation made any difference in racial equity in the lives of Black New Yorkers? If so, how? If not, why not? What should Black politicians do better or differently? There is a firm consensus among African Americans believe that government should provide for the common good of its citizens. This belief is embedded in the U.S. Constitution and is derived from America's bloody history of chattel slavery, Black Codes, Civil War, racial persecution and discrimination of Blacks as a minority.

In several historical cases, New York City's Black body politic has represented the best interests of their constituents, advancing the social, economic, political, and civil rights of their people at local, state, and federal government levels. Black politicians have had a positive impact on a range of substantive policy and programmatic initiatives. They have achieved these goals despite the macroeconomic and institutional forces they have had to contend with and compete against. Some examples follow:

1. Legislative Redistricting

Redistricting, the process of geographically designing political districts, has been a signature issue over the past 50 years. When they are created, districts can afford constituents a political voice where they may not have had one before. Now individual views can be heard on important legislation, budget appropriations, and government program and service delivery. Over the last 50 years, the combined efforts of Black politicians, community advocates, civil rights attorneys, researchers, and a fair judiciary have resulted in a greater than 100 percent increase in New York Black elected officials and political districts.

2. State Political Leadership

In 2015, the Black, Puerto Rican, Hispanic, and Asian Legislative Caucus played a pivotal role in getting New York State's first Black assembly speaker, Carl Heastie, elected. He replaced former-Assembly Speaker Sheldon Silver, who had been forced to resign due to a federal indictment and subsequent conviction. NYC's Black state assembly members form a critical mass of state legislative representation and leadership. Black political power, when unified, and in coalition with others, can achieve important political victories. Black constituents are not the only people to have benefitted from these achievements. On balance, New Yorkers have done well due to their leaders' progressive advocacy on measures relating to the environment, education, tax policy, housing, jobs, health and human services.

3. Criminal Justice Reform

Civilian complaint review boards and human rights agencies have fought hard to bring about reforms in the area of police misconduct, and to find ways to obtain redress for the citizenry. "Stop and Frisk" police policies have been changed based on recent city council legislation which now requires police to report their public contacts by race. A new NYPD program has all police officers wearing body cameras. Other recent reforms have increased cultural awareness and sensitivity training for police officers, have reduced the number of state prison cells, and eliminated both federal and state "three strikes" legislation. State inmates imprisoned under the "Rockefeller Drug Law" have been released. Some had been in jail for over 30 years for minimal drug possession. Sentences for crack cocaine possession have also been reduced.

4. Anti-Redlining and Affordable Housing

New York politicians have passed bills similar to federal legislation, championed by the Congressional Black Caucus, forbidding banks from conducting racially discriminatory lending practices. As a condition of state licensing for bank expansion, the legislation requires Community Reinvestment Act (CRA) which targets lending to underserved neighborhoods. Black, Latino and other politicians have helped create a myriad of low- and moderate-income housing programs for their neighborhoods and constituents. Both Governor Cuomo and Mayor de Blasio are implementing multibillion dollar affordable housing programs. In an appearance at Medgar Evers College in March 2017, Governor Cuomo announced a $1.4 billion, multifaceted, Central Brooklyn Revitalization Plan, including $700 million for health and wellness programs, and the construction of 3,000 affordable housing units. Black political leverage, public policy research, and advocacy played vital roles in shaping these initiatives.

5. Minority & Women Businesses: 30 percent City and State Government Contracting

In 1990, New York's first and only Black mayor, David Dinkins, initiated a Minority and Women Business (MWBE) program for city contracts via mayoral executive order. His successor, Mayor Giuliani subsequently eliminated this order. In 2016, City Comptroller Scott Stringer announced that MWBEs had received only five percent of $14 billion in city contracts. Notably, the Black business share was only a fraction of this five percent, in a city that is 25 percent Black. Clearly, Black elected officials and their allies must do more to close the Black business income inequality gap in relation to being awarded a fair share of state and city contracts. Officials have recently negotiated with the governor, and mayor, each of whom has now instituted 30 percent MWBE programs in government contracting. This is a historic first. The next stage is implementation and accountability for these goals.

A Black New Yorker's Five-Year Strategic Plan: 2020–2024

To ensure that important work is done, a series of community, borough, and citywide conferences should be convened. These conferences need to embrace a diverse and inclusive cross section of New York Black political representatives, civic, community, and professional leaders, and academicians. Together those parties will develop a joint public policy agenda, define implementation strategies, and performance evaluations for a five-year plan of collective action and shared responsibility. Their measures could include:

1. By 2024, a 20 percent increase in math and reading scores in grades K–12; reaching an 80 percent high school graduation rate and meeting a 50 percent college readiness goal for NYC Black public school children.
2. Increased state and city funding of high quality, preventive, community-based health care, to replace anticipated federal cuts in Obamacare, Medicaid, and Medicare. This includes implementation of Governor Cuomo's $1.4 billion Central Brooklyn Revitalization Plan.
3. By 2024, a 20 percent reduction in the state prison population, a $50 million increase in support services for the formerly incarcerated, and reducing barriers for former prisoners to gain access to higher education and employment.
4. Free CUNY and SUNY tuition for the working and middle class and a 25 percent reduction in student loan debt.
5. Black, minority, and women-owned businesses should be awarded thirty percent of the available state and city government contracts per state and city law.
6. Access to the capital fund in the amount of $400 million, and full access to public–private economic development tools.
7. A moratorium on foreclosures; restitution for Black homeowner victims of the subprime mortgage scandal; financial penalties for offending lenders and realtors.
8. A 50 percent increase in affordable housing production, with Black, minority and women as co-developers.
9. Zero racial discrimination in construction trades, and an increase in the number of jobs for Blacks, minorities, and women.

10. A 15 percent increase in per capita income of Black New Yorkers by 2024.

11. A 15 percent increase in voter registration and turnout for Black New Yorkers in 2020, 2022, and 2024 elections.

12. Zero percent undercount of Black New Yorkers in the 2020 Census. $50 million in education and outreach funding to target and mobilize "hard to count" Black communities.

Conclusion

In the 2017 municipal election, a low turnout of the five million registered voters reelected their city government, including their sole citywide Black elected official, Leticia James of Brooklyn, as New York City public advocate. Also, the first Black and woman city council majority leader, Hon. Laurie Cumbo of Brooklyn, was appointed; Brooklyn Black borough president Eric Adams was reelected; and another first, a Black woman, Darcel Clarke, was elected Bronx district attorney. Upstate, Buffalo, and Rochester reelected their Black mayors; and there are now fifty-five Black, Latino, and Asian members of the New York state legislature, mostly from New York City.

In the 2018 general election, Democrats took control of the US House of Representatives. Several prominent New York congress members were empowered; they included Black members Hakeem Jeffries, Democratic conference chair, and Yvette Clarke, both of Brooklyn. Gregory Meeks of Queens was elected the first Black Democratic county leader in 2019; and Antonio Delgado was elected the first Black congressman from the Hudson Valley region.

The 2020 U.S. Census will reset federal resource formulas and will determine which states, local governments, and cities throughout this nation will receive hundreds of billions of dollars in allocations from federal programs and services. Data gathered in the 2020 census count will also reset all federal, state and local political representation through reapportionment and redistricting. Historically, New York City has had an egregious census undercount, both in its Black communities and for undocumented immigrants. Trump administration policies and actions regarding illegal immigration and sanctuary cities may further exacerbate the census undercount.

Well-funded state and city census education and outreach efforts need to be well underway to avoid a fiasco with the 2020 census. In addition, 2020 is when the next presidential election takes place. That election will be a referendum on the Trump presidency, and will again determine who will have political control of the national government and state legislatures. Legislative redistricting will take place in 2021 and 2022, based on the 2020 census population counts, as prescribed by the U.S. Constitution.

A U.S. Supreme Court with Trump appointees could change the rules from previous redistricting cycles and court cases. Once again, the question will arise as to whether or not Black political representatives in New York will gain or lose seats, or hold their ground. Only through aggressive, strategic, resourceful, and vigilant execution will Black New Yorkers successfully go forward, further closing their political inequality gap.

In the past decade, the dynamics of banking, real estate, and housing have converged to threaten Black political representation. Black displacement via gentrification was accelerated by the 2008 Wall Street housing market collapse. Since then, Wall Street has recovered, and the Dow Jones industrial average has ascended from 7,000 to 20,000 points as of April 2017. However, the displacement of Black homeowners continues unabated in the form of the mortgage foreclosures, property tax liens, subprime lending, and real estate fraud.

These forces are rapidly eroding Black progress in housing, and wiping out the possibility of Black wealth. The effects have been devastating for Black tenancy in Black middle class and working class neighborhoods throughout South East Queens, Central Brooklyn, Central Harlem, and North Central Bronx. When Black homeowners and tenants are forced out of neighborhoods, the political result is a shrinking population and a diminished political base on which to anchor present and future Black political representation.

It should be clear that Black political power in New York is currently in a very precarious position. If Blacks do not choose to work in a coalition, Black power is facing stiff competition from rising Latino and Asian political power, and from resurgent young, White reformers gaining ascendency from the gentrification of Black neighborhoods. In addition, the internal competition among African American, Caribbean American, Continental African, and Afro-Latino constituencies continues.

Black political power is facing public policy challenges due to marginalized, underperforming non-profit institutions that are under assault. This is dangerous because these organizations are an essential institutional support base for Black political power. Furthermore, a voracious prison industrial complex is neutralizing an inordinate number of Black adults who have lost their political right to vote, their economic right to work, and their sociocultural right to family and community.

It is important to note that there is historical amnesia and rising political cynicism among Black millennials. Many of them are in the vanguard of today's critical protest politics via Black Lives Matter. Many question and reject the value and effectiveness of voting, the electoral process and the foundations of blood and sacrifice on which these political rights are built. This same demographic had the worst voter participation rates of any group in the 2016 presidential election. Moreover as Browning, Marshall and Tabb (1997) have noted in minority incorporation theory, "protest is not enough."

Black New York is facing a future where their political representation could decline in numbers. However, strong political advocacy, strategic mobility and multiracial appeals by Black elected officials could make it possible for them to sustain their tenure and even grow, even if the Black political population base shrinks. Demographics are not political destiny. Black candidates David Dinkins, Bill Thompson and Letitia James, all won citywide elections with just a 30 percent Black electorate. I worked on these campaigns and saw the process firsthand. In state legislative districts in Brooklyn, White incumbents Marty Markowitz and Rhoda Jacobs, who were in office for decades, represented districts where Whites were only 25 percent of the population. In Queens, the recently deceased Honorable Helen Marshall was elected the first Black borough president in 2001, with a 25 percent Black electorate. Proudly, I served as her campaign manager.

In the past 50 years, Black New Yorkers have closed the political inequality gap on the electoral front, achieving nearly proportional representation. However, institutional racism is still an American fact-of-life. Things can change because multiracial generations seem to be less wedded to old cultural norms, or notions about race in American society. In fact, right now, half of America under five years of age is nonwhite: the browning of America is well underway, replete with its forces of resistance.

Notes

1. *United States v. Cruikshank*. 92 U.S. 542 (1876).
2. *United States v. Reese*. 92 U.S. 214 (1876).
3. *Cooper v. Powers*, Federal Court. EDNY (1966).
4. *United Jewish Organizations of Williamsburgh, Inc. v. Carey*. 430 U.S. 144 (1977).
5. *Andrews v. Koch*. 528 F. Supp. 246 (E.D.N.Y. 1981).
6. *Flateau v. Anderson*. 537 F. Supp. 257 (S.D.N.Y. 1982).
7. *Ashe v. NYC Board of Elections*. 1988 US Dist. LEXIS 1006788 (E.D.N.Y. 1988).
8. *Morris v. NYC Board of Estimate*. 489 U.S. 688 (1989).
9. *PRLDEF v. Gantt*. 796 F. 677 Supp. (E.D.N.Y. 1992).
10. *Diaz v. Silver*. 978 F. Supp. 96 (1997).
11. *Favors v. Cuomo*. 866 F. Supp. 2d 176 (2012).

References

Browning, R., Marshall, D., and Tabb, D. (Eds.). (1997). *Racial politics in American cities* (2nd ed.). New York, NY: Longman.

Dawson, M. C. (1994). *Behind the mule: Race and class in African American politics.* Princeton, NJ: Princeton University Press.

Du Bois, W. E. B. (1998). *Black reconstruction in America.* New York, NY: Free Press.

Flateau, J. L. (2016). *Black Brooklyn: The politics of ethnicity, class and gender.* Bloomington, IN: AuthorHouse.

Franklin, J. H. (2004). *From slavery to freedom.* New York, NY: Alfred A. Knopf.

Hayduk, R. (1996). *Gatekeepers to the franchise: election administration and voter participation in New York.* (Doctoral dissertation). City University of New York, New York.

Holder, C. (1990). "The rise and fall of West Indian politicians in New York City, 1900–1987." *Political Behavior and Social Interaction Among Caribbean and African American Residents in New York.* Brooklyn, NY: Caribbean Research Center, Medgar Evers College, CUNY.

Irish, G., & Riviere, W. (Eds.). (1990). *Political behavior and social interactions among Caribbean & African American residents in New York.* Brooklyn: Caribbean Research Center, Medgar Evers College, City University of New York.

U.S. Census Bureau. (2015). *American Community Survey (ACS), 2010–14, 5 Year estimates; and 2015, 1 Year Estimates.* Washington, DC: U.S. Government.

Wilkerson, I. (2011). *The warmth of other suns.* New York, NY: Vintage Press.

Chapter 15

Social Capital

Social Capital, Gentrification, and Inequality in New York City

James Rodriguez, Robert L. Hawkins, and Andrew Wilkes

In 1903, W. E. B. Du Bois wrote, "The Negro race, like all races, is going to be saved by its exceptional men. The problem of education, then, among Negroes must first of all deal with the Talented Tenth; it is the problem of developing the Best of this race that they may guide the mass away from the contamination and death of the worst" (1903, p. 33). Northern philanthropists first espoused this concept of the Talented Tenth, although Du Bois is often credited with it. People believed that, if one Black person out of ten could improve his or her intellect through education, including insights into political and social change, that one person could become the catalyst for other African Americans to improve their economic standing, as well (Gates & West, 1996).

Underlying Du Bois's theory of the Talented Tenth is the belief that a few intellectual role models could in turn foster more networks of highly educated mentees, who in turn would produce even more exemplary individuals. In time, these coalitions could improve the conditions of all African Americans. Although scholars have debated Du Bois's idea of the Talented Tenth, the concept, if actualized, could lead the masses to build strong social networks to do positive things based upon shared connections, reciprocity, and common goals. Individuals would be willing and able to give to and learn from each other things that would uplift the race. This is a description of how groups advance through social capital and what actualizing the promise of social capital can do for the African American community.

The social capital concept theorizes the benefits of what well-resourced individuals would be willing and able to do for the less privileged with their connections and social currency. In a burgeoning urban center such as New York City, several generations of scholars and politicians have proposed that this is the remedy to urban poverty and the reduction of inequality. Despite Du Bois's explicit call for social capital to address the plight of African Americans and other people of color, racialized inequality has persisted for over a century after the Talented Tenth premise was put forward.

Perhaps, it is time for a critical look at this theory, and it's potential. This chapter explores social capital's historical and contemporary usefulness for people of color, especially for those living on the economic margins. From a historical perspective, we argue that developing social capital and sharing its potential benefits have been limited by the fact that people of color have been marginalized socially for so long. We will use a case study of renters of color in New York City to explore the contemporary usefulness of the concept.

Defining Social Capital

According to social capital theory, racialized inequality is the result of people of color, and their communities, lacking the opportunities and resources others have. It is not due to inherent defects in either culture or biology. Racialized inequality is hard to reconcile with traditional American values and beliefs. It does not conform to the enduring notion of American individualism and faith in the American dream (bootstraps and all). Many attribute racialized inequality to the basic inferiority of nonwhites asserted in discredited notions of scientific racism and white racial supremacy. Racialized inequality based upon institutional barriers and imbalance in resources provides an alternative explanation and offers a way to understand how one might work toward reducing urban inequality.

Social capital has been defined in many ways. It is "the byproduct of social interactions that are embedded in and accessed via formal and informal social relationships with individuals, communities, and institutions" (Hawkins & Maurer, 2010, p. 356). It is a concept that operates at the micro, mezzo, and macro levels; it builds from an awareness of interactions between individuals and their environmental influences (Lin, 2001). Many experts now suggest social capital should be seen as a dynamic set of relationships that has an impact on individuals, families, communities, and surrounding institutions (Hawkins & Maurer, 2011; Kawachi, Kim, Courts, & Subramanian, 2004; Portes, 2000).

Three kinds of social capital are most germane to our analysis. They are bonding, bridging, and linking (Gitell & Vidal, 1998; Szreter & Woolcock, 2004).

Bonding exemplifies relationships with the closest ties among members of a group or network who have similar characteristics and backgrounds. Bridging occurs among people and groups who are dissimilar in some demonstrable way, such as race, ethnicity, age, or education (Szreter & Woolcock, 2004). Linking exists when individuals and communities build relationships with systems, institutions, and people who have power over them. These structures often provide access to services, jobs, or other resources (Szreter & Woolcock, 2004; Woolcock, 2001).

Whether in a political, social, or economic context, social capital analysis is used to understand relationships between groups in stratified societies. In addition, it can be used as a way to derive a possible solution to various social problems, especially those that are economic or health-related (De Silva, McKenzie, Harpham, & Huttly, 2005; Kim, Subramanian, & Kawachi, 2008). The concept is most useful for people of color about its functional aspects. However, social capital for people of color must still contend with racism, both individual and institutional (Hamilton & Carmichael, 1967).

Social Capital, Race and Social Inequalities

Embedded structural inequalities in American society have a strong impact on people's social position, and consequently on how effective social capital can be in helping them. Depending on a person's position in society, social capital can provide limited advantages, or even put people at a disadvantage. It can perpetuate social inequalities because hierarchies exist among those who have resources, and those who do not. In fact, social capital has been criticized since its utility is based largely upon an individual's social position related to race and socio-economic status (Das, 1998). Because of economic and racial stratification, African Americans, and other people of color have historically been excluded from cross-racial or economic ties that provide useful information, financial opportunities, or other advantages. Blacks have not benefitted from social capital in the same way Whites have (Loury, 2003).

Low-income African American communities suffer from more than just poverty. They also have to contend with a combination of economic deprivation and structural racism, which serve as barriers to constructive social capital (Quillian & Redd, 2008; Warren, Thompson, & Saegert, 2001). Social capital grows from social networks that generate resources. People in socially isolated, low-income, and low-resource communities have limited access to such networks. Living in social worlds in which racial discrimination exists has the same outcome (Dominguez & Watkins, 2003; Leonard, 2004; Sampson, 2012; Wilson, 1996; Wilson, 2012). Several studies have concluded that the discriminatory racial politics of mainstream institutions dilutes the positive effects of social capital among poor communities. This leads to further social isolation (Sampson, 2012). In addition, disparities in the norms of respectability between low-income people of color and affluent Whites strains or even blocks social relations. This limits poor people's social capital even further.

All three forms of social capital must exist as preconditions before the concept can benefit people looking to escape poverty. First, those seeking change must be organized and cohesive, bonded as a group. Next, at the bridging and linking levels, there must be demonstrable differences within the population if social capital is to help the disadvantaged group. Next, those with power and resources must have the desire to share their knowledge and links. They must have the will to facilitate and support change. Without the transfer of social capital, any effort at social change is unlikely to succeed (Smith, 2005).

African Americans Historical Social Capital

The struggle to gain social capital has been a historic issue for African Americans in New York City. As far back as 1781, African Americans developed mutual aid societies in places such as Philadelphia and New York City. Some of these societies were established to help Blacks who were fleeing slavery; others were dedicated to advancing African American community life and culture. Societies in free states, along with the civic efforts of Black churches and fraternal organizations, also assisted people throughout slavery. In 1808, the New York African Society for Mutual Relief was founded to assist free Black communities in Manhattan. Other aid societies included the New York Manumission Society, the Phoenix Fund, the Abyssinian Benevolent Daughters of Esther Association, and the African Free School.

Mutual aid societies were funded by a combination of contributions by individual Blacks and by liberal Whites. A range of social services were offered including helping the sick, providing burial insurance to families, and offering aid to widows and children. Some aid organizations were funded independently; others were tied to secret fraternal orders that worked behind the scenes. That was because, in the 1800s, it was still dangerous to speak openly about Black empowerment and Black improvement in New York City. There were also social clubs for the small number of Black business owners who wanted to focus on civic causes (Gates & West, 1996). These Black mutual aid societies provided services during Black Reconstruction (1865 to 1898), and again during the Great Depression and Migration (1900 to 1940). From the late 1800s on, some Black banks, insurance companies, and colleges were founded as well to help advance African Americans (Glenn, 2001).

Collectively, these efforts transformed Harlem from a predominantly White and Jewish neighborhood into a Black neighborhood by the 1920s. The successes of Black mutual aid societies and real estate agencies made the Harlem Renaissance possible, and the successive generations of Black cultural and civil rights activism. Harlem eventually elected the first Black city council member, and later, the first Black member of Congress, Adam Clayton Powell, Jr. Harlem served as a role model for successful self-help efforts and as a base and source of social capital to combat racial discrimination in New York and Jim Crow in the South.

The American South remained the heart of racial oppression in the United States. Jim Crow cast a long shadow over racial discrimination in the rest of the nation. African Americans were excluded from jobs, schools, colleges, housing, and public accommodations nationally, but more severely in the South. Civic organizations, mutual aid societies, and cooperatives used their resources in the struggle for civil rights from the beginning of Black community life in New York. By 1960, Harlem and other New York Black communities had sufficient resources to support national civil rights organizations: the Southern Christian Leadership Conference (SCLC), the Student Nonviolent Coordinating Committee (SNCC), the Congress of Racial Equality (CORE), and the NAACP. Their joint organizational efforts were instrumental in passing the 1964 Civil Rights Act, the 1965 Voting Rights Act, and in defining President Johnson's War on Poverty, and "Great Society" initiatives (Nembhard, 2014).

Successful Use of Social Capital

At the foundation of the civil rights movement's success was the effective use of financial support and social capital from supportive Black and White communities and organizations, including labor unions and churches. During the 1970s, Blacks from across income and education strata used bonding capital to reduce race-based income and educational inequality. Civil rights gains in New York City, and beyond, required bridging and linking social capital, White investment in Black organizations, and support by the federal government and courts. Despite these impressive gains, social capital could not eradicate ad hoc racial and economic discrimination. Just as African Americans saw large social gains due to the civil rights movement, progress halted when it came to efforts to address racial inequality in the economic realm.

In retrospect, a consensus formed among White liberals who dominated Congress and the Courts during the 1960s. It was that de jure racial segregation had to go; Jim Crow was an anachronism. Sufficient social capital was transferred during the decade to Blacks to enable them to participate in American civil society as equals. However, the consensus stopped at leveling the economic participation playing field. Racial inequality in New York City over the past 50 years is an outcome of this economic barrier. African Americans never had the same financial and social capital as Whites, nor are Blacks able to make progress without large transfers of White social capital (money, support, and expertise). African Americans simply do not have the resources they need to compete with the power of White elites.

The question remains, can African Americans in New York City still leverage White social capital 50 years after the height of the civil rights movement, and after such a long tradition of aiding one another? Can people of color overcome the economic barriers to racial equality using social capital? This chapter is both an exploration of the economic barriers that stand in the way as well as what is possible if the right bonding, bridging, and linking were achieved.

Social Capital in Contemporary New York City

Today, the racial limitations of social capital are becoming more convoluted. The deprivations that racially and economically segregated communities experience have been studied, quantified, and discussed at length (Massey & Denton, 2003; W.J. Wilson, 2012). Academic and policy circles have debated such issues at length, and the wider public has been exposed increasingly to the plight of the disadvantaged through the media (Massey & Denton, 2003).

Creating so-called "integrated" or "inclusive" communities has been hailed as a solution to segregation, based on a belief in the power of social capital. Gentrification is mentioned as an example. Neighborhoods undergoing gentrification are historically low-income or working class. People believe these communities stand to benefit the most from improvements made by wealthier, and generally White, new residents.

This may be true in theory. However, the reality for people of color is more nuanced than that, because efforts toward inclusion reproduce, or even exacerbate, the very same structures of racism and inequality they were supposed to eliminate. This logic is perhaps best illustrated by New York City's approach to public housing.

The Next Generation Plan

For decades, the New York City Housing Authority (NYCHA) has faced a number of challenges and criticisms. Chief among them is the "concentration of poverty" caused by the program's income eligibility measure. Many believe the established income cap favors low-income and working-class residents, thereby limiting economic variety among residents. This arbitrary cap also curtails NYCHA's ability to fund its properties via rent collection. Also, people often malign the "tower-in-the-park" design of many NYCHA buildings. Many say these large tracts of campus-style public housing have sidelined these neighborhoods, both physically and socially, from the rest of the city. The results have been increased crime and reduced safety for the residents.

NYCHA is currently addressing both of these shortcomings through its "NextGeneration" (NextGen) plan to build private-market, mixed-income towers on public housing grounds. This comprehensive vision of New York City's future public housing applies as well to revisions in NYCHA administration, financing, and management practices. The most controversial change calls for the "infill development" of market-rate and mixed-income residential towers on existing public housing campus space. Rents from these buildings could increase NYCHA's revenues, and allow the NYCHA to do critical repairs to all its buildings. Private, for-profit developers would construct new towers on what NYCHA deems "underutilized" space within public housing communities, including parking lots, seating areas and playgrounds. NYCHA's primary motivation behind NextGen is to raise enough revenue to erase their massive $17 billion deficit.

The Authority's Web site extols the virtues of mixed-income neighborhoods that would "become more enmeshed in the fabric of the community and the city." NextGen endorses the additional employment opportunities that would be available for public housing residents. Agency spokesperson, Aja Worthy-Davis, stated, "By building both affordable and mixed-income housing, we will protect NYCHA housing, expand affordable housing options for everyday New Yorkers, and bring small businesses and services like supermarkets and restaurants closer to NYCHA developments. We will, in turn, use this growth to connect NYCHA residents to new employment opportunities" (Blumgart, 2016).

Despite the ostensible gains of such modified social capital and employment opportunities, as well as funding for the much-needed capital repairs, NextGen has met with strong opposition in neighborhoods across the city. Tenant activists renamed the plan, "NextGentrification," and have staged several protests. They expressed their concerns to NYCHA administration and City Hall. Beverly Corbin, a longtime resident of the Wyckoff Gardens development, expressed her concerns to *The Daily News*, "With the market rate income, what's going to be happening to a neighborhood that's already stressed? The people who are high income, they're not going to be shopping at the local bodega. We already lost a Chinese restaurant and a laundromat"

(Warriner, 2015). Just as NYCHA NextGen was unveiled, the NYU Furman Center for Real Estate released its 2015 study, "The Effects of Neighborhood Change on NYCHA Residents." It states, "NYCHA residents could be priced out of new private amenities, and new, higher-income neighbors may not contribute to accessible community resources" (Dastrup et al., 2015).

The distinct disconnect between the city's progressive-sounding NextGen vision for the future of public housing and the backlash from actual public housing residents illuminates the tensions on the ground. This is what happens when theories of social capital encounter real-life situations such as the city's housing market, municipal administration, and the ingrained legacy of structural racism.

As described earlier, linking and bridging are two of the three levels of social capital. In principle, they should work. Under the right circumstances, they should work to assist those on the economic and racial margins. However, on closer inspection, the resources that make up social capital are not themselves equally distributed or available to working class people of color.

The NYCHA NextGen project shows how deeply committed the administration is, in theory, transferring positive social capital to its residents. It also clearly points out that linking capital has little value for public housing residents, or even for the rest of the city's tenants. At the same time, the city was defending the merits of inclusion, while residents' protests over the NextGen gentrification plan were being largely ignored.

NYCHA continued to roll out its mixed-income developments at select sites across the city, promising that residents would be stakeholders in the process. Residents involved in the planning, particularly at Wyckoff Gardens in Brooklyn, and at Holmes Towers in Harlem, were predictably dissatisfied with the process, and the outcome. A letter from the stakeholder committee at Holmes Towers on the Upper East Side, another NextGen site, expressed their concerns over the elimination of their playground for redevelopment. On this occasion, city residents lost interest in receiving social capital in the way it sold its plan. By dismissing the valid concerns of residents, and by marginalizing their role in the planning process, the city also undermined the utility of linking capital for public housing residents.

ZQA and MIH Rezoning

Public housing in New York City has long been a stark example of structural racism and inequality, both of which are still present in even the most progressive cities. There are two other examples of structural racism that compromise the transfer of social capital. They are the massive, citywide rezoning plans,

Zoning for Quality and Affordability (ZQA), and the Mandatory Inclusionary Housing (MIH) program. Both ZQA and MIH rezoning plans were lauded by New York City's progressive administration and hailed as a model for affordable housing nationwide.

MIH mandates that a percentage of affordable housing must be included in any market-rate development. When this was proposed, working-class renters and preservationists fiercely contested the rezoning. Organizers, activists, and tenants throughout the city objected to several specifics in the plan. They complained about the paltry number of mandated affordable units and disagreed with what was classified as affordable, and for whom. Rachel Rivera, a member of New York Communities for Change, had been displaced twice from Brooklyn. She voiced her disappointment with the mayor's rezoning plan:

> [De Blasio] needs to make affordable housing affordable for myself and for people that are in my same predicament, people that are struggling, people that are homeless and on fixed incomes. If this mayor does not change this plan to make it real affordable, I will be doing civil disobedience with my kids. (Mays, 2016)

The plans were met with a widespread outcry, protests, and civil disobedience throughout the city. The overwhelming majority of community boards voted against both MIH and ZQA. However, the city council passed the plans with a comfortable margin. Once again, it was clear that in the face of political opposition and market prerogatives, linking capital offers few benefits to people of color, or to members of the working class.

Limitations on the transfer of social capital and rejection of the plans by residents are evident in the tenuous linkages between people of color and the state, and in bridging the differences that exist between races and classes. The NYCHA's NextGen plan, the mixed-income developments of MIH/ZQA, and the broader gentrification of the city have made it easier for wealthier, Whiter residents to move into working class communities of color. While a growing city economy should be ideal conditions for bridging resources and networks, the reality is that the enduring structures of race and classism foreclose this possibility.

New York City's "poor door" mishap presents a more flagrant example of the failure to understand the interests of potential participants who might have transferred capital. In this case, developers provide affordable units so they can take advantage of the city's generous tax breaks. However, this has not kept them from favoring market-rate renters over the "affordable" tenants. In their projects, mixed-income buildings were equipped with separate, but unequal amenities, furnishings, and even entrances referred to as "poor doors." These poor doors are commonly located in the back, or on the side of, high-income tower apartment buildings. Market-rate tenants approved of such measures because they believe reduced-rent, lower-earning residents do not deserve the same amenities. For example, Courtney Harding, a market-rate tenant made the following revealing statement about the amenities in her Williamsburg mixed-income condo: "If you're not paying the doorman's salary, is it fair for you to use the doorman?" (Peltz, 2014). The city outlawed poor doors, this is one more illustration of how social capital cannot work without explicit measures to dismantle the broader framework of inequality.

Developers have found new and creative ways to discriminate between high- and low-income tenants. Now they are constructing smaller, affordable towers next to their market-rate high-rises. One of the city's most prominent developers, Extell, first came under fire when it installed a poor door in one of its buildings. They found a way to work around the poor-door ban when they put up their next luxury condominium development on the Lower East Side. This building, called One Manhattan Square, uprooted the Pathmark store, a low-cost neighborhood supermarket that had been in that location since 1983. Of course, Extell's plan to displace the store met with strong opposition. Betsy Gotbaum, the city's Public Advocate in 2007, stated: "We need this Pathmark to remain open as a symbol of our commitment to listening to New York's communities" (Warren, 2007). That did not matter: the Pathmark was closed anyway. It was completely demolished, and in its place now stands 80-stories of luxury condominiums, literally towering over a much smaller, separate affordable building under the premise of inclusion.

Social Capital and Social Relations

To be clear, both New York City and its real estate market are much less concerned about developing positive social capital than they are about financial capital, with yields well into the billions in both profits and tax breaks. Nonetheless, urban planners and political progressives alike retain the goal of increasing the poor's social capital. Gentrification is the latest chapter in the struggle that organizers, activists, and tenants are waging against the displacement of the poor, and in the pursuit of social capital. Organizers, activists, and tenants, in pursuit of social capital, are now struggling to curtail gentrification to prevent the further displacement the poor.

Implicit in gentrification strategies is the assumption that the social and economic integration of a former low-income community will change that community for better. However, the unacknowledged consequence of gentrification is the disruption of existing economic, social, and cultural norms of neighborhoods. Specifically, often affordable grocery shops and bodegas are displaced, 311 complaints about noise and loitering increase and other quality of life offenses help quantify the stark divisions, discrimination, and segregation by race and class, despite the diversity and density of gentrifying neighborhoods.

A high-profile example of a quality-of-life complaint, and of respectability politics, occurred in Marcus Garvey Park, in Harlem. Every weekend since 1969, an African diasporic drum circle has played their drums in the park. In recent years, newly arrived residents have begun to complain about the practice. "African drumming is wonderful for the first four hours, but after that, it's pure unadulterated noise. We couldn't see straight anymore," said Beth Ross, a resident of a nearby luxury building (Dobnik, 2007). This sentiment encouraged residents to call the police to request the drumming be stopped. In Harlem, a historic hotbed of political and cultural capital for people of color, the community drum circle has become a point of contention, and a flashpoint.

Gentrification has led to further marginalization and displacement for people of color, rather than providing them with tangible benefits or resources. The gap continues to grow, rather than close. Harlem, a historic model of functioning social capital for people of color, has seen its black population fall, its community institutions and businesses close, and even its cultural history challenged by the people with the resources that were supposed to help improve it.

Collectively, the conflicts seen in New York City's contemporary housing market point to one more blind spot in social capital theory: one that Du Bois foresaw in 1903. New York's renters have expressed these realities repeatedly. With the influx of well-resourced residents comes a shift in the goods, services, and ambiance of a community. Playgrounds turn into towers, supermarkets give way to condominiums, and traditional drumming becomes a disturbance. Du Bois said there has to be "a common set of goals" between those who have the capital and people of color if inequality is ever to be reduced. A common set of goals existed when people found the bonding capital that helped spur the Harlem Renaissance. Shared goals generated the bridging capital that encouraged Northern abolitionists and philanthropists to join forces. Then mutual interests spawned the linking capital used by the state and Black leaders during the Civil Rights Movement.

Unfortunately, things are different now. City developers and government entities have opposing views on how to manage public housing, rezoning, and gentrification. There is no shared city vision among New York's working-class renters, city administrations, and affluent newcomers. The social capital required to reduce racial inequality is being withdrawn, rather than continued.

Social Capital and Community Organizing

Community organizing works to construct an "enduring network of people, who identify with common ideals, and who can engage in social action on the basis of those ideals" (Stall & Stoecker, 1998). Community organizing is a distinct form of social interaction that is change-oriented, highly relational, and time-intensive. Organizing requires a cause to be effective. It also calls for a nexus of personal relationships that can be called on to sustain routine and impromptu group actions.

Community organizing groups may vary in their missions and memberships, but they share the goal of building social capital. In East Harlem, Community Voices Heard (CVH) is one such collective. Founded in 1994, CVH defines itself as a "member-led organization by low-income people, predominantly women of color, to build power in New York City and State to improve the lives of our families and communities." CVH has a distinctive history, in that women of color established the organization, and continue to lead and maintain group membership. This is rare because CVH meets the bonding and bridging preconditions for successful transfer of social capital. All they need is linking with those who have the capital and interest in reducing racial and economic inequality among poor women of color. For some time now, CVH and its members have been actively organizing around public housing issues, and have worked against gentrification, including the NYCHA's NextGen plan.

CVH also mobilizes its resources to enact social change at the local and state level. This sense of scale distinguishes CVH's mission and operational practices from other community groups that focus only on neighborhood and citywide agendas. For example, in 2015, CVH coordinated a Lobby Day in Albany, New York's state capitol. Over 500 public housing residents, advocates, and partner groups attended the event to demand state funding for public housing. Two weeks later, Governor Cuomo announced a $100 million investment in NYCHA: the first such state funding since 1998.

To gain a greater understanding of how social capital can be developed, we surveyed several CVH's members and asked them about their experiences relating to social capital, resource access, relationship formation, and the consequences of participating in CVH. Three survey responses are particularly worth noting. First, responses confirm that CVH's main mission is to mobilize low-income individuals for social change. The majority of respondents indicated that their annual household income is less $44,875, with some reporting earnings of less than $21,783. Second, members believe CVH makes it possible for them to connect with needed resources, and to strengthen key relationships. In the context of social capital, these are both bridging and linking effects. This means CVH members can access resources that help them to develop knowledge, skills, and abilities that are meaningful to them. CVH membership functions as a bridge to opportunity, and by increasing linked social capital, the organization strengthens members' political capacity to advocate for institutional change.

Finally, survey respondents felt that CVH had an auxiliary effect—it enhanced the lives of neighbors who were not members of CVH. This finding is critical because it indicates that social capital may also augment the lives of individuals who are not a formal part of an organization. CVH's advocacy approach can explain this. When nonmembers hear what CVH has accomplished in the policy arena, they are impressed. They see that the organization goes to bat for the entire community, as opposed to only being interested in the needs of CVH's members. In this way, Community Voices Heard builds bonding social capital and extends its reach into the wider community.

Conclusion and Takeaways

This chapter has explored the history of social capital, and its capacity to help African Americans, and other people of color, to reduce successfully racial inequality, and to exercise political power. We have explored the multiple layers of social capital, and its utility for people of color. The concept of social capital assists people in understanding past successes and helps to plan future efforts. The concept does have its limits, however. Ultimately, just as single transfers of social capital cannot permanently erase structural racism. If done on a large enough scale, social capital transfer can reduce institutional racism by challenging and changing institutional arrangements—for example, the civil rights movement. However, for the transfer of social capital to succeed on a case-by-case basis, those with the resources and those who need them have also to challenge or at least neutralize racism, even temporarily.

Furthermore, the concept of social capital is an analytic device and way to orchestrate social change. It works only when people are willing to share and accept resources. Today, conflicting goals are tearing at New York City's housing future, and the potential to transfer social capital is reduced rather than increased in the fight for racial equality. Linking capital has been withdrawn between renters and the city administration, as has bridging capital between wealthier residents, developers, and the city administration.

We know the transfer of social capital has the potential to succeed when we see bonding capital being built by community-based groups and grassroots organizations. Change-based community organizing, led by working-class residents of color, all fighting to dismantle structural inequality are clear evidence of the effectiveness of social bridging and linking. We will know that social capital has been transferred effectively when residents can organize to bring about specific changes through legislation and resources. They are not only heard but favorably responded to, as well.

Race and class barriers erected by state and city governments limit broad-based support for organizing and community self-determination. An important way to expand social capital is to devote time and energy to getting affluent newcomers to embrace the ideal of class and race diversity. Then, for instance, a place such as historically Black Harlem could stand as an enduring model, rather than a fading memory.

As we review the historic gains and contemporary limits of social capital, we are reminded of how important local efforts are in reducing racial inequality. Whether it is in Harlem during its Renaissance, or in Harlem today, local advocacy and the use of social capital have proven to be effective in slowing gentrification. Now, unfortunately, social capital is being used against people of color. It is advancing gentrification, displacing tenants, and further increasing racial inequality. Communities of color throughout the city and the nation are damaged by persistent racial and economic discrimination and segregation.

How to Regain Momentum

Things can change. Steps can be taken to improve the benefits of social capital for people of color, and simultaneously erode structural racism. Higher-income Blacks and liberal Whites could be encouraged to invest their social and financial capital in black mutual aid societies, whether in Harlem or elsewhere. With full awareness, we can avoid the mistakes of the past. This time around, we need to avoid speculative investment, gentrification controlled by Whites, and top-down urban planning. We need to be more precise in how we invest in communities of color, by targeting residents and local institutions that are dedicated to community empowerment and interested in providing social as well as economic integration. Black mutual aid societies, such as Community Voices Heard, would benefit greatly from direct investment in their work.

Gentrification has made land remarkably valuable, vulnerable, and unavailable in New York City, as it has in cities across the country, and indeed, the globe. That means controlling land is one of the most direct and impactful ways communities can achieve self-determination and advance their own goals. Community land trusts (CLTs) could be the solution. CLTs vary in how they are organized and carried out, but the fundamental principle remains the same. You remove a designated piece of land from the conventional housing market, and you put it in the hands of the community itself.

There are numerous benefits of employing CLTs.[1] They represent one of the few ways communities can guard against the gentrification and displacement that occurs in the private market. NYCHA's NextGen project is an example of how land can be withdrawn from public and affordable housing. Furthermore, by keeping land out of the hands of developers, and by returning it to community stewardship, residents can retain a measure of self-determination over how the land is used, and people can envision the future of their own neighborhoods. In addition to using CLTs, city residents can employ community planning and participatory budgeting to gain a degree of decision-making power. Both social capital and living conditions for the most marginalized will be improved.

None of these tactics are silver bullets against inequality. However, these mechanisms do help to move people closer to self-determination and to increase their decision-making power. These measures would blunt the ongoing displacement and gentrification of people of color, and their communities (Angotti, 2011).

At the end of his life, Du Bois expressed disappointment in the concept of the Talented Tenth, and he made it clear that he recognized its limitations. This chapter has explored how the concept of social capital can have limited impact on low-income, urban communities. However, there are lessons to be learned, as well. When social capital diminishes, it is up to committed individuals and groups to make a collective, coordinated, and continuous effort to change things in vulnerable communities. This effort must come not only from "exceptional Black men," but also from other fair-minded people keen on making positive change. Community organizing is a product of the collective understanding of the living conditions in neighborhoods that are chronically underserved and exploited by both the state and the private market. The need for grassroots organizing grows more critical each year.

Notes

1. The Cooper Square Community Land Trust is one example of a CLT in New York City.

References

Angotti, T. (2011). *New York for sale community planning confronts global real estate.* Cambridge, MA: MIT Press.

Blumgart, J. (2016). New York wants to close the gap between public housing residents and Wall Street bankers. Retrieved from https://nextcity.org/features/view/new-york-public-housing-authority-changes-gentrification.

Das, V. (1998). Wittgenstein and anthropology. *Annual Review of Anthropology, 27*(1), 171–95.

Dastrup, S., Ellen, I., Jefferson, A., Weselcouch, M., Schwartz, D., & Cuenca, K. (2015). *The effects of neighborhood change on New York City Housing Authority residents.* Bethesda, MD: Abt Associates.

De Silva, M. J., McKenzie, K., Harpham, T., & Huttly, S. R. (2005). Social capital and mental illness: A systematic review. *Journal of Epidemiology & Community Health, 59*(8), 619–27.

Dobnik, V. (2007, August 11). Drummers clash with new Harlem residents. *The Washington Post.* Retrieved from http://www.washingtonpost.com/wp-dyn/content/article/2007/08/11/AR2007081100624_pf.html.

Dominguez, S., & Watkins, C. (2003). Creating networks for survival and mobility: Social capital among African American and Latin-American low-income mothers. *Social Problems, 50*(1), 111–35.

Du Bois, W. E. B. (1903). *The souls of Black Folks.* Chicago, IL: A.C. McClurg.

Gates, H. L., & West, C. (1996). *The future of the race.* New York, NY: Alfred A. Knopf.

Gitell, R. V., & Vidal, A. (1998). Community organizing: Building social capital as a development strategy. Thousand Oaks, CA: *Sage Publications.*

Glenn, B. J. (2001). Understanding mutual benefit societies at the turn of the twentieth century. *Journal of Health Politics, Policy and Law, 26*(3), 639–51.

Hamilton, C., & Carmichael, S. (1967). *Black power: The politics of liberation.* New York, NY: Vintage.

Hawkins, R. L., & Maurer, K. (2010). Bonding, bridging, and linking: How social capital operated in New Orleans following Hurricane Katrina. *British Journal of Social Work, 40*(6), 1777–93.

Hawkins, R. L., & Maurer, K. (2011). You fix my community, you have fixed my life: The disruption and rebuilding of ontological security in New Orleans. Disasters. *Journal of Policy & Management, 35*(1), 143–59.

Kawachi, I., Kim, D., Courts, A., & Subramanian, S. (2004). Commentary: Reconciling the three accounts of social capital. *International Journal of Epidemiology, 33*(4), 684–90.

Kim, D., Subramanian, S. V., & Kawachi, I. (2008). Social capital and physical health: A systematic review of the literature. In I. Kawachi, S. V. Subramanian, & D. Kim (Eds.), *Social Capital and Health* (pp. 139–90). New York, NY: Springer.

Leonard, M. (2004). Bonding and bridging social capital: Reflections from Belfast. *Sociology, 38*, 927–44.

Lin, N. (2001). *Social capital: A theory of social structure and action.* Cambridge, UK: Cambridge University Press. https://www.cambridge.org/core/books/social-capital/E1C3BB67419F498E5E41DC44FA16D5C0.

Loury, G. (2003). *The anatomy of racial inequality.* Cambridge, MA: Harvard University Press.

Massey, D. S., & Denton, N. A. (2003). *American apartheid: Segregation and the making of the underclass.* Cambridge, MA: Harvard University Press.

Mays, J. (2016, February 23). Groups promise civil disobedience if mayor's zoning plan isn't changed. *DNA Info.* Retrieved from https://www.dnainfo.com/new-york/20160223/civic-center/groups-promise-civil-disobedience-if-mayors-zoning-plan-isnt-changed.

Nembhard, J. G. (2014). *Collective courage: A history of African American cooperative economic thought and practice.* University Park, PA: Penn State University Press.

Peltz, J. (2014). "Poor door" apartment buildings a burgeoning trend in NYC. Retrieved from http://www.nbcnewyork.com/news/local/Poor-Door-Separate-Entrance-Extell-Affordable-Housing-Manhattan-Brooklyn--271685631.html.

Portes, A. (2000). The two meanings of social capital. *Sociological forum, 15*(1), 1–12.

Quillian, L., & Redd, R. (2008). Can social capital explain persistent racial poverty gaps? In A. Lin & D. Harris (Eds.), *The colors of poverty: Why racial and ethnic disparities exist* New York, NY: Russell Sage Foundation.

Sampson, R. J. (2012). Neighborhood inequality, violence, and the social infrastructure of the American city. In W. F. Tate (Ed.), *Research on schools, neighborhoods, and communities: Toward civic responsibility* (pp. 11–28). Blue Ridge Summit, PA: Rowman & Littlefield.

Smith, S. S. (2005). Don't put my name on it: Social capital activation and job-finding assistance among the black urban poor. *American Journal of Sociology, 111,* 1–57.

Stall, S., & Stoecker, R. (1998). Community organizing or organizing community? *Gender & Society, 12*(6), 729–56.

Szreter, S., & Woolcock, M. (2004). Health by association? Social capital, social theory, and the political economy of public health. *International Journal of Epidemiology, 33*(4), 650–67.

Warren, M. (2007, December 20). A YIMBY crowd rallies on the Lower East Side. *The New York Times.* Retrieved from https://cityroom.blogs.nytimes.com/2007/12/20/a-yimby-crowd-rallies-on-the-lower-east-side/?_r=1.

Warren, M. R., Thompson, J. P., & Saegert, S. (2001). The role of social capital in combating poverty. In S. Saegert, P. Thompson, & M. Warren (Eds.), *Social capital and poor communities.* New York, NY: Russell Sage Foundation Press.

Warriner, J. (2015, September 13). NYCHA tenants fear they'll lose homes if luxury apartments are built on grounds. *Gothamist.* Retrieved from http://gothamist.com/2015/09/13/nycha_tenants_fear_theyll_lose_thei.php.

Wilson, W. J. (1996). When work disappears. *Political Science Quarterly, 11*(4), 567–95.

Wilson, W. J. (2012). *The truly disadvantaged: The inner city, the underclass, and public policy.* Chicago, IL: University of Chicago Press.

Woolcock, M. (2001). The place of social capital in understanding social and economic outcomes. *Canadian Journal of Policy Research, 2*(1), 11–17.

Conclusion and Recommendations

Benjamin P. Bowser and Chelli Devadutt

It has been more than 150 years since this country fought a bloody Civil War to end slavery. Yet the legacy of slavery lives on. In addition, it is more than 50 years since the modern Civil Rights movement began, yet racial inequality has only increased, and the advances advocates of Civil Rights fought for remain under constant assault. The chapters in this book paint a clear picture of how inequality persists in our nation's largest city. This leads us to ask, what have we done since 1965, and what can we do going forward?

Since 1965, there have been drastic changes in both our national and city economies. De-industrialization, globalization, automation, out-sourcing, technical innovations, decentralization of production and management, and international trade have all had their impact. Surprisingly, the growth in racial inequality over the last half-century is not primarily due to these developments.

In chapter 1, James Parrott asserts that the rise in racial economic inequality is due, instead, to the elimination of federal policies and regulations that made a large middle class possible in the years after World War II. Since the first Reagan administration began in 1981, corporations have been deregulated, labor unions have been constrained, government expansion has been resisted, and changes in business practices, financial markets and consumer treatment have all outpaced business taxation. In effect, the federal government has been unable to respond to a half century of changes in the economy under both Republican and Democratic federal administrations.

Because this discrepancy exists between economic change and public policy (see chapter 1), income inequality for all Americans has been increasing rather than decreasing over the years. Whenever the gap widens between the highest and lowest income levels, inequality in racial and social classes increases, as well. So, if we want to reduce racial inequalities, we first have to reduce social class inequality.

It is important to note the historic relationship between class and race. Since colonial times, the concept of race has been used to conceal the presence and functioning of a distinctly American social class hierarchy, and to disguise overall economic inequality. For example, in the 1970s, the focus was on White flight (race) from New York City. Certainly, during those years, many Whites left New York City because of crime and fear, as did many Blacks. It would have been more accurate, however, to focus on the social class related cause of this flight, namely, the loss of working-class jobs, which affected everyone.

White ethnic New Yorkers, whose economic situation was declining, blamed Black and Latino gains for the deteriorating class circumstances of Whites. After 1970, it became even easier to racialize their perceptions, and to create the storyline of embattled White ethnicities. When the 1964 Civil Rights Act and the 1965 Voting Rights Act were passed, Ronald Reagan's campaign manager, Lee Atwater, devised "the Southern Strategy." Throughout Southern history, Whites spoke indirectly to one another about Black threats and called for White unity. Atwater used this racial indirection in national political campaigns to assert that declining White economic and social status were the result of Blacks' civil rights gains. This was precisely when White New Yorkers began to oppose their city government's efforts to eliminate racial discrimination, and reduce racial inequality (see chapter 4, Jarrett Murphy). When Black and Latino demands were sufficiently contained, it became apparent that overall working-class economic losses were massive, regardless of race. This was the beginning of White alienation from established political parties, which first led to the creation of the Tea Party, and later to the Donald Trump presidency. New York White economic losses independent of Blacks became obvious during the Giuliani administration, but by then, it was too late to stop the decline. Race had been used again to distract from the real cause.

In large cities such as New York, it had long been the case that Blacks were "the last hired and the first fired." For the White ethnic working class, economic participation had moved from "the first hired and then retired" to "the first hired and now fired." Their work was no longer secure, nor was it guaranteed that they could retire from it. Where previously Whites could get living-wage work with just a high school education, now the prerequisite is a college education. In 30 short years, this trend became painfully apparent, but the possibility of reversing the trend, or somehow intervening in it, was missed because of decades of a single-minded focus on race.

There was a second major change in New York obscured by race. In the city's evolving economy, White and Black, native-born labor, which had occupied the bottom rungs of the occupational hierarchy, was replaced again by immigrant labor. This happened before in the 1800s. The improvements in wages and benefits that workers enjoyed by 1960, came about because of labor movement agitation during the 1930s Great Depression. Immigration virtually ceased during the Depression and stopped altogether during World War II. Women and Blacks were hired during the war to do jobs generally done by White men. There was no reserve labor pool available to threaten the wage and benefit demands of regular labor. By 1965, support for organized labor eroded and immigration resumed, so the door opened once again for immigrants to serve as a reserve labor force. They could be hired for lower wages, work longer hours, and receive fewer, if any, benefits. All this cut business costs and increased profits, but depressed general wages.

Black and Latino citizen labor faced the same plight as Whites. As citizens, they were too expensive to employ in the new service sector. Their unemployment levels rose, and they had nowhere to go in a cruel game of job-related musical chairs. The outcome was increased racial income inequality. This all came about because the federal government no longer protected the middle class. Then, rising class and racial inequality in turn reinforced already existing racial segregation in New York housing and education.

Housing

New York's streets and other public spaces are the most diverse in the nation, thanks to the city's well-developed system of public transportation. People of all races, classes, lifestyles, and religions share the same sidewalks, streets, trains, and buses. That is not the case when New Yorkers go home, because New York City is, in fact, the most racially segregated city in the United States. However, some key shifts have occurred. Chapter 2 tells us that the number of all-White communities in New York has declined since the year 2000. Asians and Latinos, followed by Blacks, are making inroads into many all White communities, which should show up in future censuses as having reduced neighborhood racial segregation. Selected Black and Latino communities in Manhattan and Brooklyn are in the midst of gentrification, which reflects in the short term a trend toward residential racial desegregation. However, there is reason for caution.

If you look at racial desegregation in New York as a series of independent episodes, or as a set of still photographs, then it appears that residential desegregation is underway. On the other hand, if you view the city as a slow-motion video over 50-year periods, a very different picture emerges (chapter 7). New York City is undergoing a great residential class and race inversion (Ehrenhalt, 2012). Renewed urban development is gentrifying central-city districts and attracting an affluent middle class to them. The poor and working classes in these communities are being displaced to two locations. First, they are moving to older residential areas, farther from the city's downtown on the edges of the outer boroughs. Second, the poor and working classes are relocating to low-income residential areas in New Jersey, Westchester, and Suffolk counties. In another 50 years, we can surmise that most of Manhattan will house affluent residents, as will areas in the outer boroughs, along the East River and downtown Brooklyn and Queens. There will still be the five New Yorks, as outlined in chapter 12, but their locations relative to one another will have shifted, and the "gilded" and opportunity-rich New York will be proportionately larger.

Chapters 2 and 5 show that gentrification is part of a larger change process. While primary attention and angst has been focused on the gentrification of Harlem, Crown Heights, and Bedford-Stuyvesant, virtually no attention is being paid to the greater movement of Black and Latino New Yorkers into other areas in Brooklyn, Queens, and the Bronx, all farther away from Manhattan. Ninety percent of tracts integrated between 1980 and 2010 were predominantly White. The tracts that Blacks and Latinos are moving into, in relatively large numbers, contain aged and nearly exhausted housing. These were older White ethnic neighborhoods located on the edges of the city. Blacks and Latinos are not disappearing, and the proportion of Blacks and Latinos in the city's population has not gone down. Instead, people of color are being pushed from the central city to the outer boroughs and suburbs.

The inversion of class and race in New York actually continues a historic pattern of class and racial residential succession. The first half of the last century was characterized by flight of the affluent and middle classes away from all but the central city's "gold coast" communities. That exodus is over. Now, the poor, the immigrants and the least affluent must move away, and face the one-hour-plus commutes, increased dependence on cars, and growing gas and home heating prices that will eventually become prohibitive for them.

This great inversion by class and race does not suggest reduced racial segregation. When the inversion is complete, income class and racial segregation will remain. However, there is a new development, which may muddy this picture. Virtually every White residential tract has been integrated racially. Even the most affluent midtown, upper-East and upper Westside Manhattan communities now have a small number of minority residents. Formal racial segregation has broken down sufficiently to allow Asians, Latinos, and Blacks, who can afford it, to buy or rent in formerly all-White communities. Their appearance is deceptive and suggests that there is more racial integration in New York City than there actually is.

Education

Residential segregation engenders school segregation. They cannot be separated. One can see this as Blacks and Latinos move into the outer parts of each borough. School enrollments for these two groups are declining in the central-city communities. Concurrently, school enrollment of Black and Latino students is increasing in the Brooklyn, Queens, and Bronx districts that are farthest from Manhattan. In chapter 3, Norman Fruchter, suggests that this population shift could present an opportunity to improve school academic performance after nearly 50 years of failing performance in hypersegregated districts. On closer inspection, however, the low academic performance in these districts is more a function of poverty than it is of race. As the number of students from impoverished backgrounds increases in a school, the more its academic performance drops, regardless of race.

Newly integrated districts may experience some improvement in their academic performance, but the long-term prospects suggest these new districts will become hypersegregated in time. Shifting demographics cannot fix the city's failure to educate children and young adults from poor and impoverished backgrounds, most of whom are Black and Latino. Many of their parents suspect that teachers do not think their children are capable of doing higher-level work. They are correct. However, the students are not the only underperformers. Until 1999, 90 percent of the uncertified teachers in the entire state of New York taught in lowest performing New York City schools (Wrigley, 2003). Since then, the certification standard has changed, but it is doubtful that the quality of teachers has improved much. In turn, many teachers feel that Black and Latino parents do not know or care about education, nor do these parents provide educationally supportive environments at home. District administrations jump from one reform idea to another, as if looking for some magical solution. Since 1965, two generations of students have been poorly educated in this impasse, and there is no improvement in sight. It does not matter whether teachers are in unions or not, or whether schools are charter schools or not. It does not matter whether low-performing schools are closed or stay open. The outcome is still the same. The majority of low-income students in the system do not get the education they need and deserve.

The NYC school system, like other urban systems across the United States, will continue to fail until the districts they are in steps up to the specific task of educating low-income Black and Latino students in the same way they educated the children of European immigrants early in the last century. Educational excellence is not a mystery. There are ample examples of effective schools in New York. Certainly, there are students in elite private and suburban public schools who have barriers to learning, including poverty. Nevertheless, many of these same students end up prepared to do college-level work. They succeed because their teachers and their schools devote the time, attention and resources that are necessary for these students to meet academic standards high enough for college admission. The urban public school systems that have a high proportion of low-income and impoverished students of color should follow this example, because the real problem is not the students. The problem is in the city's political leaders and public who do not believe that "other people's children," meaning Blacks and Latinos, are worth the effort and resources.

Experience shows us repeatedly that whenever Black and Latino low-income students are given the attention they need, their academic performance improves. This is why the addendum to chapter 3, by Adriana Villavicencio, et al., is so important. It shows that low-income Black and Latino students in NYC schools can perform on par with college-going students if they are given the time, attention, and resources, with higher expectations thrown in for good measure. Rather than being the exception, programs such as these should be the norm.

Not everyone can or should go immediately from high school to a four-year college, but those who do not need to attend college should have other options. Before 1965, a high school diploma was all someone needed to get a good job, but this is no longer the case. Today, high schools should prepare students for at least two-year community college programs, or for a living-wage vocation (see recommendations to follow). The economy has changed a great deal, and work requirements have transformed a lot, too. It is time to rethink the purpose and outcomes of a secondary education and align them with current reality.

Government Leadership and Public Policies

Government institutions, whether federal, state, or municipal, are the only entities that have the constitutional mandate to care for common good of citizens. Since 1966, New York City's seven mayoral administrations have each had their own interpretation of providing this care (see chapter 4). John Lindsay struggled to address racial inequality. Abraham Beame was consumed by the city's fiscal crisis. Ed Koch and David Dinkins were constrained by a White ethnic electorate that was hostile to any attempts to address racial inequality. Then for eight years, Rudy Giuliani explicitly represented the hostile electorate, and refused to address racial inequality at all. Michael Bloomberg's wealth insulated him from the ethnic fear Whites had of Blacks and Latinos.

Despite repeated failure, he tried to improve city schools, three times. When these mayors spent time on issues related to race, they did not focus primarily on lack of jobs, or the poor quality of housing and schools. Instead, their attention was primarily focused on avoiding racial conflict between Black communities and the city's predominantly White ethnic police force.

The Police

Cheered on by New York's tabloids, the 36,000-member NYC Police Department has spent much of its time turning White working-class beliefs, attitudes, and fears into punitive action against the millions of Blacks and Latinos in the city. For the past 50 years, the police department has had a clear public mandate to combat drug trafficking and to reduce crime rates. However, in executing the "war on drugs," the police had a serious problem. Many officers chose not to distinguish between Blacks and Latinos who committed crimes, and the vast majority who did not. In their minds, Blacks and Puerto Ricans were criminals by definition—all were treated as criminals. This problem was compounded by the fact that many officers could not distinguish one Black person from another. So, virtually every Black and Latino "fit the description," and, therefore, was guilty until proven innocent. White racial prejudice was the operative code of justice; civil criminal codes and due process were secondary (chapter 10).

Confounding the misalignment of policing and justice is what happens once a Black or Latino defendant goes to trial. George Woods and Stephen Greenspan call attention to unexplored bias on the part of expert witnesses (chapter 10, addendum). They charge that defendants of color often are not examined for brain damage, mental illness, or physical illness that might account for their behaviors and be mitigating circumstances. Equally damaging is that other experts, defense, and prosecutors alike, may attempt to explain or convict a defendant by exaggerating cultural and environmental factors, ignoring compelling personal factors. Either bias adds damage by the courts to the damage already done by the police.

Any mayor who did not defend police racism was labeled as "weak on crime" by the police and press. In which case, the police union would charge that the mayor personally endangers cops on the street and is responsible for rising crime rates. The outcomes of these charges are tragic. Individuals are arrested and convicted of crimes they did not commit. Unarmed Black men who commit no crimes are shot dead, because they "fit the description." Hostility between the police and Black communities could erupt into a riot at any time. The police and the community do not share the trust and cooperation needed to solve crimes. In the largest city in the nation, a succession of mayors have been held hostage by the police's informal redefinition of justice. However, mayoral leadership and the police were not the only places in city government where racial prejudice have an effect. At least police failures are public and are described in the news. The actions of other city agencies, which do even more damage to the city than the police do, go completely uncovered in the news.

Community Destruction

Starting in the late 1960s, "benign neglect" became New York City's undisclosed new method for dealing with Black and Latino inner-city communities. The city withdrew fire companies, stopped enforcing housing safety codes, quit repairing streets and traffic lights, ceased cleaning streets, limited garbage pickups, closed medical facilities and libraries, and stopped responding to any crime other than shootings, murder, and violent drug offenses. The city withdrew essential and nonessential services just as it faced serious drug trafficking and HIV/AIDS epidemics. Defenders counter that all of this happened during the City's 1975 fiscal crisis. However, this benign neglect started before the crisis, went on during the crisis, and continued afterward. In chapter 11, Robert Fullilove documents this neglect and its outcomes. As a result of the city's withdrawal of services, entire communities faded away as viable social entities. Residents who could, fled the gang violence and drug dealing. Others were forced out of their apartments and buildings because landlords were unable or unwilling to provide heat, repair elevators, stairs, windows, doors, or even to exterminate rodents. By 1985, entire city blocks were abandoned, looking as if they had been bombed. Dispersing the population in this way led to HIV in the South Bronx and Harlem spreading to other low-income areas of the city. The result: a full-blown AIDS epidemic that killed thousands. A continuation of inequity in city services by race shows up as disparity in health service access. Gusmano and Rodwin address this issue in their addendum to chapter 11.

Without external efforts to monitor and end the AIDS epidemic, the connection between the city abandoning these communities, and their collapse as social and physical entities, might have gone unnoticed. The concealed decisions that resulted in the vast destruction of neighborhoods also opened the door a decade later to the gentrification of the very same communities. Mayor Koch's five-billion-dollar effort to preserve affordable housing led to a wider effort to renew housing in formerly all-Black and Latino communities. Policies that led to the social destruction of these communities also erased residents' fierce opposition to any redevelopment for the benefit of affluent White residents. In chapter 13, Victor Bach documents how the policy of benign neglect continues today in the form of systematic federal and state disinvestment from New York City's public housing. If this pattern of underfunding endures, public housing will become so unviable that residents will be forced out, and the city will have to abandon public housing altogether. Developers would welcome this outcome, because it would provide them with hundreds of redevelopment sites throughout the city.

Municipal public policies and the execution of those policies, good or bad, do not just happen—city administrations are responsible for them. New York City mayors have continually had to balance between addressing the common good of all citizens and dealing with the fear and hostility of a reactionary electorate and police force opposed to confronting racial inequality. That electorate's opposition has been unwavering, even though they would benefit from actions taken to address racial inequality. Since 1966, New York City mayors have not been able to implement progressive, multisector, measures to reduce social class bias or racial inequality. Perhaps, in the long-term, if enough people of color vote, as did the descendants of European immigrants, reforms can be undertaken. Racial inequality can resolve itself as White ethnic inequality seemingly did a generation ago.

New Ethnicities

New York City's racial "others" now include Asian, Latino, Caribbean Americans, both native and foreign-born, in addition to African Americans. Like European ethnics in 1900, these others are close to a majority of the city's population. These groups provide basic labor and services, are flexible reserve labor forces, and receive the lowest wages. Four chapters in this book offer background to each. Like the European immigrants who came before them, Asian, Latino, and Caribbean immigrants have come to recognize American racial stratification: Blacks are at the bottom of the spectrum, and Whites are at the top. They see who they must avoid and who they must imitate, and that a good education is imperative for upward mobility.

African American (Black) New Yorkers

African Americans are unique among ethnic-racial groups in New York City. Blacks are the only group with a consistent physical presence, and a persistent place at the bottom of the social class hierarchy since 1624, a total of 393 years. Other ethnic groups have come and gone, but Blacks remain, first as slaves and then as an alleged "inferior race." Their place at the bottom has not changed, even temporarily when slavery ended in 1865, nor did it happen in the 1960s, after the civil rights movement. This lowermost status is not self-imposed, nor does it just happen and continue by chance. Black subordination by others has an objective and a function that goes well beyond historically maintaining a permanent source of cheap labor.

Consider this: for hundreds of years, the British, Irish, Welsh, Scots, Germans, Italians, Dutch, and Greeks regularly fought each other, and among themselves, all for the sake of their royalty, land, wealth, and religion. It would have been disastrous if these conflicts continued among immigrants and factory workers living in close proximity in New York City tenements. Yet in two generations, these same people would forego their histories, subordinate their ethnicity, learn English, and become indistinguishable from the very people who had exploited and belittled them as immigrants. What circumstance was strong enough to make this happen? Chapter 5 tells us it was the concept of race that overrode ethnicity. By assimilating so quickly, earlier immigrants were rewarded with Whiteness and the higher status and class privileges that go along with it. It is important to remember, however, that the unifying concept of whiteness succeeds only if there is a loathed and feared inferior race in place at the bottom of the social hierarchy, as an alternative to whiteness, where no one wants to end up.

New Yorkers who exist at the bottom of the social hierarchy, are not just another ethnic group moving toward eventual assimilation into the White population. The bottom of the social hierarchy awaits any other ethnic group who holds their ethnicity over assimilating a racial identity as Whites. Being consigned to Blackness is the fate of any ethnic group that does not learn English, does not assimilate American values, does not internalizing racism, and does not become White. In this context, it is logical that Blacks should do the least desirable work, live in the poorest housing, and have the poorest educational outcomes. As a permanent reserve labor force, they can be mobilized to undercut any immigrant, or counter White labor demands for higher wages and benefits. Chapter 7 covers the history and use of racial stratification in the areas of housing and community longevity.

Latino New Yorkers

Hector Cordero-Guzman informs us in chapter 6, that speaking English is the great divide for recent Latino immigrants, just as it is for Asian immigrants. Monolingual Spanish speakers are virtually excluded from economic mobility and are immediately sent to the bottom rung on the job ladder. They must depend on English-speaking Latinos to get work. Like their European counterparts in the prior century, it is hoped that the children and grandchildren of Latinos will benefit from their parents' sacrifices. Young Latinos are expected to be upwardly mobile, but fulfilling their dreams depends totally on whether they have access to a good education. Unfortunately, the New York City school system is failing to educate the majority of low-income and immigrant Latino students.

One only has to look at the educational outcomes for prior generations of Cubans and Puerto Ricans to recognize the key role education plays in Latinos' lives. However, the success or failure of these earlier groups appears largely based on their social class and color. The children and grandchildren of fair-skinned Cubans and Puerto Ricans have achieved parity with Whites. They are accepted as White, as were preceding Irish, Italian, and Jewish immigrants. This is not the case for darker-skinned Cubans and Puerto Ricans of African and Native American ancestry, particularly those from rural family backgrounds. Latinos from the Dominican Republic and from Central and South America are now facing the same racial divide in their schools, and in their communities.

New Latino immigrants come from virtually every country in Central and South America. This level of diversity is a challenge to Latino unity and identity. This diversity is also a dilemma for those who provide social services. Effective services for one group of Latinos may not work for another: not all Spanish-speakers are alike. Educators and service providers look for one-size-fits-all solutions, but this ignores the new ethnic and cultural multiplicity among Latinos in New York City.

West Indian New Yorkers

In chapter 7, Calvin Holder and Aubrey Bonnett document the continuing inequality between West Indians and Whites. Analyzing census data for 2011 to 2013, the authors focus on English-speaking, foreign-born West Indians, who identify as West Indians in New York State, New York City, and in Brooklyn. The one factor that distinguishes West Indians from their Black and White peers is the preponderance of two-parent households in the immigrant generation. Holder and Bonnett underscore a mounting concern among West Indians. They worry subsequent generations of American-born Caribbean youth may not match their parents' degree of educational attainment. These young people are struggling, especially outside of large West Indians enclaves where they are not identified clearly as West Indians and are regarded as African Americans.

Asian New Yorkers

Howard Shih's overview of Asian American experiences in chapter 8 illustrates how education alone may not be enough for others to escape racial discrimination. Asian-Americans in New York City achieved education parity with Whites by 1960. For decades, Asian students have gone to the City's most competitive high schools. They have graduated with exceptional academic records and gone on to colleges nationally. However, their achievement is limited by an occupational glass-ceiling. So, even if Blacks and Latinos achieve educational parity with Whites, racial discrimination will still be an issue. Another caveat is that English language skills are essential. Non-English speakers, in particular, are marginalized in the main economy, and must depend on jobs and housing in exclusively Chinese, other Asian and Latino enclaves. Their mobility is severely limited within these ethnic islands. To become competitive in the broader economy, and on par with other ethnic groups, English proficiency is a prerequisite.

Skin color is also an issue for Asians, with darker skin color leading to increased racial discrimination. The influence of skin color, while not acknowledged or discussed, has growing ramifications for dark-skinned East Indians, Pakistanis, and Southeast Asians. As these groups assimilate into American life, many may lose their foreign identities where their immigrant experience is protective against racial discrimination. No one can say what race they will be members of after two or three generations in New York and the United States.

Finally, Asian-Americans are called the "model minority," because of their educational and occupational achievements, even under the glass ceiling. However, it is primarily the second and third generation Chinese and Japanese Americans, who have accomplished so much. This obscures the fact that more recent Asian immigrants from India, Pakistan and Southeast Asia still live in significant poverty, and lack the same human capital as other Asian immigrants.

Ethnic Conflict

Chapter 9 reviews the incidences of conflict and violence between and among Whites and people of color in New York between 1965 and 2015. New York City has a long history of violent conflict between ethnic-racial groups going back into the nineteenth century. The potential and threat of open street violence, especially among ethnic youth, has been omnipresent, and its prevention has been a major preoccupation of virtually all of the city's mayors. With its large population size and density and the diversity of ethnic-racial groups, one would think that the potential for conflict and riot would be greater now than ever before. However, the evidence suggests just the opposite.

There have been 10 highly publicized conflicts between ethnic-racial groups in the last five decades. Four were initiated by police violence and shootings of Black and Dominican young men. Looting during a blackout characterized a fifth case. Three other cases were over schools and education. The remaining cases were a Black boycott of Korean grocery stores and a struggle over the placement of sanitation facilities. We hypothesize there are other ethnic-racial conflicts that did not get the same attention as the listed cases. There is conflict on the job in multiple industries with different classes of ethnic workers vying for mobility. There is rivalry between ethnic-racial groups for political office. Then, there is potential conflict over admissions to selective high schools and over gentrification. Finally, what needs to be explained is why there is not more conflict between ethnic-racial groups in New York City; the rest of chapter 9 is devoted to exploring this question.

Gentrification

Gentrification can be defined as the redevelopment of central-city housing and urban spaces currently occupied by Blacks and Latinos for reoccupation by the White middle class. Gentrification is the most obvious manifestation of a process that has been going on since the founding of New York City—social class and ethnic residential succession. Early in the last century, the upper classes began purchasing country estates in upstate New York and on Long Island to expand beyond their gold coast urban residences. Advances in transportation made it possible for the White middle class to follow the upper class out of the city, and to commute back and forth daily for work. In the last 25 years, outward expansion into the suburbs has stopped and reversed. In economic terms, the value of central-city land dropped enough below suburban values to make central-city space more profitable for development. The higher economic costs of maintaining suburban housing, and the social cost of commuting, have made central-city living more convenient and more attractive.

Urban living spaces that Whites abandoned to Blacks and Latinos, almost 100 years ago, is now available once again. The benign neglect of Blacks and poor people in the 1970s and 1980s, socially and physically gutted these communities, and drove land values well below the threshold for redevelopment. After surviving three decades of heroin and cocaine drug trafficking, plus an AIDS pandemic, Black central city survivors have come to welcome, though reluctantly, the new attention to, and upgrading of their living spaces. However, long-term, lower-income renters are priced out, and long-term owners are bought out. Older housing is renovated, new housing is built, and long-term residents are displaced further away from the downtown. Central-city residents, who move, may not realize it immediately, but their new housing is once again in the basement of the housing market. This is how Harlem and Bedford-Stuyvesant developed a century ago.

Ghettos?

There is sentimental attachment to and personal identification with one's living space. However, the fact is, in New York City, the vast majority of Blacks and Latinos are renters and do not owned most of the residential and commercial properties in Black communities. For most, these communities are ghettos, reserved for them by outsiders. People who live there have few other housing options in the city. Furthermore, residents are exploited in ghettos: charged high rents for substandard housing, used as convenient market places for prostitution, drug and alcohol sales, sold inferior products for high prices and provided with "failure factories" for schools. In chapter 10, Natalie Byfield describes the operative reality of policing in Black and Latino communities. It seems that police believe Blackness and criminality are one in the same. Even though the vast majority of residents do not commit crimes, everyone is suspected and feared equally. This is the only logical explanation for the fact that police "stopped, questioned, and frisked" more young Black and Latino men in one year than live in the entire city. The way police treat Blacks and Latinos day after day is the clearest indication that Blacks are at the bottom of New York City's social hierarchy, and live in communities that are considered ghettos.

What Can Be Done?

In the 15 chapters in this book, the authors have explored ways to reduce racial inequality as well. Scores of community-based agencies and nonprofit organizations have done what they can locally, and lobby all levels of government. Hundreds of individuals have taken independent actions and achieved small victories. No chapter mentions religious communities. With only a few exceptions, it appears that overall religious leadership in the city has had little success in making structural differences in racial inequality. Perhaps they have motivated individuals to take action instead. The truth is that government is the only institution that can make any difference. Government alone has the power to influence business and shape the economy. The federal government is best positioned to act, followed by state and city governments.

The only way Black New Yorkers can achieve racial and social class equality is to work through government. That means having political representatives working on their behalf to reduce racial inequality. In chapter 14, John Flateau outlines this struggle. His portrayal of government stands in sharp contrast to Jarrett Murphy's narrative on how city administrations have addressed inequality. Flateau's chapter depicts a victory lap for just managing to get representation. The number of New York's Black elected officials is noteworthy. However, chapter 14 highlights a particular problem. Even after getting political representation in Washington, Albany, and on the city council, inequality has hardly budged. This is despite the fact that some representatives have been in office for decades. Emerging Latino and Asian political representation face the same dilemma.

Perhaps, one can argue that without new Black representatives the possibility of successfully addressing inequality would be even more remote. The bottom line is that, even with political representation, unemployment has remained high, Black and Latino communities have been destroyed, gentrification continues, schools continue to fail, the war on drugs (Black people) persists, and "stop and frisk" went on. What Black political representatives now have on their to-do list for 2022, has been on it for some time. Because of gentrification, we may be at the high point of Black political representation in New York City. However, as Black people are dispersed farther from Manhattan and central Brooklyn, we may see a decline in the number of Black political representatives. It will be interesting to see if the politicians who assume office after them will do better or worse in addressing racial inequality.

Chapter 15 brings us full circle. It explains the theory of social capital, and how inequalities can be reduced through social change. There are people who find themselves at the bottom of the social order, who managed to counteract their plight. These individuals need allies who are willing to share their expertise, contacts, and resources. Together, they can create mutually beneficial change. For instance, during the civil rights era, victories were achieved because several coalition partners worked on behalf of and transferred social capital to activists and their organizations. The last 50 years have seen nothing like this. Chapter 15 suggests that Blacks and Latinos have not had enough partners, or sufficient capital transferred to them to move the inequality mountain.

Until coalitions rebuild, and activists are empowered further, little change can take place. Kenneth Clark (1965) believed the main problem of people in ghettos was their lack of power to make changes to improve their living circumstances. Poverty, low-income, and poor housing are not why Black communities are physical and psychological ghettos. Ghettos exist because of the lack of material, human and political resources—social power—to change them. If that power existed, it would not matter whether the mayor was Koch, Dinkins, Giuliani, or Bloomberg, and anti-Black, White ethnic sentiment would have no impact. What people need are changes that reduce racial and social class inequality. Hopefully, by the time another 50 years has passed, New York City will have evolved, and found ways to address its most intractable problem of racial inequality.

Recommendations

The following list of recommendations is derived from the research presented in the fifteen chapters and three addendums in this book. They have two objectives. The first is to suggest structural changes that will permanently alter the architecture of racial inequality in New York City. The second objective is to suggest ways to improve conditions for ethnic-racial groups in New York City. There are author recommendations and then there are editors' recommendations most of which cut across sectors. For a more specific policy-centered exploration with recommendations, see Mollenkopf (2013).

Economy and Jobs (Chapter 1)

Infrastructure Investments: Blacks and Latinos in NYC have started to realize sustained wage and income gains for the first time since the 1980s. In part, these gains result from the continued growth in NYC's employment levels and sustained reductions in the unemployment rate. Federal government and Federal Reserve policies to continue the expansion and avert an economic slowdown are perhaps the most important policy factors affecting well-being in NYC. Local policies, particularly infrastructure investments, are essential to maintain job levels in the event of a national economic slowdown.

Insure Minimum Wages: The increase in NYS minimum wages since 2013 (from \$7.25 in 2013, the NYS minimum wage for employers with 11 or more employees reached \$11 at the beginning of 2017 and will rise to \$15 by the beginning of 2019). This will tremendously benefit hundreds of thousands of low-wage workers in NYC (more than one-third of all city workers will benefit from the $15 minimum wage floor when fully implemented). It is important that the city and the state ensure that the implementation of this phased-in $15 minimum wage continues, and that wages are increased for the tens of thousands of underpaid nonprofit human services workers providing public services under government contracts. This workforce is predominantly women of color.

Support for Higher Education: It is essential that city and state efforts continue to bolster the City University of New York (CUNY) system and improve quality for pre-K through grade 12 public education. Investments in vastly improved early childhood education, including better funding for child-care programs from birth to age three, are particularly important for working-poor families.

Response to Federal Budget Cuts: Now that employment opportunities are improving for low- and moderate-income Blacks and Latinos in NYC, it is particularly important that the city succeed in its efforts to preserve and expand the supply of affordable housing. In addition, the city and the state need to respond appropriately if federal budget cuts reduce the availability of federally funded Section 8 housing subsidies, or if the financial condition of the City's Housing Authority is made even more precarious.

Change Tax Structure: The city and the state need to make the state and local tax structure (personal income, sales, and residential property taxes) less regressive by reforming NYC's local property tax system. This is where renters currently pay the highest effective property tax rates. This is also where they enhance child and dependent care and earned income tax credits.

Other Economic Recommendations

Outflow of State Taxes: Serious consideration should be given to advocating a reduction in the outflow of New York State and New York City federal taxes to fund the needs of other states. These revenues are needed for local needs. As a gateway city, NYC supports a disproportionately higher immigrant, low income, and working poor population. Providing adequate infrastructure and municipal services to a growing population requires additional revenues.

Monitor Living Wage: A minimum wage level in the City of New York should be a living wage. There should be continuous research and monitoring of what constitutes a minimum living wage in New York City. Particular attention should be given to those who do not receive the minimum wage or benefits (temporary, part-time, and contract workers). This research should include estimates of the health, social services, and criminal justice costs to the city for not maintaining minimum living wages. The living wage should be reviewed and updated regularly by the New York City Council in cooperation with the Mayor's office.

Non-Exploitation of Immigrants: All workers in NYC, noncitizen immigrants and U.S. citizens, should be paid the same minimum living wages and benefits. Living wages and benefits for all workers should be a local law.

Lay-off Transition: Businesses and corporations that plan to lay-off employees should provide at least six months advance notice. These employees should be provided with on-site counseling, retraining and assistance in finding new jobs.

Training Tax Incentives: Employers who provide on-the-job training, in-service education, and skills and craft development should receive tax incentives.

Public Economic Education: City government should mount a public awareness campaign that educates city residents about the critical role city regulations, living wages, and public education play in creating and sustaining a middle class in the city.

Housing (chapters 2, 13)

Dispersal of Public Housing: Low-income housing should be distributed fairly throughout the city and not be concentrated in largely Black and Latino communities and areas of high poverty. This will require locating and building new affordable housing in higher income areas, while prioritizing the preservation of existing low-income housing.

Location of Affordable and Inclusionary Housing: The city should build and preserve more affordable housing in neighborhoods undergoing gentrification. It should also adopt mandatory inclusionary housing.

Housing and School Zoning: The city should assess the role of school zones in deepening racial and class divisions. Many school districts are oddly shaped and homogenous. More diverse districts could be created without resorting to busing.

Housing Vouchers: The city should do more with its housing choice voucher program. It could encourage and assist eligible residents to consider moving to a broader set of neighborhoods and encourage landlords in a broader set of neighborhoods to participate. This could be done by offering larger rent subsidies to households renting in higher-rent areas.

Neighborhood Equity: The city should ensure that their policies and regulations do not have disparate impact on low-income neighborhoods.

Eligibility Rules: The city should reform eligibility rules for its own housing to ensure that the homes it subsidizes are open to a range of applicants and that certain criteria (like credit scores and criminal records) do not disproportionately exclude minorities, especially in higher income areas.

Admission Rules: The city should revisit its community preference rule for admission to affordable housing. http://furmancenter.org/research/iri/discussions/community-preferences-and-fair-housing.

Anti-Discrimination: The city should invest in enforcement of antidiscrimination laws, including the city law prohibiting discrimination against someone with a voucher.

Regional Planning: Finally, city should work with neighboring municipal governments to promote the creation and preservation of affordable housing and invest in improving transit throughout the NYC metro area.

Federal Operation Funding: The city should demand full federal funding of public housing operating subsidies.

Housing in National Infrastructure: The city should advocate for the inclusion of public housing infrastructure in the national infrastructure initiative, along the lines recommended by the Senate Democratic blueprint. https://www.dpcc.senate.gov/files/documents/ABlueprinttoRebuildAmericasInfrastructure1.24.17.pdf.

Other Housing Recommendations

Integrate Social Services and Education into Housing: Public housing was intended originally to help residents become upwardly mobile by providing safe and humane housing with onsite social and educational services. Once residents were able, they were encouraged to transition into regular housing. On-site social and educational services were an intrinsic part of the public housing mission. Collaboration between housing, social services and education needs to be reenvisioned and reinstated.

Strategic and Critical Needs: Federal Section 8 programs should be extended to cover city residents who provide critical services in the areas of education, first responders and transportation personnel. These essential workers are currently priced out of market rate housing in the city where they work and are needed.

Provide Equitable Services: It is essential that the City of New York consistently monitor and enforce health and safety codes and maintain city services and infrastructure in low-income communities as it does in other communities. City services should be provided equitably.

Community Liaisons: There is a critical need for liaisons between low-income community residents and city service agencies, including the police. Liaisons will be a corps of residents trained and deployed to serve as health, education, and security outreach workers. Their mission is to link hard-to-reach residents with services 24 hours a day, seven days per week, to enhance community health, education, and security.

Education (Chapter 3)

Equity Audits: The mayor and the schools chancellor should issue an annual Equity Audit detailing the extent and intensity of school segregation within each community school district. They should require each hypersegregated district to develop and implement integration plans to increase district diversity.

Equity in High Schools: The mayor and the chancellor should require all the city's high schools to reserve specific percentages of their seats for students with disabilities, English Language Learners (ELLs), and Over the Counter (OTC) students. The percentage of reserved seats in each high school would be equivalent to the percentages of each category of students within the citywide high school system, and those reserved seats would be assigned through a computerized selection process. Since students with disabilities, ELLs and OTCs together comprise about 40 percent of the citywide high school population, reserving 40 percent of the seats in every high school would significantly increase integration across the city system.

Magnet Schools: The chancellor should develop new magnet schools on the boundaries between hypersegregated and less segregated community school districts, to draw students from both hypersegregated and less segregated schools into more diverse new schools.

Dual Language Schools: The chancellor should establish more dual language schools or programs, especially in the hypersegregated school districts, because dual language efforts have demonstrated some success in creating more school diversity.

De-Segregation: The chancellor should revise the boundaries of the city's community school districts to increase school-level integration and petition the New York State legislature to authorize those district boundary changes to increase diversity within the city school system.

Resources and Personnel to Fulfill Mission: For the majority of students of color in the school system's hypersegregated school districts, diversity is unlikely to be increased by shifting students or school/district boundaries. The following will produce what integration ultimately aims for—the elimination of race- and class-based achievement gaps in the outcomes of the city's schools.

1. Massive infusions of resources.
2. Preparation and training of effective teachers of students of color.
3. Intensive recruitment of teachers of color.
4. Thoroughly revised curricula and pedagogy focused on culturally responsive and supportive education for students of color.

Education Cross-Sector

Expanded Success Initiative: New York City Schools need to implement to scale the Expanded Success Initiative in high schools with low performing students of color as part of their standard curriculum (see chapter 3, addendum).

Enhanced Teaching Mission: Teachers and principals should be provided with the resources and authority they need to devise ways to address the educational needs of their students and to meet grade goals and standards. Their strategies should be independently evaluated and effective best practices should be shared with other teachers and principals.

Excellence Pay Incentives: Teachers and principals who demonstrate that they are effective in educating low-income traditionally difficult to teach students should receive an excellence supplemental to their salaries.

Role of Social Services: Primary and secondary schools should work closely with social service agencies to address the individual and family needs of low-performing students. Case management should be available for students and families in need. Teachers and case managers should meet and work as a team to address the educational needs of these students.

Parents as Partners: School should have the option of starting parent academies that provide orientation and training for parents in after work and weekend sessions on how to support and provide optimal learning environments for their students.

After-School: Comprehensive after-school programs are essential to student educational goals and to youth development. There should be after-school tutorial, sports, arts, music, and science programs available to all public school students.

Community Colleges: Community colleges' vocation education mission needs to be revitalized with staffing and funding to do vocational education, retraining and reemployment preparation that works closely with public education and with employers.

City Government (Chapter 4)

Hiring: Create or expand paths to city jobs for young people of color so that agencies better reflect the city they serve and diverse communities get access to the unionized, civil service posts that can anchor a middle-class life.

Health: Retool the city's crumbling public hospital system to attack health disparities.

Justice: Give communities a role in determining how they are policed and establish more restorative justice mechanisms so neighborhoods can get the quality of life they deserve without unnecessary arrest or incarceration. Close Rikers Island and build much smaller jails in each borough.

Transit: Dramatically improve bus service in isolated outer borough minority neighborhoods to make it easier for people to get to work and school and make transit far cheaper for the poor.

Planning: Create a citywide comprehensive land-use planning process to ensure all neighborhoods are part of the conversation about how New York City should grow, with burdens and benefits spread logically and fairly.

Economic access: Establish broad public Wi-Fi and community banking programs to make sure people are connected to the Internet and financial system.

Education: Expand school zones and implement a citywide controlled choice admissions system so each elementary and middle school looks broadly like the neighborhood it is in. Ensure that specialized and selective high schools use multiple bases for admissions decisions.

Political Participation: Make voting easier with weekend voting and same-day registration. Reduce campaign contribution limits, lower the caps for campaign spending and increase the bonus for candidates who participate in the matching-funds system running against candidates who do not.

Police (Chapter 10)

Police Commission: Elimination of the police commissioner's veto power over the disciplinary rulings of the Civilian Complaint Review Board (CCRB). In disciplinary cases, discrepancies between the CCRB and the Police Commissioner should be settled in the courts.

Personal ID Data: Create an oversight community-based body similar to the CCRB to monitor the police department's storage and use of all personal identification data.

Crime Assessment Algorithms: All algorithms used by police in the assessment of crime data should be considered public property.

Precinct-Level Crime Assessment: The city should fund research collaborations between university researchers and community organizers in each precinct whose work will define current policing practices in the precinct (An example is the Morris Justice Project).

Police Cross Sector

Expert Court Testimony: There is a need for research to explore cultural shadowing in forensic mental health and other expert witness testimony in New York City court system. That is the extent that experts either exaggerate or omit social and cultural factors as evidence in cases with Black and Latino defendants. Depending on the extent to which cultural shadowing exists, how much effect does it have on case outcomes? How might any effects be mitigated? The research needs to answer these questions (see chapter 10 addendum).

Community Policing: Community policing is essential to build trust and communications between residents and the police. Officers should patrol communities on foot to get to know people and businesses in their patrol area. Police officers should work with community liaisons teams to work proactively to address community needs in crime prevention.

Face Recognition Training: Police officers need training in face recognition of members of ethnic/racial groups other than their own. They need clearer rules as to when and under what circumstances deadly force is appropriate.

Mobile Video Systems: The police should experiment with using mobile video camera systems that can be deployed to crime hotspots to provide 24-hour surveillance as a crime prevention measure.

Case Manage Hot-Spots: When police deploy additional officers to neighbors in response to increasing crime, that neighborhood should also be the topic of review by a social service taskforce. They should determine if there are particular services missing and needed in these communities. The social service taskforce should answer the following question: Can city agencies do anything in the long or short-run to prevent future crime surges from happening?

Post-Crime Forensics: There should be post-crime forensic investigations of selective crimes to understand why a crime occurred and what can be done to prevent its reoccurrence. These investigations could be used to enhance community policing and the work of community liaisons.

Public Health (Chapter 11)

Drug Abuse: The most effective way to reduce drug abuse in Black and Latino communities is to promote drug abuse prevention and treatment, and to foster job opportunities. The war on drugs approach has failed because of over reliance on incarceration. Drug trafficking is a crime, but drug addiction is not. Addiction is a medical problem with medical solutions. Local drug trafficking is also an economic problem that arises when young people have no viable options for earning a legitimate living wage. Instead, they seek ways to survive through the underground economy by drug trafficking and dealing.

HIV/AIDS: The most effective way to reduce HIV rates is through risk-reduction practices. Injection drug users must not be driven underground and forced into needle sharing that virtually guarantees HIV infection. This could be accomplished by withdrawing needle and injection paraphernalia possession laws, and replacing them with needle exchanges, prescription opioid substitutes, and HIV/AIDS treatment and prevention plans.

Support for Low-Income Communities: Withdrawing municipal services, especially fire services, from the most vulnerable New York City communities was the 1960s and 1970s equivalent to the more recent pumping of contaminated water into Flint, Michigan's water supply. It was a racially motivated act of genocide, and clearly a criminal offense. The outcome has been devastating to low-income Black and Latino New Yorkers and has set the stage for gentrification of these areas. As an act of restitution, and of practical necessity, the City of New York needs to devise public policies to preserve rather than destroy low-income and below-market rate housing, and racially diverse communities. Low-income workers are vital to the city, and stable, equitably resourced communities are essential for effective education, public health, and drug abuse and HIV prevention.

Improve Health Care Access: Research is needed on how New York City health services might reduce infant mortality, heart disease treatment, treatment for breast cancer and access to community-based ambulatory care for low-income residents. Research is needed to determine if racial health disparities exist in each boroughs, and if so, what can be done about them (see chapter 11 addendum).

Anti-Racism and Economic Inequality

Anti-Racism Efforts: The New York City Human Rights Commission needs to start a taskforce that will explore developing educational, public service and outreach efforts to address the presumption of racial superiority and inferiority that has been so central to racial and ethnic discrimination in the City's history and present life (chapter 5).

Use of Human Development Index: There is need for an annual report using the American Human Development Index as a tool to measure progress and regressions in economic and racial inequality. There is also a need for continued research on and refinement of the Human Development Index for use in New York City (chapter 12).

Social Capital Transfers: There is need for private foundations to set-up social and economic capital transfer programs between community-based organizations working for local change and external entities with the resources to facilitate mutually desired change (chapter 15).

References

Clark, K. B. (1965). *Dark ghetto: Dilmemmas of social power.* New York, NY: Harper and Row.

Ehrenhalt, A. (2012). *The great inversion and the future of the American city.* New York, NY: Alfred A. Knopf.

Mollenkopf, J. (Ed.) (2013). *Toward a 21st century city for all: Progressive policies for New York City in 2013 and beyond.* New York, NY: The Center for Urban Research, The Graduate Center CUNY.

Wrigley, J. (2003). The public school systems of New York and Los Angeles. In D. Halle (Ed.), *New York and Los Angeles: Politics, society and culture* (pp. 225–50). Chicago, IL: The University of Chicago Press.

Contributors

Maxwell Austensen has been data manager at the New York University Furman Center since 2015. Maxwell received a MPA from NYU Wagner School of Public Service specializing in Policy Analysis, and a BA in Political Science from the University of British Columbia in Vancouver, Canada.

Victor Bach is senior housing policy analyst at the Community Service Society of New York (CSS), a nonprofit, anti-poverty organization that seeks to improve conditions and opportunities for low income New Yorkers. Since 1983, he has directed the organization's housing policy research and advocacy agenda and provided technical assistance to community and resident organizations. Prior to that, he was a faculty member at the Lyndon Baines Johnson School of Public Affairs, the New School for Social Research, and a research associate at the Brookings Institution. He received a PhD in Urban Studies and Planning from Massachusetts Institute of Technology and a BA from Brooklyn College. His major focus has been on the preservation of New York City's affordable housing. Most recently, his work has focused on the issues that face public housing and its residents. Some of his published work is available at www.cssny.org.

Aubrey W. Bonnett is professor emeritus in the Department of American Studies at State University of New York, the College at Old Westbury, where he served under two presidents as the vice president of academic affairs. He has served in a number of capacities: dean emeritus and professor of the College of Social and Behavioral Sciences, at the California State University, San Bernardino; chairperson of sociology at Hunter College; a presidential intern, office of the provost at Hunter College; faculty fellow in administration and assistant dean at the City University of New York central office; and deputy head of the PhD Program in Sociology at the CUNY Graduate School and University Center. He has also taught medical sociology to the physician assistant (PA) Program, Sophie Davis at CCNY Harlem Hospital.

He has authored and coauthored four books, more than 100 scholarly articles, popular directed newspaper, and other pieces in the areas of migration and development, diaspora studies, political sociology, race and ethnic relations and administrative leadership. His last book, *Continuing Perspectives on the Black Diaspora* (2009), is coedited with Calvin B. Holder. He has a BA from the Inter American University of Puerto Rico, magna cum laude, where he was a Jessie Smith Noyes Foundation scholar. He has graduate degrees from the University of Alberta, 1969, and the CUNY Graduate School and University Center in 1976. In 1977, the Social Science Research Council awarded him and Frank Douglas a postdoctoral fellowship to study the psychosocial adaptation of Black medical students in predominantly White institutions.

Benjamin P. Bowser is from New York City and is emeritus professor of sociology and social services, California State University East Bay in Hayward, California. He was the university's outstanding professor in 1996. As a sociologist, he specializes in research methods, public health, community assessments and evaluation research. He has served on three Institute of Medicine (National Academy of Science) expert panels focused on drug abuse and HIV risk, and has published over forty peer reviewed papers and chapters. He has recently authored *The Abandoned Mission in Public Higher Education: The Case of the California State University* (2017), and coedited with the historian Paul Lovejoy a book that looks at the long-term impacts of slavery in the Western Hemisphere, *The Transatlantic Slave Trade and Slave: New Directions in Teaching and Learning* (2012).

He has several award-winning books: *The Black Middle Class: Mobility and Vulnerabilities* (2007), and edited works, *When Communities Assess their AIDS Epidemics: Results of Rapid Assessment of HIV/AIDS in Eleven U.S. Cities* (2007); *Against the Odds: Scholars Who Challenged Race in the Twentieth Century* (2002); and the classic, *Impacts of Racism on White Americans* (1996, 1981). He was part of the collaborative team that won the James H. Nakano Citation for Outstanding Scientific Paper by the U.S. Centers for Disease Control and Prevention in 1995. He was elected president of the Association of Black Sociologists in 2004, served as interim dean of his college and department chair. He was a visiting professor at the University of Paris (La Sorbonne) in 2005, and Board Chair of the American Social Health Association in 2001 (Durham, NC). He received his PhD from Cornell University.

Sarah Burd-Sharps is codirector of Measure of America of the Social Science Research Council. Her work is focused on broadening the discussion about societal well-being beyond today's overreliance on financial and economic metrics to often overlooked measures of health, education, and economic security. She is the coauthor of two volumes of *The Measure of America* (2010). She has written state and local human development reports for California, Louisiana, Mississippi, and Los Angeles, Marin, and Sonoma Counties, and a set of quantitative assessments of civil liberties topics for the ACLU on domestic violence, discriminatory housing lending, and online voter registration. Prior to this position, she worked for the United Nations for over two decades with a focus on economic empowerment, democratic governance, and gender equity. Before leaving the U.N. in 2007 to found Measure of America, she was Deputy Director of the U.N. Development Program's Human Development Report Office. She received a masters degree in International Affairs from Columbia University.

Natalie P. Byfield is the author of *Savage Portrayals: Race, Media, and the Central Park Jogger Story* (2014). She is a cultural sociologist, who has taught in the fields of sociology and media studies. She is an associate professor at St. John's University in Queens, New York, where her research centers on the subjugation of Black people in its examinations of the construction and reproduction of inequalities under capitalism. The components of the society that she explores in her studies are language, media systems, technologies, and research methodologies. Through those explorations, she writes most frequently on the reproduction of race, class, and gender inequalities in institutions related to policing, journalism, social science research, and higher education.

Héctor R. Cordero-Guzmán is a professor at the Austin Marxe School of Public and International Affairs at Baruch College of the City University of New York (CUNY). He is also a professor in the PhD Programs in Sociology and in Urban Education at the CUNY Graduate Center. For the last three years, he was the codirector and coprincipal investigator of Human Services Research Partnerships in Puerto Rico funded by DHHS Office of Policy, Research and Evaluation. He has published research and taught graduate courses on issues related to youth development and outcomes; education outcomes, processes, and institutions; labor markets and employment; poverty and inequality; economic and community development; nonprofit organizations and philanthropy; microfinance and small business development; international migration; race and ethnic relations; and aspects related to education, health, labor, employment, welfare, and social policy.

His most recent book is *Poverty in Puerto Rico: A Socio-Economic and Demographic Analysis* with Raul Figueroa and Alberto Velazquez (2016). Over his career, he has collaborated and worked as a consultant to many government, research, and community-based organizations and worked as a program officer in the Economic Development and the Quality Employment Units of the Asset Building and Community Development Program at The Ford Foundation. He has also served on the board of directors of the Afro-Latin Jazz Alliance, the Economic Policy Institute, Association for Research on Non-Profit Organizations and Voluntary Action (ARNOVA), El Museo Del Barrio, and New York City's Economic Development Corporation (NYCEDC). He received his MA and PhD degrees in sociology and demography from the University of Chicago.

Chelli Devadutt has more than 40 years of experience working in NYC government and with nonprofits. Serving as a frontline caseworker in the Lower Eastside of Manhattan has informed all of her subsequent work. She helped develop affordable housing under the Model Cities program in Bedford Stuyvesant as a project coordinator, and later helped implement employment training under CETA for at-risk low-income youth. At the NYC Public Development Corporation (Now EDC), she created a job-match partnership program for unemployed residents between Local Development Corporations and non-profit organizations. Then, at the NYC Community Services Society, she successfully advocated for NYS funding for job training and education programs for at-risk youth when federal funds were cut severely. While at CSS, she and Walter Stafford designed a first source hiring agreement in the 1980s that would have mandated every city agency contracting with private sector employers to hire low-income minority city residents. This proposal is now standard practice. During the Dinkins administration, she headed the city's day care system with 60,000 children of poor and working poor families by contracting with 400 community-based organizations in all five boroughs. When Rudi Giuliani became mayor, she started an independent consulting practice focusing on program and organizational development, change evaluation and policy analysis. Her clients include grassroots and large voluntary organizations, intermediaries, and management consulting firms.

Devadutt has a BA from Kalamazoo College, MAs from SUNY Brockport and Harvard Kennedy School. She has been a resident of New York City for more than 45 years.

Ingrid Gould Ellen is the Paulette Goddard Professor of Urban Policy and Planning at NYU's Robert F. Wagner Graduate School of Public Service and faculty director of the NYU Furman Center. Her research centers on neighborhoods, housing, and residential segregation. She is the author of *Sharing America's Neighborhoods: The Prospects for Stable Racial Integration* (2000) and editor of the Dream Revisited blog at the Furman Center. She works at the intersection of economics, public policy, and urban planning and has authored numerous articles and book chapters related to housing, segregation, and neighborhood change. She has held visiting positions at the Department of Urban Studies and Planning at the Massachusetts Institute of Technology, the U.S. Department of Housing and Urban Development, the Urban Institute and the Brookings Institution. She attended Harvard University, where she received a BA in Applied Mathematics, an MPP, and a PhD in Public Policy.

John Flateau is professor of public administration and political science at Medgar Evers College, CUNY, where he is director of the Du Bois Bunche Center for Public Policy and U.S. Census Information Center. He has served as vice president, dean, and department chair. He is a commissioner on the NYC Board of Elections; was chief of staff and campaign coordinator for Mayor David Dinkins; senior vice president, Empire State Development Corp.; and executive director, NYS Black, Hispanic and Asian Legislative Caucus. He was deputy secretary for intergovernmental relations, NYS Senate, and comanaged the 2010 Census and Federal Stimulus Program. He was also chairman of the U.S. Census Advisory Committee on the African American Population. He is a strategist on historic federal, state, and local campaigns, election reform and voting rights litigation empowering communities of color. He has coauthored major foundation and government research studies on job creation, business finance and public contracts for Minority and Women businesses. He worked on New York's $1.4 billion "Vital Brooklyn" initiative. His published work includes *Black Brooklyn: The Politics of Ethnicity, Class and Gender* (2016); and *The Prison Industrial Complex: Race, Crime and Justice in New York* (1996). He earned his BA in English literature, New York University; MPA, Baruch College; MPhil., MA, and PhD in political science from the Graduate Center, City University Of New York. He has received numerous academic, professional and community awards; he is a trustee of Bridge Street AWME Church, a life member of the NAACP, and intergenerational member of Brooklyn's Bedford Stuyvesant community.

Norman Fruchter is currently a deputy director for policy, research, and evaluation at NYU's Metro Center. He was formerly a senior scholar at the Annenberg Institute for School Reform at Brown University, and a mayoral appointee to the New York City Panel for Educational Policy. He founded and directed NYU's Institute for Education and Social Policy for more than a decade and spent eight years as the Aaron Diamond Foundation's Education Program Officer. He has directed an alternative high school for dropouts in Newark and an alternative BA program for community activists and public sector workers in Jersey City. He served 10 years on his local Brooklyn school board, and published *Urban Schools, Public Will* (2007). He is a coauthor of *Choosing Equality: The Case for Democratic Schooling* (1985), and of *Hard Lessons: Public Schools and Privatization* (1996) as well as several other education policy texts and many articles. Fruchter also published two novels and codirected several award-winning documentaries. He was one of the founders of the Campaign for Fiscal Equity (CFE).

Robert E. Fullilove is the associate dean for community and minority affairs, professor of clinical sociomedical sciences and the codirector of the Cities Research Group at Columbia University. He has authored numerous articles in the area of minority health. From 1995 to 2001, he served on the board of Health Promotion and Disease Prevention at the Institute of Medicine (IOM) of the National Academy of Sciences. Since 1996, he has served on five IOM study committees that have produced reports on a variety of topics including substance abuse and addiction, HIV/AIDS, tuberculosis, and damp indoor spaces and health. In 2003, he was designated a National Associate of the National Academies of Science. In 1998, he was appointed to the Advisory Committee on HIV and STD Prevention (ACHSP) at the Centers for Disease Control, and in July 2000, he became the committee's cochair. Finally, between 2004–2007, he served on the National Advisory Council for the National Center for Complementary and Alternative Medicine at the National Institutes of Health [NIH]. Since 2010, he has taught public health courses in six New York State prisons that are part of the Bard College Prison Initiative (BPI) and serves as the Senior Advisor to BPI's public health program. He serves on the editorial boards of the journals *Sexually Transmitted Diseases*, and *The Journal of Public Health Policy*. He has been awarded the Distinguished Teaching Award at the Mailman School of Public Health three times (in 1995, 2001, and 2013), and in May 2002, he was awarded an honorary doctorate from Bank Street College of Education.

Shifra Goldenberg is a senior policy analyst at the New York City Mayor's Office of Operations, where she provides project management, analytical, and technical support for projects of strategic significance, focused on improving the efficiency and effectiveness of intra- and interagency operations. Previously, she was the communications coordinator for the Research Alliance for New York City Schools, where she edited and produces publications, and managed the organization's website and online presence. This included leading the launch of "Spotlight on New York City Schools," a web-based series of data analyses and visualizations. Before joining the Research Alliance, she supported marketing for RKT&B Architects and client management for Luca Bonetti, Corp., a painting conservation studio. She was an editorial assistant for *A*

Curator's Quest: Building the Museum of Modern Art's Painting and Sculpture Collection, 1967–1988. She holds an MPA in public and nonprofit management from New York University's Wagner School of Public Service and a BA in anthropology with a concentration in art history from Columbia University.

Stephen Greenspan grew up in New York City, where he was one of the few students at the Bronx High School of Science more interested in social than in physical science (his exact age-mate, Stokley Carmichael was another). He earned a doctorate in developmental psychology at the University of Rochester and followed that with a post doctorate in developmental disorders at UCLA. Prior to becoming a psychologist, he earned a MA in political history at Northwestern University and worked for several years doing urban policy research at the Rochester (NY) Center for Governmental Research. He has held a number of academic positions, retiring as professor emeritus from the University of Connecticut. Now living in Colorado, he has combined his two interests (policy and disability) by becoming highly cited in disability policy studies (most recently on cultural and racial injustice in criminal justice and disability services), for which he has won several awards. His most recent award was added to the wall of fame of the National Organization for Fetal Alcohol Syndrome.

Michael K. Gusmano is an associate professor in the School of Public Health's Department of Health System and Policy at Rutgers, the State University of New Jersey. He is also a research scholar at the Hastings Center and a visiting fellow at the Nelson A. Rockefeller Institute of Government of the State University of New York. His research examines the politics of health and social policy. He codirects the World Cities Project, which compares large city health systems across the world. He is the coauthor of *Health Care in World Cities: New York, London and Paris* (2010), of *Healthy Voices/Unhealthy Silence* (2007), *Growing Older in World Cities* with Victor G. Rodwin (2006) and more than 100 scholarly articles. From 1995 to 1997, he was a Robert Wood Johnson Scholar in Health Policy Research at Yale University. He serves as the international editor of the *Journal of Aging and Social Policy*, associate editor for *Health Economics, Policy and Law*, and is on the board of editors of the *Journal of Health Politics, Policy and Law* and the editorial committee of the *Hastings Center Report*. He received his PhD in political science from the University of Maryland College Park in 1995.

Robert L. Hawkins is the McSilver Associate Professor in Poverty Studies and the assistant dean and director of undergraduate education at NYU Silver School of Social Work, where he also directs the Restorative Justice Lab. He is an expert on poverty, race, social capital, and social policy in the United States. His current research focuses on the concept of complex poverty and understanding and improving the lives of low-income families and individuals through the integration of policy and psychological interventions. He consults, speaks, writes, and presents nationally and internationally on a range of topics related to social problems, including poverty, structural racism, oppression, and community economic development. He has developed research in New York City, New Orleans, Germany, and the Philippines. He did predoctoral studies at Harvard University School of Medicine and received his PhD and MA in social welfare policy from Brandeis University. He also holds an MPA from the University of North Carolina at Chapel Hill, and a BA in speech communications from Appalachian State University in North Carolina. He is the recipient of the Silver School of Social Work Distinguished Teaching Award at New York University.

Calvin Holder is professor of history and African American studies at the College of Staten Island, City University of New York. He earned his MA and PhD from Harvard University. His research and scholarly interests are American immigration and African-American history. He has published in both areas.

Sarah Klevan is a research analyst for the Research Alliance for New York City Schools. She conducts qualitative research as part of the Research Alliance's evaluation of the Expanded Success Initiative. She works as well on the Safe Public Spaces evaluation, and other projects related to school climate, safety, and discipline. She has coauthored a number of Research Alliance reports and has presented her work at meetings of the American Educational Research Association and the Eastern Sociological Society. She has also presented at practitioner-focused events, such as Eskolta's annual conference for school leaders, educators, and staff. She is a doctoral candidate in NYU Steinhardt's Sociology of Education program. The overarching question that frames her research is: How and in what ways do schools simultaneously reproduce and disrupt patterns of inequality? Her dissertation research examines restorative approaches to discipline in NYC high schools. Earlier in her career, she taught fifth and sixth grade in Philadelphia. She was also a fellow of the Jewish Organizing Initiative in Boston.

Kristen Lewis is a codirector of Measure of America, a program of the Social Science Research Council, and coauthors of two volumes of *The Measure of America* (Columbia University Press, 2008 and NYU Press, 2010). With Burd-Sharps, their studies have created well-being reports for California, Louisiana,

Mississippi, and Marin and Sonoma Counties. Before founding Measure of America, they both worked extensively with the United Nations.

Christina Mokhtar was a principal research associate at the Annenberg Institute of School Reform (AISR) at Brown University where she directed and managed a public education data archive for New York City public schools. The team she directed also provided data and research support to community organizing efforts to improve New York City's schools. As a member of AISR's Research and Policy Team, she conducted research and data analyses examining the enrollment, educational opportunities and outcomes of student groups traditionally underserved by public schools. Her AISR work resulted in several published reports and presentations, such as *Over the Counter, Under the Radar: Inequitably Distributing New York City's Late-Enrolling High Schools Students* (2013) and *Opportunity and Equity: Enrollment and Outcomes of Black and Latino Males in Boston Public Schools* (2014). Most recently, she coauthored a book chapter in, *The Shifting Landscape of the American School District: Race, Class, Geography, and the Perpetual Reform of Local Control, 1935–2015* (2018). She also served as a research officer at the Social Disadvantage Research Center, University of Oxford, where she managed and analyzed large administrative data sets and small area statistics. She holds a PhD in social policy from the University of Oxford, England.

Jarrett Murphy is the executive editor and publisher of *City Limits*, a nonprofit news agency founded in 1976. A native of Lynn, Mass., who grew up in New Britain, Conn., he graduated from Fordham University in the Bronx and later received a diploma in public financial policy from the London School of Economics and a MA in economics from the New School. He joined *City Limits* as investigations editor in 2011. Earlier he worked at WFUV-FM, the Hartford Advocate, CBSNews.com and the *Village Voice*. His work has appeared in *The Nation, Newsday, the Daily News, Columbia Journalism Review, the American Prospect,* and *AlterNet*. Jarrett won the 2007 James Aronson Award for Social Justice Journalism, the 2007 PASS Award from the National Council on Crime and Delinquency and the Deadline Club's 2011 award for best coverage of issues affecting minority groups. A little league coach and the bass player/vocalist for Fort Indy, a rock band, he lives in the Norwood section of the Bronx with his wife and two sons.

James A. Parrott is the director of economic and fiscal policies at The Center for New York City Affairs at The New School. The center is an applied policy research institute that drives innovation in social policy, focuses on how public policy impacts low-income communities, and strives for a more just and equitable city. In previous positions, Parrott worked for the Fiscal Policy Institute, the Office of the State Deputy Comptroller for New York City, the City of New York (as chief economist for economic development), and for the International Ladies' Garment Workers' Union. Parrott regularly analyzes New York City's economy and job market. He has written extensively on topics including income inequality, the New York City and State budgets and tax policies. His research helped bring over $20 million in federal funds to New York following 9/11 to aid dislocated workers. He coordinated the economic research in support of New York State's $15 minimum wage policies adopted in 2015 and 2016. Parrott has served in various city and state advisory positions, including on Governor Andrew Cuomo's Tax Reform and Fairness Commission. He received his BA in American studies from Illinois Wesleyan University and his MA and PhD in economics from the University of Massachusetts at Amherst. He teaches public policy at the Roosevelt House, Hunter College.

James Rodriguez was born and raised in New York City public housing. Currently, he is assistant professor of history at CUNY Guttman Community College, where he teaches and writes about gentrification, race, housing, and urban policy. He recently completed his doctorate in American studies at New York University and has previously worked as a land use and public housing organizer on the Lower East Side.

Victor G. Rodwin is professor of health policy and management at the Wagner School of Public Service, New York University and codirector (with Michael K. Gusmano) of the World Cities Project, a joint venture of Wagner/NYU, the Butler Columbia Aging Center and the Hastings Center. He teaches Wagner's introductory course on health policy and classes on comparative analysis of health systems and healthcare reform. He is the author of numerous articles and books, including *The Health Planning Predicament: France, Quebec, England, and the United States* (1984); *The End of an Illusion: The Future of Health Policy in Western Industrialized Nations* with J. de Kervasdoué and J. Kimberly (1984); *Public Hospitals in New York and Paris* with C. Brecher, D. Jolly, and R. Baxter (1992); *Japan's Universal and Affordable Health Care: Lessons for the U.S.?* (1994); *Growing Older in World Cities: New York, London, Paris and Tokyo,* edited with M. Gusmano (2006); *Universal Health Insurance in France: How Sustainable? Essays on the French Health Care System* (2006); *Health Care in World Cities: New York, London and Paris* with M. Gusmano and D. Weisz (2010); and *A La Santé de l'Oncle Sam: Regards croisés sur les systèmes de santé Américains et Français* with D. Tabuteau (2010). His most recent work (in collaboration with Michael K. Gusmano and Daniel Weisz) has focused on health care system performance in world cities, as measured by amenable mortality, hospitalizations for ambulatory-care sensitive conditions and rehospitalizations. He is currently studying health systems and big pharma in Brazil, Russia, India, and China.

Howard Shih is the research and policy director for the Asian American Federation. He has authored or coauthored a number of reports on Asian Americans, including *NYC'S Economic Engine: Contributions & Challenges of Asian Small Businesses*; *Asian American Seniors in New York City: An Updated Snapshot, Analysis of City Government Funding to Social Service Organizations Serving the Asian American Community in New York City;* and *Making America Work: Asian Americans, Native Hawaiians and Pacific Islanders in the Workforce and Business. He* has also written two articles for UCLA's AAPI *Nexus Journal*, one on poverty among Asian New Yorkers and another as a coauthor comparing the state of Asian Americans in the New York and Los Angeles metro areas.

In addition, he is responsible for the Federation's Census Information Center (CIC), officially designated by the Census Bureau as a repository of Census data for improving data access to underserved communities. The CIC collaborates with Asian American community-based organizations to effectively utilize data to serve and advocate on behalf of their constituents. He also led the Federation's 2010 Census outreach initiative to encourage Asian Americans to participate fully in the decennial census.

Adriana Villavicencio serves as the deputy director of the Research Alliance for New York City Schools at New York University. In this role, she helps to shape the Research Alliance's research agenda, works to enhance relationships with external partners and key stakeholders, and leads many of the organization's large-scale research projects focused on the NYC school system. Her research has focused on identifying both the causes and potential solutions to educational inequities. This includes a four-year evaluation of the Expanded Success Initiative (ESI), a precursor to My Brother's Keeper and one of the country's largest initiatives targeting Black and Latino male students. She is currently leading a three-year mixed-method study on schools that serve recently arrived immigrant youth and a series of targeted multi-method studies called *Equity, Access, and Diversity in New York City Schools: Steady Progress and Stubborn Barriers*.

She has conducted research at MDRC, the RAND Corporation, and Westat. She is a recipient of the Founders Fellowship from New York University and a graduate student fellowship from MDRC. Previously, she served as a department chair and interim principal at a charter high school in Oakland, California. She has also taught high school English at East New York Middle School of Excellence in Bushwick, Brooklyn, and worked on the development of a new school in Bangalore, India. She earned her PhD in education leadership and policy from the NYU Steinhardt, holds an MA in English education from Teachers College, Columbia University, and a BA in English from Columbia University. She is president of the board of directors for the Latino Alumni Association of Columbia University as well as a member of NYC's Advisory Council for the Young Women's Initiative, and New York State's Board of Regents Research Workgroup on Integration, Diversity and Equity.

Andrew J. Wilkes is an associate pastor, public speaker, writer, and husband. He is a graduate of Hampton University, Princeton Theological Seminary, and has the Coro Fellowship in Public Affairs. He is the former executive director of the Drum Major Institute in New York City, and is currently a PhD candidate in political science at the CUNY Graduate Center. He lives in Harlem, New York.

George Woods, MD, DLFAPA is a practicing neuropsychiatrist and internationally known mental health expert. Over the past several decades, his clinical practice focuses on neurodevelopmental disorders and geriatric psychiatry. He is immediate past president of the International Academy of Law and Mental Health, and then the academy's secretary general. He is also vice-chairperson of the Challenging Behaviors Special Interest Research Group of the International Association for the Specialized Study of Intellectual and Developmental Disabilities, and associate editor of *The Journal of Policy and Practice*. Since 2002, he has taught clinical aspects of forensic psychiatry at Morehouse School of Medicine in Atlanta, Georgia, and is a lecturer at the University of California, Berkeley, School of Law. He has published extensively on topics including neurobehavioral assessment in forensic mental health, fetal alcohol spectrum disorder, cultural factors in assessing the mentally disordered, trauma, financial fraud, and intellectual disability. He has also consulted with forensic systems internationally in Malawi, Pakistan, The Hague, Uganda, Kenya, Zanzibar, Senegal, Tanzania, Italy, and Japan. He is the recipient of the 2018 distinguished alumnus for the University of Utah School of Medicine.

Jessica Yager is the executive director at the NYU Furman Center. She has led the NYU Furman Center's policy work since 2012, first serving as policy director and then as deputy director. Prior to joining the NYU Furman Center, she was the founding director of the Foreclosure Prevention Project at Queens Legal Services. She worked as a senior staff attorney at the Office of the Appellate Defender; held a clinical teaching fellow at the Center for Social Justice at Seton Hall University School of Law; and was a law clerk to the Honorable Napoleon A. Jones, Jr., United States District Court for the Southern District of California. She received a JD from NYU School of Law, where she was a Root-Tilden-Kern Public Interest Scholar. She received her BA from Wesleyan University.

Index

Bold type indicates contributors and their chapters in this edited volume.

www.ingramcontent.com/pod-product-compliance
Lightning Source LLC
Chambersburg PA
CBHW030633270326
41929CB00007B/62